"This book is the paramount resource for practitioners who seek to provide interventions for anger control problems. It is masterfully composed, conveying deep knowledge about anger and offering an impressive range of evidence-based treatment procedures. Among its superb features are a rich array of case illustrations and an abundant supply of clinical tools to facilitate case formulation, client engagement, developing pathways for therapeutic change, and gauging outcomes. It puts two top expert consultants right there on your bookshelf or laptop."

—**Raymond W. Novaco, PhD**, professor in the department of psychological science at the University of California, Irvine; author of *Anger Control*; and coeditor of *Using Social Science to Reduce Violent Offending*

"Although anger is considered a universally experienced emotion, most practitioners feel ill-equipped when treating clients who struggle with it. In this book, Howard Kassinove and Raymond Chip Tafrate—two well-established experts on anger—provide current, effective, and empirically based techniques in a manner that is clear and easy to read. The book is very thorough, covering a number of aspects of treatment, from the basics of relaxation and cognitive restructuring to those typically neglected in other manuals (e.g., assessment, happiness, lifestyle changes). This book is a necessity for any practitioner who works with clients who experience anger (i.e., everyone)."

—**Michael J. Toohey, PhD**, clinical psychologist, and core faculty of the clinical psychology PsyD program at Antioch University Seattle; and director of the Anger, Aggression, and Irritability Research Group for Antioch University Seattle

"Rather than simply telling you what to do, this book carefully explains how to best talk to someone about their anger, and how to conceptualize the key issues in a way that identifies which interventions are likely to prove most effective. You can then choose from a menu of carefully constructed activities—tried and tested through clinical experience, and firmly grounded in contemporary science—to best suit the circumstances in which you work. Written by internationally renowned anger practitioners and researchers, this really is a fabulous resource for anyone who wants to help someone to manage problematic anger. Essential reading!"

—**Andrew Day, DClinPsy**, enterprise professor in the department of criminology at the University of Melbourne in Australia; registered clinical and forensic psychologist who has previously worked in forensic settings in both Australia and the UK; and published in the areas of offender rehabilitation and violence prevention

"*The Practitioner's Guide to Anger Management* by Kassinove and Tafrate is an outstanding book for any clinician or mental health provider who deals with anger. And that includes all of us. This is an intelligent, practical, and informative guide by two outstanding clinicians that provides the reader with all the tools you will need to help clients cope with anger. Should be required reading for all clinicians."

—**Robert L. Leahy, PhD**, director of The American Institute for Cognitive Therapy, and author of *The Jealousy Cure*

"Grounded in science, filled with informative case examples, and brimming with illuminating exercises and step-by-step instructions, this book is a must-read for all practitioners interested in intervening effectively with angry and aggressive clients. As highly respected and vastly experienced clinicians and researchers, Kassinove and Tafrate have written the definitive 'how-to' guide for treating anger-related disturbances using the outstanding SMART anger program. Whether a trainee or a fully licensed clinician, readers will find the book's writing style highly accessible and clinically powerful, yet also empirically based and theoretically relevant. Without a doubt, the authors have written the definitive handbook that provides clinicians with a wide array of tools to effectively understand and intervene with clients whose lives are in ruin because of dysfunctional anger."

—**Christopher I. Eckhardt, PhD**, professor and director of clinical training at Purdue University, and coauthor of *Treating the Abusive Partner*

The Practitioner's Guide to

Anger Management

Customizable Interventions,
Treatments, and Tools for Clients
with Problem Anger

HOWARD KASSINOVE, PhD, ABPP
RAYMOND CHIP TAFRATE, PhD

Impact Publishers, Inc.

Publisher's Note

Distributed in Canada by Raincoast Books

Copyright © 2019 by Howard Kassinove and Raymond Chip Tafrate
      New Harbinger Publications, Inc.
      5674 Shattuck Avenue
      Oakland, CA 94609
      www.newharbinger.com

Cover design by Amy Daniel

Acquired by Tesilya Hanauer

Edited by Xavier Callahan

Indexed by James Minkin

All Rights Reserved

Library of Congress Cataloging-in-Publication Data on file

Printed in the United States of America

21   20   19

10   9   8   7   6   5   4   3   2   1   First Printing

Contents

PART 6: Interventions to Alter Internal Experiences and Urges

PART 7: Interventions to Alter Anger Expression

PART 8: Going Beyond Anger Management and Putting It All Together

Online Resources

Preface and Acknowledgments

When we published *Anger Management: The Complete Treatment Guidebook for Practitioners* (Kassinove & Tafrate, 2002), anger was understudied, as it is even now, and there were few high-quality programs that focused specifically on treating clients with problematic anger. Our goal was to provide professionals with interventions and tools that could be used to help those clients. The book and our program were well received. Editions were published in Arabic, Korean, Spanish, Chinese, and Russian. Reviews were very positive, and we received many letters and emails from practitioners who told us how useful the program was in their professional practices.

Yet we knew that most people don't go to a professional for help with their anger. Therefore, we published *Anger Management for Everyone: Seven Proven Ways to Control Anger and Live a Happier Life* (Tafrate & Kassinove, 2009) as a self-help book. It was directed at adults and adolescents who were interested in learning about anger on their own and helping themselves live more effective, peaceful lives. New findings and techniques continued to emerge, of course, and we shared them in the second edition of the book, *Anger Management for Everyone: Ten Proven Strategies to Help You Control Anger and Live a Happier Life* (Tafrate & Kassinove, 2019). The updated edition incorporated many new materials, including tips for lifestyle management, information about mindfulness and meditation, strategies for disconnecting from the thoughts that drive anger reactions, and guidance for improving social and interpersonal skills.

The present, treatment-oriented guidebook is new. It is aimed at professionals who want to help others better manage dysfunctional anger. Knowledgeable practitioners often want to know about the scholarly underpinnings of the interventions they are using. We provide this information and also thoroughly describe how to use a broad menu of tools to help bring clients' dysfunctional anger under control. Many of the book's practitioner scripts, client information sheets, and client worksheets are also downloadable from www.newharbinger.com/42877 (see the very back of the book for more details).

Our overarching goal is to provide you with the knowledge and skills to deliver a solid, research-supported anger management program that actively engages clients in developing new thinking and improving their reactions to a wide range of challenging life scenarios. The consumer-oriented *Anger Management for Everyone* can be incorporated into treatment as a companion volume so that clients, on their own, can further practice the skills you have taught them.

As always, we recognize the important work of colleagues who have made significant contributions to the study and treatment of anger. Over the years, they have added much to our understanding of this normal but sometimes dysfunctional emotion; while pioneering the development of positive life skills for happiness, they have also created techniques for minimizing excessive anger reactions. Some professionals with whom we have worked closely deserve mention. They include Jerry Deffenbacher, Thomas DiBlasi, Raymond DiGiuseppe, Christopher Eckhardt, Albert Ellis, Jeffrey Froh, Damon Mitchell, Raymond Novaco, Joseph Scardapane, Denis Sukhodolsky, Junko Tanaka-Matsumi, and Joseph Wolpe. We also thank our many clients, patients, and students who have shared their personal anger experiences with us. Our knowledge and our personal growth improved as we traveled with them through their individual anger journeys.

We have been fortunate to work with our very helpful editor, Xavier Callahan, as well as with Tesilya Hanauer and the production team at New Harbinger, who provided thoughtful guidance and helped shape this book's final form.

We are also grateful to our respective academic institutions, Hofstra University and Central Connecticut State University, for supporting our study of anger treatment. Of course, our work would not have flourished without the encouragement of our families. We appreciate their love and patience.

We hope that our experiences in professional practice, coupled with academic and personal support, have led to the creation of a down-to-earth, evidence-based, practical guidebook for those working on the front lines of anger treatment.

—Howard Kassinove
Hofstra University

—Raymond Chip Tafrate
Central Connecticut State University

Introduction

Anger leads to all sorts of human suffering. At the milder end, it contributes to everyday conflicts and problems; at the extreme, it can be deadly. Anger is also commonplace. A survey of thirty-four thousand adults from the United States by Okuda et al. (2015) found that 8 percent of respondents admitted to poorly controlled anger, as defined by answering yes to questions such as "Have even little things made you angry?" and "Have you had difficulty controlling your anger?" and "Have you often had temper outbursts or gotten so angry that you lose control?" This suggests that about twenty-six million adults in the United States have significant anger problems. Anger difficulties may actually surpass many more commonly diagnosed psychological conditions. For example, according to the National Institute of Mental Health (https://www.nimh.nih.gov/health/statistics/index.shtml), the past-year prevalence in adults was less than 5 percent for agoraphobia, binge eating disorder, borderline personality disorder, bipolar disorder, generalized anxiety disorder, persistent depressive disorder, post-traumatic stress disorder, panic disorder, and schizophrenia. It was about 4 to 8 percent for suicidal thoughts in adults. Therefore, anger seems to be an important dysfunctional emotional reaction for adults that is more common than many others. Also troubling is a study by Swanson et al. (2015), which found that 9 percent of adults have a history of impulsive, angry behavior *and* have access to guns. Anger, as emotional excess, may play a central role in epidemics of gun violence.

Of course, anger is not just confined to the United States. Millions more around the world are likely to be suffering from dysfunctional anger that leads to noteworthy interpersonal and intrapersonal problems. Similar findings emerged from a survey of two thousand people by Richardson and Halliwell (2008). Here are some of the key findings from that study:

- Almost one-third of people polled (32 percent) said they had a close friend or family member who had trouble controlling anger.

- More than one in ten respondents (12 percent) said they had trouble controlling their own anger.

- One in five respondents (20 percent) said they had ended a relationship or friendship with someone because of how that person had behaved when angry.

- Fewer than one in seven respondents (13 percent) who said they had trouble controlling their anger had actually sought help for their anger problems.

- Almost six in ten respondents (58 percent) said they wouldn't know where to seek help if they needed it for an anger problem.

For somewhat younger folks, a study of almost 6,500 adolescents by McLaughlin et al. (2012) found that nearly two-thirds (63 percent) reported lifetime anger attacks that were severe enough to involve threatening or engaging in violence and/or destroying property. Although the program described in this book is aimed primarily at adults, anger is an important mental health problem that appears across the adult and teenage years. Fortunately, many of the interventions we present here can be applied to people from the late teenage years to late adulthood.

Anger is also a bit of a conundrum. It's universal and familiar but also misunderstood by the public and well-meaning practitioners alike. Practitioners across different care settings are looking for interventions and tools to be effective with their clients; in the absence of good science, however, misconceptions and myths often fill the void.

SMART Anger Management

Recognizing the dearth of high-quality materials to help angry clients, we developed our customizable Selection Menu for Anger Reduction Treatment (SMART) anger management program and wrote this how-to book for case managers, clinical practitioners, counselors, educators, health service personnel, people working with justice-involved individuals, psychologists, social workers, and students in training. Together, we have more than seventy-five years of combined experience with community adults and families, hospital outpatients, clients in mental health centers, university students, and adults involved with the criminal justice system. On the basis of scientific evidence, we developed our Anger Episode Model and a series of up-to-date treatments and interventions that can be used to help people who experience and express dysfunctional anger. We also wrote a self-help book, the second edition of *Anger Management for Everyone* (Tafrate & Kassinove, 2019), to serve as companion reading for your clients who are using our SMART model.

Because the SMART model can be used to help clients of many ages and in many settings, we have included case examples that range from mild to quite extreme, and that represent anger problems as they appear in relationships, in the community, on the job, in institutional settings, in mental health clinics, and so forth. Do not be dismayed if the case examples seem too mild or too extreme by comparison to the anger you see in your own setting. Anger shows itself in many ways, and the cases, while real, are simply meant to illustrate elements of our anger interventions.

The SMART program evolved from earlier works for practitioners (Kassinove & Tafrate, 2006, 2010) in which we recognized that working to change anger triggers, along with learning to accept and adapt to them, would be central to any set of interventions. We also recognized that anger was tough to treat (Kassinove, 1995) and that special attention had to be given to early phases of treatment in order to overcome roadblocks that were likely to appear because of a poor therapeutic alliance (Tafrate & Kassinove, 2003; Kassinove & Tafrate, 2010). As practitioners ourselves, we recognized early on that the best approach to anger treatment would likely involve a menu-driven approach that was flexible, rather than a rigid manualized approach (Tafrate & Kassinove, 2006). Many, confirming our early conclusions, have now recognized that manualized treatments are *not* better. For example, one set of researchers reviewed six studies that directly compared manualized and nonmanualized psychological treatments as well as eight meta-analyses that looked at effect sizes of manualized treatments and control conditions; they concluded that manualized treatment "is not empirically supported as more effective than nonmanualized treatment" and went on to say that manualized treatment "may be attractive as a research tool" but "should not be promoted as being superior to nonmanualized psychotherapy for clinical practice" (Truijens, Zühlke-van Hulzen, & Vanheule, 2019, 323). Manualized treatments seem attractive because they can potentially be carried out by practitioners with lower levels of training, or even as computer programs. The burden on practitioners who use flexible programs is that they have to be familiar with a variety of intervention strategies and feel confident that they can select strategies likely to be helpful to a particular client. The SMART approach helps you make such decisions.

Foundational Principles

All around the world, and in all segments of society, anger is part of the landscape of felt emotions. When we are exposed to the slings and arrows of life's adversities, anger typically emerges first. Yet anger and especially its cousin, aggression, are rarely the most useful responses in modern society. They developed thousands of generations ago in our evolutionary history as reactions to threat, to help ensure we would have food and shelter, opportunity for reproduction, and opportunity to protect our offspring. Today there are many other ways to solve conflicts and deal with threats, without resorting to anger and aggression. For example, an issue might be taken for resolution to a counselor, a lawyer, small claims court, a mediator, a parent, a respected religious leader, a teacher or school principal, a senior manager at work, and so forth. In the modern world, even though anger is rarely necessary to ensure our survival, it remains with us.

Human beings are complex, and anger often emerges along with anxiety, cognitive rumination, depression, jealousy, shame, guilt, and other feelings that produce the richness of our personal lives. We were aware of these complexities as we developed our program. Because anger is often an immediate response to many kinds of perceived threats and attacks, however, we tackle it directly as a primary and key emotional reaction. Our goal is to provide you with guidance as you help your clients develop the skills to experience anger in a reasonable manner, bring it under control when it's dysfunctional, and live fruitful and enriched lives.

Practitioners sometimes have limited personal experiences with the problems they focus on with their clients. But anger is different. All of us have dealt with troublesome family issues, school and work problems, dating and marital conflicts, excessive demands on our time, occupational misfortunes, and other stressors. We have all been rejected, neglected, and misunderstood. We have all felt angry, and we have all been the target of someone else's anger. As a result, it is likely that you have developed your own anger awareness skills and personal coping responses. Because anger is not foreign, you know what your clients go through. Anger reactions, of course, vary widely across individuals, and your own anger may be far less problematic than that of your clients. Nevertheless, you can use your own experiences to better understand theirs and, in addition to the research-tested tools we present, you can sometimes use your personal solutions to help others deal with their problems. Awareness of and openness about your own anger can be used to increase empathy, develop a stronger therapeutic bond, and model emotion management skills.

We suggest you consider yourself to be a *coping model*—that is, a person who has read and studied, thoughtfully engaged in self-reflection about anger, and found some personal solutions that may be of help to others. The alternative is known as a *mastery model.* That term refers to a top-down approach in which you see yourself as a person who is in charge—an expert who has fully conquered anger and can now tell others how to do the same. In our experience, that model leads to practitioner overconfidence and a poor therapeutic relationship. Collaboration and the recognition that we all struggle with anger, to a greater or lesser degree, are most likely to lead to success with your clients.

Across official diagnostic systems, such as the *Diagnostic and Statistical Manual of Mental Disorders* (DSM) and the *International Statistical Classification of Diseases and Related Health Problems* (ICD), there are, strangely, no anger disorders (that is, disorders where anger is the primary focus). Perhaps some professionals think that an official disorder would lead to sympathy, as when we feel sorry for highly anxious people who are frightened when they have to get on an airplane or give a public speech. Sympathy is also granted to people who feel deep shame about their personal histories, their family background, or their limited educational or vocational achievements. Adults who admit to having been sexually, physically, or emotionally abused also get our sympathy. Such problems often lead to social support: "Oh, I'm so sorry to hear that. You're a really smart, wonderful person. What can I do to help you?" Understanding is also usually given when people are depressed, have low self-esteem, and feel hopeless. In contrast, when people show moderate to strong anger, it's often believed that they are just impulsive or immature, or that they possess a deep character flaw. Their anger may be followed by such statements as "Why are you so angry? What's wrong with you? Grow up and get a grip on yourself! Just face reality as it is! Don't be such a hothead." They may also be the subject of gossip that labels them as childish, naive, emotionally sensitive, or unworldly. The truth is that we all have to learn how to manage anger, which is a natural and common response to the challenges of life.

An adult has an anger problem when his or her anger experiences and expressions can be accurately described in the following ways:

- They are too frequent.

- They are too intense.

- They last too long.

- They are out of proportion to the triggering events.

- They lead to problematic life outcomes.

Accordingly, for persons whose anger is dysfunctional on a regular basis, anger management can be very helpful. The term "anger management" refers to the reduction of maladaptive, disruptive, and excessive angry arousal and expression. Anger management does not mean complete anger elimination. The goal is teaching clients to be aware of their anger, to react with minimal and infrequent anger to perceived conflicts and struggles, to express anger appropriately when they feel it, and, when possible, to use anger functionally to resolve life's problems.

SMART anger management is based on the view that this is best accomplished by a combination of three factors, experienced in the context of a supportive, collaborative, engaged relationship with a practitioner:

1. Knowledge development: It's important for clients to understand exactly what anger is, how it can lead to narrow thinking about problems and restrict the development of solutions, how it can lead to major life problems in unexpected realms (such as anger-related medical issues), and how it can fester and morph into damaging verbal responses and aggressive behaviors. We want clients to be able to figure out when their anger is adaptive versus maladaptive, and why it's important to reduce dysfunctional anger.

2. Behavioral practice to foster change: With your guidance, clients engage in office-based imaginal and/or in vivo practice, developing skills and adaptive reactions to real or perceived aversive triggers.

3. Acceptance: Sometimes there is no possible resolution to a perceived conflict. Clients may indicate that the source of their anger is a deceased person, someone from childhood who cannot be located, a former spouse who sees herself or himself as perfectly okay, an unknown person, a narcissist who denies any role in producing anger in others, or the unbending rules of an institution (such as a workplace, a higher education facility, or a prison). In such cases, only acceptance can be of help, for without acceptance, anger is likely to continue to fester.

It is wise for practitioners and clients to share the same base of knowledge about anger. This knowledge base includes the following elements:

- A shared definition of anger, to allow for its differentiation from other emotional states

- Awareness of the uniquely personal stimuli that may trigger anger in any particular client

- The understanding that anger does not just happen but occurs in episodes that can be examined, with your guidance, to begin the process of improvement

- An understanding of the difference between adaptive and maladaptive or dysfunctional anger

- Awareness that most (but not all) of the consequences of moderately intense, frequent, and enduring anger are negative

- Recognition and agreement that, irrespective of the objective trigger, clients contribute significantly to the development and maintenance of their own anger reactions

SMART anger management rests on two foundational principles:

1. *Increased client awareness, motivation, and knowledge are central to change.* Engagement is the initial key to treatment success. Understanding a client's perspective and the unique context of how anger emerges in his or her life is an important starting point. Knowledge about the characteristics and causes of anger, and about the problems associated with frequent, strong, and enduring anger, will increase the client's awareness about dysfunctional anger reactions and enhance the client's motivation to reduce them.

2. *The client's active participation in developing anger management skills must be fostered.* Clients are not merely along for the ride. Actual change comes from practitioner-guided discussions that reinforce the practice of new thinking and behaviors, and from acceptance of transgressions that cannot be changed. The practitioner initiates the change process, but in the end it's the client who gets credit for doing the actual work to make change happen.

Organization of This Book

Although this is a how-to book, we briefly review the fundamentals of anger and anger management. Readers who want more science, history, or philosophy may consider the following sources:

- *Understanding Anger Disorders* (DiGiuseppe & Tafrate, 2007)

- *Anger Disorders: Definition, Diagnosis, and Treatment* (Kassinove, 1995)

- *International Handbook of Anger* (Potegal, Stemmler, & Spielberger, 2010)

For readers interested in basic and historical articles, we recommend the following works:

- "Studies on Anger and Aggression: Implications for Theories of Emotion" (Averill, 1983), a classic in the field

- "Anger Episodes in High- and Low-Trait-Anger Community Adults" (Tafrate, Kassinove, & Dundin, 2002)

- "A Brief History of Anger" (Potegal & Novaco, 2010), an excellent contribution to the *International Handbook of Anger* (Potegal et al., 2010)

In this book, the chapters are organized into eight parts. In part 1, "Anger Treatment Basics," we present an overview of the origins of anger, formally define anger and differentiate it from hostility and aggression, and identify characteristics of normal and dysfunctional anger. We also discuss common challenges that emerge in the effort to engage angry clients in the treatment process. We encourage empathic listening, with a de-emphasis on logical explanations, shaming, and confrontation. We also answer the biggest of all questions: Can anger really be managed? That is, do we have a firm scientific basis that leads to a degree of certainty that anger management works? (So as not to keep you waiting, we will tell you now that the answer is a resounding yes.) We also consider whether anger reduction comes from so-called common factors (such as a good interpersonal relationship between you and your client) or from specific interventions. We conclude that both are important in producing maximal change, and therefore both are part of the SMART program.

In part 2, "Case Formulation and Treatment Planning," the Anger Episode Model is presented. It is noted that anger occurs in shorter or longer episodes and that these episodes can be analyzed and dissected for treatment-planning purposes. Occurring in the context of pre-anger lifestyle issues, the model shows that anger episodes consist of triggers, cognitive appraisals (that is, thoughts) about the triggers, and physical activation and sensations. Each of these is typically accompanied by an urge to act. The model then explores expressive patterns as well as the outcomes related to specific episodes of anger. Each of these elements may be a useful target for intervention, and each can be directly addressed in a customizable treatment plan. At the heart of any intervention plan are change targets that emerge from good assessment. Therefore, we also provide recommendations for assessment tools that are *not* based solely on tradition (such as the tradition of always giving a good personality assessment). Rather, our recommendations are based on elements of the Anger Episode Model as well as on assessment tools that address shame, guilt, and self-deception.

Part 3, "Preparing Clients for Change," may turn out to be the most important part of anger treatment. Relatively few people look deeply into their lives and decide on their own to seek help for anger. Rather, most are coerced by friends or colleagues or family members, or they are mandated to treatment by an employer or the criminal justice system. As a general rule, self-referred clients arrive with greater motivation to work on their anger, whereas those who have been nudged by others tend to have less motivation. Those who are forced or mandated into treatment activities usually show up with the lowest level of insight and motivation; they require more time in the initial phases of treatment before you can move on to active interventions. Preparation consists of increasing clients' awareness that a problem exists, evoking clients' own reasons for why anger management would be beneficial, and resolving clients' ambivalence about changing their long-held angry reaction patterns. Psychoeducation, which also occurs here, helps with knowledge development, awareness, and motivation to change.

Part 4, "Interventions to Alter Anger Triggers," consists of strategies to help clients change pre-anger lifestyle elements in ways that may quickly lead to decreased anger reactivity. Although practitioners often want to jump in with a mental health–based or skills-based intervention, sometimes significant reactivity reduction can occur through simple changes in eating habits, sleep habits, or the kinds of colors and music in the client's environment. On occasion, the best intervention is to help a client effectively sidestep conflicts in the short run until coping skills can be developed. And sometimes the development of social problem-solving skills can significantly enhance a client's ability to navigate common anger triggers.

Part 5, "Interventions to Change Thoughts: Accepting, Adapting, and Adjusting," addresses anger management from a different perspective. In life, we all deal with the issue of change versus acceptance. This recognition is part of dialectical behavior therapy and has always been a main tenet of Alcoholics Anonymous (AA). For example, one version of AA's Serenity Prayer is, "Give us the serenity to accept what cannot be changed, the courage to change what can be changed, and the wisdom to know the one from the other." In part 5 we present techniques to help clients adapt when changing anger triggers is unlikely or impossible. We begin with classic cognitive interventions, based on the contributions of Albert Ellis and Aaron Beck, which are aimed at reducing distorted and exaggerated thinking and accepting reality, even aversive reality. Then we move on to interventions that use perspective taking, compassion, and forgiveness to change perceptions about existing problems and reduce anger.

In Part 6, "Interventions to Alter Internal Experiences and Urges," we present ways of helping clients take charge of their lives by reducing impulsive urges and learning to engage in relaxation, mindfulness, and meditation procedures. We also show how deliberate and repeated exposure to anger-provoking situations (see Grodnitzky & Tafrate, 2000; Brondolo, DiGiuseppe, & Tafrate, 1997) may be some of the best medicine for reducing maladaptive anger reactions.

Part 7, "Interventions to Alter Anger Expression," addresses a crucial unawareness on the part of most clients—they often don't realize that one key to solving a problem is to look less angry to the other person than they may actually feel. Adopting certain facial expressions, exhibiting a domineering posture, and standing too close to others can serve as signals of excessive anger and will likely increase negative reactions from others. Apart from describing these kinds of behavioral issues and how they can be handled, in part 7 we discuss verbal assertiveness training as a powerful way to increase effective communication and resolve conflicts.

In part 8, "Going Beyond Anger Management and Putting It All Together," we conclude the intervention package, present ideas to help clients increase their day-to-day happiness, and note that happiness enhancement and anger management go hand in hand. We also present a sample case to illustrate how the SMART program works. This will give you a practical model for approaching individual cases.

Throughout the chapters of this book, you will find practitioner scripts to structure discussions, client information sheets that can be given out, and client worksheets that reinforce different skills. Many of these materials are provided at the end of their respective chapters and can also be downloaded from www.newharbinger.com/42877. In addition, clients can download a parallel assortment of SMART practice exercises from www .newharbinger.com/42266; these are resources from our self-help program (see Tafrate & Kassinove, 2019) and will reinforce the interventions described in this book.

A Word About Labels and Language

Throughout the book, we decided to use the word "client" while recognizing that "patient," "student," "inmate," "parishioner," "group member," or other terms may be more common in your setting. Using this single term makes the chapters more uniform, but there is also a more important reason to use "client." In our judgment, for anger management to work, practitioner-led intervention programs have to be at least partially based on the collaborative efforts of all the parties involved. The term "client" nicely fits this conception.

Similarly, there are many terms for the professionals who provide anger management services—"counselor," "case manager," "educator," "probation officer," "parole officer," "psychologist," "social worker," and "pastor," to name just a few. We decided to use the term "practitioner" to describe professionals who work across a range of settings where anger management might occur.

Services are often described differently across settings—"counseling," "programming," "psychotherapy," "case management," and so forth. We use the terms "treatment" and "intervention" to describe the anger management activities presented throughout this book.

Finally, the term "tools" refers to the specific techniques, exercises, and worksheets that are part of our SMART model.

We commend you for investing your time and effort in becoming a SMART anger management specialist. Let's begin!

PART 1

Anger Treatment Basics

CHAPTER 1

Anger Fundamentals and SMART Anger Management

It is better to light a candle than curse the darkness.

—William L. Watkinson

Anger is natural. It developed as part of the evolutionary fight, freeze, or flee reaction that most animals use to deal with adversity. As a method of protection when they feel threatened, animals sometimes move *toward* the threat. They puff themselves up, show their fangs to look intimidating, change to bold colors, and hiss or make other noises. These displays of strength, like human anger, make it clear that anger, at its base, is an *approach* reaction that emerges to deal with a perceived threat or an imminent attack. In contrast, anxiety is essentially an *avoidance* reaction. When those same animals perceive the threat to be stronger than they are, they make themselves look smaller, change color to blend with the environment, and either freeze or run away to avoid the danger and survive another day.

Anger also serves a communicative function. Much of the time it's easy to spot someone who is angry. We have more than forty muscles on our face that are stimulated by the seventh cranial nerve. They determine how we look to others and also provide a feedback loop that contributes to how we feel in any given moment. If asked to pick the angry face from the two shown in figure 1.1, there is no doubt. It's an easy task. Note the differences in the shape of the eyebrows, the furrow in between the brows, the width of the mouth, and the shape of the lips.

Figure 1.1. Facial Expressions of Anger and Happiness

Facial muscles certainly *communicate* anger and other emotions. Yet they also partially *cause* us to experience feelings. Try to feel happy while mimicking the face at the left in figure 1.1. It doesn't work. Now think of something unfair that was done to you, and try to feel angry while mimicking the face at the right in the figure. Again, it's almost impossible. You can see that facial expressions both communicate anger and partially lead us to experience anger. It turns out that it's a useful and practical step to teach your angry clients about facial communication, although we recognize that few practitioners coach this basic skill.

Anger on the face has also been empirically linked to transient myocardial ischemia (restricted blood flow to the heart). Rosenberg et al. (2001) had 115 men with coronary artery disease undergo a videotaped interview about their pet peeves and situations that led them to feel aggravated. Their facial expressions were recorded, as were their cardiac wall motion abnormalities and left ventricular ejection fraction. It turned out that those who exhibited ischemia showed significantly more anger expressions than smiles. Anger on the face can be threatening and shut down communication. More than half a century ago, Salter (1949) suggested that good psychotherapy includes behavioral exercises such as teaching *facial talk* to clients. We agree! For that reason, we return to the topic of facial talk and body language in chapter 14.

Anger, however, is obviously more than facial talk. It's a complex construct that consists of thoughts and overt verbalizations, mental images, physiological reactions, action urges, and blatant motor behaviors. Because anger is a construct, no single characteristic defines it. Of course, the same is true of anxiety, depression, guilt, and other emotions. They are all complex reactions that we place under a single label for convenience.

In addition to facial reactions, anger has specific vocal components. It's typically characterized by loud and fast speech, as seen in people who are yelling or arguing. Anger usually has a higher pitch than the pitch of contempt, grief, and indifference, and one that is lower than the pitch of fear. When these vocal qualities are combined with certain words and phrases, and with the facial talk just noted, we usually find it straightforward to recognize anger in others.

Verbalizations are among the most obvious and common expressions of anger. Consider these:

- I'm going to completely lose it.

- I get really agitated when I think about what she said about me.

- Are you calling me lazy? You're such a disrespectful ass!

- When I see him tomorrow, I'm going to let him have it.

- No fucking way you're gonna talk to *me* like that!

Obviously, along with other anger elements, words matter because they signal emotional states to others. In a thoughtful and complete anger management program, it will be worthwhile for you to address all the components that both signal anger to others and escalate the personal experience of anger. These components include facial expressions, words, thoughts, desires, and actions.

Universal Sources of Anger

At the human level, our anger reactions come from three fundamental sources:

1. Evolution

2. Personal learning

3. Sociocultural influences

These powerful forces can foster the misconception that anger reactions are entrenched, automatic, and impossible to change. The good news is that with proper focus and repetition of new skills, clients can overcome these influences and change their patterns and habits.

Evolutionary and Biological Roots of Anger

Anger has an evolutionary history that enabled us to survive in the face of danger. Our animal ancestors learned when to be aggressive and when to run away. If they made the wrong choice, they died. Today, anger is thought of as being *partially* controlled by different brain structures, such as the limbic system (for example, the amygdala) and the prefrontal cortex. The limbic system developed as part of our evolution and is considered to be a lower or more primitive part of the brain. It contributes to nonconsciously controlled, impulsive angry and aggressive reactions. In contrast, the prefrontal cortex contributes to slower, more thoughtful responses. When we are threatened, the amygdala is automatically activated and leads to a rapid fight-or-flight response unless it is controlled by prefrontal cortical activity.

If the response that is activated by the amygdala can be delayed, then thoughtful actions determined by the prefrontal cortex can take over. In each of us, the more primitive brain structures develop earlier than others; the prefrontal cortex is not fully developed until we reach approximately the age of twenty-five. This somewhat explains the unhelpful emotional reactivity that occurs in teenagers and young adults. In addition, for some adults, frequent experiences of anger may be the result of having an energetic amygdala that stays in "on" mode, not giving higher prefrontal processes a chance to kick in. Also, some anger can be accounted for by a higher level of such neurotransmitters as dopamine and serotonin. All of this means that anger is partially a built-in, immediate biological reaction to perceived threat. Therefore, interventions to slow actions down are worthwhile, because they give the prefrontal cortex a chance to do its job. That's why relaxation, mindfulness and meditation training, problem solving, and exposure practice are included in the SMART program. This evolutionary underpinning is also why the term "anger *management*" is used. Although we cannot eliminate anger, we can learn to manage behaviors that may exacerbate anger reactions.

A comment on medications is warranted here. We are not aware of any medications developed specifically for anger. Yet, because anger can co-occur with other disorders, such as post-traumatic stress disorder, oppositional defiant disorder, attention deficit and hyperactivity disorder, and various personality and psychotic disorders, you may have clients with anger problems who take antidepressants, antianxiety medications, or drugs for psychotic-spectrum conditions. All medications have side effects, some of which are severe. It is important to understand that the science in this area is quite limited.

Individual Learning Histories

In addition to our evolutionary history, each of us has an individual learning history that continues to develop throughout our lives. This learning history leads to a set of anger-associated habits. Clients who were *reinforced* for anger displays when they were frustrated or disrespected are more likely to react with anger in future, similar situations. In addition, if clients observed older siblings, other family members, or friends acting with strong anger during disagreements and conflicts, then angry behaviors were modeled for them as a way of reacting to the offensive behavior of others, and those clients will likely show anger in similar situations. Also, some young adults learn to bully and demean others as part of the process of being initiated into a club or a gang. This behavior is then reinforced by group cohesion and acceptance into the group, leading to a pattern of repeated angry and aggressive responding.

Social and Cultural Influences

There are also sociocultural forces that encourage or discourage the display of anger and aggression. Although there is a biological universality to anger, culture calibrates responses to perceived aversive threats by teaching display rules (social norms) to its members. For example, Asian cultures are more likely to promote respect for the elderly, which leads to less demonstrated anger at older parents and grandparents.

Culture teaches us when to amplify and when to diminish anger reactions. Therefore, our anger displays are strongly influenced by our culture, our geographic region, our socioeconomic group, and our environment. Some cultural groups, such as the Hutterites of Canada and the northwestern United States, the Hopi of the southwestern United States, the Norwegians, and the Laplanders, are known for their nonviolent perspectives. And all cultures certainly have individual members who model nonviolence; consider Martin Luther King Jr., Mohandas Gandhi, John Lennon, Rosa Parks, and the "flower power" movement of the mid-1960s hippie subculture (you may have seen photographs of young people placing flowers in the muzzles of National Guardsmen's rifles during the antiwar demonstrations of the period). It is also interesting to note that the modern-day Kingdom of Bhutan developed the concept of measuring the nation's "gross national happiness," placing a higher value on kindness, equality, and humanity than on anger and aggression.

In other societies, people are entertained by anger and violence, and they may engage in it at significant levels. For example, violent films dominate theaters and television programs in the United States; violent video games are among the most often played; and gun control is still debated, despite the frequency of street-level gun violence and mass shootings, which are often based on anger and desires for revenge. Finally, in some subcultures, displays of anger are commonly used to achieve respect and enhance or maintain a high rank in the social hierarchy. This phenomenon occurs in gangs, some work environments, and prisons—and, as noted earlier, it contributes to the individual learning histories of some clients.

Client Types: A Tailored Approach

In addition to recognizing that these three sources influence anger reactions, we developed our program with the understanding that there are large individual differences among clients. For example, working with highly verbal and insightful adults is different from working with persons who possess intellectual or developmental disabilities. It is wise to consider age, gender, education, and literacy levels in the development (case formulation) of a successful anger management program for any particular client. Other factors, such as family situation, physical health, financial security, and employment status, can also affect baseline stress levels and responsiveness to treatment. Because the variables for each case will be unique, the SMART program is delivered with a non-manualized and individually tailored approach.

A Brief History of Defining Anger

What, exactly, is anger? Philosophers and scholars have pondered this question for centuries. Definitions are important. They subtly, and not so subtly, frame how we view a phenomenon. Definitions also set the stage for conceptualizing effective treatments. For example, if anger is defined as the activation of the sympathetic nervous system, then interventions that calm the body and mind would be central. A definition of anger that emphasizes distorted thinking leads to the conclusion that cognitive therapy is necessary. If anger is solely about neurotransmitters, then drug treatment holds the most promise. If social and environmental deprivation are central to one's definition of anger, then solutions can be found in the alteration of social dynamics and the situations in people's lives…you get the idea.

The early Greek and Roman philosophers, such as Aristotle, Seneca, and Plutarch, defined anger as a strong emotion or passion that is triggered when people suffer pain, insult, or injury; once aroused, anger motivates action against the offending person. The Greco-Roman philosophers were among the first to identify anger as a potential human problem that can have insidious effects on individuals and entire societies. At the core of anger's damaging effects is its capacity to cloud judgment and impair interpersonal effectiveness (for historical reviews, see DiGiuseppe & Tafrate, 2007, and Potegal & Novaco, 2010).

For extended historical periods, anger was not defined as a legitimate problem in its own right. For example, in psychiatry from the sixteenth through the nineteenth centuries, anger was viewed as a subtype of melancholia. This notion lingers today, as evidenced by the absence of psychiatric diagnoses for anger disorders and by the popular but mistaken view among some practitioners that anger is a secondary emotion and is part of depression.

Darwin (1872) proposed that anger is linked to expressive behaviors (snarling, growling, certain postures, and so forth) that have species-specific survival value. Sigmund Freud, in the twentieth century, expanded on the idea of a biological relationship between anger and aggression, adding that all humans inherently possess aggressive drives and urges that periodically must find expression (be vented) to avoid a buildup of excessive aggressive energy. As we discuss in later chapters, it is unfortunate that some practitioners still see this discredited "catharsis" hypothesis as viable. Similarly, behaviorism, another school of thought that developed during the twentieth century, failed to define anger as an emotional construct worthy of attention; for many behaviorists, anger is defined simply as a diminished form of aggressive motor behavior.

Emotion researchers such as Ekman (1984) and Izard (1977) clearly identify anger as a basic and universal emotion, and these researchers' conclusions are more consistent with the positions of the early Greek and Roman philosophers. Most practitioners today are understandably unfamiliar with the conclusions of emotion researchers, but their findings explain why, in this book, we view anger as a primary problem to be addressed independently from other sorts of behavioral and emotional distress.

Other attempts to define anger include the investigations of Ax (1953) and Schachter (1957), who focused on specific physiological reactions that might serve as markers to differentiate anger from fear. For example, Schachter's subjects with recording wires attached to them were asked to lie down on a bed. In a fear condition, they were told that a possible life-threatening electrical short circuit could occur, and in an anger condition, they were insulted, criticized, and handled roughly; the results showed that angry subjects, in comparison to those in the fear condition, showed larger increases in diastolic blood pressure, muscle tension, and skin conductance responses. A more recent meta-analysis of fifteen studies conducted by Stemmler (2004) concluded that anger provocations, in comparison to fear experiences, led to larger changes in facial temperature, diastolic blood pressure, total resistance of arteries to blood flow, and muscle tension. These findings suggest that physical activation may be a relevant treatment target.

As time went along, interest in the clinical management of anger developed. Novaco (1975) ignited the treatment revolution with his text *Anger Control*. He noted that anger serves six functions—it is energizing, disrupting, expressive, defensive, instigating, and discriminating. Anger can both lead to positive social change and be disruptive to relationships. In this way, anger came to be considered as more than a mild form of aggressive behavior and a simple physiological reaction. It began instead to be identified as a multidimensional state comprising physiological, cognitive, and behavioral elements.

Kennedy (1992) focused on the urgelike nature of anger, noting that it is usually experienced in terms of motivation to act in ways that warn, intimidate, or attack others who are perceived as threats. Accordingly, anger is coupled with sensitivity to the perception of threat.

Novaco (2003, 1) noted not only that "anger is a normal emotion that has considerable adaptive value for coping with life's adversities" but also that anger, as a clinical feature of many disorders, can "become 'dysregulated' so that its activation, expression, and effects occur without appropriate controls." He also noted that anger can be both helpful and unhelpful, can damage social relationships, can activate aggressive behavior, and is often entangled with other, potentially problematic physical health–related behaviors and emotions, such as fear, sadness, and disappointment.

Taylor and Novaco (2005, 17) gave a broader definition of anger as "a negatively toned emotion subjectively experienced as an aroused state of antagonism towards someone or something perceived to be the source of an aversive event." This definition focused on the interpersonal nature of anger—on the fact that anger usually involves a perceived aversive stimulus, and that it includes motivational aspects. They referred to anger as an emotion, a broader term than "feeling." The word "feelings" has traditionally referred to subjective experiences, whereas the word "emotions" has referred to the constellation of subjective experiences, motor behaviors, and changes in the physiology of the body.

Spielberger (1999) suggested that anger is a personally experienced, negative feeling state. He said it can vary in intensity (from annoyance to fury, for example) and in duration (from fleeting to enduring states). He also noted that anger can occur either infrequently or frequently and is associated with negative images and thoughts about the instigating event. Other writers have recognized that angry states may or may not be associated with physiological and motor reactions; further definitions can be found in DiGiuseppe and Tafrate (2007).

Taylor and Novaco (2005), Spielberger (1999), and others make it clear that anger is primarily negative. Most triggers, such as unfair treatment at the hands of others, criticisms, rejection, verbal put-downs, and physical assaults, are objectively unpleasant or aversive and lead to an unpleasant feeling state. At the same time, we acknowledge that anger can have positive outcomes, and that some clients say they want to feel angry in specific situations. Indeed, there are some scenarios where anger can be functional. Some people see anger as beneficial, because it may energize them to face a relationship problem, may enhance social status, or may keep them from being disrespected or treated poorly by others in the future. As we discuss in later chapters, displays of anger are sometimes effective in the short term (that is, they are reinforced) and thus they become hard to eliminate. Nevertheless, few people get up in the morning and say, "I hope I feel pissed off today." Anger is most often viewed as a negative experience.

Elements of truth seem to exist in all the philosophical and historical attempts to define the phenomenon of anger. In our opinion, any definition of dysfunctional anger needs to account for the long-standing acceptance of anger as a basic human emotion that is woven into the fabric of human nature. Therefore, a useful definition of anger will cite its complex, multidimensional makeup, which includes provocations, physical arousal, cognitions, motives, and behaviors. As stated earlier, a definition of anger sets the stage for treatment.

A Working Definition

It is useful to have both a simpler definition of anger, which practitioners can use for everyday work with clients, and a comprehensive definition for scholarly and professional work, when practitioners talk to each other. Our simple definition is in sync with that of Kassinove and Sukhodolsky (1995) and Taylor and Novaco (2005):

> Anger is a transient, negatively experienced emotional state of antagonism or antipathy toward someone or something perceived to be a source of an aversive event, and it typically generates desires to harm or get even.

Our comprehensive definition is in line with that of DiGiuseppe and Tafrate (2007, 21):

> Anger is a subjectively experienced emotional state that is typically, but not always, associated with autonomic arousal (e.g., heart rate increases, sweating, etc.). It is elicited by a perceived threat to one's family, personal well-being, property, or social status, or by violations of rules that regulate social life. It may be shown immediately and also may linger for long periods of time after the threat has passed. As a negative approach-oriented feeling state, it motivates desires to act against others, to warn, intimidate, control, attack, or get retribution. It is associated with distorted thoughts, such as misappraisals about the importance of events or about the ability to cope with problems, demands for justice, global evaluations of others, dichotomous thinking, overgeneralizations, attributions of blame, and fantasies of revenge. Anger is expressed in facial expressions, postural gestures, vocal inflections, aversive verbalizations, and aggressive behavior. Whether it is actually expressed is influenced by social, contextual, and cultural contingencies that define when and how to act when angry.

For practitioners, a comment is in order here about our statement that anger is typically, but not always, associated with physiological changes (such as higher heart rate and blood pressure, sweating, and so forth). In the heat of the moment in everyday life, when clients are yelling and waving their hands, their anger is very likely to be associated with physiological activation. But when you see them days or weeks later in an office setting, their anger is probably more cognitive in nature and only a remembrance of their past experience. Unless you use techniques to evoke anger in the office, as we recommend in the SMART program, the physiological components will often not be present. We discuss tools for safely evoking the experiential element of anger in chapter 13.

Differentiation of Anger, Hostility, and Aggression

Another challenge is differentiating the term "anger" from the related terms "hostility," "aggression," and "violence," since these terms are often used interchangeably in both the scientific and the professional literature as well as in everyday discourse. This has led to confusion and difficulty with diagnosis, assessment, case formulation, and treatment.

We use the term "hostility" to refer to semipermanent negative attitudes that set the stage for anger and aggression. These attitudes represent an overgeneralized way of thinking about a person or groups of people, a way of thinking that leads to response tendencies for anger development. Suppose, for example, that your client's attitudes consist of biased beliefs like "Women are so self-involved" or "Jews are always looking out for themselves" or "Atheists have no morals" or "African Americans are genetically inferior." Such negative attitudes increase the probability that your client will interpret neutral acts by women, Jews, atheists, or African Americans as unfair, deliberately aversive, and preventable, or that your client will believe that negative acts by women, Jews, atheists, and African Americans represent fundamental and permanent group characteristics. And because much of what goes on in life is legitimately ambiguous, with members of all groups varying widely on a variety of characteristics, your client's biased, hostile attitudes will often lead to increased anger and prejudicial behavior.

The term "aggression" refers to observable, gross motor behavior carried out with the *intent* to harm. Behavior that inadvertently hurts another person, such as procedures by a physician that cause pain during an examination, is not considered aggressive. But repeatedly spanking a misbehaving child certainly is aggression, as is shoving a spouse as a "reminder" for him or her not to break a promise again in the future. The word "intent" in our definition of aggression makes it clear that practitioners cannot simply assume all behavior to be automatically and mechanistically elicited by the environment. Rather, our definition assumes that there is some degree of conscious planning and forethought in much of the motor behavior that we label as aggression.

Aggression that immediately follows anger is often called *impulsive emotional aggression* or *reactive aggression,* as when an insult leads to immediate anger and a physical conflict, or when an eruption of road rage quickly leads to retaliation, such as dangerous tailgating. Alternatively, *planned emotional aggression* occurs when, for example, a spurned romantic partner thinks he has been consistently ignored, unappreciated, or humiliated. His anger may be maintained by rumination about the perceived unfair treatment and may eventually lead to a plan to carry out a vengeful, retaliatory, aggressive act against his former partner. Planned emotional aggression may also occur in the workplace or in prisons, or even in a household where a family member perceives disrespect by others, feels angry, and carries out a formulated retaliatory act.

Aggression that occurs in the relative absence of anger is sometimes called *proactive* or *instrumental aggression.* Such aggression is intended to achieve a goal. Much of the aggression that arises in animals, for example, fits this model, as does aggression that emerges in sporting competitions: among animals, the aim is to obtain food; among sports competitors, the aim is to get an opponent out of the way in order to score a run, a touchdown, a point, or a goal and ultimately win the game or the match. This type of aggression is also present in certain types of crime, such as shoplifting, purse snatching, or armed robbery. In a startling example of instrumental aggression, we recently lost a psychologist colleague in New York City when a stranger rushing to enter a subway car before the door closed pushed him over on the platform; our colleague hit his head on the concrete, developed a brain bleed, and never recovered. The outcome in this case was tragic, and yet we realize that the behavior of the perpetrator, who was never identified, was proactive, driven not by anger toward our colleague but by the desire to catch a train.

In these ways, then, *anger may appear in the absence of aggression* and *aggression may appear in the absence of anger.* Anger can be connected both to impulsive aggression and to planned emotional aggression but is less likely to be a precursor of instrumental aggression. In the real world, of course, it is often difficult to neatly categorize clients' observed aggression as exclusively reactive, retaliatory, or instrumental. Instances of instrumental aggression can involve some degree of emotional arousal, and anger can lead to behavior that is goal-oriented.

The good news is that even aggression-prone individuals can learn strategies for inhibiting their aggressive behavior, often through anger reduction (as noted later in this chapter, anger is one of the factors that amplify the urge to aggress). Anger and aggression are also partially connected to the following phenomena and issues:

- A client's testosterone level

- The client's age (with respect, for example, to development of the prefrontal cortex)

- Alcohol and drug intake

- Hot weather

- Uncontrolled pain

- Daily hassles and frustrations

- Relative deprivation

- Social rejection

- Neglect

- Exclusion

- Taunting

- Learning from others in real life, by way of television, or perhaps by way of computer games

These connections highlight the importance of adequate assessment in treating any single individual.

Although there is some overlap between the various definitions and manifestations of anger and aggression, we hope you will think of anger and aggression as different phenomena. After all, as the object of an aversive verbal trigger such as an insult, you *can* learn not to react with anger, whereas you *cannot* learn not to bleed when you're punched in the nose.

Our definition of aggression also overlaps with our definition of violence, which is often thought of as severe aggression. Rape, assault, and murder, not to mention the decapitations that occur in international warfare, are appropriately seen as violent acts.

Anger occurs frequently in daily life but rarely leads to aggression or full-blown violence. Yes, most of us have yelled and broken a pencil, kicked a suitcase, or thrown a book against the wall in a moment of frustration. And if we're honest, most of us can also cite at least one instance in our lives of pushing or shoving someone or destroying property when we were angry. But this is not likely our typical behavior, because the link between anger and aggression is not that strong for most of us. When we were angry, most of us have not seriously punched someone else, pushed someone down the stairs, maimed anyone, or murdered another person. (If you are working in a controlled psychiatric or criminal justice setting, however, you may be dealing with persons who have committed these kinds of violent acts.)

Acts of aggression that make the news are often preceded by anger, and we hear about such acts all the time. But if there is a common perception that anger and aggression are closely linked, it's because the link between them is exaggerated by newspapers, radio, television, and articles on social media that report severe cases of aggression. In our much more common daily experience, anger is not often linked to or followed by aggression. Our more typical experiences of anger never make the headlines.

Does Anger Cause Aggression?

Since most daily anger is not followed by aggression, it's wise to ask why aggression sometimes happens. If we look at individual studies that have examined precursors to one type of aggression—violence directed at an intimate partner—dozens of risk factors can be found. Therefore, an overarching model is needed to account for those times when violence does occur. The I^3 model (pronounced "I cubed"; see Finkel & Eckhardt, 2013; Finkel, 2014) does just that. It suggests that aggression emerges as a function of three interacting factors, all of which begin with the letter I:

1. *Instigation:* In the I^3 model, some sort of instigation is required. The term "instigation" refers to a situational event that normatively triggers an urge to aggress, and that produces a rudimentary form of anger. For most adults, instigation might take the form of being called an offensive name, or suddenly learning that our marital partner has been unfaithful, or being rejected, or being disrespected at work, or suffering from chronic pain.

2. *Impellance:* The term "impellance" refers to a force that increases the urge to act in response to an instigating stimulus. Impelling forces increase the base level of aggressive urges. They may be cultural, evolutionary, biological, or based on subgroup-level social norms. For a client who discovers a spousal transgression, impelling forces to act may be based on beliefs (such as "Honesty and respect are paramount in relationships" and "Disrespect absolutely must be dealt with") or on a high level of dispositional jealousy. In addition, the client may be impelled to act aggressively because he has witnessed aggression in his family of origin.

3. *Inhibition:* The term "inhibition" refers to typical counteracting forces of aggression, such as cultural norms, the awareness of negative consequences, or the capacity for perspective taking and empathy. Such counteracting forces are probably diminished, however, for a client who has had a few drinks or who is not cognitively sharp because of fatigue or drug use or who has experienced head trauma or who is sleep-deprived or who perceives little risk of negative outcomes from acting aggressively.

Aggression and violence against a partner are most likely, and most severe, when the instigating and impelling forces are strong but the inhibiting forces are weak.

So how does anger fit into the I³ model? Anger is an instigating and impelling force that, combined with reduced inhibition, produces interpersonal aggression. It follows, then, that *if anger can be reduced, both the urge to aggress and actual aggression will also be reduced.*

Four Questions for Differentiating Normal from Dysfunctional Anger

Anger can be both psychopathological and normal, since it is a function of our evolutionary past and appears in everyone. But anger is manifested differently at younger ages, and in varying degrees among adults. Children under the age of five have limited cognitive development and often react with temper tantrums. For example, when a two-year-old discovers that her favorite toy is broken, she may express immediate, full-blown rage by yelling, throwing her other toys, and crying uncontrollably, but her reactions may end within five minutes if a parent consoles or distracts her. Things are quite different after the prefontal cortex is more fully developed (that is, by late adolescence or early adulthood); at this age, an undesirable work schedule or a misplaced set of keys may lead to nothing more than annoyance. And yet psychopathological anger—an adult tantrum, in effect, which is a sign of emotional dysregulation—is still possible and may lead to strong anger and a desire for revenge, as when your client learns that a close friend has been spreading lies and nasty rumors about him.

What, then, differentiates normal anger from psychopathological anger? When we evaluate a client, we start by asking four questions that involve the *frequency, intensity, duration,* and *effectiveness* of the client's anger.

1. How Often Is the Client Angry?

It turns out that normal adults may feel some degree of anger once or twice a week (Tafrate, Kassinove, & Dundin, 2002). The frequency of a client's anger will depend on a variety of objective life factors. Living with an alcoholic or verbally abusive spouse will generate more anger than living in a well-functioning family. Likewise, being harassed or bullied by a nasty neighbor may lead to frequent (if suppressed) anger, and an adult whose work is constantly criticized by a supervisor will likely feel more frequent anger in the workplace than someone whose work performance is often appreciated.

2. How Intense Is the Client's Anger?

Although we are not surprised when a child under the age of five throws a tantrum, we expect the intensity of an adult's anger to be in proportion to the triggering stimulus. It's normal to feel more anger when you discover that your friend and business partner has stolen money from your company than when you discover that your refrigerator has broken and you need to replace the milk. That is, some situations deserve more anger than others. When we say "deserve," we simply mean that there are unspoken cultural rules about anger reactions, and well-adjusted adults learn those rules and abide by them. We support the minimization of anger in most circumstances, but we also understand the strength of anger in reaction to the infliction of severe suffering. For example, who can't understand intense anger toward Farid Fata, a Michigan oncologist who got rich by administering needless or excessive chemotherapy to his patients, many of whom did not have cancer (Allen, 2015)? Some of Fata's victims lost their teeth or their ability to walk, and many suffered excruciating pain from his interventions. Fata was ultimately sentenced to forty-five years in prison, but we certainly understand the continued anger of his victims. And yet their anger does little good. (In chapter 11 we discuss how some people have found ways to overcome anger, even in extreme situations like this one.)

3. How Long Does the Client's Anger Last?

Most anger lasts from a few minutes to a few hours. When it festers for weeks or even years, and if there is continued rumination about the event, it has gone beyond the common experience of anger and may lead to more serious consequences.

4. Is Clients' Anger Working for Them?

There are both benefits and costs to anger. If a client's mild, moderate, or temporary anger is useful in a specific situation because she finds it energizing and motivating, then her anger may not become the focus of treatment. But if her anger leads to more serious consequences—road rage, for example, or relationship-damaging arguments with friends, family members, and colleagues, or problems with the criminal justice system, or marital conflict, or conflict with former romantic partners, or dismissal from her job, or expulsion from school—then we're dealing with something else.

Can Anger Be Managed?

In most cases, the goal of treatment will be to diminish anger so that your client will experience reduced negative affectivity to daily stressors (see McIntyre et al., 2018), suffer fewer negative life consequences, and live a more fulfilling life. It makes sense, then, to ask an important question before you learn skills to promote anger management: *Are anger management programs effective?*

As this book went to press, there were more than a dozen meta-analyses and reviews indicating that, across various populations, people who received treatment for anger had more positive outcomes than people in control or no-treatment conditions (Lee & DiGiuseppe, 2018). Since meta-analysis is a statistical technique for combining findings from independent studies, our belief in the effectiveness of anger management is well supported by the available science. The reviews we cite have demonstrated moderate to strong overall mean-effect sizes. On the basis of these results, we conclude that there is good evidence for the effectiveness of psychological treatments for anger.

As just one example, a meta-analysis by Saini (2009) included 96 studies and 139 treatment effects. Most of the studies were conducted in the United States, and nine different types of treatment were examined:

1. Cognitive therapy

2. Cognitive behavioral therapy

3. Exposure

4. Psychodynamic therapy

5. Psychoeducation

6. Relaxation-based interventions

7. Skills training, including assertiveness training

8. Stress inoculation

9. Multicomponent interventions

The results were quite positive. According to Saini (2009, 476), "Within adult populations, the meta-analytic reviews provide evidence that treating anger is effective across diverse groups including persistently violent male prisoners, adults with intellectual and learning disabilities, forensic patients, angry parents, female batterers, mental health patients, undergraduate students, incarcerated male juveniles, male batterers, aggressive drivers, faculty members, Vietnam War combat veterans, and patients with schizophrenia." Saini found significantly larger effect sizes for programs that used multiple interventions, as compared with single-modality approaches like cognitive therapy, psychoeducation, and relaxation-based interventions. Also, larger effect sizes emerged in university and community treatment programs than in correctional facilities, psychiatric facilities, and hospitals. Yet even studies with special populations (such as developmentally delayed individuals, and people in forensic facilities or incarcerated samples) showed positive results. The mean number of treatment sessions in the studies reviewed was 8.5, with a range of 3 to 40. As expected, the data suggested that more sessions are better. As programs required more sessions, however, dropout rates also increased. Therefore, a smaller number of sessions—say, eight to fifteen—may represent a nice balance.

In contrast to these positive conclusions from meta-analytic data, Olatunji and Lohr (2004) reviewed evidence for the efficacy of psychological interventions for anger. They concluded that much of the change we see in clients is due to nonspecific or *common* factors, such as attention, support, reflective listening, and expectation for an intervention to work. Since the SMART program focuses both on the therapeutic relationship and on specific interventions, it is fully aligned with both sets of findings.

SMART Anger Management

As noted in the introduction to this book, the SMART program is based on findings from the scientific literature as well as on our combined seventy-five years of experience providing psychological treatment to clients in a variety of treatment settings (including community mental health centers, hospitals, prisons, university clinics, probation departments, criminal justice community programs, and independent practice). These experiences have led us to conclude that manualized, rigid programs are likely to provide only limited success in the real world. They may have *efficacy* in research studies, but their *effectiveness* in real-world clinical settings will probably be limited.

We recognize that the readers of this book work in a wide array of treatment settings, including outpatient practice, hospital or university clinics, religious institutions, criminal justice programs, and the like, and offer anger management services to persons who differ on a range of characteristics, such as age, literacy level, socioeconomic status, motivation, ethnicity, comorbid mental health problems, and so forth. Moreover, many treatment settings restrict what can be offered to clients, how treatment can be offered, and how long it can be delivered. For example, insurance companies may decide whether to reimburse a hospital for continued services. In a school, services may have to end in June, when the institution closes for summer vacation. In a university, administrative officers may impose limits on the number of treatment sessions that can be offered to a student, and the services usually end when the student graduates. In a prison, services may abruptly conclude if the client is transferred to another facility. For security reasons, one of our colleagues who works with inmates at a maximum-security state prison was able to deliver anger management services only by way of the prison mail system and never saw his clients in person. Then, in probation departments, treatment ends when probation ends.

As also noted in the introduction, clients have their own preferences and expectations regarding treatment, which may lead them to consider some interventions acceptable and others unacceptable. For example, a client may accept a relaxation procedure but bristle at the idea of forgiving a perceived enemy. Some clients want to incorporate religious teachings into their progress, whereas others reject any kind of spiritual component. These factors all argue for the development of customizable programming—and that is what you will develop as a SMART anger manager.

Elements That Lead to Change

Our recommendations regarding the multiple elements that lead to anger reduction are based on current thinking in the fields of counseling and psychotherapy. For example, Johnsen and Friborg (2015, 748), cite four sources of improvement that are associated with efficacious treatment in psychotherapy research trials:

1. Client-related factors: These include the client's personality traits, temperament, motivation for treatment, and experience of significant life events.

2. Therapist-related factors: These include the practitioner's education, training, skill level, knowledge of interventions, and competence in engaging the client and establishing the therapeutic alliance as well as such personal factors as gender, age, and even height and appearance.

3. Common factors: These include factors important across all models of psychotherapy, such as the context of therapy, the presence of an acceptable rationale for the interventions to be used, the achieved client-practitioner relationship, expectations for improvement, and perceived social support.

4. Technique-specific factors: These include the interventions specific to a particular treatment model, such as a focus on particular constructs (the client's cognitions, relationships, behaviors, family of origin, and so forth), the implementation of specific procedures (use of metaphors or cognitive restructuring, for example), the number of sessions, and possible use of out-of-session assignments).

So here is the big question: *To what degree does each of these four factors relate to the outcome of an intervention?* According to Johnsen and Friborg (2015), common factors account for the greatest amount of change (about 40 percent), client factors are next (approximately 35 percent), therapist factors explain approximately 10 percent of outcomes, and only 15 percent is attributable to specific techniques. There are also important changes over the course of treatment to consider. Common factors are more important in the beginning phase of intervention, and technique-specific factors become more important as time goes on (Honyashiki et al., 2014). Thus you can see why the SMART program, although based in science, is not rigidly limited to a single psychotherapeutic orientation and is not highly manualized. Rather, the SMART program includes interventions and tools from behavioral, cognitive, client-centered, constructivist, cultural, and humanistic orientations.

Takeaway Messages and Tools

In the end, a flexible and uniquely customized program is most likely to be successful. Nevertheless, such a program places emphasis on your judgment with respect to which of the many available intervention options will probably be successful with clients in your particular setting. Once interventions are selected, it will be important for you to be skilled in delivering them so that they are carried out correctly. It is also helpful for you to be aware of your own anger issues, biases, and interpersonal skills so that they do not interfere with treatment.

The SMART program requires you to understand and address the elements of good anger treatment:

- Client engagement and preparation

- Assessment and case formulation

- Skills for altering clients' anger triggers, restructuring their thinking, lowering their internal anger experiences, reducing their urges to act, improving their expression of felt anger, and helping them create a path to a life worth living

These elements are not sequentially fixed; rather, they are overlapping targets for change. Nevertheless, we stress again that treatment is unlikely to be successful unless careful consideration is first given to issues of engagement and preparation.

To help guide your learning and skill development, figure 1.2 presents the broad stages of a SMART anger management intervention plan. We hope you will find it useful as you conceptualize your cases. And, since engagement is a primary factor for treatment success, we address it fully in chapter 2.

Engagement

Expect client motivation and engagement levels to vary widely. Many angry clients will arrive at least partially against their will, coerced into treatment by family members, friends, employers, or the criminal justice system. Some may participate simply because they believe it will look good on their "record." Therefore, the first consideration for any case centers on the engagement process (see chapter 2).

Case Formulation

Use a good interview as well as selected assessment instruments to develop an understanding of how anger looks in your client's life. How frequent, intense, and enduring is it? What recurring triggers have set off angry reactions, and what kinds of thoughts exist about those triggers? What is the anger experience like, and how is anger typically expressed? What have been the shorter- and longer-term real-world outcomes and repercussions of the client's anger? Said another way, what impact does anger have on the person's everyday life (see chapters 3 and 4)?

Preparing Clients for Change

The term "change" refers to the development of skills to deal with perceived aversive situations. Nevertheless, clients may show resistance or lack of enthusiasm to work on the development of better reactions. You may have to consider whether there is adequate awareness regarding the dysfunctional and destructive nature of the anger experiences and expressions, and whether there is enough motivation to change. Evoking and reinforcing the client's own reasons for changing anger reactions is to be emphasized in the early phases of treatment. Psychoeducation can also be helpful in bringing some of the critical issues regarding anger into the forefront so they can become a focus of discussion (see chapters 5 and 6).

Interventions to Change Triggers

Once you have established a good working relationship, developed a case formulation, and gained a clear sense of what anger looks like in the client's life, and once your client is prepared to work on change, the active treatment process can begin. At this point, the goal is to deal with the actual triggers that repeatedly lead to dysfunctional anger. There may be particular pre-anger lifestyle changes (such as improving the quality of sleep) that can be put into practice to reduce stress and anger. You may be able to teach clients to skillfully sidestep certain provocations. It may also be worthwhile to teach problem-solving techniques so the client can more effectively deal with certain anger triggers (see chapters 7, 8, and 9).

Interventions to Change Thoughts

In cases where the likelihood of change in a situation or other people is minimal or nonexistent, clients will benefit from interventions that aim to reduce their distorted and exaggerated thinking and to help them accept the realities of their lives. These aims can be achieved through clients' development of a flexible life philosophy, through recognition of their own ability to deal with adversity, through their becoming compassionate, and through their learning to take a perspective other than their own (see chapters 10 and 11).

Interventions to Alter Internal Experiences and Urges

Tools to reduce impulsive urges to act include training and exercises in muscle relaxation, meditation, and mindfulness. It may also be useful to remind clients that thoughts are just thoughts, and that thoughts do not have to be acted on. By safely and repeatedly exposing clients to their common anger triggers, you can significantly reduce internal activation and improve reactions (see chapters 12 and 13).

Interventions to Alter Anger Expression

Much anger arises from interpersonal conflict, with clients misunderstanding social dynamics and how to verbally express themselves. Here, the goal is to teach clients about facial expressions, tone of voice, interpersonal distance, and similar factors. They also learn about the differences among assertive expressions of annoyance, aggressive verbalizations, and unassertive or passive responses. Conflicts have the greatest chance of being resolved if the parties express their concerns in reasonable ways and search for mutually beneficial solutions (see chapters 14 and 15).

Going Beyond Anger Management

Once you reach the point where successful anger reduction has occurred, it's time to move to another level. A reduction in your client's anger is not a guarantee that your client will flourish in his or her family relationships, career, or other aspects of life. We want clients to give some thought to how they might increase their overall happiness, and to whether they are living a life they will be proud of in the years ahead. Apart from helping the client review accomplishments and successes, and how to maintain gains when the intervention is over, the culminating goal of the entire SMART anger management program is to help the client create a life worth living (see chapter 16).

Figure 1.2. SMART Anger Management: Intervention Plan Overview

CHAPTER 2

The Initial Sessions: Engagement

Three things in human life are important. The first is to be kind. The second is to be kind. And the third is to be kind.

—Henry James

Mark is thirty-three and currently married, with two daughters, eight and nine years old. He sought counseling because his wife said she just couldn't put up with his temper and drinking any longer. She complains about having spent years tiptoeing around him, trying not to say or do anything that might trigger his anger.

There is also concern about the effect that Mark's anger is having on their daughters, who are becoming increasingly distant from him. A recent altercation between Mark and his brother-in-law at a family picnic prompted the referral for treatment: what had started as a verbal argument quickly escalated into a brawl involving several family members; the police were called, but, fortunately, no arrests were made.

Mark's in-laws now refuse to have any contact with him. Following this incident, Mark's wife insisted that he seek treatment. She is adamant about seeing real change, in order to stay married.

A review of other areas of Mark's life revealed that he is a man with a high school education and a sporadic work history. During the past decade, he has worked for a few different companies, primarily in construction. Although he is generally viewed as a skilled employee, his disagreements with supervisors and colleagues have derailed his long-term employment and advancement opportunities.

Mark acknowledges that he drinks at the end of the day to relax, but what used to be one beer during dinner is now supplemented by two or three hard drinks. Overall, Mark is not sure that anger is the cause of his family and work problems. Discussing some recent anger-related negative incidents, he was quick to point out reasons why others were at fault, and why his actions were justified. At the same time, he expresses a desire to keep his family intact, be a good father, and find steady employment with a company where he can get along with people.

Mark's story is typical of many adults referred for anger treatment:

- *He is seeking counseling because of external pressures.* It's common for people like Mark to be coerced into treatment. Concerned friends and family members, sometimes employers, and, in more extreme cases, the criminal justice system may serve as the primary motivation for clients to show up, at least initially. Therefore, in adults with problematic anger reactions, as compared to adults suffering from anxiety and depression, intrinsic motivation to change is often lacking. When anger is a presenting problem, we recommend that you carefully consider the sources of subtle and overt coercion as well as the degree to which such factors are influencing the client's decision to seek intervention.

- *There is evidence of significant damage to relationships, both at home and at work.* Relationships of chronically angry individuals are marked by high rates of verbal and physical conflict and by overall life dissatisfaction.

- *There appears to be a connection between Mark's anger and his comorbid substance use.* One explanation for this link is that people who experience chronic anger turn to alcohol and other drugs as a means of reducing their negative internal arousal. For some individuals, over time, this pattern of substance use becomes entrenched through negative reinforcement, whereby unpleasant bodily activation is dulled by alcohol or drugs. For others, substance use reduces inhibition and increases verbal and physical expressions of anger. The result can be enhanced feelings of self-efficacy and power in dealing with interpersonal conflicts and life's stressors. Of course, when an individual is intoxicated, such feelings are illusory; risky behavior and damage to important relationships are more often the reality.

- *Mark is like many other individuals referred for anger counseling in that his attitude toward treatment can be described as ambivalent.* The prevailing mind-set of most people when they are experiencing anger is to see themselves as having been transgressed upon and treated unfairly, and to believe that others should have acted differently. In addition, people recalling the circumstances surrounding their anger typically view their own actions as justified.

- *In Mark as well as in other angry clients, we have noticed a set of beliefs that are less obvious but that are clinically important because they underlie and support motivation to change.* These beliefs, which can be elicited with skillful interaction on your part, are related to clients' recognition of the costs associated with their anger reactions, and to their desire to improve in specific life areas. It's common for clients to come to treatment focusing on the unfair behavior of others but at the same time to have some awareness that their anger is not working for them. It's this ambivalence—their feeling two ways about their anger—that makes it so challenging to engage angry clients.

Four Beliefs Likely to Impede Engagement

On the basis of our experience and research on treatment dropout (Mitchell, Tafrate, Hogan, & Olver, 2013), we recommend your consideration of four beliefs about anger that, when endorsed by clients, may hinder treatment engagement. These four beliefs inhibit the self-reflection that people often need in order to reach the conclusion that reducing their anger reactions is important. Note, however, that it's a mistake to directly confront these beliefs too early in treatment. Rather, we recommend that you listen for these themes, be patient, explore, and gently guide the person to consider alternative views.

1. It's Healthy for Me to Express Anger

Our culture continues to promote the idea that cathartic expression is healthy and desirable. Further, venting anger often feels right and may provide the temporary illusion of relief (in the same way that leaving a party feels right for people with social anxiety). This is highlighted by a disturbing trend—the marketing of "anger rooms" for overly stressed businessmen and businesswomen (http://www.angerroom.com/about-us-old). In contrast, very few credible professionals argue that venting makes people less angry. The notion that if anger is not expressed, it will build up and lead to physical illness or increased aggression has been largely debunked. Most experts agree that catharsis as an intervention makes people worse (Bushman, 2002; Lohr, Olatunji, Baumeister, & Bushman, 2007). To help your client challenge the venting hypothesis, you can explore the consequences of anger expression, how others view the client's outbursts when they occur, and the deleterious effects that anger expression is having on the client's existing relationships.

2. My Anger Is Controlled by External Sources

You will commonly hear clients say, "He/she/they/it made me angry." The downside of this belief is that if people see the cause of their anger as wholly externally based, they will be unlikely to think they can change it. It is certainly wise to begin by acknowledging the perceived transgressions of others; there is simply no shortcut for this. Over time, however, conversations with SMART anger managers shift away from the "bad," "immoral," or "unfair" behavior of others and explore the extent to which anger is helping the client face problems effectively, negotiate desired outcomes, and live a happy life. Also, lack of interpersonal, cognitive, and problem-solving skills can contribute to the belief that anger is an automatic and uncontrollable reaction to adversity. Assisting clients in developing new skills will provide strong evidence that clients can actually manage their anger reactions, and that it is useful for them to do so.

3. Anger Gets Me What I Want

Anger reactions often produce short-term compliance from others. Parents who harshly yell at their children may get them to temporarily stop arguing or do their homework. Supervisors who scold their employees may push them to meet deadlines, and angrily confronting a family member may produce an apology. At the same time, there are longer-term costs associated with such outbursts. Rather than strengthening bonds, anger is likely to create resentment, bitterness, and distance in relationships. Examining the longer-term social consequences of anger expression is often worthwhile, since many clients are not aware of them.

4. Anger Protects Me

For some clients, anger expression is part of projecting a tough image. They believe that if they give up their anger, others will take advantage of them. In these cases, it's useful to explore the person's history in order to determine the etiology of this idea. Experiences of adversity, trauma, and abuse may be part of the clinical picture. For other clients, anger is more connected to a peer or family environment that reinforces anger and its expression. As treatment progresses, explore the possibility that your client, with the addition of new anger reduction skills, can still be respected, strong, and effective in the world.

Six Behaviors for Practitioners to Avoid in the Initial Sessions

Being successful at engaging angry clients often means pulling back from some common ways you may be used to acting as a practitioner. Here, we suggest six behaviors for you to avoid in the first couple of meetings and sometimes in later sessions as well.

1. Being Confrontational

Here are some examples of the "get tough" approach:

- You're just a bully who tries to control everyone with your anger.

- Your anger is ruining your life. When are you going to wake up?

- I'm not putting up with your nonsense. I won't hesitate to call your probation officer.

It may look good on reality TV, but this approach will generally backfire; for example, this kind of confrontation usually perpetuates the client's defensiveness and damages the opportunity to form a productive working relationship. Also, angry clients are generally ambivalent about their anger reactions to begin with. When you confront such individuals, you are firmly placing yourself on one side of the ambivalence equation by communicating that anger is a problem that needs to be changed. This stance naturally leads the client to jump to the other side and explain why anger episodes are reasonable and justifiable given the circumstances.

2. Asking Closed-Ended Fact-Gathering Questions

To gather relevant information, there is often the temptation to engage the client with a barrage of closed-ended questions:

- How long have you been married?

- Have you hit your children?

- Have you ever been arrested?

These types of fact-gathering questions are problematic because they immediately narrow the conversational focus to what the practitioner thinks is most important. This line of questioning will unintentionally produce an interrogative quality to the session, render the client passive, and result in lack of depth.

3. Performing a Comprehensive Assessment

We recommend that you pull back from lengthy assessment activities in the initial session or two. Engagement is the first priority. Consider assessment to be an ongoing process that will be more valid once engagement is established. (A range of recommended assessment strategies, to be used once a working relationship has developed, is discussed in chapters 3 and 4.)

4. Making Judgmental Statements

A common error in angry individuals is to simultaneously misinterpret another person's neutral communications and to attribute malevolent intentions to the other person. Even an offhand or well-intentioned comment by a practitioner—"It might be difficult for you to get hired, with your history of anger outbursts" or "Your kids are going to grow up repeating your angry patterns because that is what you are showing them"—can be perceived as judgmental and can damage the foundations of a working relationship. It will be difficult to move treatment forward with clients who do not think you understand their perspective, or who do not believe that you have their best interests at heart.

5. Debating the Client

It is very unlikely that you will be able to debate your clients out of their problematic anger reactions. Disputing is a foundational element of traditional cognitive interventions, but presenting logical arguments too soon (that is, prior to successful engagement) will often backfire because such discussions run the risk of coming across as invalidating. The goal is to have the first sessions feel more like dancing together than like wrestling or tussling, and debate will not produce that outcome.

There are two issues that practitioners commonly want to debate with their angry clients, and each is likely to quickly throw engagement off track. The first issue has to do with the excessiveness of clients' anger reactions in relation to triggering events (sometimes referred to as the *transgression-to-retaliation ratio*); debate about this ratio will cause clients to defend their actions and verbalize their reasons for believing that their behaviors are appropriate. The second issue has to do with getting the client to replace demanding and inflexible beliefs with more preference-based views. For example, you may want to make a philosophically reasonable point by asking, "Why *must* your supervisor always treat you with respect?" But this maneuver will not enhance engagement; it's counterproductive when presented too early, and will probably be met with an argument about why the boss is at fault, and why life would be better if everyone were respectful.

6. Being the Expert

A range of behavior on the part of practitioners falls under this category, such as giving advice, providing solutions, presenting educational information about anger, identifying faulty thinking, and recommending new behaviors. Although some of these activities are central to the SMART change strategies we present in later chapters, they tend to be less optimal in the early, engagement phase of treatment.

There are two reasons to initially pull back from such activities:

1. As noted earlier, pushing for change places you squarely on one side of the ambivalence equation, leaving clients to once again verbalize why their anger is necessary, useful, and not a big deal.

2. Being the expert too early can come across as condescending and demeaning.

In training workshops, we sometimes make the second point by having someone present a challenging real-life personal problem that is connected to anger (this presentation is also called a *real-play*). Perhaps, for example, the person talks about a problem—with in-laws, or teachers, or children—that has been associated with anger. As the other workshop participants take turns "helping," it quickly becomes apparent that giving advice is a frequent but ineffective strategy. After ten minutes or so, we debrief the group and discuss why providing advice didn't work. From the perspective of the real-play client, the same reasons emerge in group after group. Keep in mind that these same client responses are usually unspoken in real-world sessions. We bring them out in our workshops in order to illustrate the unspoken dynamics that can occur within a session. Here are some common, unspoken reactions that clients may never communicate to you aloud when you give advice:

- I have been struggling with my problem for ten years. How do you think it comes across when you tell me what to do after five minutes?

- You are condescending. You make it sound like I am really stupid not to have thought of such an obvious solution.

- What's the likelihood that in ten years I have already tried what you suggested? I have, and it didn't work.

- You have been thinking about my problem for about ten minutes. Don't you think there are more details surrounding my problem that you are not yet aware of? Actually, there are many details and nuances that you don't know about yet. I don't trust that you understand me enough, so I'm not willing to accept your advice after just a few minutes.

- Is there a simple solution, like the one you are suggesting, that fixes this problem? No! You don't seem to understand that some life problems don't lend themselves to quick solutions. Many, like this one I am having, require longer-term adaption and adjustment rather than a simple quick fix.

Even if you are well-meaning, positioning yourself as an expert in the first meeting or two is unlikely to produce successful engagement with angry clients.

Foundations for Successful Engagement

Now that we have presented some information about beliefs that may diminish engagement and about behaviors to avoid in initial sessions, let's move on to some truly helpful ways to begin treatment. What are the ingredients for quickly and successfully engaging difficult cases?

The Therapeutic Alliance

We begin with the recognition that the interpersonal therapeutic alliance is central to success. One widely accepted model of the therapeutic alliance, (Bordin, 1979) highlights three components of successful engagement:

1. A warm, accepting, mutually respectful relationship

2. Agreement on the goals of treatment

3.   Agreement on the tasks or steps needed to reach those goals

The therapeutic or working alliance has also received considerable attention from other researchers (see, for example, Muran & Barber, 2010). Here are a few key findings:

- The therapeutic alliance is very important across treatment modalities and clinical problems.

- The therapeutic alliance is established early in treatment, usually by the third or fourth session.

- The alliance is dynamic; once established, it can rupture or collapse.

- A weak alliance is strongly associated with client dropout.

Our position is that a positive and productive working relationship can be developed with most (but not all) clients who present with anger problems. As a general rule, however, more coercive referrals require longer engagement-oriented activities. Because of the typical mind-set of blaming and denying, agreement on the goals of treatment is typically more difficult to achieve with angry clients than with those suffering from anxiety or depression, who tend to have a more internal focus and a desire to alleviate their distressing symptoms.

The good news is that once angry clients come to the realization that their anger reactions are not working for them, agreement on active steps toward change can be surprisingly straightforward. Angry clients often possess a willingness to practice new skills and engage in exposure activities; clients suffering from anxiety, by contrast, usually show strong tendencies to avoid unpleasant scenarios. Angry clients also show less helplessness and inaction and have more energy to implement new ways of thinking and behaving than do depressed clients.

Motivational Interviewing, the Four OARS Skills, and Four Dynamic Processes

Our approach to engaging clients with anger problems rests on a foundation of *motivational interviewing*, or MI (see Miller & Rollnick, 2013). Our decision to incorporate MI as a central component of SMART anger treatment was made because of failures we experienced when trying to implement evidence-based interventions in real-world settings. Much of the published literature on outcomes of anger treatment comes from studies conducted with analog populations (such as high-anger college students) or volunteer participants who had already decided to seek treatment to reduce their anger. It became apparent to us that empirically supported interventions, when transferred to settings with mandated clients, did not get off the ground so easily. Something more was needed to be successful. In the 1990s, the first MI training videos showed a way of working with such traditionally "resistant" client problems as intimate partner violence, prostitution, and alcohol and drug use; these videos demonstrated an approach that diverged significantly from the more authoritarian, confrontational, and directive approaches that dominated clinical practice. As the MI treatment literature grew, it was shown to have a synergistic effect with respect to other approaches. Our perspective is that MI complements the interventions we outline in later chapters.

Miller and Rollnick (2013, 13, 21, 29) define MI in three ways:

1.   Their simplest definition of MI is "a collaborative conversation style for strengthening a person's own motivation and commitment to change."

2.   With respect to why a practitioner would want to learn and use MI, they define it as "a person-centered counseling style for addressing the common problem of ambivalence about change."

3.   Their technical definition is that MI works as "a collaborative, goal-oriented style of communication with particular attention to the language of change," a style that is "designed to strengthen personal motivation for and commitment to a specific goal by eliciting and exploring the person's own reasons for change within an atmosphere of acceptance and compassion."

Overall, MI is based on a spirit of partnership, acceptance, compassion, and evocation from the client. It is also understood to be a communication style built on what are known as the four *OARS skills:*

1.   Open questions

2.   Affirmations

3.   Reflections

4.   Summarizations

The OARS skills themselves are used across four *broad and dynamic processes* whose objective is to elicit and explore the client's own motivations to make changes:

1.   Engaging

2.   Focusing

3.   Evoking intrinsic motivation

4.   Change planning

We will have more to say about the OARS skills later in the chapter (see "Using the OARS Skills"). For now, let's take a look at the four processes just mentioned, with an emphasis in this chapter on engagement in the first session (the other four processes are touched on in later chapters). In using these four processes, flexibility is key because the amount of time spent on each process will vary considerably across different clients. Also, the processes are best thought of as fluid and overlapping rather than as simple, discrete stages. Although you will likely begin with engaging and end with change planning, you will find yourself shifting back and forth as challenges arise. In that sense, there is no precise beginning or end to each process.

1. ENGAGING

The first process, *engaging*, is about connecting and establishing a productive working relationship. With a focus on listening skills, the goal is to fully understand your client's perspective, without an agenda for change. Here, your job is to avoid "fixing" the anger problem. Your first priority is to foster the working relationship with your client.

2. FOCUSING

The second process, *focusing*, occurs when you and your client clarify a general direction and establish agreed-upon targets or goals. Ask your client what he or she sees as important to change, and what he or she desires to be different.

3. EVOKING INTRINSIC MOTIVATION

At the heart of MI is the third process, *evoking*, which involves eliciting clients' own motivations to make changes. Here, your goal is to listen for, selectively reinforce, and sometimes actively elicit client verbalizations in favor of moving in a direction of less anger. This type of client language, referred to as *change talk*, is further discussed in chapter 5; the opposite type of client language is referred to as *sustain talk*, which means verbalizations about not changing. Again, we recommend against making suggestions, giving advice, or coming across as the expert. Instead, use probes: "What has led you to think that your anger is a problem?" or "What makes you feel confident that you can actually reduce your yelling when conflicts with your colleagues at work occur?" Then be prepared to reinforce change talk. For now, see if you can discriminate between change talk and sustain talk by looking at the statements presented in table 2.1. Which statements might you reflect and reinforce? Which would you pay less attention to?

We would try to verbally reinforce A2, B1, C2, D1, and E2 with reflective statements like these:

- A2: "So one reason you would like to work on your anger is to reduce your chances of having an early heart attack."

- B1: "You seem confident that you can make things better."

- C2: "You would like to have a better connection with your kids. Being a good listener might help improve things."

- D1: "You are aware that your relationship would probably get better if you reduced your yelling."

- E2: "You want to be a more thoughtful and calmer boss. One of your goals is to stop blowing up at your employees."

Table 2.1. Change Talk or Sustain Talk?

A1. My whole family yells. I think it's in our blood.	A2. My whole family yells and screams, but I don't want to wind up like my father, who had a heart attack at the age of forty-nine.
B1. If I put in some effort, I know I can make our relationship better.	B2. We fight a lot. But it's not a big deal, because we make up a few days later.
C1. I'm constantly trying to give my children good advice, but they don't often come to me.	C2. I noticed that Jack is a good listener, and his children always go to him for advice.
D1. If I stopped yelling, I might get along better with my spouse.	D2. My spouse and I argue almost every day. It's just the way we are.
E1. My employees only listen to me when I am angry. Then they do what I tell them to do.	E2. I'd like to be a good boss, the kind who doesn't blow up at his employees.

4. CHANGE PLANNING

The fourth process, *change planning,* is about establishing realistic and manageable steps to reach agreed-upon goals. Here, it's wise to reinforce another type of client language known as *commitment language:* "I'm going to buy that anger management book I saw at the bookstore" or "I will call the high school tomorrow morning to inquire about their parenting course for adults" or "I'll spend fifteen minutes just listening to my son." Commitment language is often captured in verbalizations in which the client communicates a specific next step. This topic is covered again in more detail in chapter 5.

Seven Behaviors for Practitioners to Emphasize in the Initial Sessions

Here, we present seven behaviors, consistent with the underlying spirit of MI, that we recommend you use in the first couple of meetings and sometimes in later sessions as well.

1. Start with Listening

First and foremost, be a good listener. People tend to reveal more to those who listen well. In addition, when a high level of listening is perceived, it enhances likeability and trust as well as persuasive influence and increases the likelihood of future interactions. As a general guideline to begin successful engagement, we suggest that you encourage your clients to talk as much as or more than you do. Although it may seem more efficient to simply jump right in and offer suggestions, this approach rarely succeeds with angry clients and frequently leads to superficial plans that clients cannot or will not follow. Being a good listener in the initial sessions will save time in the long run.

2. Meet Clients Where They Are

There is a good deal of variability among angry clients in terms of awareness and motivation. For example, suppose that client A says, "I don't have an anger problem. She starts all the arguments, and I wind up loudly defending myself. She should be here, not me." In this scenario, it is important to acknowledge the perceived unfairness; you might respond, "It seems like you think it's unfair that everyone is focused on you and no one is acknowledging her role in the arguments." Or suppose that client B says, "I'm not sure anger management will work for me, but there has been so much drama in my family that I'm willing to try anything to make it better." Here, it's important to emphasize the person's desire for a more peaceful family life: "You're willing to give this a try because you want better family relationships." One key to engagement is simply to meet clients where they are and not take it personally if they are not ready to work on their anger. In a case where there is lack of agreement on whether anger is a problem for the client, it is better to avoid forcing an agenda and instead simply agree to explore the impact of anger on the client's life.

3. Seek to Understand the Client's Perspective

As we have noted, expressing empathy for individuals who suffer with anxiety and depression comes easily to most practitioners. In contrast, having empathy for angry clients can be more challenging. Angry individuals tend to justify their destructive actions and minimize the effects of their angry behaviors on others. Assaults, harsh verbalizations, and acts of revenge are common in the anger landscape. It's understandable that practitioners may experience automatic, negative reactions to individuals who have caused harm and suffering to others. Having empathy may require effort on your part. At the same time, most people who are angry see themselves as victims rather than perpetrators. Therefore, understanding your client's perspective is crucial to successful engagement. As Moyers and Miller (2013) document, low practitioner empathy is associated with a range of poor outcomes, such as a weaker therapeutic alliance, higher rates of dropout, and less client change.

4. Convey Compassion

Compassion, which Kolts and Chodron (2013, 7) define as "sensitivity to the suffering of others and the desire to alleviate it," is foundational in helping relationships. Angry clients usually have messy lives, with an assortment of social, interpersonal, economic, medical, and occupational problems. Although their anger may be excessive, the situations they experience are often truly negative. Genuine caring about their struggles is an essential ingredient for establishing a productive working relationship.

5. Evoke Inner Motivation for Change

Recently a physician friend of ours was seeking advice on how to motivate a patient, a young man who had visited our friend's emergency room several times after overdosing on drugs. When we asked our friend what he and the patient had talked about in the emergency room, he listed all the information he had imparted to the patient, but he looked puzzled when we asked him about the patient's part in these conversations. "He didn't say anything," our friend replied. "I was giving him the information he needed."

Our friend failed to realize that what a patient says during an interaction is critically important. When it comes to changing entrenched patterns, much more is required than simply dispensing educational information. We do believe that education is important in terms of engaging clients and enhancing their motivation for change, but there is a bottom line—what clients hear *themselves* say is more important than what they hear *you* say. It's always the client's reasons for change, not yours, that win the day. So look for opportunities to evoke clients' personal reasons for the importance of changing their anger reactions.

6. Instill Hope

Hope in clients is a nonspecific or common factor associated with treatment outcomes (Irving et al., 2004). After all, if clients do not have hope that treatment will help them change, then there is little reason for them to continue attending sessions.

When it comes to anger, optimism is certainly warranted. As noted earlier, comprehensive meta-analytic reviews over the last twenty years all converge on the same conclusion: anger treatment is effective. Be upbeat and positive about the benefits of working with your clients.

7. Be Up Front: Reveal What You Know About the Referral

In the setting where you work, you may have information about why the client was referred. In most such cases, we recommend that you show your cards in the first meeting and reveal the information you have. For example, you might let the person know that you have spoken to an employee assistance program coordinator, a probation officer, or a concerned family member who recommended treatment. It is important in these situations to quickly reassure clients that you are open to their perspectives, concerns, and priorities, and that you will be transparent with them.

Initial Approach and Opening Statements

Engagement happens quickly and effortlessly with some clients. With others it can move at a snail's pace, requiring multiple sessions over a period of weeks or months. And with still others, treatment never gets on track. Since a client-centered interaction style is more effective in engaging most angry clients, begin by positioning yourself as a good listener, and strive to maintain a respectful, curious, supportive, empathic, compassionate stance. Resist the temptation to get too far ahead of your client; just maintain a more moment-to-moment focus. Shifting to a more client-centered and present-moment approach requires a leap of faith on your part that the interaction will go somewhere useful. It usually does. Being present-moment-focused is often more efficient than attempting to be overly directive and clinging to a rigid game plan.

For the initial session, keep goals modest. When we are engaging clients who are challenging and angry, our checklist of reasonable goals for the first meeting includes the following elements:

- Getting the person to talk

- Understanding the circumstances that brought the person into treatment

- Understanding the role that anger plays in the person's life

- Eliciting reasons why intervention might be beneficial at this time

- Increasing the person's willingness to return for another session

During the initial contact, the stage is often set for successful (or unsuccessful) engagement. The way you introduce yourself and describe your role will influence how clients respond. It is worthwhile to develop a thoughtful and welcoming opening statement. Practitioner script 2.1 shows two examples of opening statements that you can use as a general guide.

PRACTITIONER SCRIPT 2.1. Sample Opening Statements

1. Hi, Mark. I'm Dr. Kassinove. It is a pleasure to meet you. I'm a clinical psychologist, and I work to help people develop skills to improve their lives. These skills often involve learning new ways to solve problems and react to life's challenges. On the

phone, you told my secretary that there have been some family problems that brought you here. I'd like to hear your perspective about them and find out what is most urgent for you right now, so that I might be helpful. Tell me, what's been happening?

2. Hi, Hannah. I'm Dr. Tafrate. It's good to meet you. I know that your probation officer referred you. She told me a little bit about your case, why you are on probation, and about the problems you have been having. Today I would like to find out what you think is most important. Then we can decide together what would be most helpful for you. Tell me about some of the things you have been struggling with.

Using the OARS Skills

The OARS skills are common across many models of counseling and psychotherapy, but they are used in MI with a level of precision not typically found in other models. In general, MI conversations are characterized as nonjudgmental, nonconfrontational, respectful, inquisitive, supportive, and collaborative, with an emphasis on client autonomy and self-direction. Generally, MI practitioners use at least as many reflections as questions, place strong emphasis on open rather than closed questions, and skillfully reinforce the client's own reasons for change. Many practitioners are surprised by our recommendation to use more reflections than questions, yet mastering the skill of reflecting works best, and we hope you will give it a try.

The OARS skills may seem simple, but sustaining an OARS communication style throughout a conversation is not easy. Developing fluency in these skills is an essential foundation for successfully engaging angry clients. Let's briefly review each of the OARS skills and show how they can be integrated into a session with Mark.

Open Questions

Most practitioners intellectually grasp the difference between open and closed questions. Closed questions can be answered with minimal information, whereas open questions require more elaboration. Yet emphasizing open questions in real sessions is more challenging than it seems. When you are asking open questions, it's important to communicate an exploratory and curious stance ("I am interested in what you are most concerned about in your relationship with your wife's family?") rather than attempting to fix anything or find solutions ("How can you make things better with your brother-in-law?"). Here are some open questions that would be useful in an initial session with Mark:

- How do things stand in your family relationships right now?

- What are your major concerns regarding your relationship with your wife?

- How has your relationship with each of your daughters changed over the last two years?

- What happened at the family picnic? Walk me through it.

- What have been your major successes at work?

- What are your major regrets in your career?

- What effect has your anger had on your career?

- Moving forward, what are your hopes for your career?

- Where do you see things headed if you don't make a change in how you handle your anger?

- In terms of changing something, what seems most urgent for you now? Why?

Affirmations

In the initial session, it is crucial to demonstrate that you can quickly grasp the problem areas in the client's life. Equally important is showing that you recognize competencies, strengths, and areas that are going well. Keying into positive aspects of your client's life is validating and will reduce defensiveness and enhance engagement. In addition, affirming provides opportunities to selectively reinforce specific behaviors.

An affirmation is a statement to a client that highlights the person's strengths, abilities, good intentions, or efforts and is formulated according to a specific structure:

- Organizing the statement around the word "you" and resisting the temptation to start with the word "I"

- Identifying specific behaviors and giving descriptions of those behaviors

- Attending to strengths rather than deficits

- Being genuine by identifying legitimate strengths and avoiding compliments that might seem superficial or insincere

Here are some affirmations that might be used in an initial session with Mark:

- It is obvious that you want to be a good father.

- Your relationships with your daughters are very important, and you work hard to make sure you are there for them.

- Despite the disappointments in your career, you have never given up.

- It comes through loud and clear that you value your relationship with your wife. You want to make it right.

- Even though you have been pressured into coming here, you seem determined to improve your family relationships.

Reflections

A key skill for conveying empathy is reflective listening. Skillful reflections involve more than parroting back what the person said. A reflection is a reasonable guess, delivered in the form of a statement that emphasizes the meaning behind what a client has communicated (Miller & Rollnick, 2013). For most practitioners, becoming proficient in forming reflections will take time, so expect a bit of a learning curve because it can feel unnatural at first. One way to develop fluency in this skill is to pay attention to clients' reactions after your reflections are delivered. Reflections that are on target produce continued talking, nodding, and sometimes enthusiastic agreement: "Yes, you understand what I am saying!" When a reflection misses the mark, the reaction is a facial expression of nonagreement, or the client may correct your statement and possibly provide additional information: "No, I don't think much about it. My anger just comes over me, and then I say things I later regret." Once you know what to look for, you will have continued feedback to increase your reflecting skills.

In the initial sessions, reflections are designed to clarify meaning, express understanding, reduce defensiveness, and move the interaction forward. Reflecting becomes incredibly valuable once a level of fluency is reached, allowing constructive responses to all sorts of challenging client statements. There are many ways to launch into a reflection, but we recommend starting with the following sentence stems:

- It sounds like…

- You're feeling…

- It seems…

- So you…; so…, and…

- You…

Rosengren (2018) has provided a workbook that offers guidelines and examples for constructing more complex reflections. It contains many useful examples for you to consider.

Keep in mind that in real-world sessions conducted by skilled MI practitioners, reflections are used most often, with open questions, affirmations, and summarizations used the rest of the time, in the frequency just given (of course you will be intermixing all the OARS skills in your interactions). Reflections are used almost exclusively in the following sample dialogue:

Practitioner:	Walk me through what happened at the family picnic.
Mark:	My brother-in-law was bragging about the new contract his company just got. He was rubbing it in. He knew I was going to be out of work in a few weeks.
Practitioner:	*You thought* he was trying to embarrass you.
Mark:	Yeah. We both work in construction and he is always trying to show what a big shot he is in his business.
Practitioner:	*Sounds like* there has been friction between you two in the past.
Mark:	He has been putting me down for years. He never thought I was good enough for his sister. Behind my back, he always tells her that I'll never amount to anything.
Practitioner:	*You don't feel* respected by him, and that really bothers you.
Mark:	Yes, it does. I feel bad enough that the economy is so crappy, and I have to hustle from job to job. The guy is not supportive in any way. He seems to take pleasure in tearing me down in front of my family.
Practitioner:	*So* the part that is most upsetting is that he was doing this in front of your wife and kids.
Mark:	Yes, and everyone else in my wife's family. I tried to brush if off and said, "Maybe we shouldn't talk so much about work." He says, "Guess Mark's about to lose another job." That's when I lost it.
Practitioner:	*It sounds like* that's when you pushed him.
Mark:	Yeah. Then it got crazy—we started swinging, and other people jumped in. My kids saw the whole thing, and that really bothers me the most.
Practitioner:	*You* don't like the idea of being out of control in front of your kids.
Mark:	It's ugly. That is not the kind of father I want to be.

Summarizations

In contrast with reflecting, which involves conveying a moment-by-moment understanding of what the client means, when you are summarizing you reach back further and capture larger amounts of information, helping clients organize their experiences. Summarizations are a common ending in MI conversations. Common phrases for launching into a summarization might include "Let's pull together what we have been talking about" or "Let me see if I understand what you have told me so far" or "We're running low on time, so let's pull together what is most important." When you're ending a session, you will make strategic decisions about what parts of the conversation are important enough to include in the summarization. The most common mistake is to include too much. The art of developing effective summarizations is related to decisions about brevity and selectivity (Rosengren, 2018). Highlighting three or four of the important issues is usually sufficient. In the following example, the practitioner's summarization includes Mark's employment stress, the disrespect shown to him by his brother-in-law, and Mark's sense that being out of control is incompatible with his views about being a good father:

Practitioner: Mark, let's pull together what we have been talking about. You have been under a lot of stress during the last few years to stay employed. It's not been easy. The incident at the family picnic is somewhat connected to what's been happening at work. But it's also related to a long history with your brother-in-law. You have often felt disrespected by him. Being put down in front of your family was the last straw, and that's what led to the brawl. When you look at this situation now, you are not happy with how you handled it. You don't want to be out of control in front of your kids. It's not consistent with being the good father you want to be.

Using OARS Skills to Respond to Difficult Client Statements in the Initial Session

Things do not always go as planned, so expect the unexpected when working with angry clients. Provocative, antagonistic, outrageous statements can and do emerge in the first meeting. Be calm and patient, and steer away from confrontation as much as possible. Responding to such statements skillfully will often get treatment back on track. Reflections and open questions like those shown in table 2.2 will elicit more information about clients' concerns and will usually work best. With practice, you can learn to sidestep arguments and smoothly move the interaction in a productive direction.

Table 2.2. Responding to Difficult Statements in the Initial Session

Client's Difficult Statement	Practitioner's Response
I'm just defending myself. She's the one who gets physical first. She should be here, not me. You're focused on the wrong person.	(Reflection) It seems unfair that everyone is focused on you and not seeing her role in the fighting.
I've been to an anger management program before. Obviously, it didn't work.	(Open question) What have you tried and how did that go?
I don't see why I have to come and see you. It was just an argument that got out of hand. I'm not an abuser.	(Reflection) This incident doesn't reflect who you are. You do not see yourself as someone who harms others.
Nobody is going to tell me to stop yelling. The hell with you. I like yelling, and I'll do what I want.	(Open question) When you think about your life, what's good about yelling?
I know what's going on. You're not here to help me. My boss is just looking for a reason to fire me. You're gonna write a negative report so she can get rid of me.	(Reflection) You think this whole thing is about trying to find a reason to fire you, and no one is really here to help you.
My probation officer sent me. Let's be honest. I don't want to do this, and I don't need this. I'm here so I don't go back to prison. How about I give you some gift cards to the restaurant and you sign the paperwork so I get credit for completing this program? We both win.	(Reflection) You want to figure out the easiest way to get through this, and you also want to make sure you don't have any problems with probation and end up back in prison.
I'm only here because my attorney thinks it would be a good idea. It is not because I have any problems. I'm just fine.	(Reflection) You're not sure there is anything you need to work on. You're here only because your attorney thinks it will help with your legal problems. That's the only reason you're here.

Takeaway Messages and Tools

Angry clients show up differently for treatment than clients who suffer from problematic anxiety and depression. The mechanisms of referral often include some degree of external pressure or coercion. Given the mind-set that accompanies anger, the client tends to see himself or herself as a person who has been wronged, and this perception is often combined with a demand for others to change their behavior. Clients' attitudes toward changing their anger reactions will vary and are usually ambivalent at best. Practitioners who are unaware of these challenges run the risk of not successfully engaging angry clients and of having anger treatment get off track in the first session. Engagement skills are essential to working with this client group. Therefore, create a strong opening statement that works in your setting. Remember to position yourself as a good listener, to convey strong empathy and compassion, to practice increasing your reflections, to emphasize open questions, to weave occasional affirmations into the conversation, and to end sessions with summarizations that highlight the most important things discussed. Our hope is that, with practice and repetition, your engagement skills will come alive in your daily practice. And while you are working to strengthen engagement, you will also be thinking about conceptualizing your clients' anger reactions in ways that set the stage for effective treatment. We deal with issues related to case formulation and treatment planning in chapters 3 and 4.

PART 2

Case Formulation and Treatment Planning

CHAPTER 3

The Anger Episode Model

Mankind must put an end to war, or war will put an end to mankind.

—John F. Kennedy

It's common for people to describe their own anger by saying things like, "My anger just comes over me and I explode" or "Shit happens, and I lose it." Similarly, when describing others, phrases such as, "He's a crazy hothead," "She's got a volatile temper," and "He's an angry dude" are commonplace. The problem with such statements is they suggest that anger is a confusing cluster of triggers, sensations, thoughts, and behaviors that emerge automatically and uncontrollably. The truth is that anger occurs in specific, understandable episodes. It has a clear cycle with identifiable components. Anger begins (often very quickly), intensifies, and then diminishes (often quite slowly). Understanding the cycle will help you find potential treatment targets that you can work on with your clients. Let's consider the case of a typical marital argument:

> Dyson is a thirty-five-year-old self-employed carpenter who did well in high school. Customers like his work, and he has lots of repeat business. Following high school, he attended a liberal arts college, majoring in chemistry. He was the first in his family to attend college, but he found academic work difficult and received a series of poor grades that led to his dismissal.
>
> He met his wife, Janet, during his second year at the college. Janet, like her father, eventually completed a master's degree in engineering, with outstanding grades. Although Dyson is proud of her academic accomplishments, he also feels envious that she has achieved a higher level of education than he did. Married twelve years ago, they now have three sons, ages eight, ten, and eleven. The kids are well adjusted and do well in school.
>
> Dyson and his family live in a small rented apartment. Although Dyson and Janet want to eventually buy their own home, Dyson has not earned enough to save a down payment, and the couple's parents are not in a financial position to help. This has been a cause of strife, since Janet has refused to go to work, even on a part-time basis, saying that taking care of the children comes first.
>
> Janet is relatively frugal, although Dyson thinks she spends too much money on personal-care items, such as "expensive" makeup. Last month Dyson was doing a

weeklong home repair for a thirty-five-year-old divorcee, an attractive woman who was clearly interested in him. What started as flirting ended up as a brief affair that ended after three weeks. Dyson feels guilty about what happened and has told no one about it, yet he ruminates about his behavior, no longer sleeps well, and had one episode of drinking to the point of blacking out.

Last weekend Janet asked him to watch the children for about three hours while she went to a cosmetics demonstration at the local department store. He asked (that is, told) her not to go, and he refused to watch the children. Janet, not willing to alter her plans, said, "I have been looking forward to this all month, and I'm going!"

They began to argue and yell loudly at each other. The children became scared and began to cry. Then, in a particularly heated moment, Dyson called his wife a bitch and threw a laptop computer at her. He missed, but he also put a hole in the wall.

Janet called the police, and Dyson was arrested. After two days in jail, he returned home and is now sleeping in the living room because Janet put a lock on their bedroom door. In a court hearing, the judge ordered Dyson to attend anger management sessions. Janet is happy with that because she thinks it will be helpful, but she will not let him return to their bedroom.

Let's analyze the situation. On the plus side, we can see that Dyson is moderately well educated, with some college experience, and probably has adequate verbal skills to profit from intervention. Their twelve-year marriage, their well-adjusted children, and his solid work history also bode well for improving his anger reactions. On the other side, Dyson's angry response to Janet's statement that she was going to the cosmetics demonstration was likely increased by their financial stress, Janet's refusal to work, his perception that she spends too much on cosmetics, his envy of Janet's education, and his rumination and guilt about the hidden sexual indiscretion. Dyson might not have reacted so strongly if Janet worked part time, if they had extra disposable income, and if he had not been feeling guilty about his sexual encounter.

When you are working with angry clients, we urge that you assess and consider stressful life circumstances and lifestyle issues that may be increasing clients' overall reactivity to aversive triggers. These factors include those listed here and a few others discussed in chapter 7 (also, chapter 4 includes an interview form to help you assess such contextual factors):

- Lack of educational achievement

- Poor language skills

- Economic stressors

- Relationships with family and friends who serve as flawed models for dealing with frustration

- A dearth of satisfaction with work or school

- Inadequate sources of support

- Feelings of shame and guilt

- Poor nutrition

- Lack of sleep and fatigue

- Alcohol misuse

- Lack of opportunity for enjoyable recreational activities

- Secrets (as in Dyson's case)

Nevertheless, even though looking at such background factors is important, the analysis of individual episodes of anger is central to the SMART treatment approach. We consider the anger episode to be the primary unit of analysis that forms the foundation for treatment. The current argument between Dyson and Janet is but a single anger episode, but it is probably repeated periodically. They surely have many areas of conflict, and it will be to their benefit if they understand the way in which anger develops so that they can figure out how to reduce it. Dyson in particular is most likely to be able to reduce his dysfunctional anger after multiple anger episodes have been systematically examined. In that way, he will become sensitive to the factors that initiate his anger eruptions and exacerbate his anger and will begin to see useful and acceptable solutions. We recommend exploring the nature of the client's anger episodes collaboratively, using the motivational interviewing skills discussed in chapter 2. Doing your best to collaboratively analyze anger episodes with clients will allow for the development of a treatment plan that has the greatest likelihood of success.

Anger Episode Analysis

You will need a clear road map to make sense of your client's often jumbled and disorganized descriptions of his or her anger experiences. Our Anger Episode Model, shown in figure 3.1 and downloadable from www.newharbinger.com/42877, has six specific components, each of which suggests a potential target for intervention. The goal is to use the model to understand anger episodes, reduce confusion, and formulate a customized treatment plan to address those areas most relevant to your client's anger patterns. We usually have an enlarged copy of the model on our office wall so that it can be openly discussed. Let's go through it step by step.

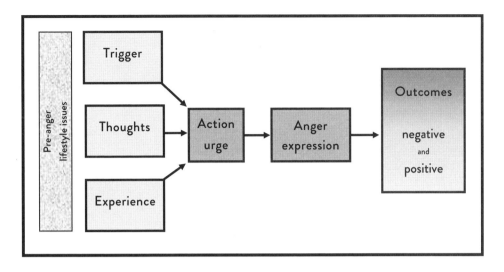

Figure 3.1. Kassinove and Tafrate's Anger Episode Model

PRE-ANGER LIFESTYLE ISSUES

A variety of environmental factors and habit patterns can make anger episodes more likely to occur, even though they are not specific elements of an anger episode. Major culprits include poor nutrition, lack of sufficient sleep, alcohol misuse, and unpleasant background noises and smells. In case formulation, most practitioners rarely consider changes in the client's environment, routines, and other background factors. These lifestyle issues are often important and are discussed in detail in chapter 7 along with suggestions to help clients rearrange their daily worlds to make angry, aversive interactions less likely.

Trigger

Anger begins with a triggering event. As we saw earlier, our evolutionary history mandates anger displays and aggressive responses to some triggers, such as threats to our children or our physical well-being and actual attacks. But much of clients' anger arises in response to far less serious triggers. Most of those triggers are negative and interpersonal in nature. For example, according to Kowalski (2001, 3), "When most people think of aversive interpersonal behaviors, they think of acts of aggression or violence, such as physical abuse, murder, and rape…[but] these extreme forms of aversive behaviors are relatively rare"; instead, she says, aversive anger triggers commonly include those listed here:

rudeness	neglect	using the silent treatment
gossiping	intentional embarrassment	incompetence
swearing	infidelity	sabotage
failing to control bodily functions	criticism	defensiveness
complaining	betrayals	forgetting commitments
narcissism	violating confidentiality	not listening
teasing	moodiness	incompetence
excessive reassurance seeking	jealousy	spreading rumors
ostracism	disappointment	passive-aggressiveness
deception		

Such triggers represent the *unwanted* and *unexpected* actions (or inaction) of other people that are perceived to be aversive and that commonly set the stage for anger to emerge. They are the instigation forces of the I^3 model noted in chapter 1.

Also, anger most often involves people who are well known to the client, including people the client likes or loves (family members, work colleagues, schoolmates, friends and neighbors, romantic partners, and so forth). Anger does emerge in response to the actions of strangers, but it's the people close to clients who usually set their anger off. In addition, we have never heard of a client who became angry at a carpet or a box of tissues. It's true that there are some middle-ground triggers, as when anger emerges in response to a character in a computer game, or when a cell phone suddenly stops working, but most triggers for clients will be interpersonal in nature. Moreover, most triggers are objectively negative. It is rare to become angry in response to a true compliment, a hefty salary increase at work, or a dentist's report of no cavities.

Triggers are frequently *verbal*, as when a client is insulted or teased, learns that others are gossiping about him or her, is the target of a racial slur, is wrongly accused of misconduct at work, or is verbally disrespected, unappreciated, or lied to. Triggers can certainly be *motoric*, as when a client has been pushed or shoved or hit, as may occur in cases of intimate partner violence or bullying. In some cases, clients may be spit at, held down, or have something thrown at them. This may lead to fear as well as anger and a desire for revenge. Triggers can also be *visual*. Imagine seeing your spouse walking in a mall with an unknown but attractive person, or seeing your romantic partner holding hands with, hugging, and kissing someone else. You do not have to look far to find such examples of anger combined with jealousy.

You can surely think of other scenarios that set the stage for anger. Many triggers are combinations of verbal, visual, and motoric stimuli, although some are pure. The immediate trigger for Dyson was Janet's verbal statement "I have been looking forward to this all month, and I'm going!" Identification of the particular trigger for the specific episode under discussion serves two purposes:

1. It keeps the discussion focused (a session is generally unproductive when it drifts into the client's complaining and moaning about all the other times he or she has become angry because of others' poor behavior).

2. It can initiate awareness in the client about whether his or her anger reaction to the trigger was or was not helpful in bringing about desired outcomes.

Thoughts

At some point in our evolution, humans developed language and thinking skills. These skills allow us to recall the past, evaluate the present, and think about the future. With the development of language and thinking skills, our displays of emotion were no longer automatic stimulus-to-response behavioral acts; rather, they became refined by our enhanced cognitive and linguistic capacities. We began to evaluate and appraise situations and the behavior of others, and to formulate ideas about what was good or bad. Evaluative thinking now plays a central role in our emotions and behaviors. A few years ago, for example, both of us were lecturing in Oklahoma and were taken to a restaurant that served Rocky Mountain oysters (you can look that delicacy up to see what it is). We stopped at one bite—the taste was not bad, but our cognitive appraisal of what was, to us, an unusual food was the primary factor in our decision to stop eating it. Similarly, in almost every anger situation that clients report, you will find thought processes that will become a critical target for treatment.

Thoughts related to triggers occur automatically. According to Wranik and Scherer (2010), four types of cognitive appraisal are always in operation as we constantly scan and evaluate our environment, try to make sense of the world, and experience emotions (such as anger) when we consider a particular event to have personal significance or importance:

1. *Relevance detection:* Is the event pleasant or unpleasant? Is it relevant to me or my social group?

2. *Implications:* Who is responsible for this event? Did I expect it to happen? Is it favorable? Do I have to take immediate action?

3. *Coping potential:* Do I have the power to do something about this event? What are its consequences?

4. *Normative significance:* Will the event influence what others think about me?

Of course, some thinking on the part of your clients is helpful. Suppose, for example, that your client is facing a challenging but potentially beneficial task and thinks, *I can do this—I'm sure I have the skills to master it.* In this case, your client will probably persist at the task. Now suppose that your client fails at the task and thinks, *I'm very capable and I'm determined to do better next time—trying and failing is better than not trying at all.* In this case, your client may be more likely to reattempt the task.

Anger-prompting thoughts are problematic, however. Let's return to Dyson, who threw a laptop computer at his wife, and look at some of his thoughts at the time of this incident. A handful of thoughts might fit his case. In contrast to the generic list of cognitive appraisals offered by Wranik and Scherer (2010), clinically oriented lists of negative thoughts that promote maladaptive feelings and behaviors have been around for many years (Beck, 1967; Ellis, 1962, 1994). We hope that even those readers who are generally familiar with processes of cognitive appraisal will take time to consider how thoughts manifest themselves specifically in anger.

AWFULIZING

This is the tendency to magnify and blow things out of proportion. Legitimate difficulties and unwanted situations are described with such words as "appalling," "atrocious," "awful," "calamitous," "catastrophic," "disastrous," "dreadful," "horrible," "ruinous," and "terrible." People with a tendency to awfulize lack wisdom about what is and what is not a big deal in life. Some events are, of course, truly very bad. But most of the time when clients awfulize and catastrophize, their magnification of an aversive event's hardship is wildly out of proportion with reality.

Is it bad for their relationship that Dyson's wife unilaterally refuses to work? Yes.

Is it bad that they are economically challenged? Yes.

Is it bad that Dyson is jealous of Janet's academic achievement? Yes.

Is it bad that she would not agree even to discuss not going to the cosmetics demonstration? Yes.

But *bad* is not *awful* or *catastrophic*. Evaluating a situation as bad is usually realistic, since the word "bad" indicates some legitimate loss of satisfaction. For example, less money means less opportunity for gratifying experiences. Failing a college course, losing a wallet, or being dismissed from a job or from university studies is bad because it may mean reevaluating life goals and putting some of them on hold for a while.

But clients who are chronic awfulizers engage in continual evaluation of and verbalization about situations that they regard as incredibly overpowering, and this type of thinking and behavior diverts time and effort from productive problem solving. Awfulizing may initially lead to sympathy from listeners, but in the longer run it makes clients less appealing—no one wants to be around a perpetual whiner. Putting energy into solving problems is generally much better than catastrophizing and complaining.

According to Peterson, Seligman, Yurko, Martin, and Friedman (1998, 130), "A cognitive style in which people catastrophize about bad events, projecting them across many realms of their lives, foreshadows untimely death decades later," a conclusion they reached after tracking mortality rates over a number of decades for 1,182 subjects who had completed questionnaires about difficult life events, and whose thinking style included poor problem solving, social estrangement, and risky decision making. These researchers also found a global catastrophizing style of thinking to be a good predictor of death by accident or violence as well as from unknown causes, as opposed to death from cardiovascular disease or cancer.

LOW FRUSTRATION TOLERANCE

How often have you heard a client say, "I can't take my husband anymore" or "I can't stand my job" or "I've had it with my children fighting with each other"? These statements, of course, are all untrue. Husbands, jobs, and children do present challenges now and then. And some of the problems can be rather objectionable. Yet most clients do tolerate these situations, and sometimes for a very long time. They don't die. Their ears don't fall off. They don't melt into a pile of mush. Their words, however, suggest that something dire will happen to them if their husband (or wife) continues to be a slob, if their job continues to be boring, or if their children continue to argue. These verbalizations suggest that clients are underestimating their ability to cope, whereas the objective data suggest they usually do cope. When clients combine awfulizing statements with statements expressing low frustration tolerance, they set themselves up for anger and other emotional problems and for poor coping in the face of life's difficulties.

DEMANDINGNESS

One of us (Howard Kassinove) used to have a coffee cup that had this saying on it: LIFE STINKS AND THEN YOU DIE. It did not represent pessimism but rather realism. Life is filled with all kinds of disappointments, rejections, discomforts, and difficulties, many of which are definitely not fair. Some people are born into wealth and privilege, and into supportive families with well-adjusted parents. Others are born into dysfunctional families, with alcoholic or drug-addicted parents who argue, steal, and engage in criminal behavior. There is little sense in demanding that life be any different from what it is. So it's useful for you to help clients understand that making demands on other people rarely helps. Life just *is*. With your help, clients can work to improve the odds that their lives will be better, even when they have been dealt some bad cards. They can complete advanced education, wear seat belts, stop smoking, and reduce their drinking. They can come to you for marriage counseling, parent education, and of course anger management. Each of these interventions, hopefully, will lead to an improved life. But they are not guarantees. Life is probabilistic. Some statements that you hear from clients suggest they do not understand this. In fact, demandingness seems to be the most common thought that drives people's anger (Tafrate, Kassinove, & Dundin, 2002). Consider these statements by three adult clients:

- Enrique: "I work so hard for my company. My boss *should* give me the raise I asked for!"

- Adriana: "My professor *must* give me an A on that term paper, or I won't pass the course."

- Ramin: "My wife *has to* stop interfering when I discipline the children."

Each of these adults is actually stating a demand, as reflected in the words "should," "must," and "has to." They are saying, "Because I expect something to happen and want it to happen, and because it often *does* happen, it absolutely *must* happen now."

Dyson, no doubt, had more than a simple expectation of and desire regarding Janet's behavior when he threw the laptop at her. In his mind, his *expectation* for Janet not to go to the cosmetics demonstration had been elevated to a *demand* that she do what he wanted. Obviously, demandingness will lead to anger because lots of times the expected does *not* happen. That's the probabilistic nature of the world. Your client may have a great résumé for a job but not be hired. Your client may have excellent credentials for admission to Harvard or Yale but still not be accepted. A long-awaited vacation may be disrupted by bad weather that interrupts air travel. At times life stinks, and we all have to adjust to that reality. How? By improving the odds that life will be better rather than simply making demands.

RATINGS OF OTHERS AND OURSELVES

Rating others is part of what we all do naturally—we can't help ourselves. Sometimes a rating is helpful, especially when it's a global positive rating. Consider love, which can be regarded as a very, very strong attraction to another person, to the point where reality can sometimes get distorted. We have all heard people say, "That girl is just perfect" or "I can't find anything that he does wrong." Or in the business world an employer might say, "That new guy is absolutely perfect for the job," and in the world of medical professionals a colleague might say, "She's absolutely the best internist in the city." Well, no one is perfect! We all do lots of good and bad things, and probably the internist physician is not the best physician for every medical case. These global positive ratings are unrealistic, and they wear off, just as time passes and initial infatuation and love diminish. For a time, however, they enhance relationships, build trust, and can bring people closer together.

And yet it's probable that your angry clients often engage in global negative ratings:

- Dyson: "My wife is a liar."

- Ellen: "My husband, Karl, is totally lazy."

- Mickey: "My boss is a real ass."

Here, the problem arises from use of the word *is*. Clients' anger is more likely to emerge when they give another person a generalized negative label regarding that person's totality, but on the basis of only a few of the person's actions. It's always better to describe individual behaviors rather than totalities, and clients can be taught to do this:

- Dyson: "My wife, Janet, sometimes lies about how much money she spends on cosmetics."

- Ellen: "My husband, Karl, frequently promises to clean the garage and then doesn't."

- Mickey: "I have noticed that my boss asks me to work harder while he takes two-hour lunches."

When a client describes specific behaviors rather than globally rating another person, the client's anger diminishes, and improved relationships can be developed.

Similarly, some people tend to rate themselves in overly harsh, negative, and extreme terms when they make mistakes. So angry clients who are severe in describing others' faults may be equally prone to self-criticism and self-denigration when they blunder. Being overly self-critical can feed guilt, shame, and sadness in addition to anger.

DISTORTION OR MISINTERPRETATION

There are other appraisals, cognitive distortions, and thinking patterns that you may catch as you listen to your clients. For example, your clients' evaluations of other people's motives and intentions may be distorted or exaggerated:

- Maria: "I didn't get the part in the play because the director doesn't like Latinas."

- Frank: "He's not listening to my proposal because he dislikes me."

- Yvonne: "If my husband respected me and our relationship, he would stop coming home so late."

Of course, Maria might objectively not be a good fit for the part. Frank may have written a flawed proposal. Yvonne's husband may have taken on extra hours at work in order to surprise Yvonne with a vacation. So listen carefully for evidence that your clients, without seeking out all the facts, are misinterpreting actions and jumping to negative conclusions about the people in their lives.

Experience

When triggers and thoughts combine, they result in an experience of anger. We use the word "experience" to mean what Skinner (1974) referred to as a private event, since it can be perceived by only one person—your client. Classical behaviorism was based on the study of such animals as rats and pigeons. Their behaviors could be seen, heard, and felt by experimenters. In contrast, human anger experiences are internal, and only some parts can be measured. We can see clenched fists, shaking hands, sweating, and a red face as well as behavior like pointing, glaring, and the like. But most anger is simply verbally reported to practitioners. It involves clients' sharing of internal reactions that may consist of self-monitoring statements ("I feel like I am about to boil over"), thoughts ("I hate him and hope that he fails"), desires ("I'd like to slap her"), and images ("I can just see the police coming and arresting him, and then he'll be out of my life").

These anger experiences are communicated to you in words, and that is both useful and a challenge. It's useful because clients can tell you quite a lot in a short period of time. The challenge is that verbal behaviors, just like motor behaviors, are controlled by carrots and sticks (that is, by incentives and punishments). For example, some clients lie to themselves and their practitioners. Despite objective evidence to the contrary, they describe themselves as calm, fair, and kindhearted. Others know they are lying—their verbal fabrications are designed to influence and manipulate consequences. Consider justice-involved individuals. Some of our probation-referred clients are quick to say, "I've learned so much about anger, and I'm feeling much more in control now," since they want us to send a positive report to their probation officer. Prison inmates will sometimes lie to parole boards when asked, "Do you still think about doing harm to your ex–business partner?" A positive verbal response will surely lead to a denial of parole. In any case, it's important for you to be savvy and consider the potential motives of clients' self-reports.

Before we move on, it's useful to review some information about the frequency, intensity, and duration of self-reported anger experiences. This will provide some normative data against which you can judge your clients' reports. Various studies have shown that anger is quite frequent. Averill (1983, 1146), after looking at data from as early as World War I, concluded, "Depending upon how records are kept, most people report becoming mildly to moderately angry anywhere from several times a day to several times a week." Scherer and Wallbott (1994, 318), using information provided by respondents from seventy-three countries who recalled events in which they had experienced anger and other emotions, also concluded that anger experiences are frequent: "Almost half of the respondents need[ed] to think back only days or weeks to remember an appropriate episode." Our own data show that normal adults report that they are typically angry at least once a week. In our current and ongoing anonymous Internet surveys, two-thirds of respondents say they "often feel angry" and "quickly fly off the handle." We often begin professional presentations and workshops by asking audience members to think of a time during the past few weeks when they felt angry; then we ask for a show of hands to tell us how many people were able to do so, and almost all hands immediately go up. These are not random samples, but the findings suggest that anger is frequent in community samples as well as among professionals. The data also suggest that people often label their anger as quite intense; for example, 80 percent of our Internet survey participants describe the anger they recall as having been strong, even to the point of fury and rage. These findings may not represent the reported anger intensity of your clients, since our respondents were motivated enough to take our survey. Across all adults, most anger is probably in the milder range.

Perhaps the good news is that most anger experiences are short-lived—50 percent of anger episodes are reported to last less than an hour, and the intensity of anger experiences is generally reported to quickly decline. In contrast, approximately 30 percent of anger episodes seem to be enduring and to last more than a day. In practice, we have run across clients who reported anger toward people who were perceived to have done them harm many years ago. The longer the anger lasts, the more likely it is to be doing harm to your client.

Action Urge

As noted by Carver and Johnson (2018), it is well known that impulsiveness—an urgency to act—is related to various types of psychopathology. Internal urges and actual impulsivity involve quick, unplanned reactions, with no consideration of potential negative consequences. As shown in figure 3.1, an impulse to act may be influenced by a trigger, a thought, and/or an experience. Because of both the evolutionary history of our species and our cultural norms, a trigger may immediately lead to arousal and an impulse to act. An impulse to act may also be enhanced as a function of maladaptive thought processes. In other scenarios, the impulse to act may arise from a felt internal experience.

Actual behavior is a possible consequence of an action urge, not a definite consequence. Berkowitz (1993) has noted that anger experiences may or may not be connected to an urge to act—anger, as a private event, may just sit there. It may or may not be goal-directed, and for a period of time a client may just angrily stew, without much desire to act or get even.

For many clients, however, the experience of anger is linked to a goal-directed urge to act. According to Wranik and Scherer (2010), urges may be related to anger that is *malevolent* ("She's a bitch, and I'll get even"), *constructive* ("I'm going to talk to her and find out why she did that—maybe we can work it out"), or *fractious*, which is to say unrelated to the actual situation ("I'm going to the gym to let off steam"). Sometimes clients we see in treatment say, "I plan to get even. He will pay for what he did. I'm gonna make things right!" Because a client may be planning a very serious act of revenge, you would be wise to take goal-directed anger verbalizations seriously. Approximately 25 percent of the respondents to our Internet survey have said they *want to* or *did* get even:

- "I decided to shine my high beams into that person's car."

- "I threw a wrench through the wall."

- "I want to get some type of sexually transmitted disease and give it to him."

- "I want to physically hurt all the people who caused me pain tonight—not kill them, just hurt them."

To assess risk, we look for the time frame, specificity, and actions related to the verbalized intentions. "I just feel so pissed" is obviously different from "I'm gonna wait for Sally until she gets off work tomorrow night and teach her a lesson." Also, a verbalization is more serious if it indicates that a behavioral step has already been taken toward harming someone else ("I bought a gun for the next time I run into Jim"). These scenarios require thoughtful decision making on your part and may warrant violation of confidentiality and a duty to warn the target.

Urges can lead to immediate action, as when a drunk customer in a bar called Lexi a dumb broad and she threw her drink at him. Such immediate actions represent impulsive anger and aggression. But urges may also lead to postponed and planned vengeful actions. For example, a survey of more than two thousand students in grades seven through twelve found that the respondents saw revenge as the strongest motivator of school shootings; more than 87 percent said that school shootings are motivated by the shooters' desire to get back at those who have hurt them, and 87 percent said that teenagers turn to lethal school violence as a result of being picked on, made fun of, or bullied by other kids. Delayed urges may also lead to passive-aggressive behavior in the workplace or in Internet chat rooms, where, following some rumination, sensitive and embarrassing information is revealed about a former friend or romantic partner. So even though your clients may not bring up their urges to act, it is always wise to inquire about such desires.

Anger Expression

Although most expressions of anger are verbal, motor behaviors connected to anger range from pushing, shoving, and throwing objects, at the milder end, to the extremes of rape, murder, torture, setting fires, workplace shootings, and bombings. In most cases that we see, fortunately, expressions of anger are milder and are generally limited to verbal behaviors. If you work in settings with justice-involved clients, of course, you will see many people who have expressed anger in motor behaviors. And if you work in a school or university setting or at a community mental health center, you won't be surprised to hear that a large number of anger-induced fistfights occur in these settings, nor will it surprise you if a client complains about having been pushed, hit, or sexually abused in such a place.

Spielberger's (1999) model posits anger experiences as being expressed outwardly, held in, or controlled:

- An *outward expression* of anger is a verbal or motor reaction such as yelling, accusing, pouting, cursing, using sarcasm, throwing something, slamming a door, demanding, speaking fast and loudly, or talking more.

- When anger is *held in*, your client is aware of the anger but does not express it outwardly, at least for the moment. (By contrast, a person who is engaging in self-deception is unaware of his or her anger, although others may observe it in acts like banging on a table or becoming flushed in the face.) Held-in anger may share some characteristics of controlled anger, as when your client feels angry at her former spouse but does not show her anger in court, where it might affect a decision about child custody.

- When anger is *controlled* or reduced, your client says, for example, "I'm the guy who keeps my cool—I can just decide to go with the flow." With some success, your client may be able to relax or soothe himself or reinterpret a situation to reduce his anger. If his anger is not truly reduced, however, he may internally hold grudges, setting the stage for additional problems. Also, as we'll discuss in chapter 4, it's wise to assess for anger avoidance or substance abuse as indirect expressions of anger.

Outcomes

We recognize that anger can be a positive, motivating force. The #MeToo movement, for example, has energized both women and men to recognize and deal with inappropriate gender relationships; historically, many injustices against women, members of ethnic minority groups, gay individuals, and people with physical challenges have been remedied after anger provided enough of a tipping point to encourage social change. Anger may also provide a degree of confidence about the future. For example, Lerner, Gonzalez and Small (2003) showed that people who were angry (rather than anxious) about incidents of terrorism were more optimistic and expected fewer attacks in the future. The possibility of an optimistic forecast emerging from anger seems to be related to a greater perceived sense of control. Moreover, in some business situations that require negotiation, displays of anger have been shown to lead to increased concessions from negotiating partners and are therefore a useful strategy (Van Kleef, De Dreu, & Manstead, 2004). In addition, about 50 percent of respondents to our own self-report studies (Kassinove, Sukhodolsky, Tsytsarev, & Solovyova, 1997; Tafrate et al., 2002) have said that anger had led to good outcomes, and 33 percent have said that anger has given them insight into their own faults. Anger, then, can be mobilizing, can encourage a sense of personal power, and can lead to positive short-term results.

When you get to discussing outcomes with your clients, you may find that some of them emphasize the positive side of anger. That's fine. You would be wise to agree that some anger is no doubt helpful—because it is. From our perspective, however, the negative consequences far outweigh the positives, so keep exploring additional episodes. The issue reminds us of the smoking controversy that went on for fifty years. The short-term effects of smoking cigarettes may be satisfying, but the longer-term outcomes are very different; similarly, angry business negotiators, lawyers, teachers, parents, and others may gain some advantages in the short term. But in the long run the consequences of frequent, intense, enduring anger are many and can be quite destructive, even fatal.

One way to make clients aware of the negative outcomes of anger is to leave an anger information sheet in your waiting area, or to send such a sheet to potential clients by mail or email (see client information sheet 3.1, included at the end of this chapter and downloadable from www.newharbinger.com/42877). This kind of document can provide information that may serve to increase clients' engagement as well as their motivation to change their anger reactivity. You can also provide a copy of the Anger Episode Model for clients to review at home (see client information sheet 3.2, also included at the end of this chapter and downloadable from www.newharbinger.com/42877).

INTERPERSONAL PROBLEMS

Have you ever invited a few people over for a barbecue? Did you invite only your six angriest friends? Probably not; after all, "nobody wants to hug a porcupine" (DiGiuseppe & Tafrate, 2007, 358). Porcupines, sea urchins, angry adolescents, and hostile adults are filled with barbs that keep others away. And, clearly, one of the most common negative outcomes of inappropriate anger is poor interpersonal relationships.

Angry folks tend to be strongly opinionated and argumentative, and they make poor team players. They see the world from their own perspective and resist looking at and accepting the opinions and desires of others. These tendencies often distance them from their colleagues, friends, and family members. And, unfortunately, angry people often do not see this. Client information sheet 3.3, included at the end of this chapter and downloadable from www.newharbinger.com/42877, is a semiplayful handout that you can give clients to highlight some behaviors that can intensify anger and lead to interpersonal problems.

AGGRESSION

We have already noted that anger and aggression are relatively independent of each other. Yet anger, along with such instigations as verbal conflict and such disinhibiting factors as alcohol use, is an impelling factor that can set the stage for aggression. Once an instigating trigger is present and angry arousal has occurred, a client may have trouble inhibiting impulsive, aggressive behavior.

POOR DECISION MAKING AND INCREASED RISK TAKING

Angry clients engage in self-defeating thinking, selective and skewed information processing (they attend to a limited set of cues), and risky actions. By comparison to fearful people, who hold back, angry people make overly optimistic risk assessments, and their views about available options to resolve their problems become narrow. Angry people are more willing to suffer penalties in their attempt to be victorious and win interpersonal battles. They exhibit defensive optimism (Hemenover & Zhang, 2004), whereby they de-emphasize both the importance of negative events and the impact of those events on themselves. They may gamble more often, place higher bets, increase their use of drugs or alcohol, and make accusatory and inflammatory statements. And yet, according to Litvak, Lerner, Tiedens, and Shonk (2010), chronically angry people also see themselves as much less likely than most others to suffer from cardiovascular illness, get divorced, and have problems in the workplace.

DECREASED FOCUS AND PERFORMANCE

Some activities clearly require a cool, steady hand. Would you want a preoccupied, angry dentist to perform oral surgery on you? What about a neurosurgeon who has just had a massive argument with his wife and is on the brink of divorce? When clients are angry, they have diminished capacity to perform all kinds of complex tasks.

ROAD RAGE

Anthony, a fifty-five-year-old unemployed electrician, was driving on the freeway with his adolescent nephew when another driver accidentally cut him off. Anthony perceived the other driver's behavior to have been intentional, and so he sped up and forced the other car off the road.

Anthony and the other driver got out of their cars, and a heated argument ensued. Anthony then got back into his car. He slowly and intentionally drove toward the other driver and knocked him to the ground.

The police were called, and Anthony was arrested. After spending a few months in jail, he was sentenced to anger management and came to our clinic.

Our intervention began as interventions often do—that is, with Anthony minimizing and justifying his actions. For example, the police report clearly stated that Anthony had deliberately hit the other driver, but Anthony said, "In one way, you could say I hit him. In another way, you could say he just fell down."

People who are normally calm and reasonable may turn into combatants behind the wheel. When they perceive a provocation—a slow driver in front of them, a tailgater, the high beams of an oncoming car, a honk, a flip of the bird—they may yell obscenities, make wild gestures, honk in retaliation, swerve in and out of traffic, and return the flipped bird. This is road rage, defined as hostile or angry action directed at other drivers. It is one of the most important anger-related motor behaviors for you to consider, since it affects a very large number of adults.

High scores on standardized anger tests seem to be useful predictors of road rage. For example, Sullman (2006), after collecting responses from middle-aged drivers in New Zealand who had completed Deffenbacher's Driving Anger Scale (1994) in addition to a questionnaire about driving behavior, found trait anger to be positively related to aggressive verbal expression (such as audibly calling other drivers names) and use of a vehicle to express anger (such as following another driver while shining one's high beams). Similar results were found by Sullman, Stephens, and Yong (2015), who reported significant relationships among anger, aggressive forms of expression while driving, and such crash-related variables as loss of concentration, loss of control of a vehicle, and involvement in near misses.

RUMINATION AND REVENGE

According to Sukhodolsky, Golub, and Cromwell (2001), anger-related rumination consists of repeatedly remembering a prior anger trigger, placing one's focus on the experience of anger, and having distorted thoughts that are contrary to what actually happened. There are also repeated instances of condemning others, holding grudges, and having revenge-oriented thoughts and desires. The cognitive repetition is believed to sustain and increase the original anger experience, without further transgression by the offender. Ruminative thoughts lead to further unhappiness and diminish interpersonal relationships as well as personal and work-related productivity. Have you ever been able to read a complex novel while ruminating about an unfair situation? We can't; we have to read the same paragraph over and over again. Our attention and thoughts keep drifting back to the perceived transgression.

ADDITIONAL NEGATIVE FEELINGS

In terms of clinical experience and research findings, adults who are anger-prone report that other negative feelings follow their anger episodes. These include depression, disgust, foolishness, and guilt or shame (Tafrate et al., 2002). Interaction of various emotions is also evident in the case of Dyson, who argued with his wife, Janet, and threw a laptop computer at her.

PAIN

Fernandez and Wasan (2010) have suggested that anger may be a consequence of pain, may simply be a correlate of pain, or, more interestingly, may be a predisposing factor for pain, as shown by studies in which adults prone to migraine headaches and tension headaches were placed in anger-provoking situations and then developed headaches; these researchers have also reported that anger can exacerbate and perpetuate existing pain (that is, pain can increase in intensity and duration as a function of anger).

Burns et al. (2015), examining anger in patients with chronic back pain, had 105 married couples (where one of the spouses was a pain patient) complete diaries to assess various elements of anger, as measured by the participants' reports of having done one or more of four things—speaking or shouting about their anger, taking physical action (such as gesturing, pounding a table, slamming a door, or throwing something), keeping their anger or annoyance to themselves, and concealing the extent of their anger and annoyance from others—in response to having felt irritated, annoyed, or angry during the preceding three hours. These researchers found that pain patients' increased reports of anger were directly related to their reports of increased pain, that their increased behavioral expression of anger was related to the increased intensity of their pain and to their decreased functioning, and that pain patients' increased reports of anger were also related to their spouses' increased reports of the intensity of the patients' pain and to the patients' pain-related behaviors.

MEDICAL PROBLEMS

Some medical problems have been linked to anger. Most likely this is because anger is part of the fight, freeze, or flight response, in which the adrenal glands flood the body with stress hormones, such as adrenaline and cortisol. Heart rate, blood pressure, and respiration increase during an anger episode, and body temperature rises. These changes cause harm to multiple body systems. Health problems associated with anger include headaches, indigestion, and even stroke and heart disease. Evidence that persistent, longer-term anger is associated with these medical conditions has existed for some time:

- Williams et al. (2000), using a sample of almost thirteen thousand middle-aged men and women who were initially free of cardiovascular disease and had normal blood pressure, followed these individuals for a mean of fifty-three months in order to complete a prospective study about the relationship of anger to cardiovascular heart disease. The researchers concluded that high trait anger is associated (independently of other biological risk factors) with a significantly higher risk of coronary heart disease and other cardiovascular events than is a low level of trait anger.

- Evidence has also emerged to suggest that anger can be an immediate cause of heart problems. Mostofsky, Penner, and Mittleman (2014), with a sample of nearly four thousand participants from more than fifty medical centers in the United States, sought to determine whether the intensity of anger outbursts is associated with the risk of acute myocardial infarction events (that is, obstruction of blood flow). They found a more than twofold increase in such events within two hours after an anger outburst, an association that was also found to be stronger with increasing intensity of anger. In addition, they noted that anger has previously been associated with a greater risk of acute coronary syndrome, ventricular arrhythmia, myocardial ischemia, and ischemic and hemorrhagic stroke.

- Similarly, Buckley et al. (2015), in a study of nearly seven hundred Australian hospital inpatients admitted for myocardial infarction, found an eightfold higher risk for an infarction in the two hours after an anger episode to be associated with higher self-ratings on standardized measures of anxiety and anger (the anger triggers most often reported were arguments with family members, problems at work, and incidents that occurred while patients were driving).

Takeaway Messages and Tools

Once you are confident that a good working relationship has been developed, we suggest that you present and discuss the Anger Episode Model with your clients to begin the process of case formulation and treatment planning. Several client information sheets may be helpful as you take this step. Remember that the anger episode is the primary unit of analysis underlying the SMART program. Try to avoid vague and philosophical discussions about anger. Your goal is to understand how anger is actually experienced and expressed in your client's real-life interactions. The six components of the Anger Episode Model are a trigger, thoughts, experience, an action urge, anger expression, and outcomes; you should also consider the possibility of pre-anger lifestyle issues.

Much can be accomplished in the SMART approach through a review of the Anger Episode Model. Sometimes, however, formal assessment adds important information about client functioning. For that reason, we turn to formal assessment procedures in chapter 4.

CLIENT INFORMATION SHEET 3.1.
Anger Reduction Is Important for You

Many people come for help with anger. You may be having problems with your spouse, boss, children, or friends, and your interactions with them may often lead you to feel angry. Or you may simply feel angry while driving, or thinking about past crises, or waiting in line, and so forth. We all get annoyed and angry on occasion, but frequent and intense anger that lasts for a long time is a real problem.

Anger is toxic. It causes many more problems than it solves. You may experience some positive payoffs from your anger. People may listen to you when you are in their presence, and they may even do what you want—for a while. So it seems to pay off. The long-term effects of anger are very negative, however, and they far outweigh the short-term benefits.

Having an interest in anger reduction is a positive first step. By reducing your tendency to become angry, you are more likely to live a happy, healthy, and interpersonally fulfilling life.

Problems Associated with Anger

1. Anger leads to conflicts with others and worsens conflicts that already exist.

2. Anger leads others to evaluate you negatively and dislike you. This affects family happiness, job advancement, social opportunities, and so forth. Since angry people are disliked, others are less likely to invite angry people to social events, for fear of the anger-based conflicts that are expected to occur. Anger leads to isolation and loneliness.

3. Major medical problems, such as cardiovascular disease, stroke, and cancer, appear more often in angry people. Long-term studies also show that people who are frequently angry die earlier than other people.

4. When you recognize the negative social outcomes of your anger, you realize that you have been the cause of much family and interpersonal disruption. That's no fun.

5. Anger leads to verbal outbursts or physical assaults, including conflicts and altercations with people we supposedly love and respect. Angry people say and do things they later regret, including calling other people names and making inappropriate gestures.

6. Anger leads to erratic driving, which may lead to involvement with the law.

7. Anger may lead you to destroy property in a fit of anger, when you're out of control.

8. Anger leads to occupational dissatisfaction and maladjustment, problems with co-workers, lowered productivity, and increased probability of job failure.

9. Anger leads to poor decision making and inappropriate risk taking. In the long run, these are quite self-defeating.

10. Very strong anger can be highly disruptive, can cloud thinking, and can lead to (or become a justification for) crimes of passion committed while you are in an "insane" state. It can also cause you to believe that you need to drink, use illegal drugs, gamble, or engage in other bad habits.

Does your anger place you at risk for any of these problems? Talk to your mental health practitioner about anger.

Howard Kassinove, PhD, and Raymond Chip Tafrate, PhD

CLIENT INFORMATION SHEET 3.2.
About the Anger Episode Model

Anger Does Not Just Appear

Many people believe that anger "just happens." They don't understand why they become angry and agitated, sometimes about very little things. In fact, people who become angry often say, "I don't know. It's just me. It's the way I always react. I get that way with everyone."

A number of lifestyle issues can increase the likelihood that you will react with strong anger in aversive situations. For example, being hungry, tired and fatigued, intoxicated, or hungover can set the stage for anger and conflicts with others to emerge. These issues are like kindling, making your anger more likely to ignite.

Without understanding how anger develops, it's easy for you to feel overwhelmed and to become pessimistic about bringing your anger under control. Anger usually follows a clear pathway to expression. This pathway can be presented in the form of a model, a simplified way for you to think about anger episodes. In addition to considering pre-anger lifestyle issues, the anger model has six parts and applies to everyone. It is wise to ask your mental health practitioner to help you understand how your anger develops.

1. Trigger

A *trigger* is the first part of the sequence. It can be something another person says ("You're lazy") or does or doesn't do, as when you discover that your child has failed to do his homework, or when there is a slow-moving car in front of you. It can be a minor event, as when your supervisor abruptly asks you to work overtime. Or it can be a major event, such as physical abuse. The trigger does not have to be an external event. It can be a memory of the past (like a daydream about your neglectful spouse) or a reflection on a major period or event in history (such as slavery or the Holocaust).

2. Thoughts

Every trigger is appraised or evaluated according to your *thoughts*. It is rare to "just" think about a trigger. For example, when you discover that your child has failed a test at school *or* helped a neighbor with yard work, you place the trigger into the category of "bad" or "good," respectively. When you discover that a friend is telling others that you are trustworthy *or* not to be trusted, you also categorize that trigger. A trigger, unfortunately, is often exaggerated or magnified out of proportion. Anger is often caused by such thoughts. For example, suppose your friend promised to pick you up at 7 p.m. to go to the movies. It is now 7:45, and your friend has not arrived. In fact, your friend never arrives. When you call your friend, she claims to have forgotten about the whole thing. Your friend's action might be categorized as fine, bad, absolutely disgusting, or catastrophic. Most people would agree that "bad" is the rational category. But we all know people who magnify such an event and say something like, "That was *terrible*. I can't take it anymore! She should have remembered. What a jerk!" Such exaggerated thoughts are frequent causes of anger.

3. Experience

Your *experience* of anger is the personal part. It consists of your private thoughts and images as well as your goals for resolution of the problem. No one knows about this self-talk but you. It also includes the physical sensations you experience, such as a rapid heartbeat or muscle tension. Your private anger can range from mild to intense, and you may feel angry rarely or quite frequently.

4. Action Urge

The trigger itself (as when you are neglected or insulted), or your thoughts about the trigger, or your physical sensations can all contribute to an *action urge*—that is, a strong desire to express your anger and take action. An action urge does not reflect a deliberate decision. Instead, it seems to encourage you to do something automatically and sometimes impulsively. It's important, however, to recognize that an action urge does not (and need not) always lead to action.

5. Anger Expression

Each person has a unique pattern of *anger expression*. Some people yell, scream, and let it all hang out. Others mope and pout. Some people's anger goes away after a short time. Other people dwell on an anger-provoking event for hours, days, months, or even years; they say, with pride, "I'm like the elephant who never forgets." Talk with your mental health practitioner about your own pattern of anger expression, since there are real costs to these patterns.

6. Outcomes

Your mental health practitioner will ask you to examine the effects, or *outcomes*, of your anger. In the short run, your family members or colleagues may do what you ask when you act in anger. In the long run, you may lose the respect of people who are the targets of your anger. You may also suffer in other ways, such as with medical problems. Your mental health practitioner is an expert, so ask him or her what you are trying to achieve with your anger, and whether there is a better way for you to accomplish your goals.

Howard Kassinove, PhD, and Raymond Chip Tafrate, PhD

CLIENT INFORMATION SHEET 3.3.
Ten Rules to Help You Become a Really Angry Person

1. *Confront every injustice.* Don't let anything go, whether it's big or small.

2. *Jump to negative conclusions about the actions and intentions of others.* Interpret any potentially negative or ambiguous behaviors as a deliberate and malicious attack on you.

3. *React quickly and impulsively to life's challenges.* When you face difficult people or situations, don't spend time considering options or consulting others to find a reasonable solution.

4. *Insist that other people agree with your opinions and views.* Relentlessly argue until they see things your way.

5. *Harbor grudges.* Never forgive anyone who has harmed or wronged you.

6. *Demand that other people act the way you want them to.* Insist that situations must turn out the way you want.

7. *Don't make a distinction between a minor hassle or inconvenience and an issue that is really important.* Treat every difficulty and challenge as a highly significant loss or setback.

8. *Practice using your anger to get compliance from others.* Repeatedly criticize, make nasty remarks, and use intimidating behaviors to get others to comply with your demands. It's all about you, not about achieving a balance between what you want and what the other person wants.

9. *Ruminate about unfair situations and poor treatment by others.* Regularly recall negative experiences, especially times when you were not treated the way you wanted to be treated. Ignore feedback from others about how they appreciate you and your own thoughts about being grateful for what is going well.

10. *Avoid self-reflection.* Spend no time considering whether your anger is working to make your life better. Tell yourself there is no need to take responsibility for your angry reactions, because other people and unfair situations caused you to become angry in the first place.

Howard Kassinove, PhD, and Raymond Chip Tafrate, PhD

CHAPTER 4

Assessment

I believe in observation, measurement, and reasoning, confirmed by independent observers.

—Isaac Asimov

Engagement, as we have noted, is the first priority in working with angry clients. It's only when the basics of a good therapeutic relationship have been established that we move on to assessment. We try not to skip assessment, because the costs of pursuing intervention without assessment can be significant.

There are three key anger-related questions to answer during the assessment phase of treatment:

- How does anger fit into the larger constellation of problems in the client's life? This will require an understanding of the client's full range of disorders, clinical signs and symptoms, and problem areas. It's best to make decisions (collaboratively) about which problems are to receive immediate attention. Focusing on a goal not shared by the client will usually result in disengagement.

- To what degree do your client's anger patterns deviate from normal or useful experiences of anger? The goal here is to understand where the person stands as compared to others. It will be useful to look at this question from the perspective of different anger dimensions (intensity and frequency of anger experiences, frequency of verbal outbursts, rumination, desire for revenge, physical aggression, and so forth).

- What does anger look like in the person's day-to-day life? It doesn't make much sense to talk about anger in the abstract. You will be more effective if you focus on the specific elements of anger episodes as they emerge in clients' daily lives.

A comprehensive assessment includes several information-gathering strategies and channels:

- *Verbal reports* gathered through interviews and discussions are most common. Although such reports can have drawbacks (unreliability, for example, and factors related to impression management), they are useful in accessing information about subjective experiences (such as thoughts, fantasies, immediate urges, longer-term desires, and physical sensations).

- In some situations, *reports from significant others*, such as family members, close friends, and romantic partners, can be obtained. Angry clients often minimize the degree to which anger interferes with significant relationships, and so reports from others can provide both a valuable perspective and additional information.

- Another channel of information is *observations* of facial expressions, body language, and vocal indicators of anger. This is a relatively indirect way of gathering information in that you will be observing bodily and verbal signs of anger that occur during clients' descriptions of their education and employment problems, relationship difficulties, and challenges in multiple life areas. Such observations can be useful, and that is why we examine awareness of body language in chapter 14.

- *Self-monitoring* provides a precise ongoing record of the client's anger experiences as they occur between sessions. Asking clients to actively engage in monitoring helps them attend to anger patterns of which they may be unaware.

- *Standardized anger-specific tests* yield a different stream of information about the client's anger experiences and expressions. Tests are beneficial because they can be efficient in highlighting problematic patterns and will clarify how your client compares to others on important dimensions of anger.

Assessing General Psychopathology: Comorbidity and Collateral Issues

More than two decades ago, we learned an important lesson about working with angry clients. We wanted to better understand anger in community adults and to study the effectiveness of a new treatment. The idea was to identify a group of adults whose primary issue was problematic anger. So as not to contaminate our findings, we set our study up so that adults who suffered from psychopathology other than anger were not to be accepted into the project. Therefore, we naively launched into our first treatment study, looking for adults with "pure" anger problems. We placed advertisements in local newspapers, and potential study participants called the office to set up screening appointments. During the screening sessions, respondents were asked questions about their anger experiences and about their histories of other psychological problems. Two months in, there was no one left who could participate in the study! We had received many calls from adults who suffered from difficulties with anger, but all these potential participants had been excluded because they had other problems, too. The lesson? *Comorbidity is the norm when you're working with angry clients.*

Four specific observations emerged from this early study:

1. The most common comorbid problems clustered around substance-use disorders.

2. Subjects presented with a range of diagnosable problems, including anxiety and mood disorders.

3. An assortment of self-defeating personality styles (such as borderline, antisocial, and paranoid) was evident.

4. Collateral issues that often complicated the clinical picture included vocational maladjustment, relationship conflicts (with marital partners, other family members, and friends), reckless driving, problematic gambling, and involvement in the criminal justice system.

Studies conducted more recently have supported our early observations about complex comorbidity patterns. Mood, anxiety, and substance-use disorders are often associated with anger (Barrett, Mills, & Teesson, 2013). Other associations have been noted with trauma (Gonzalez, Novaco, Reger, & Gahm, 2016) and paranoia (Darch, Ellett, & Fox, 2015). With respect to personality pathology, anger tends to be most common among persons diagnosed with borderline, antisocial, narcissistic, and paranoid styles (Distel et al., 2012).

There are mixed findings regarding anger and criminality. One study found anger to be a poor predictor of criminal behavior (Mills, Loza, & Kroner, 2003), whereas others have found stronger associations between anger and assaultive behavior (Novaco & Taylor, 2015). One of our early studies, which compared high-anger adults to their low-anger counterparts, found that those with high levels of anger were more than twice as likely to have been arrested and three times more likely to have served time in prison (Tafrate, Kassinove, & Dundin, 2002). For a comprehensive CBT approach to working with justice-involved clients, see Tafrate, Mitchell, & Simourd (2018).

All of this means that angry clients are likely to have a variety of other problems. Nevertheless, this complicated pattern will also be true for other "pure" clinical problems, such as anxiety, substance use, and personality and mood disorders. If investigators earnestly look for clients with "pure" disorders, their studies may never get off the ground. At the level of the practitioner, this means that even though anger may be the central presenting issue, full-spectrum assessment is important.

Conducting a Full-Spectrum Assessment

Because your angry clients are likely to show complex comorbidity patterns, we generally recommend a comprehensive assessment. This may mean administration of standard tests such as the Minnesota Multiphasic Personality Inventory scales (Butcher, Graham, Yossef, Tellegen, & Kraemmer, 2009), the Sixteen Personality Factor Questionnaire (16PF; see Cattell & Mead, 2008), the Symptom Checklist-90 (Derogatis, 1994), or a similar instrument, but you would be wise to conduct a full clinical interview that allows you to fully assess problem areas while building trust and rapport.

Figure 4.1 shows a general interview form, which we regularly use for adults and adolescents, filled in for the case of Dyson (see chapter 3). A blank interview form (see practitioner script 4.1, included at the end of this chapter and downloadable from www .newharbinger.com/42877) can be used with your own clients; note that the questions are often but not always open-ended.

If areas of concern are found, you can further explore the frequency, intensity, and duration of the problems and determine how they may interface with the anger problems of your client. A verbal interview—if you conduct it in a nonjudgmental manner, listen attentively, and incorporate MI skills—also provides an opportunity to continue building the relationship and engaging your client.

Some anger-related signs and symptoms to look for are associated emotions, such as guilt feelings about hidden transgressions and shame about the client's family background. Other clients suffer from anger-related jealousy, as when they learn that a colleague was promoted at work, or when they discover that their best friend has found a long-term partner and is now less available for leisure-time activities. Situations that lead to guilt, shame, regret, envy, and jealousy often lead clients to experience and express anger.

If you are looking for a DSM-based diagnosis because it's required in your setting, you may find it useful to consult the Mini-International Neuropsychiatric Interview for DSM-5 (Sheehan, 2015) or the Millon Clinical Multiaxial Inventory (Millon, Grossman, & Millon, 2015). Both instruments are keyed to the DSM and can be completed in a relatively short period of time. Note, however, that the existing diagnoses are mainly summaries of symptoms, not explanations of anger's etiology, and often do not help much, since they do not capture unique elements of anger episodes. In fact, the DSM considers anger only as a symptom of other diagnostic categories; anger is ignored as an emotional entity deserving of its own diagnosis. This is astounding, given the high frequency of common and highly maladaptive anger experiences and expressions. Since we believe that a good clinical interview is very important, and that it can contribute to the therapeutic alliance, we always begin there.

Client's name: Dyson Williams

Address: 25 Park Road, Tempe, AZ

Location of clinical interview: Central Mental Health Clinic, Tempe, AZ

Greeting

HK: Hi, Dyson. I'm Dr. Howard Kassinove. It's good to meet you. [Observe interviewee's eye contact, handshake, dress, comportment, loudness and tone of voice, and so forth.]

Presenting Problem

HK: I know that you were sent by the judge, but tell me in your own words about what brings you to see me at this point in your life.

DW: I'm kind of embarrassed to say this, but in the heat of an argument I threw a laptop at my wife. She called the police, and I was arrested. The judge at my hearing said I had to come for anger management.

HK: It must be difficult to share that with me. I can hear your discomfort. Even though you were sent here by the judge, I want to say thanks for being here and being up front with me. Tell me, how long has the tension with your wife been going on?

DW: We've been married for twelve years, and we argue, like most couples, I guess. But I never did anything like this before.

HK: Sounds likes even you are surprised by what you did.

Background

HK: I'm going to talk with you more about your concerns as we go along, but first I'd like to learn about your background. My goal is to get a full picture of your life, so I can be most helpful. Would this be okay?

DW: Sure.

Age/Family

HK: Tell me, how old are you?

DW: I'm thirty-five.

HK: And who do you live with? [Obtain names and occupations of spouse, parents, and children, as appropriate.]

DW: My wife, Janet, and our three sons. Stephen is eleven, Alex is ten, and Billy is eight.

Marital/Relationship/Family Problems

HK: How is your marriage going? [Look for financial, sexual, occupational, or medical stressors.]

DW: It's generally fine. But lately we've been fighting more than usual.

HK: You seem to be aware of changes that are occurring. Tell me a bit about those changes.

DW: Life used to be easier before the kids were born. I work for myself as a carpenter, and things are now going only fair. I make enough to pay our bills, but it's hard with three kids. My wife refuses to even consider working, so it's real hard. She won't even talk about it. Lately she's been spending more and more money on fancy cosmetics, and that's been really hard on me. In fact, that's what got me arrested. I got so angry when she said she was going to a cosmetics show that I threw a laptop at her. Now things are really tense at home. Needless to say, sex is gone, and I'm locked out of the bedroom until she thinks it's safe to let me back in, and now here I am.

HK: Let me see if I have this straight. Things were good in the marriage until the stress of having to provide for children made things tight. Janet doesn't work, and to your way of thinking she spends too much on cosmetics. When she said she was going to a cosmetics show, you got angry and threw the laptop at her. That led to the arrest and to your being sent here.

Education

HK: Let me see if I can learn a bit more. How far did you go in school?

DW: I completed two years at Green Park College. It was okay, but I didn't finish. I got some good grades, but not enough to graduate.

Occupation

HK: You said you're a carpenter. Do you like that job? [Dyson has already said that he is a carpenter, and so the question "What do you do for a living?" is not asked.]

DW: Actually, I do. I like to be creative, and I meet a whole bunch of people. Mostly they are very nice.

Religion/Culture

HK: You seem happy about work and are probably quite talented. That's good news. Now tell me about your religious and cultural background.

DW: We were both brought up as Christians, but we never go to church.

HK: How is your religion a source of comfort for you?

DW: It's not, really.

Hobbies/Sports

HK: What do you do in your spare time?

DW: Not much. Mostly watch TV or play video games.

HK: Tell me about your athletic interests.

DW: I used to play tennis in college, but I have no time for anything now.

Medical Issues

HK: Do you have any medical problems that I should know about?

DW: No, just some allergies.

Previous Psychotherapy

HK: Have you seen a mental health practitioner before?

DW: Nah.

Emotional life

HK: Now I'd like to learn a bit about your emotional experiences. Would that be okay?

DW: Sure.

Anxiety

HK: In what kinds of situations do you become nervous or anxious?

DW: Mostly around not having enough money to survive.

HK: Do you worry a lot about those situations? [Look for frequency, intensity, duration, and behavioral avoidance patterns related to worry.]

DW: Not often. I'm hoping my business continues to grow.

HK: Do you have any specific fears, like fear of elevators or high places?

DW: No.

Depression

HK: Are you sad or depressed?

DW: No.

HK: Have you been thinking or have you ever thought about killing yourself?

DW: No.

Guilt/Shame

HK: Tell me about any feelings of guilt or shame that you have.

DW: Uh-oh. Are you going to tell my wife about what we say?

HK: You sound concerned. Mostly what we talk about is between us. But, as I said before this interview began, if you were to tell me that you are suicidal or homicidal, I'd have to reveal that. Also, as I said earlier, I'll probably have to make a report to the judge who sent you here. In that report I will make a number of statements, including whether I think you are stable enough to live with your family. That's probably tough to hear. None of us likes to be evaluated in that way. On the other hand, many things that you tell me won't be relevant to my report, so I won't include them…. Dyson, I hear your concerns. You seem to want to tell me something but don't know if it's safe to do so.

DW: Okay. Here's what happened. I had a three-week affair with one of my customers. She was coming on to me, and there wasn't much sex happening between me and Janet. Now I feel guilty about it, and I don't want it to ruin my marriage.

HK: Thanks for letting me know about it. If it's okay with you, we can talk more about that later, unless you feel it's urgent to talk more about that now.

DW: That's okay. We can do it later.

Anger

HK: What leads you to become angry?

DW: Usually not too much.

HK: Tell me more. [Look for additional anger triggers; for frequency, intensity, and duration of anger; and for behavioral outcomes.]

DW: The kids fighting with each other. When a customer treats me poorly. And when Janet spends money on those cosmetics.

Happiness

HK: Do you feel generally happy?

DW: Yeah.

HK: Are there times when you feel really happy or joyous?

DW: Sure.

HK: What do you get most happy about?

DW: When I am with my friends and my kids, and when I get new creative jobs.

Love

HK: Do you often feel warm and loving?

DW: Yeah, but it used to be more often.

HK: Who are you closely attached to?

DW: I'd say my kids, Janet, and my mother.

HK: Okay. Let's see if I have this all correct. From an emotional perspective, you are not particularly anxious, fearful, depressed, or overly angry except for the laptop incident. One issue that is lingering is guilt about a short affair you had with a customer, and you are probably trying to figure out what to do about that situation. We may be able to talk about that over the next few weeks.

DW: Yes. I think you understand what I have been saying.

Thinking/Cognitive Issues

Obsessions

HK: Do thoughts run through your head over and over that you can't get rid of?

DW: No. Just about the affair.

Compulsions

HK: Do you find that you do some things over and over, and you can't stop?

DW: Nothing in particular except for making sure my figures are correct for my job estimates.

Unusual Thoughts

HK: From time to time, we all have some unusual thoughts that go through our head. Tell me about some surprising or unusual thoughts that you have.

DW: Nothing really weird. Sometimes I wonder why I don't have more friends.

HK: Again, Dyson, thanks for sharing all this with me.

Behaviors/Habits

Sleep

HK: How have you been sleeping?

DW: Okay—about six to seven hours a night.

Eating

HK: And how are your eating habits?

DW: Okay. I guess I eat too much junk food.

HK: Is your weight okay?

DW: Yeah. I'd like to lose about five pounds, but I'm okay.

Alcohol and Drugs

HK: Tell me about your drinking.

DW: I have one or two beers now and then. Nothing more. Hard liquor makes me dizzy.

HK: Tell me about your drug history.

DW: I smoked pot in college. Nothing since the kids were born.

Gambling

HK: How often do you gamble?

DW: Ha! I have no money for gambling. Sometimes I buy a lottery ticket. That's it.

Sexuality

HK: Now, Dyson, I'd like to know about your social and sexual history. For some people, this is a sensitive area, but would it be okay if I proceed?

DW: Yeah, it's fine. We are doing okay with each other so far.

HK: What kinds of sexual concerns have you had? [Dyson has already said he is married with children, and so the question, "Have you had a relationship with another person?" is not asked.]

DW: I guess, like most guys, I used to wonder if I was big enough to satisfy a woman. Now I realize how silly that stuff is.

HK: Have you ever been interested in or had a sexual experience with a person of your own gender?

DW: No. That stuff is okay, but it's not for me.

HK: Have you had difficulties achieving or maintaining an erection, coming, or ejaculating?

DW: When I was younger, I used to come really quick. Now it's all A-okay.

HK: Do you worry about your sexuality?

DW: No.

Final Inquiry

HK: I've asked you quite a few questions, Dyson, and I think I've learned a lot about you. Thanks for sharing so much about your life with me. Although you were sent to see me because you had that anger incident with your wife, I can tell that you also have many strengths. Is there anything more that you think I should ask you about?

Figure 4.1. Dyson's Completed Clinical Interview

Using Standardized Anger Tests and Related Instruments

In comparison to what is available for assessing other emotions, such as anxiety and depression, the number of scientifically acceptable anger instruments is limited. Self-styled "anger tests" can certainly be found on the Internet, but we advise caution in using any of them because they do not meet basic psychometric standards. For any test of anger that you consider using, ask yourself three questions:

1. Is it based on an accepted theory of anger?

2. Does it give data about reliability and validity?

3. Does it provide adequate normative data?

Standardized anger tests can be easily integrated into intake procedures and are an efficient way to understand how clients score on important dimensions of anger, as compared to the scores of a larger reference group.

Anger-Specific Instruments

We believe that the following four anger-specific instruments are acceptable for use in practice; each is administered in a self-report format, and each examines anger as a multidimensional construct (they all emphasize different dimensions of anger, however, and they provide different ranges of scores):

1. State-Trait Anger Expression Inventory-2 (STAXI-2): This widely used forty-four-item anger scale (Spielberger, 1999) focuses on the elements of state and trait anger. (A *state* is what one feels in the moment; a *trait* is one's general propensity to experience anger states in multiple situations.) Spielberger has proposed that people tend primarily either to express anger outwardly or to experience it inwardly. Therefore, the STAXI-2 includes subscales for state anger, trait anger, anger expression–out, anger expression–in, and anger control. Most adults can complete it in about twelve to fifteen minutes.

2. Novaco Anger Scale and Provocation Inventory (NAS-PI): Novaco (2003) has proposed a model of anger that includes four domains: eliciting environmental events, thoughts, arousal aspects of anger, and behavioral reactions. Therefore, the NAS-PI contains subscales that highlight dimensions of anger that can be targeted in treatment, such as specific cognitions, arousal patterns, angry behaviors, and common provocations (disrespect, unfairness, and frustration, for example). The NAS-PI can be completed in about twenty-five minutes.

3. Anger Disorders Scale (ADS) and Anger Regulation and Expression Scale (ARES): The ADS (DiGiuseppe & Tafrate, 2004) and the ARES (DiGiuseppe & Tafrate, 2011) assess angry feelings, thoughts, and behaviors. Both instruments provide a comprehensive profile of anger characteristics that can be addressed in treatment. The ADS is focused on adults and is organized across three higher-order factors: reactivity/expression, anger–in, and vengeance. Eighteen clinical subscale scores are provided, including scores for rumination, verbal expression, impulsivity, suspiciousness, physical aggression, and indirect aggression. The ARES, designed for adolescents, is also organized around three higher-order factors: internalizing anger, externalizing anger, and extent of anger. Both the ADS and the ARES can be completed in fifteen to twenty minutes, and short screening versions are available.

4. Anger Parameters Scale (APS): The APS, still in development by Fernandez, Arevalo, Vargas, and Torralba (2014) and Fernandez, Kiageri, Guharajan, and Day (2017), is based on the idea that forensic samples differ from community samples when it comes to anger and on the desire of these researchers to provide enhanced norms for both types of samples. The APS measures anger in terms of frequency, duration, intensity, latency, and threshold. The thirty items on the APS do not yield a total score but allow for examination of individual dimensions. Of interest to readers who work in forensic settings is the APS's finding that adult jail detainees experience anger more frequently, more intensely, and for longer durations than do nonincarcerated individuals. This finding is consistent with the idea that clinical and forensic populations, in comparison to general community samples, may represent the extreme end of the spectrum for anger and violence.

Paulhus Deception Scales

Some self-referred adults are typically aware of their maladaptive anger and may be ready to work with you as soon as they enter treatment. In contrast, clients referred by others (such as marital partners, parents, probation officers, or supervisors in the workplace) may truly be unaware of their anger and of the negative impact it is having on their lives. They often believe that others are making too much of their anger reactions. Mandated justice-involved clients may consciously know that their anger is problematic but still have an incentive to minimize or totally deny it, since to admit to having continuing anger problems may lead to additional sanctions. To assess this issue and gain some insight into whether clients are aware of their maladaptive anger, the Paulhus Deception Scales (Paulhus, 1998) are often useful. This forty-item instrument assesses impression management (defined as the conscious use of inflated self-descriptions, faking, and lying) as well as self-deceptive enhancement (defined as a tendency to use self-descriptions that are perceived as honest but that lack insight into problems).

Readiness-for-Change Instruments

A final concern regards readiness for an intervention. The term "readiness" refers to characteristics of the client indicating that the client is willing, prepared, or even eager to participate in treatment. Practitioners, friends, family members, and others often recognize how important it is for treatment to be helpful to the angry client. The client, however, may not be ready and may still think of his or her anger as not being bad enough to require intervention. The Readiness to Change Questionnaire, developed by Heather and Rollnick (1993), assesses readiness for intervention in problem drinkers. Williamson, Day, Howells, Bubner, and Jauncey (2003) have reported on modifications of this instrument that are specific to angry clients. In addition, Boudreaux, Dahlen, Madson, and Bullock-Yowell (2014) have reported on initial development of the Attitudes Toward Anger Management Scale; developed for college students, it contains thirteen items that assess two factors: belief in treatment, and receptiveness.

Assessing Individual Episodes of Anger

Standardized tests provide scores that indicate how a client compares to others, but they do not yield rich information about what anger looks like in a particular client's life. To get an in-depth understanding of the unique features of your client's anger, it is critical that you explore specific episodes of anger. As described in chapter 3, an anger episode consists of six elements that make up the larger chain of events. When you explore multiple episodes of anger over time, your interventions can target key features of anger for your particular client. Our Anger Episode Model (see figure 3.1) provides a framework for a shared understanding of the client's anger, and it forms the foundation for developing a treatment plan and selecting change strategies.

Anger Episode Record

The Anger Episode Model, discussed at length in chapter 3, has been translated into the Anger Episode Record (see client worksheet 4.1, included at the end of this chapter and downloadable from www.newharbinger.com/42877), an easy-to-use assessment tool that gives you a simple way to help your clients understand the various elements of their anger reactions. A good starting point is to use the record as a structure for a conversation about a recent and significant anger episode. The record is used to guide your questions. We recommend a casual conversational tone that allows your client freedom to expand on each area. We have found this strategy useful in developing clients' awareness and strengthening the therapeutic relationship.

It's important to stay focused on a single anger episode, to be concrete and specific, and to avoid fuzzy theoretical discussions about anger in general. Reviewing one anger episode in this manner can take about fifteen minutes or longer, depending on the client's verbal abilities (practitioner script 4.2, included at the end of this chapter and downloadable from www.newharbinger.com/42877, provides sample questions to help you elicit information).

Once the Anger Episode Record has been introduced, it can be easily incorporated into subsequent sessions. One approach is to ask the client at the beginning of the first meeting, or in the waiting room prior to a session, to complete a single Anger Episode Record for the most significant anger experience that occurred since the last meeting. This works best after the client has had previous experiences completing the record with you. Since your goal is to have a shared understanding of what anger looks like, we do not recommend just giving the client the Anger Episode Record with little or no explanation. (Most clients can complete the Anger Episode Record on their own in less than ten minutes—after they have completed one with you.) Responses are then discussed and can become the starting point for the session. This approach allows you to efficiently "take a pulse" of how anger has emerged since you last saw the client.

Aside from using the Anger Episode Record to structure a conversation about the client's anger, enhance the client's awareness, and strengthen the therapeutic alliance, you can use it as an ongoing self-monitoring tool, and completed Anger Episode Records can provide an indicator of treatment progress. Ask the client to complete the Anger Episode Record for each significant episode of anger experienced between sessions. You can suggest that clients fill the record out at the end of each day. That way, instead of asking the client to try to recreate an entire week (or more) of Anger Episode Records in your waiting room before a session, you can reinforce the client's daily self-monitoring. The number of anger episodes reported early in treatment can serve as a baseline from which improvement can be measured. Other dimensions of anger can also serve as indicators of progress, depending on the areas you wish to target. These may include the intensity of anger episodes, their duration, and/or the number of episodes containing negative verbalizations or physically aggressive behaviors.

Takeaway Messages and Tools

Assessment sets the stage for effective treatment because understanding the unique details of the client's anger experiences allows for the development of clear treatment targets and planning. Good assessment is the foundation of case formulation; when done properly, it promotes a collaborative working relationship. To fully understand most clients, we recommend that you assess general psychopathology, conduct a comprehensive interview, use anger-specific tests, and have the client (initially with your help) complete the Anger Episode Record on a regular basis (as guides to your assessment activities, see practitioner scripts 4.1 and 4.2 and client worksheet 4.1, included at the end of this chapter and downloadable from www.newharbinger.com/42877).

If you and your client do not share an understanding of what matters most, then your client is not likely to put in the effort required to be successful with the SMART intervention strategies introduced in later chapters. Therefore, in chapter 5 we discuss additional strategies for enhancing awareness and motivation that can be tied to assessment.

PRACTITIONER SCRIPT 4.1. Clinical Interview

Client's name: _____

Address: _____

Location of clinical interview: _____

Greeting

Hi, _____. I'm _____.
It's good to meet you. [Observe interviewee's eye contact, handshake, dress, comportment, loudness and tone of voice, and so forth.]

Presenting Problem

What brings you to see me at this point in your life?

[For court-mandated clients] I know that you were sent here by
_____. In your own words, tell me what happened.

Background

I'm going to talk with you more about your concerns as we go along, but first I'd like to learn about your background. My goal is to get a full picture of your life, so I can be most helpful. Would this be okay?

Age/Family

Tell me, how old are you?

And who do you live with? [Obtain names and occupations of spouse, parents, and children, as appropriate.]

Marital/Relationship/Family Problems

[For married clients] How is your marriage going? [Look for financial, sexual, occupational, or medical stressors; also determine whether this is the first marriage.]

[For unmarried clients] How is your relationship going? [Look for financial, sexual, occupational, or medical stressors]

[For adolescents] How are things between your parents? [Look for financial, sexual, occupational, or medical stressors.]

[It's often useful to give a short summary at this point.]

Education

How far did you go in school?

[For college students] How far along are you in college?

Are you satisfied with your education [so far]?

Occupation

What do you do for a living?

Are you satisfied with your job?

Religion/Culture

Tell me about your religious and cultural background.

How is your religion a source of comfort for you?

Hobbies/Sports

What do you do in your spare time?

Tell me about your hobbies [and/or athletic interests].

Medical Issues

Do you have any medical problems that I should know about?

Previous Psychotherapy

Have you seen a mental health practitioner before?

Emotional Life

Now I'd like to learn a bit about your emotional experiences. Would that be okay?

Anxiety

In what kinds of situations do you become nervous or anxious?

Do you worry a lot about those situations? [Look for frequency, intensity, duration, and behavioral avoidance patterns related to worry.]

Do you have any specific fears, like fear of elevators or high places? [If yes] Tell me about them.

Depression

Are you sad or depressed? [If yes] What do you think led to your depression?

Have you been thinking [have you ever thought] about killing yourself?

Guilt/Shame

Tell me about any feelings of guilt or shame that you have.

Anger

What leads you to become angry?

Tell me more. [Look for additional anger triggers; for frequency, intensity, and duration of anger; and for behavioral outcomes.]

Happiness

Do you feel generally happy?

Are there times when you feel really happy or joyous?

What do you get most happy about?

Love

Do you often feel warm and loving?

Who are you closely attached to?

[It's often useful to give a short summary at this point.]

Thinking/Cognitive Issues

Obsessions

Do thoughts run through your head over and over that you can't get rid of?

[If yes] Tell me a bit about them.

Compulsions

Do you find that you do some things over and over, and you can't stop?

[If yes] Tell me a bit about them.

Unusual Thoughts

From time to time, we all have some unusual thoughts that go through our head. Tell me about some surprising or unusual thoughts that you have.

Behaviors/Habits

Sleep

How have you been sleeping?

Eating

And how are your eating habits?

Is your weight okay?

Alcohol and Drugs

Tell me about your drinking.

Tell me about your drug history.

Gambling

How often do you gamble?

Sexuality

Now, _____, I'd like to know about your social and sexual history. For some people, this is a sensitive area, but would it be okay if I proceed?

Have you had a relationship with another person?

Have you been sexually active?

Were you sexually active in high school or college?

What kinds of sexual concerns have you had?

Have you ever been interested in or had a sexual experience with a person of your own gender?

Have you had... [difficulties achieving or maintaining an erection, coming, ejaculating; having an orgasm, pain during intercourse]?

Do you worry about your sexuality? [If yes] Tell me more about that.

Final Inquiry

I've asked you quite a few questions, _____, and I think I've learned a lot about you. Thanks for sharing so much about your life with me. Is there anything more that you think I should ask you about?

[Give final summary here.]

Summary of Interview

So as I understand your life, here is what is going on...

It looks like your main issues are...

Some of your most positive skills and talents are...

Some of your goals seem to be...

Remember...

Emphasize the use of open-ended questions.

Affirm the client's strengths, talents, and openness during the interview.

Be collaborative.

End with a supportive statement.

Howard Kassinove, PhD, and Raymond Chip Tafrate, PhD

PRACTITIONER SCRIPT 4.2.
Instructions for Using the Anger Episode Record

Introduction

Goal: Introduce the Anger Episode Record and provide a brief rationale for the interview.

Hi, _____. As I said before, everyone feels angry now and then. Yet anger can be difficult to understand because it is made up of different parts. Also, since everyone's life is unique, anger can be very specific to the particular difficulties each person is facing. In order for me to understand you better, and to focus our work on what is most important, I'd like to ask you questions about the specific elements that make up your anger. Would that be all right?

This form is called the Anger Episode Record, and together we are going to fill in the information for each of the boxes. Okay? To start, tell me about the strongest episode of anger you have experienced in the past month.

Trigger

Goal: To ask questions until you understand the specific and/or immediate triggering event as well as some of the context and history connected to the anger episode. You can show the client the record and ask him or her to identify the life area in which the anger emerged. Then expect the client to tell you a bit of a story.

Take a look at the list of boxes on the Anger Episode Record. These are common life areas where anger emerges in people's lives. Which area is most connected to your anger in this situation?

Tell me more about what triggered your anger.

How did it start?

What led up to the situation?

What were the circumstances surrounding this situation?

Thoughts

Goal: To identify problematic thoughts that seem connected to the anger episode. Start by asking open-ended questions about the client's thoughts that emerged during the episode. Then direct the client's focus to the record and the list of six common thoughts that contribute to anger development. Ask him or her to select those that were present. It is acceptable to identify multiple thought patterns.

What was going through your mind when you started to get angry?

What were you telling yourself right before you got angry?

Take a look at the list of thoughts on the Anger Episode Record. These are six thoughts that people commonly experience when the get angry. Usually people do not have all six of these thoughts, but they often have a few of them. Which ones did you experience when you were angry in this situation?

Experience

Goal: To explore (1) the intensity of the felt anger, (2) the duration of the anger episode, and (3) any physical sensations the client experienced. Since intensity ratings of anger may fluctuate over time, ask about the highest intensity level related to the anger episode, using the rating scale and descriptions on the Anger Episode Record. In some cases, the duration of anger may be difficult to pin down because the anger is still ongoing. If anger is ongoing, simply note it on the Anger Episode Record. In terms of exploring physical sensations, start with an open-ended question. Then ask the client to review the list of sensations on the Anger Episode Record and to indicate the sensations that were present. Some clients will not identify any sensations, because the anger episode was not strong enough or because they are not accustomed to noticing their own bodily reactions. Other clients may report several strong sensations.

On a scale of 0 to 10, where 0 is not at all angry and 10 is the most anger you have ever experienced, how angry did you get during this anger episode?

In terms of this particular anger episode, how strong was your anger when it was at its highest level?

How long did your anger last?

Is your anger about this situation still present? Do you still feel angry when you think about it?

What physical sensations did you notice in your body at the time you were angry?

Take a look at the list of physical sensations on the Anger Episode Record. These are things that people sometimes experience when they are angry. No one experiences all of them, of course. Which ones did you experience when you were angry in this situation?

Action Urge

Goal: To explore the client's automatic-like urges or impulses to react in this situation. Remember that action urges are those that occur in the moment as the anger is emerging. Urges to act are influenced by the trigger, by thoughts, and by the perceived experience itself, including the intensity of physical activation. The impulse can be to withdraw, to confront, or to try to fix the problem. Keep in mind that urges do not always translate into actual behaviors. When possible, ask about action urges in an open-ended manner.

Think about your anger in this situation. What did you want to do in the moment?

What was your autopilot directing you to do?

Did you have the sense that if you weren't careful, you might lose control?

Did you have the sense that you had to do something right away?

Anger Expression

Goal: To explore what the person actually did when angry. For example, was the response verbal? Was it a physical action against an object? Was it physical aggression against a person or an animal? Was it avoidant, passive-aggressive, socially antagonistic? Start by asking open-ended questions about angry behaviors. Then review the list of behaviors on the Anger Episode Record, and ask the client to identify which ones he or she engaged in during the anger episode. It is common for more than one behavior to be selected.

What did you actually do when you were angry during this episode?

What were some of the things you said?

Were you sarcastic or blaming?

What was your tone of voice like? Did it get louder or lower?

What did you do with your body, such as hand gestures, glaring at the other person, or leaning forward and trying to be dominant?

What actions did you take in the moment, such as pushing, hitting, spitting, walking away—things like that?

Did you do things in the moment to avoid the situation or distract yourself, such as walking away, taking a drink, taking a drug—things like that?

How much similarity was there between your automatic autopilot urges to react and the way you actually did react?

Outcomes

Goal: To explore the client's perception of the negative outcomes connected to the specific episode of anger but also the client's perception of the positive outcomes—and do keep in mind that outcomes can sometimes be positive (for example, anger can be helpful in facing a problem, having a difficult conversation with someone, or even resolving a disagreement). It is also important to ask not only about immediate outcomes but also about longer-term consequences. Sometimes immediate outcomes are positive (for example, gaining compliance from others), whereas longer-term outcomes are negative (for example, being dismissed from a job). Explore the short-term and longer-term outcomes of anger in an open-ended manner.

What good came out of your anger in this situation?

What was not so good about your anger in this situation?

What was good about how you reacted?

What was not so good about how you reacted?

How do you think this anger episode affected your relationship(s)?

Moving forward, what do you see as the longer-term positive effects of your anger in this situation?

Moving forward, what do you see as the longer-term negative effects of your anger in this situation?

Howard Kassinove, PhD, and Raymond Chip Tafrate, PhD

CLIENT WORKSHEET 4.1. Anger Episode Record

Fill out one record for each episode of anger. Provide information in each of the six parts.

Part 1. Trigger

Place a check mark in the box next to the word(s) indicating the area of your life in which your anger was triggered.

- ☐ Work
- ☐ School
- ☐ Family
- ☐ Parenting
- ☐ Romantic relationship
- ☐ Friendship
- ☐ Other:_____

In one simple sentence, report the event that led to your anger. (Example: "My son forgot again to clean his room.")

_____

_____

_____

Part 2. Thoughts

Place a check mark in the box next to every statement that applies to this anger episode.

- ☐ *Awfulizing:* At the time, I thought this was one of the worst things that could be happening.

- ☐ *Low frustration tolerance:* I thought I could not handle or deal with the situation.

- ☐ *Demandingness:* I thought the other person(s) should have acted differently.

- ☐ *Rating others:* I saw the other person(s) as _____.

- ☐ *Rating myself:* Deep down, I thought I was less important or worthwhile.

- ☐ *Distortion or misinterpretation:* My thinking became distorted, and I didn't see things clearly.

Part 3. Experience

Place a check mark in the box next to the number that corresponds to the intensity and degree of your anger, and to how you felt in this situation.

Intensity of Your Anger	Extent of Your Anger	How You Felt
☐ 1	Almost no anger	Calm, indifferent
☐ 2	Slight anger	Jarred, moved, stirred, ruffled, challenged
☐ 3	Mild anger	Annoyed, bothered, irritated, perturbed, flustered, uneasy, provoked, impelled, cranky, crotchety, distressed, disturbed
☐ 4		
☐ 5	Moderate anger	Mad, agitated, pissed off, irked, aggravated, fired up, riled up, all worked up, peeved, indignant
☐ 6		
☐ 7	Strong anger	Irate, inflamed, exasperated, fuming, burned up, incensed, infuriated, enraged, hysterical
☐ 8		
☐ 9	Extreme anger	Frenzied, vicious, unhinged, up in arms, rabid, crazed, maniacal, wild, violent, demented
☐ 10		

Now complete the following sentence: *At the time of this specific event, I felt...*

_____

How long did your anger last? Place a check mark in the box next to the word indicating the duration of your anger.

☐ Minutes ☐ Days

☐ Hours ☐ Ongoing

What physical sensations did you notice? Place a check mark in the box next to the word(s) describing your physical sensations.

☐ Fluttering/upset stomach ☐ Warmth/flushing

☐ Indigestion ☐ Nausea

☐ Rapid heart rate ☐ Rapid breathing

☐ Dizziness ☐ Headache

☐ Fuzziness/feelings of unreality ☐ Tingling

☐ Muscle tension ☐ Trembling

☐ Fatigue ☐ Other:_____

☐ Sweating

Part 4. Action Urge

Place a check mark in the box next to the word or phrase corresponding to your action urge in this situation. Then, on the line that follows that word or phrase, briefly describe the impulse that arose for you. (Examples: "I just wanted to get in his face" or "I couldn't wait to get away from her.")

☐ Confront: _____

☐ Withdraw: _____

☐ Resolve the problem: _____

☐ Other: _____

Part 5. Anger Expression

Place a check mark in the box next to every behavior you engaged in during this anger episode.

☐ No expression (kept things in, boiled inside, held grudges and didn't tell anyone)

☐ Indirect expression (secretly did something to harm the other person, spread rumors, ignored what the other person wanted)

☐ Outward verbal expression (yelled, screamed, argued, threatened; made sarcastic, nasty, or abusive remarks)

☐ Outward expression against an object (broke, threw, slammed, or destroyed an object)

☐ Outward expression against a person (fought, hit, kicked, or shoved someone)

☐ Outward expression through bodily gestures (rolled eyes, crossed arms, glared, frowned, gave a stern look)

☐ Avoidance (escaped or walked away from the situation; distracted myself by reading, watching TV, listening to music)

☐ Substance use (drank alcohol; took medications; used other drugs, such as marijuana or cocaine)

☐ Attempt at resolution (compromised, discussed, or came to some agreement with the other person)

☐ Other:_____

Part 6. Outcomes

What was a *positive short-term* outcome of this anger episode?

_____

_____

_____

What was a *positive long-term* outcome of this anger episode?

_____

_____

_____

What was a *negative short-term* outcome of this anger episode?

_____

_____

_____

What was a *negative long-term* outcome of this anger episode?

_____

_____

_____

Howard Kassinove, PhD, and Raymond Chip Tafrate, PhD

PART 3

Preparing Clients
for Change

CHAPTER 5

Enhancing Awareness and Motivation

Everyone thinks of changing the world, but no one thinks of changing himself.

—Leo Tolstoy

Even when clients arrive with some degree of awareness that anger has been negatively affecting their lives, their automatic responses usually consist of blaming others and demanding that others around them change. Therefore, increasing clients' *awareness* of anger and its negative costs, and increasing their *motivation* to reduce their anger reactions, are related and critical goals in the early phases of treatment.

Awareness Enhancement

In this section of the chapter, we highlight awareness-enhancement strategies that are connected to the assessment procedures discussed in chapter 4. The first strategy is to focus on increasing the client's awareness while reviewing feedback from the results of standardized anger tests. The second strategy is used during reviews of the client's Anger Episode Records.

Providing Feedback from Standardized Anger Tests

Once there is a reasonable degree of engagement, we recommend the use of anger-specific tests to help clients better understand how their anger reactions are different from those of the population at large. A powerful awareness-enhancement experience can be had through sharing with the client information about how his or her scores compare with those of others. Scores are usually presented in terms of percentiles for the anger dimensions that were measured, and they can be explained in easy-to-understand language. We recommend that you limit your feedback to one or two scores representing the anger areas that are most critical. For the more comprehensive instruments, it is not essential or even useful to provide feedback on all the dimensions that were measured.

When you're having this discussion, resist the temptation to convince the client to accept the feedback. Instead, take the position that the feedback is presented simply as information for the client to consider. The client is free to reject it. If the feedback is presented properly, however, most people appreciate it, even if it is uncomfortable to hear. In addition to its usefulness as a simple awareness-enhancement tool, feedback based on standardized anger tests is also useful as a platform for exploring how anger may be negatively impacting the client's life in a more general sense. Practitioner script 5.1 presents a dialogue that shows how feedback was presented in the case of Mark (see chapter 2); only one score, for verbal expression, is reviewed in the script, but this dialogue can be used as a template for providing feedback on other scores or test results.

PRACTITIONER SCRIPT 5.1.
Providing Feedback on Standardized Anger Tests

Practitioner: Hi, Mark. Would it be okay if we spent a few minutes going over your score on one of the questionnaires that you completed at our last meeting? That questionnaire measured different dimensions of anger, and one dimension involves the level at which you verbally express your anger to others. Your score on that dimension was a high one. You scored at the 99th percentile. This means that you express anger at a level greater than what is true for 99 percent of men your age. In other words, you are among the top 1 percent of men your age in terms of yelling, arguing, or saying negative things to others when you are angry.

The following questions can be used to explore Mark's score on verbal expressiveness and to increase his awareness:

What do you think?

How does this fit with how you see yourself handling your anger?

How has being so verbally expressive with your anger influenced your life?

Give me examples of some things you have lost because of your expressiveness with your anger. [Search for lost relationships, jobs, money, health, freedom, respect, and so forth.]

How have your anger reactions undermined _____?
[Insert a word or phrase referring to something that Mark values, such as his relationships with his children.]

Where do you see things headed if you don't get a handle on your anger?

How might your life be different if you made a change in how you deal with your anger?

Practitioner: Thanks for your willingness to talk with me about this.

Keep in mind that the style of presenting feedback we describe here works best for the kinds of human problems and behaviors (such as anger, substance use, and criminal thinking) that people tend to minimize, or for which they have limited awareness regarding the longer-term consequences. This style of presenting feedback is not recommended for clients who tend to obsess or ruminate about specific anxiety- or depression-related symptoms. For example, if significant anxiety is part of the clinical picture, then telling the client that her amount of worry is greater than that of 94 percent of women her age would probably be counterproductive and might result in even more rumination. But if a client has little concern about using alcohol to manage her anxiety symptoms, then you might present feedback from the results of a standardized test that is specific to alcohol use; see Kassinove and Tafrate (2014) for access to a videotaped example of providing anger-related feedback in this style.

It is common to get agreement from clients about their high scores on anger tests, since the tests measure problem areas that have been identified on the basis of clients' self-reports. Nevertheless, clients can have a variety of reactions to hearing how their scores compare to those of a standardization group. At the same time, however, these reactions are almost always limited to a few themes. Table 5.1 shows typical reactions from clients to this kind of feedback, along with sample responses from practitioners. Even when the client disagrees with the feedback, a usually effective approach is to use open questions and reflections designed to explore the issue further and elicit change talk (a concept briefly introduced in chapter 2 and table 2.1, and discussed again later in this chapter). The one exception is for a client who reacts with confusion. In this scenario, your task is to explain the score again, in a different way that the client is more likely to understand. If the client seems confused by talk about percentiles, then we recommend that you use a simple description instead: "One area where you scored really high is…"

Table 5.1. Client's Reactions to Assessment Feedback, with Practitioner's Responses

Client's Reactions	Practitioner's Responses
Agreement: My anger has always been a problem. I know that.	This seems on target for you. Tell me how your anger reactions have created problems in your life.
Surprise: I always thought I was like everyone else. I didn't think my anger was that high.	Sounds like this information is surprising. What do you think it means for you?

Minimization: My anger is not a big deal. I know other people who do things way worse than I do.	You're not sure your verbal reactions are really a problem. You notice that other people are more out of control. What have you noticed about how others handle their anger?
Justification: I live in a rough neighborhood. I have no choice but to show a tough image. So I say "Fuck off" to people.	You have your reasons for acting the way you do. What usually happens when you angrily confront or yell at others in your neighborhood?
Disagreement: Something is wrong with your test. I'm not the one with an anger problem.	This score doesn't seem right or make sense for you. Let's put the test aside. How do you see your own anger in comparison to how others react?
Indifference: This is stupid! But, whatever... I don't believe in tests.	You're not sure this information is relevant for you. Let's not go with what the test says. I'm interested in how you see things. How would you describe your anger in comparison to others?
Confusion: Cool—99 percent is great, right?	Let's talk a bit more about what this score means. I'll draw a quick chart. When it comes to expressing your anger, this X shows where you stand compared to others. You are at the extreme high end, which puts you at risk.

Reviewing Specific Episodes of Anger

The client's awareness of his or her anger reactions in general can sometimes be enhanced when you review specific episodes of the client's anger. Anger is common, and so clients in most treatment settings often have little difficulty coming up with anger episodes. In some cases, clients are aware of their aggressive motor behaviors and often have to admit to aggression, since it may have been observed by others; it's hard to deny pushing, shoving, hitting, spitting, and so forth. And yet these clients may be less aware of their anger and may deny having been angry, because they may not be used to focusing on their internal experiences of anger. In these cases, we try first to put clients in contact with their bodily reactions and then with their anger-producing thoughts. Consider the following dialogue:

Practitioner: Belvina, you said you were unhappy when you found out that your son had copied his homework from his friend James. You learned this from James's mother.

Belvina: Yes. I was unhappy. And I told my son so. Then I punished him by sending him to his room, and I took away his game console, and I guess I yelled a lot. Actually, I screamed at him.

Practitioner: You said you felt unhappy. Were there any other feelings involved?

Belvina: No. I was just really sad and unhappy to learn that he'd cheated like that.

Practitioner: I understand. However, you also said you screamed at him. I'm wondering what was happening in your body during the incident.

Belvina: Well, I noticed a kind of uneasiness, and my heart was racing. Also, I had a drink right after the incident, and it was only 4 p.m. I never drink before dinner.

Practitioner: You seem to be aware that something more than a little unhappiness was going on in you. Tell me, when you learned that he'd copied his homework, what did you think?

Belvina: In my head, I called him a no-good little shit. Then I told him he would never get anywhere in life by cheating, and that he was a disappointment. He's very bright, and he shouldn't be cheating—period!

Practitioner: So you screamed, your heart raced, you had a drink, you called him a pretty bad name in your head, and you took away his game console. Taking away the console sounds like a calm and cool and even appropriate reaction. But the stuff you felt in your body, and what you thought to yourself—that sounds like something else, something more than a little unhappiness. What do you think?

Belvina: Yeah. I agree. I guess I was really angry. "Angry" would be a better word than "unhappy."

The goal here is to enhance awareness, as a prelude to increasing motivation to change. Once engagement, awareness, and motivation have been achieved, it will be much easier to tackle change strategies. At that point, you and your client will both be on the same page.

Here we should mention those situations in which anger reduction may be useful even though it is not the primary issue. There are potential anger management clients in community mental health centers, hospitals, religious institutions, independent practices, and even schools—clients who may not even be aware that anger management services are available. For this reason, it may be beneficial to leave a client information sheet in the waiting area so as to highlight the option of anger management services to improve the client's life. Client information sheet 5.1, included at the end of this chapter and downloadable from www.newharbinger.com/42877, may help potential clients come to the awareness that their anger is also a problem to be addressed.

Motivation Enhancement

There are a number of ways to develop a client's motivation to reduce dysfunctional anger and develop better coping reactions to perceived adversity. One way is to place emphasis on the "outcomes" portion of the Anger Episode Model and the Anger Episode Record (see chapters 3 and 4). As you and the client review the short- and long-term outcomes of specific anger episodes, the goal is to listen for and reinforce any naturally occurring change talk that may emerge about negative outcomes. Strategic questions for evoking the desire or reasons to change can be interwoven into the exploration of outcomes. Although this type of discussion will usually highlight the negative aspects of the client's anger, also look for opportunities to evoke and reinforce aspirations for better anger management and increased effectiveness in dealing with similar challenges in the future. Here is a dialogue with Keith regarding a recent argument that he had with his girlfriend at a party; the dialogue picks up at the "outcomes" portion of the anger episode analysis:

Practitioner: What good came out of your anger in this situation?

Keith: I have no regrets.

Practitioner: What was good about getting so angry in this situation?

Keith: Nothing good came out of it. Nothing good comes out of anger.

Practitioner: What was *not* so good about how you reacted?

Keith: Everything. I'm yelling at my girl, and everyone is watching. They're all thinking, *What is going on here? This guy is out of control.*

Practitioner: As you look back on it now, it seems like you're embarrassed by how you reacted.

Keith: Yes, I was raised better. It's not how I want to be.

Practitioner: How do you think this anger episode affected your relationship with your girlfriend?

Keith: She was distant for the next few days.

Practitioner: So even though she didn't bring it up, it still affected how she reacted to you.

Keith: Yeah. Big time.

Practitioner: How would you like things to be different, moving forward?

Keith: I want to learn how to slow down and not react so quickly. To let things go. To have better control.

Practitioner: Sounds like you would like to see yourself in a different place, with less anger and more patience with her in the future.

Keith: Yeah. Definitely.

Two specific skills help foster motivation in angry clients:

1. Listening carefully for verbalizations that express, however subtly or ambivalently, the client's awareness of the costs of anger and the client's desire for change, and then reinforcing those expressions

2. Intentionally evoking and reinforcing the client's verbalizations in favor of anger reduction

These two skills, which operate in tandem, are part of the motivational interviewing (MI) process of evoking clients' intrinsic motivation. At its heart, evoking the clients' intrinsic motivation is about supporting and encouraging clients to voice their own motivations to change their anger-related patterns; indeed, as we noted in chapter 2, "what clients hear *themselves* say is more important than what they hear *you* say." In other words, clients who are successful in treatment actually go through a process of talking themselves into reducing their anger.

Distinguishing Change Talk and Sustain Talk

If you were trained in classical cognitive behavioral therapy (CBT), you were taught to pay attention to specific types of verbalizations that suggest cognitive distortions, irrational beliefs, and dysfunctional schemas. Such cognitive constructs are believed to be central to various forms of psychopathology. We have already addressed some cognitions that are the focal point of anger treatment (and will do so again in chapter 10), but much of our therapeutic work in the beginning phases of treatment is based on MI, which keys into a different constellation of language constructs. Those constructs are specifically related to motivation and subsequent change. It will take time and practice for you to learn to elicit, identify, and respond to this form of language from clients; it's like putting on a set of headphones through which you will listen for specific verbalizations.

Two formal concepts—sustain talk and change talk (Miller & Rollnick, 2013)—are relevant to your understanding of clients' verbalizations that are related to change:

1. *Sustain talk* favors not changing, and maintaining the status quo.

2. *Change talk* favors movement toward and commitment to change.

With angry clients, sustain talk often takes the following forms:

Justification

- My reputation was at stake. Anyone would get angry in that situation!

- Being angry felt right. I have no regrets about what I said.

- I'm not going to be a doormat. I'm going to stick up for myself.

- That's why we say, "An eye for an eye."

- She got in my face first. I was just defending myself.

Blame

- It was her fault.

- My boss needs to treat me with more respect.

- I blame my parents. They were always getting angry with each other.

- Those kids make me so angry!

Identifying with Anger

- Anger runs in my family. I come from a passionate culture.

- My anger is part of who I am. They'd better get used to me.

- I've always been quick to fly off the handle.

- They will just have to learn to accept me.

Change talk, in contrast, may sound something like these statements:

- I have to do something about my anger before I lose my job.

- Who knows why I got so angry? Sometimes I wish I was different.

- The way I acted definitely made the problem worse.

- I don't know, maybe old dogs *can* learn new tricks!

- Okay, maybe I can learn something here, and not take things so seriously.

Change talk can sometimes be obvious and easy to spot: "Do you know of a book or something that I can read to help with my anger?" Or it can be subtle: "I could have handled that situation a little better." And it does not necessarily involve a 100 percent commitment to suddenly change destructive anger reactions. In fact, it is quite normal for angry clients—just as it's normal for you, for us, and for people in general—to have two voices bouncing around in their heads at the same time, representing both sides of the equation (that is, both for and against reducing anger).

The ratio of change talk to sustain talk during practitioner-client interactions is an important marker for subsequent change and is associated with treatment outcomes. A predominance of change talk predicts actual behavior change; a higher proportion of sustain talk, or an equal amount of sustain talk and change talk, is predictive of not changing (Moyers, Martin, Houck, Christopher, & Tonigan, 2009). The client's amounts of change talk and sustain talk can also be influenced by the practitioner's response style (Glynn & Moyers, 2010). Therefore, a core skill in work with angry clients is to facilitate their expression of verbalizations in favor of making changes to reduce their anger in the future when they are reacting to challenges and struggles. Increasing the client's change talk is always your goal.

Change Talk Subtypes: DARN CAT

Change talk is organized on two levels:

1. *Preparatory* change talk

2. *Mobilizing* change talk

PREPARATORY CHANGE TALK

Preparatory change talk signals energy in favor of change. It has four subtypes—related to clients' *desire* for change, their *ability* to change, their *reasons* for changing, and their *need* for change—which you can remember with the acronym DARN:

1. Desire: I want a better relationship with my partner, with less fighting and drama.

2. Ability: Next time I could probably listen before I react.

3. Reasons: If I could keep my cool at work, I think I would be more successful.

4. Need: I need to (*or* I should) stop and walk away before things get out of hand.

WHAT TO DO WITH "SHOULDS"?

In traditional CBT models, words and phrases like "should," "ought to," "must," and "have to" are viewed as representing irrational beliefs. In fact, demandingness, or the tendency to believe that people or life conditions should be different from what they actually are (see chapter 3), appears to be the most important cognitive irrationality underlying anger reactions (Tafrate, Kassinove, & Dundin, 2002). Because an important goal of treatment is to foster a more flexible and less demanding life philosophy, the thinking pattern of demandingness is often targeted and restructured in treatment that uses a traditional CBT model.

In the MI model, by contrast, words like "should" and "must," as they pertain to clients' discussions of their own angry behaviors, are viewed as forms of change language (that is, as "need" statements, which belong to the fourth subtype of preparatory change talk). Such words are assumed to represent the underlying construct of statements like "It would be better if..." or "I'd have a better life if..." For this reason, such statements are reinforced in the early phase of treatment, albeit with minor modifications. Thus, if a client whose "should" statement is self-directed says, "I should have kept quiet and not gotten into an argument with my mother-in-law," it would not be useful in the early phases of treatment for the practitioner to challenge this "should" language in an attempt to foster less demanding thinking. In the traditional CBT approach, the practitioner could respond by saying something like, "Why *should* you have kept quiet? It might have been more desirable, but family relationship can be challenging, and we all make mistakes." If the statement were to be handled in this manner, the client could say, "I guess you're right—family arguments happen all the time" and might then be able to adopt a more accepting view of his or her own shortcomings and perhaps feel less guilt or regret. But this response would do little to enhance the client's motivation to reduce his or her anger reactions and might even undermine the client's motivation. From the perspective of MI, it would be more effective for the practitioner to elicit, enhance, and reinforce the client's change language with a response like one of these:

- Why would it have been better if you had kept quiet?

- You really think it wasn't worth it to get into that argument?

- What is the downside of getting into arguments like that with your mother-in-law?

- How would you have wanted to handle that situation differently?

These kinds of responses from the practitioner strategically evoke *more* change talk from the client. They elicit statements on the side of the client's not arguing with his or her mother-in-law in the future.

MOBILIZING CHANGE TALK

Mobilizing change talk has three subtypes—related to clients' *commitment* to change, their *activation* of change, and their *taking steps* toward change—which you can remember with the acronym CAT:

- Commitment: I'll reach out to Casey next week and apologize for what happened.

- Activation: I'm planning to start taking a walk after work to clear my head so I don't come home angry.

- Taking steps: I looked on the Internet and found some relaxation programs that I think will help me stay calm when crap happens to me.

Recognizing Change Talk

Before you can evoke change talk, you need to tune your ear to recognize change talk when it occurs. Table 5.2 presents a list of statements we have heard angry clients say during sessions. First read over the list, and indicate with a check mark whether each statement reflects sustain talk or change talk (it may be either *preparatory* change talk or *mobilizing* change talk) as the statement pertains to reducing anger. Then go back over the list, and for the statements you marked as change talk, identify the specific subtype (*desire, ability, reasons, need, commitment, activation,* or *taking steps*), and write the name of that subtype in the space provided. Answers are provided below the table.

Table 5.2. Recognizing Change Talk

Client's Statements	Sustain Talk	Change Talk	Change Talk Subtype
1. I have my reasons for confronting her.	☐	☐	
2. My daughter wants me to be less angry at home.	☐	☐	
3. I took a different route to work so I wouldn't be so keyed up when I got there.	☐	☐	
4. I might be able to have a discussion with my supervisor so I can get more help at work.	☐	☐	

5. I say what I feel. That's who I am. I'm not going to pretend to be someone different and hold my anger in.	☐	☐	
6. I want to be a more patient father.	☐	☐	
7. My anger makes me look strong. Not sticking up for myself is weak.	☐	☐	
8. I plan to drink less at the family picnic so I won't get angry and say something I'll regret.	☐	☐	
9. I'm not going to forgive John. I'm thinking about ways to get back at him.	☐	☐	
10. I've got to work on my anger to save my marriage.	☐	☐	
11. I don't need to go to counseling. My anger is no worse than anyone else's that I know.	☐	☐	
12. Sometimes I just need to vent to get my feelings out.	☐	☐	
13. I guarantee I'll complete the Anger Episode Records for our next appointment.	☐	☐	
14. It's my house, and I'm in charge.	☐	☐	

Answers

1. Sustain talk

2. Change talk (reasons)

3. Change talk (taking steps)

4. Change talk (ability)

5. Sustain talk

6. Change talk (desire)

7. Sustain talk

8. Change talk (activation)

9. Sustain talk

10. Change talk (need)

11. Sustain talk

12. Sustain talk

13. Change talk (commitment)

14. Sustain talk

Responding to Naturally Occurring Change Talk

One of the benefits of becoming familiar with change talk is that you will begin to notice much more motivation emerging in sessions. Since many clients are ambivalent about the consequences of their anger reactions, change talk will often bubble up naturally. When it emerges, your goal is to reinforce it so that more change talk will occur. You can use the OARS skills (*open questions, affirmations, reflections,* and *summarizations;* see chapter 2), with a more strategic purpose of evoking additional change talk. Suppose, for example, that you hear statement 10 from table 5.2: "I've got to work on my anger to save my marriage." You might respond in one or more of the following ways:

- Open question: Why it is so important for you to save your marriage?

- Affirmation: In spite of all the conflict, you want to be a good husband.

- Reflection: Sounds like your marriage is important to you.

Any change talk that emerges during the session can also be incorporated into your closing summary:

Practitioner: Let's pull together what we have been talking about. The last few years of your marriage have been a struggle, with lots of arguments and disagreements. There are a couple of reasons why things have gotten so bad. As you look at what has been happening, you recognize that your angry reactions are a big part of the problem. You have decided that saving your marriage is your number one priority. Your kids are your most important reason for you to take steps to make things better. You're willing to do whatever it takes to learn some new ways to handle disagreements at home. And you're hopeful that things will get better.

Actively Eliciting Change Talk

With some clients, there may be little opportunity to reinforce change talk, because it has not emerged naturally in the session. In that situation, you can take steps to actively evoke change talk by asking strategic open questions. These are sometimes known as *change talk questions* because the answers invite DARN CAT verbalizations. Table 5.3 presents a list of generic questions that are related to anger, and that correspond to the model of change talk we have been discussing. You can create more specific questions that better fit the characteristics of a specific client.

Table 5.3. Questions Likely to Evoke Change Talk

Change Talk Subtype	Change Talk Questions
Desire	Why would you want to live your life with less anger? Why would you want to be less angry?
Ability	What gives you confidence that you can change your anger reactions? What strengths do you have that might help you be less angry?
Reasons	What might be the two most important reasons to work on your anger? What are the benefits of working on your anger?
Need	How important is it for you to work on your anger? What's at stake if you don't get a handle on your anger reactions?
Commitment	What do you see as the next step in working on your anger? What is one specific thing you can do to change your anger reactions?
Activation	What are some things you might do to get ready to change your anger reactions? In what ways could you start exploring how changing your anger would improve your life?
Taking steps	What have you done so far to move toward changing your anger? What are some of the things you have accomplished that can help you change your anger right now?

Responding to Sustain Talk

During discussions with an angry client, sustain talk (that is, the client's statements that are not in favor of reducing his or her angry reactions) will also occur naturally. The amount of sustain talk may be particularly high for an adult or an adolescent who has been coerced into treatment. The good news is that, with successful engagement, sustain talk usually decreases over time. When sustain talk emerges, it's important not to reprimand or punish clients. It is also important not to completely ignore sustain talk, with the hope of extinguishing such verbalizations. Extinction usually takes a very, very long time. You're also likely to damage the working relationship if you respond to sustain talk by reprimanding the client or ignoring such statements. It's crucial to grasp the client's perspective instead. This means that there will be times when you acknowledge the client's sustain talk. Suppose, for example, that you hear statement 5 from table 5.2: "I say what I feel. That's who I am. I'm not going to pretend to be someone different and hold my anger in." You might respond in one or more of the following ways:

Reflection: Your anger is part of who you are, and it's hard to imagine being different.

- Open question: Can you tell me the good things about being so genuine and expressive with people?

Responses such as these demonstrate good listening. Somewhat counterintuitively, however, *if you avoid the impulse to confront or challenge sustain talk, change talk will often follow* because the client is ambivalent, and both voices are naturally occurring. If change talk does not bubble up, you can attempt to actively elicit it by using questions similar to the ones we've just suggested: "Tell me anything you've noticed that is maybe not so good about being so genuine and expressive with people."

Additional Thoughts About Change Talk

During a single session, and over the course of treatment, change talk will naturally rise and fall. Even when clients have voiced strong arguments in favor of change, sustain talk will inevitably surface. Your task is to carefully listen for and differentially reinforce change talk throughout the treatment process. Reinforcing change talk is a continuous goal.

There will be times when attending to change talk will infuse the conversation with a negative and heavy tone because the content will be about bad outcomes the client wishes to avoid, such as damaged relationships, work conflicts, and other failures associated with anger. At other times, attending to talk about changing angry reactions will result in conversations that are more uplifting, more optimistic, and about hopes and aspirations for a better life, inner peace, and increased happiness. Both types of conversations are acceptable. A common progression is for conversations to center at first on the negative consequences linked to intense and frequent anger and then move on to the more positive anticipated outcomes that may come from managing anger better.

Because your task is to increase change talk, be cautious about asking questions likely to evoke sustain talk. Unfortunately, such questions are common among well-meaning practitioners. Here are some examples of questions to avoid:

- Why are you not more motivated to change your anger?

- Why haven't you taken steps to control your anger?

- Why do you find it so hard to control your anger?

- Why won't you work at managing your anger?

- What are the pros and cons of changing your anger?

The final question exemplifies what is known as the *decisional balance technique*, a very common maneuver in which the practitioner asks the client to explore the upside and downside of angry thoughts and behaviors. This technique does lead to change talk as well as to sustain talk, but it does not always lead to a *higher ratio* of change talk.

In short, these are ill-advised questions, since they are likely to increase sustain talk. Nevertheless, there will be times when they are useful for understanding a client's perspective and exploring potential roadblocks to change. So think ahead when you are constructing your questions, and if a specific question is likely to elicit sustain talk, then have a good rationale for asking it—or don't ask it at all.

Angry clients coming into treatment and describing their perspectives and reactions to their challenges and struggles often do so with very high energy, and so there are many things for you to pay attention to during conversations. One of your most important tasks as a practitioner is to tune your ear to your client's change language. Tilting the balance in favor of change talk (over sustain talk) is a subtle art. With effort and practice, you can achieve higher levels of competency with this skill. A series of self-guided and highly useful exercises for recognizing, reinforcing, and eliciting change talk can be found in the excellent workbook by Rosengren (2018).

Takeaway Messages and Tools

Engagement, as we've seen, goes a long way toward setting the stage for effective treatment. So does awareness enhancement, with the magnitude and consequences of clients' anger clarified through the use of feedback based on results from standardized anger tests as well as by review of clients' Anger Episode Records and discussions about clients' bodily and cognitive reactions to anger. Informational materials left in the waiting area of your office can also encourage awareness. In the SMART program, you enhance motivation by listening for and reinforcing change talk early on and then interweaving it throughout the treatment process. What clients have to say about their own reasons for reducing their anger is more powerful than your attempts to convince them to change or your lectures about the importance of change. Learning to identify, evoke, and respond to change talk is a core skill. To get the intervention process on the right footing, you can use engagement along with awareness enhancement, and you can do so in a coordinated way.

And yet there is one more foundational component of the work that you will do to prepare clients for the active interventions that follow the beginning of treatment. Because anger can be confusing to many people, SMART anger management includes the development of a shared understanding regarding some basic elements of anger. This psychoeducation process is addressed in chapter 6.

CLIENT INFORMATION SHEET 5.1.
Can I Benefit from an Anger Reduction Program?

You may wonder whether your anger is a true problem for you. To find the answer, read the following questions, and place a check mark in the box next to any response that seems accurate for you. There are no right or wrong answers, but your honest responses will provide you with guidance about whether you can profit from an anger reduction program.

1. I have experienced episodes of anger for six months or longer.

    ☐ Yes

    ☐ No

2. I become angry...

    ☐ more often than most other people.

    ☐ less often than most other people.

    ☐ about as often as most other people.

3. When I become angry, I feel that my anger is...

    ☐ stronger and more intense than most other people's anger.

    ☐ not as strong or intense as most other people's anger.

    ☐ about as strong and intense as most other people's anger.

4. When I become angry, it seems to me that my anger...

    ☐ lasts longer than most other people's anger.

    ☐ does not last as long as most other people's anger.

    ☐ lasts about as long as most other people's anger.

5. As a result of my anger, I have experienced the following negative consequences:

    ☐ Damage to personal relationships (with my spouse, my children, my friends, ...)

    ☐ Difficulties at work (with colleagues, bosses, people who work for me, ...)

    ☐ Reduced ability to handle difficult situations

    ☐ Experiences with the criminal justice system (traffic tickets, incarceration, ...)

☐ Physical health problems (heart palpitations, sweating, sleep disturbances, ...)

☐ Personal and emotional distress (worrying, dwelling on problems, feeling shame, ...)

6. There have been times when my anger has blocked me from achieving important life goals.

☐ Yes

☐ No

7. I would probably be more successful in life if I had better control over my anger.

☐ Yes

☐ No

Howard Kassinove, PhD, and Raymond Chip Tafrate, PhD

CHAPTER 6

Psychoeducation

Education consists mainly of what we have unlearned.

—Mark Twain

We have been making the case that SMART anger management begins with an engagement process that consists of the following behaviors and elements on your part:

- Careful listening to the problems presented by clients

- Encouragement

- Acceptance

- Compassion

- Open-ended questioning

- Reflection of an understanding of the client's perspective

- An established agreement with the client on the goals of treatment and on the methods that might be used to achieve those goals

We have also discouraged, particularly at the beginning of treatment, the following behaviors and elements:

- Closed-ended interview questions

- Giving advice to the client

- Shaming the client

- Debating the client

- Taking a judgmental stance to indicate that you disagree *or* agree with the client

- Acting like a know-it-all expert

Each of these recommendations reflects our belief that the first step to success for you and your client is for the two of you to work as a team, collaboratively moving toward problem resolution. This means that you, as the practitioner, will *elicit* rather than impart, *guide* rather than direct, *lure* rather than pull, and *consult* rather than instruct. What, then, is the role of education, especially when you may have important knowledge or expertise to share with clients?

The Role of Education

The word "education" implies a teacher-student relationship, which we have discouraged, to some extent. Yet there are three key reasons for promoting some degree of anger education:

1. To ensure that you and your client share a knowledge base regarding anger

2. To shape the client's expectations for treatment

3. To test the client's current knowledge and beliefs about anger

Establishing a Shared Knowledge Base

To move forward productively, it's useful for you and your clients to be working from the same base of knowledge about anger. You will probably have to impart this knowledge, since most clients have never thought about anger in any systematic way. The renowned behaviorist B. F. Skinner spoke about an important and yet underappreciated reason for you and your clients to have a base of shared knowledge about anger—namely, education about any subject begins when the student learns a set of facts about that subject, often by rote memorization, and those facts, although the student often can't simply recall them at will, do remain as a kind of guiding, supportive, latticelike structure (which is why a multiple-choice test is often much easier than an essay test, since recalling previously learned facts in order to write an essay is much harder than simply recognizing those facts and picking them from a list of choices). Likewise, if you impart facts about anger to your clients, that learned knowledge about anger will always be there to guide your clients in the future.

Shaping the Client's Expectations

In anger management, psychoeducation involves knowledge both about anger and about the treatment of anger, and thus arises the therapeutic issue of expectations. According to Kichuk, Lebowitz, and Adams (2015), a practitioner-delivered rationale regarding what will happen during an intervention program can enhance the client's expectations of success. Some clients, for example, come in believing that anger is caused by biological factors, or by unconscious behaviors that simply cannot be overcome with psychological treatment. But if you share your knowledge that biological factors are malleable, and that more than a dozen meta-analyses have shown positive outcomes for anger treatment, in all kinds of populations, you have a good chance of raising your clients' expectations for making improvements, increasing their motivation to engage in the treatment process, and helping them achieve success in treatment.

Testing the Client's Current Knowledge and Beliefs

Perhaps the most important reason for encouraging psychoeducation is that many "facts" whose status as truths we all take for granted are actually not facts at all, and many bits of information that seem quite wrong are actually true. Before you read any further, consider the twenty statements in table 6.1, decide which ones are true and which ones are false, place a check mark in the appropriate column. Only then should you continue reading this chapter.

Table 6.1. Truths About Our World

Statement	True	False
1. Cracking your knuckles will eventually cause arthritis.	☐	☐
2. Maine is the closest US state to Africa.	☐	☐
3. A sugar rush (from eating too much sugar) is a cause of attention deficit/hyperactivity disorcer (ADHD).	☐	☐
4. Cleopatra lived closer to the invention of the iPhone than to the building of the Great Pyramids.	☐	☐
5. In the Bible, the forbidden fruit Eve gave to Adam was an apple.	☐	☐
6. Saudi Arabia imports camels from Australia.	☐	☐
7. To prevent cramps, it is important that children wait thirty minutes after eating before they swim.	☐	☐
8. The heart of a blue whale is so big that a human can swim through its arteries.	☐	☐
9. The earth revolves around the sun.	☐	☐
10. Vending machines are twice as likely to kill you as a shark is.	☐	☐
11. Chameleons change colors to blend in to their environment.	☐	☐
12. Oxford University is older than the Aztec Empire.	☐	☐

Statement	True	False
13. George Washington Carver invented peanut butter.	☐	☐
14. Armadillos nearly always give birth to identical quadruplets.	☐	☐
15. Vincent Van Gogh sliced off his own ear.	☐	☐
16. Honey never spoils.	☐	☐
17. In elementary school, Einstein was a poor student and failed mathematics.	☐	☐
18. Hippopotamus milk is pink.	☐	☐
19. Because of technical limitations in his time, George Washington had wooden teeth.	☐	☐
20. Alaska is the easternmost state in the United States.	☐	☐
TOTAL	☐	☐

How did you do? We can tell you now that all the odd-numbered statements are false, and all the even-numbered statements are true. Most people score 8 to 10 points, which is close to what you would score just by guessing. Discussions of these truths can be found online at the following sources:

- http://www.lolwot.com/20-things-you-thought-were-true-but-arent/20

- https://en.wikipedia.org/wiki/List_of_common_misconceptions

- http://www.huffingtonpost.com/2014/02/05/history-facts-not-true_n_4696288 .html

- https://www.buzzfeed.com/daves4/77-facts-that-sound-like-huge-lies-but -are-completely-true

In any case, we all have ideas about the world, ideas that guide our actions, and those ideas include what we believe about anger and aggression. Much of what your clients think they know about anger is likely to be false. For that reason, we encourage you to spend some time reviewing the facts about anger, and to do so in a collaborative and nonjudgmental way. We usually try to inject this type of information into the early sessions, looking for opportunities to weave in relevant facts during the engagement phase of SMART treatment, but psychoeducation will continue throughout the entire intervention period. Don't overdo it, however. Be careful not to come off as too much of an expert by trying to convince your client about what is true, and about how much your client can learn from you—that will only impede engagement.

In addition to having discussions about anger with your client, you might consider using wall charts, diagrams, and client information sheets that can be referred to in subsequent sessions. We are not suggesting that you try to make your clients experts in the science of anger. Rather, we simply want them to have a basic set of facts about the characteristics and causes of anger; information about the problems associated with frequent, strong, persistent anger reactions; and optimism about the intervention they're engaged in. When you skillfully raise your clients' awareness of these issues, you enhance the therapeutic alliance that comes from a shared perspective about the facts, and you boost your clients' confidence in their ability to change.

Psychoeducation About Anger: Basic Questions

We hope that you will consider helping your clients understand the thirty basic facts about anger presented in table 6.2. Many of these facts have been or will be discussed in other chapters; here, we offer them as a set of forced-choice alternatives to be given to your client as a quiz. For discussion purposes, these facts are also presented (without the explanations) in client information sheet 6.1, included at the end of this chapter and downloadable from www.newharbinger.com/42877. Once your client has completed the quiz, you can talk about each of these thirty facts. The quiz and the client information sheet are not meant to be tough or tricky. Rather, they are meant to stimulate conversation and increase knowledge.

Table 6.2. Basic Facts About Anger

Item	Statement A	Statement B	Explanation
1	Anger is a normal, natural feeling that often does not have to be managed.	Anger is an abnormal feeling state that causes aggression and has to be managed.	Here, you have an opportunity to suggest that anger is natural, and that when clients feel mild anger that disappears quickly, they do not have to worry that they are going downhill. They can also be helped to distinguish anger from aggression, and to learn that most anger exists independently of aggression.
2	When anger occurs more than once a month, it's a sure sign that something is wrong.	Many normal people feel angry a few times a week.	Item 2 can be used to note that many people experience anger a few times a week. The key to whether anger is dysfunctional rests more in the intensity of the experience, in how long it lasts, and in whether it is associated with behavioral dysfunction and poor outcomes.
3	Basically, anger and aggression are the same thing.	Anger and aggression are actually quite different.	By reviewing item 3, clients can learn about (or solidify their knowledge about) the difference between internal personal experiences and external behaviors. A sharp distinction can be drawn between anger as a feeling (which is often acceptable and can be reduced) and aggression as a motor behavior that is usually unacceptable, since it hurts others.
4	Anger is complex and multifaceted.	Anger is pretty simple. Basically, it's a mental thing.	Here, clients can learn that an anger episode has six parts: a **trigger, thoughts, experience** (subjective intensity, and such internal physiological reactions as an increased heart rate and overall muscle tension), an **action urge, anger expression** (such as yelling, withdrawing, or throwing an object against a wall), and an **outcome** (its effect on a relationship, or success or failure in dealing with a challenge).
5	We all feel angry sometimes. Usually, anger disappears by itself.	Like elephants, we never forget—once we feel angry, the anger lingers forever.	Item 5 provides an opportunity to show clients that they have been previously able to manage many of their anger episodes. Discussion can give them an expectation that they have the personal strength to deal with life's adversities, and that time is indeed a great healer.

Item	Statement A	Statement B	Explanation
6	Dysfunctional anger occurs only in specific groups of people, such as teenagers, those who drink a lot, gang members, or people whose parents were often angry.	Anyone can suffer from dysfunctional anger.	Item 6 provides an opportunity to show that anger is an equal-opportunity experience. Clients can be shown that anyone, given the right circumstances, may struggle with dysfunctional anger, and that it is therefore always good to have an anger management toolbox at their disposal.
7	Fundamentally, the cause of anger is interpersonal stress and conflict.	There are many different causes of anger.	Often clients think simplistically about the causes of anger (that is, they propose single-variable explanations). They attribute their anger to their children or their job or their boss or their family history. In truth, however, anger has many possible causes. Item 7 provides an opportunity to discuss causes from the perspective of the biological history of our species, our individual learning history, life stressors, and culture's role in how we act. Clients can learn that they have the capacity to overcome those forces that have previously led them to respond with anger.
8	Basically, it's other people who make us angry—romantic partners, parents, friends, work colleagues, and so forth.	No one can make us angry. We do that to ourselves.	One part of the SMART model suggests that various stimuli can lead directly to an urge to act. But another part recognizes that interpretations and appraisals of stimuli are what mostly lead to anger. This recognition can be very helpful, since it increases awareness that we can all, in many ways, be in control of our anger—and, of course, that blaming others rarely leads to anything productive.
9	When things go wrong, as when you are ignored or treated unfairly or disrespected, anger almost always is the result.	Even when things go wrong, as when you are ignored or treated unfairly or disrespected, anger may not follow at all.	Clients surely know that most people do respond at least with annoyance when they are the target of unfair treatment. Clients may rarely think about people who respond differently, such as the nonviolent figures of Gandhi and Martin Luther King Jr., but highlighting the reactions of such people sets the stage for a discussion about how these people became that way, and of whether clients can learn from their example.

Item	Statement A	Statement B	Explanation
10	Many times when things go wrong, anger just comes over us like an unexpected storm.	Anger occurs in episodes and can be analyzed, understood, predicted, and controlled.	Item 10 provides an opportunity to reinforce concepts related to the Anger Episode Model. Clients can be shown that anger follows a predictable and modifiable path.
11	Once we feel angry, it's important for us to express our anger rather than hold it in. Anger is like steam in a kettle, needing to be released.	It's often best to wait a while to see what happens, and to figure out how and when to express your anger.	Anger is not like steam in a kettle; it typically does not build up until it bursts out. Rather, anger may linger for a while, or it may dissipate quickly. Sometimes, however, it is useful to express anger thoughtfully and assertively. The differentiation of assertive, unassertive, antagonistic, and aggressive responding can be introduced with item 11.
12	Since anger is a natural human response, it does not lead to significant medical problems.	Long-term anger, or even a short intense blowup, significantly increases the chance of having a heart attack.	Clients are less likely to be aware of the well-established relationship of anger to cardiac events and other negative health outcomes, such as high blood pressure and stroke.
13	Thinking about what happened, how you were wronged, and how you can get even will lead to better long-term outcomes.	Thinking about what happened, how you were wronged, and how you can get even is a sure way to make things worse.	Although many clients believe that rumination and fantasies of revenge will lead to a reduction in their anger, the evidence says this is not true. Ruminating and seeking revenge often make things worse.
14	The result or outcome of feeling and expressing anger will be known to you right away.	Some results or outcomes of feeling and expressing anger will not be known for many years.	Item 14 provides an opportunity to differentiate the shorter- and longer-term effects of anger. Most clients focus on the short term, ignoring long-term damage to relationships and careers or physical harm to the body when anger persists for years.

Item	Statement A	Statement B	Explanation
15	If you wait and tolerate the problem when you are belittled, let down, disrespected, insulted, or threatened, usually the angry feeling will lessen over time.	It's important to attend immediately to the problem if you are belittled, let down, disrespected, insulted, or threatened.	We think that in some circumstances it can be important for clients to quickly address situations in which they are belittled or disrespected or dealt with unfairly. The goal, however, is to figure out how to do it skillfully and assertively, with everyone's rights respected, rather than simply engaging in impulsive, ineffective verbal or aggressive responses.
16	Only you know about your life, and whether you have an anger problem.	It's important to listen, with an open mind, to other people who may tell you that you have an anger problem.	Many clients are unwilling to hear feedback from spouses, friends, and family members about how they come across when angry. This is an opportunity to agree that only clients know about their internal anger, but also to say that outsiders can see effects to which clients may be blind.
17	Since anger is basically a genetic predisposition to react, there is little chance of bringing it under control.	Anger is both a genetic reaction and a learned pattern of behavior, and so anger management is often quite effective.	Item 17 gives you an opportunity to note that a person's anger patterns are based both on genetics and on learned behaviors. They also provide an opportunity to show how the environment can affect genetic propensities, for better or for worse. For example, although cholesterol level begins with genetics, it can be modified by what we eat, how we exercise, and medications; likewise, the tendency to become angry may have begun in our evolutionary past, but sunshine, sleep, good food, improved emotion-regulation skills, and social support can make reaction patterns better. Indeed, evidence suggests that social support and hugs may even ward off the common cold (see Cohen, Janicki-Deverts, Turner, & Doyle, 2015).
18	If you learn what is taught in anger education classes, you will be able to reduce your anger reactions when things go wrong.	Anger education alone will not work as well as customized anger management treatment, which includes skill building and repeated practice.	Most clients do not distinguish between education and gaining knowledge, on the one hand, and, on the other, cognitive and behavioral practice undertaken to achieve less angry reactions to perceived aversive stimuli. Clinical experience and research evidence highlight the limitation of anger education alone. Fernandez, Kiageri, Guharajan, and Day (2017) have concluded that psychoeducation is instructional, not therapeutic. Item 18 allows clients to make this distinction and, hopefully, increase their desire to move beyond knowledge acquisition alone and become active participants in treatment.

Item	Statement A	Statement B	Explanation
19	Silly as it sounds, when you have been disrespected, just counting to ten may help reduce your anger.	Managing your anger when you have been disrespected is a serious issue that requires professional intervention in order for you to bring your anger under control.	Data indicate that when an aversive event is perceived, the amygdala goes into immediate but often nonthoughtful action. If a few seconds pass, the prefrontal cortex becomes activated. This is when the brain's thinking reaction occurs, and anger outcomes are likely to be better. Therefore, counting to ten turns out to be a helpful procedure because it buys time. There are many ways to program in a pause before reacting to perceived and actual aversive events. Item 19 also provides an opportunity to talk about self-help books, self-help computer programs, and other beneficial self-help techniques.
20	Most anger management requires a change in thinking. There is no sense in just getting some exercise, taking a time-out, or just listening to calming music.	Anger management treatment works best if it includes a change in thinking along with other techniques, such as exercising, taking occasional time-outs from problem situations, or listening to calming music.	This is your opportunity to make the case for a **comprehensive** and **customizable** plan of action to reduce dysfunctional anger.
21	Uncontrolled anger usually leads to aggression.	Uncontrolled anger usually results in yelling, screaming, sarcasm, and demeaning others.	Some clients are afraid to express their anger, for fear that it is likely to turn into aggression. In some cases, this is a legitimate concern. In most cases, however, anger is separate from aggression. Most angry responses are verbal. When you teach this to clients, it may be easier for you to teach them communication techniques like assertiveness.

Item	Statement A	Statement B	Explanation
22	Behind violent crimes we can usually find anger.	Strong anger does not typically lead to criminal behavior.	The relationship of anger to criminal behavior is often misunderstood, apparently because of clients' exposure to news media that focus on crime and show that anger precedes crime. But large-scale studies do not confirm the notion that strong anger typically leads to violent crime; in fact, about 90 percent of anger experiences stay at the level of yelling and verbal putdowns. **Criminal behavior** is often associated with criminogenic thinking patterns, such as the belief that it's perfectly okay to steal from rich people because they have plenty of money; **anger,** in contrast, is most often associated with preferences that have been elevated to demands on others, such as a client's demand this his wife be more respectful of him in front of their friends.
23	Anger is almost always expressed at people we consider to have done something wrong.	Anger may build and be expressed diffusely to anyone we happen to be with.	Here, clients can be taught about the broad nature of anger expression. The old notion of displacement, and the related scientific concept of excitation transfer, is sometimes valid—clients may experience frustration and disappointment at work and wind up yelling at home.
24	Anger is anger. Depression is depression. Anxiety is anxiety. People may suffer from only one of these problems, and so specialized help is always required.	Anger, depression, anxiety, and even shame and guilt overlap and often appear in the same person.	The focus of this book, and of our work as well as of yours, is anger. Yet human beings are complex creatures, and angry folks will experience other dysfunctional emotions. Therefore, item 24 may provide an opportunity to talk about shame, guilt, anxiety, and depression. Many of the techniques in our SMART program can be effectively applied to the treatment of other feeling states.
25	Sometimes anger can be experienced inside, in our thoughts and fantasies, and it doesn't become known to others.	When anger is experienced, it is almost always expressed outwardly to others.	Item 25 provides an opportunity to differentiate the **experience** of anger from the **expression** of anger. This item can even be helpful in introducing some of the ideas that we present in later chapters, such as the idea that words and thoughts are just words and thoughts, and that we can observe our own words and thoughts as if from afar, without having them drive external reactions like yelling or throwing objects.

Item	Statement A	Statement B	Explanation
26	Anger is typically tied to the thought that the behavior of others is awful and terrible.	Underneath, most anger is tied to shame and pity.	As we'll show in chapter 10, angry adults often use phrases like "The way my boss behaved today was just awful" or "I think what my husband said is terrible." These ideas suggest nonempirical value judgments that are likely to lead to unhappiness. It has often been said that one person's trash is another person's treasure. What one client views as terrible (such as polyamory, or sending a misbehaving child to military school, or telling a colleague off for not showing up on time for work) may be viewed as quite acceptable by someone else. Here, clients can be introduced to the idea of perspective taking, or seeing the world as experienced by others (see chapter 11).
27	Much of the negative, inconsiderate behavior of other people (friends, family members, and so forth) is absolutely intolerable.	Some actions taken by other people are fundamentally unpleasant to see or hear but are tolerable.	Clients who think that the behavior of their friends, family members, and associates is intolerable are fundamentally demeaning their own capacity to cope. Item 27 provides an opportunity to make that point, and to review all the ways in which the client has indeed coped with unpleasantness and disappointment at other times. Here, clients are taught that even though some kinds of behavior on the part of other people are legitimately bad or offensive, there are many ways of tolerating such behavior without liking it.
28	Focusing directly on understanding anger can lead to useful and effective treatment.	Anger cannot be treated unless underlying causes, such as depression, are dealt with.	Some professionals promote the idea that anger is not a real, independent emotion; they may say that anger is just a reaction to anxiety, and that the anxiety is what has to be treated. Others may use diagnostic categories and say that anger is caused by post-traumatic stress disorder (PTSD), and that there is no sense in treating the anger when it's the PTSD that must be treated. Still others say that anger is a defense, one that prevents clients from becoming depressed, and that it's therefore the depression that should be the focus of treatment. Clients then mimic such ideas in session. Along with most emotion theorists, our position is that **anger is a basic approach emotion and a central symptom of many life problems** and is to be dealt with directly. Yes, anger is associated with other emotions and behaviors. But those other problems are not the primary causes of anger; they can often be the outcomes of long-term anger episodes or part of the constellation of a larger problem. For example, treating PTSD symptoms in a client who has experienced prolonged sexual abuse at the hands of a family member will not make that client's anger go away, whether the anger is directed at other family members who looked the other way or at those who didn't believe the client. Similarly, treating the anger may not reduce the PTSD symptoms (such as intrusive thoughts, avoidance, or anxious activation related to specific stimuli). Effective treatment will have to address both the PTSD and the anger.

Item	Statement A	Statement B	Explanation
29	Some people are inherently bad. It's just the way they are.	All people sometimes act badly, although some act badly much more often than others.	Item 29 provides an opportunity to discuss human nature. All people are controlled by their biology, their learning histories, their culture, and their cognitive processes. Some people (Adolf Hitler, for example, or Josef Stalin, various other mass murderers, and serial killers) have behaved in exceptionally bad ways. Other people (such as some who have lived in poverty with little food, poor shelter, and abusive parents) have behaved like thugs and criminals. At the same time, the general understanding of scientists is that even tyrants and criminals, had they found themselves in different, more caring circumstances, might have turned out to be more empathetic. This possibility leads to the conclusion that people are neither inherently bad nor inherently good but instead are the products of the forces in their lives. Hopefully, an understanding of this idea will eliminate some of the blame that angry clients place on others. This idea may lead to further discussions about perspective taking and forgiveness (see chapter 11).
30	Basically, anger is a problem for men.	Anger is often a problem for both men and women.	Anger, again, seems to be an equal-opportunity experience. When it comes to anger, it makes little sense to say, "Men are just like that" or "Women get angry at every little thing." Men and women may express anger differently, but problematic anger in people of both genders can be characterized by great frequency, high intensity, and long duration. Treatment is not a cookie-cutter endeavor. In work with angry clients, the goal is always to conduct an individual case analysis and develop a customizable treatment plan instead of blaming anger on any group characteristic, such as gender.

Takeaway Messages and Tools

We hope you will skillfully look for opportunities to infuse accurate knowledge about anger into your sessions so as to supplement the formal techniques that will be presented in subsequent chapters. For SMART anger managers, engagement remains the primary goal in the first few meetings with a client, but we still try to weave psychoeducation into the early sessions.

We now move on to ten treatment strategies. We begin with strategies that address anger triggers, in particular interventions that can be used to reduce a client's reactivity to perceived nasty situations.

CLIENT INFORMATION SHEET 6.1.
A Quiz on Anger-Related Issues

For each item, on the basis of what you believe the bulk of the evidence suggests, please make a check mark next to the statement (A or B) that you believe is true.

Item	Statement A	Statement B
1	☐ Anger is a normal, natural feeling that often does not have to be managed.	☐ Anger is an abnormal feeling state that causes aggression and has to be managed.
2	☐ When anger occurs more than once a month, it's a sure sign that something is wrong.	☐ Many normal people feel angry a few times a week.
3	☐ Basically, anger and aggression are the same thing.	☐ Anger and aggression are actually quite different.
4	☐ Anger is complex and multifaceted.	☐ Anger is pretty simple. Basically, it's a mental thing.
5	☐ We all feel angry sometimes. Usually, anger disappears by itself.	☐ Like elephants, we never forget—once we feel angry, the anger lingers forever.
6	☐ Dysfunctional anger occurs only in specific groups of people, such as teenagers, those who drink a lot, gang members, or people whose parents were often angry.	☐ Anyone can suffer from dysfunctional anger.
7	☐ There are many different causes of anger.	☐ Fundamentally, the cause of anger is interpersonal stress and conflict.
8	☐ Basically, it's other people who make us angry—romantic partners, parents, friends, work colleagues, and so forth.	☐ No one can make us angry. We do that to ourselves.
9	☐ When things go wrong, as when you are ignored or treated unfairly or disrespected, anger almost always is the result.	☐ Even when things go wrong, as when you are ignored or treated unfairly or disrespected, anger may not follow at all.

Item	Statement A	Statement B
10	☐ Many times when things go wrong, anger just comes over us like an unexpected storm.	☐ Anger occurs in episodes and can be analyzed, understood, predicted, and controlled.
11	☐ Once we feel angry, it's important for us to express our anger rather than hold it in. Anger is like steam in a kettle, needing to be released.	☐ It's often best to wait a while to see what happens, and to figure out how and when to express your anger.
12	☐ Long-term anger, or even a short intense blowup, significantly increases the chance of having a heart attack.	☐ Since anger is a natural human response, it does not lead to significant medical problems.
13	☐ Thinking about what happened, how you were wronged, and how you can get even will lead to better long-term outcomes.	☐ Thinking about what happened, how you were wronged, and how you can get even is a sure way to make things worse.
14	☐ The result or outcome of feeling and expressing anger will be known to you right away.	☐ Some results or outcomes of feeling and expressing anger will not be known for many years.
15	☐ If you wait and tolerate the problem when you are belittled, let down, disrespected, insulted, or threatened, usually the angry feeling will lessen over time.	☐ It's important to attend immediately to the problem if you are belittled, let down, disrespected, insulted, or threatened.
16	☐ Only you know about your life, and whether you have an anger problem.	☐ It's important to listen, with an open mind, to other people who may tell you that you have an anger problem.
17	☐ Since anger is basically a genetic predisposition to react, there is little chance of bringing it under control.	☐ Anger is both a genetic reaction and a learned pattern of behavior, and so anger management is often quite effective.

Item	Statement A	Statement B
18	☐ If you learn what is taught in anger education classes, you will be able to reduce your anger reactions when things go wrong.	☐ Anger education alone will not work as well as customized anger management treatment, which includes skill building and repeated practice.
19	☐ Silly as it sounds, when you have been disrespected, just counting to ten may help reduce your anger.	☐ Managing your anger when you have been disrespected is a serious issue that requires professional intervention in order for you to bring your anger under control.
20	☐ Most anger management requires a change in thinking. There is no sense in just getting some exercise, taking a time-out, or just listening to calming music.	☐ Anger management treatment works best if it includes a change in thinking along with other techniques, such as exercising, taking occasional time-outs from problem situations, or listening to calming music.
21	☐ Uncontrolled anger usually leads to aggression.	☐ Uncontrolled anger usually results in yelling, screaming, sarcasm, and demeaning others.
22	☐ Strong anger does not typically lead to criminal behavior.	☐ Behind violent crimes we can usually find anger.
23	☐ Anger is almost always expressed at people we consider to have done something wrong.	☐ Anger may build and be expressed diffusely to anyone we happen to be with.
24	☐ Anger is anger. Depression is depression. Anxiety is anxiety. People may suffer from only one of these problems, and so specialized help is always required.	☐ Anger, depression, anxiety, and even shame and guilt overlap and often appear in the same person.
25	☐ Sometimes anger can be experienced inside, in our thoughts and fantasies, and it doesn't become known to others.	☐ When anger is experienced, it is almost always expressed outwardly to others.

Item	Statement A	Statement B
26	☐ Anger is typically tied to the thought that the behavior of others is awful and terrible.	☐ Underneath, most anger is tied to shame and pity.
27	☐ Much of the negative, inconsiderate behavior of other people (friends, family members, and so forth) is absolutely intolerable.	☐ Some actions taken by other people are fundamentally unpleasant to see or hear but are tolerable.
28	☐ Focusing directly on understanding anger can lead to useful and effective treatment.	☐ Anger cannot be treated unless underlying causes, such as depression, are dealt with.
29	☐ Some people are inherently bad. It's just the way they are.	☐ All people sometimes act badly, although some act badly much more often than others.
30	☐ Basically, anger is a problem for men.	☐ Anger is often a problem for both men and women.

Howard Kassinove, PhD, and Raymond Chip Tafrate, PhD

PART 4

Interventions to Alter Anger Triggers

CHAPTER 7

Lifestyle Changes

A tradition without intelligence is not worth having.

—T. S. Eliot

There are some very practical interventions that few practitioners think about when working with clients with anger management issues. We are usually so focused on standard counseling and psychotherapy intervention techniques that we ignore simple pre–anger development changes that can make a big difference in life, such as getting a good night's sleep. In order to apply these lifestyle-change tools, it is best to step back and look at your clients with a broader lens. It may even be helpful to conceptualize your clients' anger episodes as wildfires. Are there factors that make it more likely that one of these anger wildfires will ignite? This type of question is addressed by the fields of environmental psychology and biological psychology, both of which offer important insights into how a person can rearrange his or her daily world to make angry, aversive interactions less likely.

Ancillary Issues Related to Anger Episodes

In this chapter, we present information about the impact of eight ancillary issues related to shifts that can be made in the environment, and in clients' lifestyle habits, so as to dampen clients' urge to respond with anger:

1. Food

2. Alcohol

3. Sleep

4. Temperature

5. Music

6. Lighting

7. Colors

8. Smells

Although attention to these areas is not a central aspect of the SMART program, it can still benefit clients by possibly cutting down on common factors that serve as kindling for their anger to ignite. Here, for your consideration, we describe possible adjustments that have scientific support as well as those with which we have some personal experience.

Food

Greenbaum (2018, 54) writes, "What we eat—and how we eat it—directly influence[s] our mental health, according to growing research in the integrative field of culinary medicine." Many nutritionists and mental health professionals now believe that food contributes to the development of cross-situational anger. Blame for dysfunctional anger reactions is placed on consumption of too many carbohydrates as well as on deficiencies in thiamine, vitamin B_6, omega-3 fatty acids, and magnesium (which helps relax muscles). A higher copper-to-zinc ratio in the blood, along with lead, has also been linked to assaultiveness; children with this blood pattern have been described as oppositional, defiant, pathologically dishonest, and cruel (Bitsas, 2004). People who live mostly on processed foods, white flour, and white sugar are more likely to experience anger than those who consume large amounts of fruits, leafy greens, and beans. And it is relatively clear that corn-based products, including high-fructose corn syrup and cornstarch, are major problems. In addition, Sawada, Konomi, & Yokoi (2014) showed that iron deficiency in Japanese women is associated with anger and fatigue.

Okay—you may be thinking that it's a little weird for two psychologists to be writing about the use of food to minimize anger and aggression. But let's look at the issue a little further.

It is generally agreed that when blood sugar drops, people tend to become moody, foggy, and irritable. In a study conducted by Oxford University criminologist Bernard Gesch and his colleagues (Gesch, 2013), the specific relationship of food intake to anger and aggression was tested, with the purpose of looking for a potential intervention. In this study, 231 institutionalized offenders took pills that contained either vitamins, minerals, and essential fatty acids or a placebo. The study recorded the number and types of offenses that each of the offenders had committed in the nine months before receiving the pills, as well as the number and types of offenses that each of the offenders committed in the following nine months, during the research trial. The results of the study strongly favored the addition of supplements—inmates who had received the supplements committed 26 percent fewer offenses over the nine months of the study than did those who had been given the placebo, and they showed the greatest reduction in serious, violent offenses. Earlier studies (such as Schoenthaler, 1983) and reviews (Ramsbotham & Gesch, 2009) reported a reduction of 25 to 42 percent in serious antisocial behaviors when incarcerated juveniles were given vitamin-and-mineral supplements rather than a placebo.

The relationship of blood glucose to anger has also been examined in experimentally sound laboratory studies. The concept that describes this relationship is "hanger," a term that has come to refer to the anger and irritability that erupt when a person is hungry. The mechanism for this relationship revolves around the fact that ingested carbohydrates, proteins, and fats are digested into simple sugars (such as glucose), amino acids, and fatty acids. They enter the bloodstream as nutrients and are then distributed to the organs and tissues, to be used for energy. Naturally, as time passes from when the last meal was eaten, there is a reduction in the circulating amount of these nutrients. When the blood glucose level falls far enough, it becomes critical, and it becomes harder for the person to function, since the brain requires glucose; during conversations words may become slurred, and the number of minor cognitive mistakes is likely to rise. Of importance to mental and behavioral health practitioners is the fact that when glucose falls, it becomes harder for the person to behave within social norms and to respond to adversity without irritation. The person may still act appropriately in important situations, such as in his or her occupational role. But in more casual situations, the person may become irritable, and anger-generated behaviors may emerge.

Another part of the equation to consider is known as the *glucose counterregulatory response*. When glucose levels fall too much, the body compensates by releasing hormones such as adrenaline and cortisol. These are the same hormones that are naturally released during the fight-or-flight response, and so people in the grip of hanger may shout and yell as angrily as they would if they had been legitimately threatened. Hanger is probably part of an evolutionary survival mechanism. Getting food into the body was critical for our ancestors when their glucose levels dropped, since this meant survival, whereas being withdrawn, unassertive, overly cooperative, and unaggressive would most likely have meant death. When resources were scarce, being self-centered, angry, and aggressive was crucial to continued existence.

Since we present our SMART program as science-supported, studies with behavioral dependent variables are of interest regarding the mechanism of hanger. For example, a paper reporting on four studies (DeWall, Deckman, Gailliot, & Bushman, 2011) describes the outcomes of the researchers' efforts to determine whether there is a causal link between low blood glucose and increased aggression. They had their participants fast, gave them lemonade that contained either sugar or a placebo with no glucose, and then had them engage in a competitive task, with the winners given an opportunity to aggress by blasting the losers with a loud noise. Their results showed that a winning participant who had drunk the placebo-containing beverage was more likely to blast a losing partner with noise after winning in the competitive task; in contrast, a winning participant who had consumed the glucose-containing beverage was less likely to show aggressive behavior after winning. They also administered a questionnaire to adults from different US cities in order to examine relationships among diabetic status, self-control, and aggressiveness. Self-reported diabetic status (as evaluated on the basis of shortness of breath at night, aching calves upon walking, and so forth) was used because the inability to metabolize glucose is a characteristic of diabetes. As predicted, self-reported diabetic status was related to low self-control and to self-reported aggressiveness. These researchers then looked at rates of diabetes and crime for each US state, predicting a positive relationship; as expected, prevalence of diabetes was positively linked to rates of violent crime. Finally, they tested whether glucose deficiency across the world would predict violent crime; using data from 122 countries, they found that glucose deficiency predicted violent killings carried out both in war and in circumstances other than war. It's true that these are correlational data, but the studies as a whole provide clear evidence for a relationship of blood glucose level to anger and aggression.

Bushman, DeWall, Pond, and Hanus (2014) wanted to determine whether low blood glucose in the evening predicts aggressive impulses and behavior in people who are married. In order to measure aggressive impulses, the researchers asked each participant—during the evening, and over a period of three weeks—to stick up to fifty-one pins into a voodoo doll representing the participant's spouse. They also recorded the participants' blood glucose levels and found that a participant who had lower blood glucose levels at the end of the day stuck more pins into the voodoo doll. These researchers' overall conclusion was that a steady level of blood glucose is important for emotional control.

There are differences in the rates at which consumption of various foods delivers glucose to the blood, and so the foods that a person consumes are likely to affect his or her cognitive status, behavior, and emotional reactions (such as anger). The rate of glucose delivery is measured with the *glycemic index* (which assigns values to individual foods on the basis of how slowly or quickly they cause an increase in blood glucose level) and with what is said to be individual foods' *glycemic load* (which represents a more realistic number for mental health practitioners to consider when giving advice about food, since the glycemic load takes portion size into account). Low-glycemic-load foods (including beef, chicken, chickpeas, hamburger buns, ice cream, milk, oranges, peanuts, pork, salmon, tomato juice, tuna fish, and both red and white wine) produce a prolonged supply of glucose for the brain, and this is associated with emotional stability over time. Foods with a high glycemic load (including bagels, candy, couscous, instant oatmeal, French fries, macaroni and cheese, spaghetti, pizza, raisins, apple and cranberry juice, vanilla cake, and white rice) are rapidly digested and absorbed and tend to produce greater fluctuations in blood glucose, since they cause a rapid spike in blood glucose levels, followed by a sharp decline. High-glycemic-load foods may be effective at reducing immediate feelings of hunger and lowered self-control, but they do not provide enduring energy between meals. Low-glycemic-load foods are more effective at providing stable and sustained glucose release between meals; they are conducive to reducing hanger and to helping a person maintain self-control in stressful situations.

Our brief review of this topic is not enough to turn mental and behavioral health practitioners into skilled dietitians. Nevertheless, you can increase your awareness of the glycemic counts and glycemic loads of various foods by consulting the charts at https://

www.ncbi.nlm.nih.gov/pmc/articles/PMC2584181 (for information about the glycemic index) or https://extension.oregonstate.edu/sites/default/files/documents/1/glycemicindex .pdf (for information about both the glycemic index and glycemic load).

In short, we have three pieces of advice for practitioners:

1. Be aware that a food's glycemic load may be only one variable to consider. Clients may have medical restrictions on the foods they eat, and they may be guided by calories, carbs, and fats if they are trying to lose or gain weight. Also, some clients observe religious prescriptions about food, and these have to be considered. Nevertheless, it may be helpful during an anger management program to discuss dietary habits and, if possible, have clients self-monitor and adjust their food intake. This is not done in typical anger intervention programs.

2. It's probable that the best way for clients to manage their hanger is to eat at regular intervals. This prevents the low blood glucose levels that result in diminished self-control, irritability, and outbursts of anger. Unfortunately, however, your clients may often skip meals. Moreover, when clients become hungry, there is a temptation in our modern world for them to eat unhelpful foods like bananas, spaghetti, raisins, cookies, or cake. These items lead to spikes in glucose levels and may lead to additional hanger.

3. Clients can be advised to consider the times when it would be wise to work on difficult life interactions, whether these are related to family disagreements, problems with friends, or challenges at the workplace. Tackling these issues after eating (rather than before) may make the difference between an assertive discussion and an angry one, between a better outcome or one that is poorer.

Alcohol

This is not a book about alcoholism (or other substance abuse) or treatment for excessive drinking, and we don't want to stray too far into that problem area. Rather, we want to highlight the importance of inquiring about your clients' alcohol and other substance use. If a client's drinking seems to lead to angry interactions with others, you may want to guide your client toward alcohol treatment.

Alcohol affects people differently, and it is therefore wise to consider a client's unique reactions to beer, wine, and hard liquor. Some folks who drink to excess, in particular at dinnertime, become lethargic and nonreactive to social interactions; they just go to bed early. Others become angry, argumentative, and even aggressive.

The connection between alcohol use and anger is well known. For example, Weiner, Pentz, Turner, and Dwyer (2001) completed a self-report study of more than one thousand adolescents to examine the relationship between early alcohol use and anger in middle and late adolescence. Participants were asked to respond to four anger-related sentences:

1. When I have a problem, I get mad at people.

2. When I have a problem, I do bad things or cause trouble.

3. When I have a problem, I say or do nasty things.

4. I am a hotheaded person.

Two additional items asked participants to report the number of alcoholic drinks consumed over the past thirty days and the frequency of their drunkenness during the same period. After controlling for gender, age, and socioeconomic status, the researchers found early use of alcohol to be associated with later anger: alcohol use in combined grades six and seven increased the odds of doing or saying nasty things in combined grades eleven and twelve; even more problematic, being drunk in grades six and seven increased the odds of self-reported hotheadedness, as well as high scores on an anger scale and doing something bad to cause trouble, in high school.

At the behavioral level, it is also well known that alcohol use is associated with intimate partner violence, defined by the World Health Organization as any behavior within an intimate relationship that causes physical, psychological, or sexual harm in that relationship. Intimate partner violence includes acts of physical aggression (such as slapping, hitting, or kicking), psychological abuse (such as intimidation, belittling, or humiliation), forced sexual intercourse, and any other controlling behavior (such as isolating a person from family and friends). Alcohol use increases the occurrence and severity of domestic violence and is one cause of intimate partner violence. Alcohol affects cognitive and physical functioning, reduces self-control, and leaves individuals less capable of negotiating nonviolent resolutions to conflicts.

One explanation for the link between alcohol, anger, and aggression is that people who experience chronic anger turn to alcohol or other drugs to reduce their negative internal agitation; over time, drinking becomes entrenched (that is, it is negatively reinforced) because unpleasant body experiences are dulled. Another explanation is that, for some people, alcohol reduces inhibitions, removes cognitive and behavioral filters, and thus increases verbal and physical expressions of anger and aggression; such people feel more confident when buzzed (in this case, anger is positively reinforced) and are more likely to let their anger out. Yet another explanation is that cultural "belief" factors allow for more anger and aggression after drinking; this explanation is supported by reports that show increased anger and aggression both after drinking alcohol and after drinking nonalcoholic drinks simply *thought* to contain alcohol.

As noted in chapter 1, the brain's prefrontal cortex is responsible for executive decision making. In instances of perceived threat and conflict, as when a client has been insulted or demeaned, the prefrontal cortex allows for consideration of possible actions and outcomes related to the situation and leads to decisions about how to act. But alcohol impairs that ability. Consider the case of Mandy:

Mandy, a forty-year-old homemaker in an abusive relationship, drank most afternoons and was usually close to being drunk when dinnertime arrived. One Thanksgiving Day, after having four gin and tonics, she was preparing a traditional turkey dinner when her husband accused her of having been "stupid" for leaving her keys in the door. Mandy became enraged and threw the turkey out the window and into the backyard.

Alcohol use and anger also have a reciprocal relationship. Drinking can lead to more anger, and anger can lead to more drinking.

The good news is that anger management interventions can lead to reductions in both anger and problematic drinking. Walitzer, Deffenbacher, and Shyhalla (2015) had a group of alcoholic men and women receive either a six-month Alcoholics Anonymous–related treatment or an alcohol-adapted anger management treatment. At the end, the men and women in both groups showed significant reductions in drinking and anger. Anger management may be particularly important when problematic alcohol use is a concern.

As already noted, however, this is not a book about the complex issues involved in maladaptive alcohol use. Rather, we ask you to review the alcohol use of your clients and consider how it may be reducing their ability to cope with conflicts, disappointment, and other life stressors. If alcohol is a problem for your clients, many self-help and professional treatment programs are available.

Sleep

Lack of sleep can lead to all sorts of problems, including general irritability and an unusually strong tendency to respond with anger to unwanted, conflict-oriented situations. Sleep deprivation increases the anger urge. The word to describe anger that is related to sleep deprivation is "slanger."

For most people, slanger occurs in addition to feelings of sluggishness and grogginess after one or two poor nights of sleep. This leads to poor decision making and to seeking out lots of coffee or tea.

Research with healthy adolescents, male prison inmates, juvenile offenders, and others indicates that poor or inadequate sleep is associated with anger and aggression. Sleep problems are important in everyday problematic family interactions as well as in cases of intimate partner violence, school bullying, cyberbullying, and violence committed in psychiatric hospitals. For example, Ireland and Culpin (2006) studied 184 juvenile offenders to examine the relationship of sleep to anger, impulsivity, and aggression. Questionnaire responses indicated that reduced sleep hours were related to hostility and aggression. A larger review of the data by Krizan and Herlache (2016) concluded that sleep problems are important contributors to aggression, especially with respect to intimate partner violence, school bullying, cyberbullying, and aggression in psychiatric and correctional institutions.

Krizan and Hisler (2018) divided 142 community adult participants into two groups. The participants in one of the groups maintained their usual sleep routine and got about seven hours of sleep per night. The participants in the other group restricted their sleep routine for two nights and got about four and one-half hours per night. For both groups, the researchers measured anger by bringing the participants into the lab and asking them to rate different products while listening to various noises. As expected, the sleep-restricted participants felt generally more negative and were specifically more angry.

Although there are wide variations in the need for sleep, adults in the United States indicate that they get about six and one-half hours per night, with 21 percent indicating that they sleep less than six hours, according to a survey conducted by the National Sleep Foundation (2013). Yet these adults say that they need about seven and one-quarter hours each night to function at their best, and almost 75 percent report that they get less sleep than needed on work nights. Therefore, many of us function with a sleep deficit of more than forty-five minutes per night (sleep scholars have concluded that about eight hours of sleep per night helps us function at our best). In the same survey, 58 percent of respondents said that inadequate sleep affected their mood, and 24 percent said that it affected their intimate relationships. Poor sleep was also reported to affect physical health. As in the case of alcohol use, we again note that there are multiple patterns of interaction in the associations among life stress, sleep dysfunction, and anger—life stress may increase sleep disruption, sleep disruption may lead to more anger, and more anger may increase life stress and affect sleep quality.

There are many possible causes of sleep disturbances, but work scheduling is an important factor for practitioners to consider. According to Schiller, Lucas, Ward, and Peregoy (2012), almost fifteen million Americans work full time on evening, night, or rotating shifts. In addition, about 19 percent of adults work more than forty-eight hours per week, and 7 percent work more than sixty hours per week; this population includes pilots and other airline personnel, emergency room doctors, police officers, firefighters, restaurant waitstaff, and combat personnel. Mothers, fathers, and other caregivers are typically on duty all the time, never knowing when a young child will be fussy or wake up crying in the middle of the night. College students often do not get adequate sleep, because of academic responsibilities or social events, and older adults typically get less sleep than when they were younger. Also, these days of globalization have led to a twenty-four-hour-per-day economy, with many businesspeople having to work in the middle of the night to accommodate the schedule of a customer who resides halfway around the world.

There is a strong relationship between lack of sleep and the tendency to respond with irritability and anger when things go wrong. In addition, sleep deprivation can contribute to depression, headaches, memory problems, concentration difficulties, ulcers, heart disease, and occupational accidents.

The connection between sleep disturbances and anger seems to be related to disruptions in normal circadian rhythms. Human beings, other animals, and even plants and bacteria respond predictably to built-in, genetically determined twenty-four-hour cycles. We are programmed to be most alert in the daylight hours, and to sleep in darkness. We are most alert in the morning; we are most coordinated and have the greatest muscle strength in the afternoon; and we are in our deepest sleep at about 2 a.m. At about 7 a.m., our blood pressure rises, and the secretion of melatonin, which helps us sleep, stops. When this rhythm is disrupted, the likelihood of anger and aggression increases. Overall, there is a worsening of cognitive performance along with poorer decision making and impulsiveness when normal sleep patterns are disturbed.

Knowing about this relationship, you can help your clients in two ways:

1. As usual, you first need to recognize the issue—in this case, that slanger may be a problem for your clients, who may be unaware that the urge to react with anger will be more intense after a night or two of minimal or poor sleep. Clients may feel lousy, but they may not link that feeling to irritation or anger. And yet simple awareness about the effects of sleep can increase clients' thoughtfulness about when it's best to interact with others and take on conflicts and challenges. In addition to bringing up the topic of sleep in anger intervention sessions, you may find it useful to leave an information sheet about slanger in your waiting area for clients to peruse while waiting to see you (see client information sheet 7.1, included at the end of this chapter and downloadable from www.newharbin ger.com/42877).

2. You also need to be aware that for some clients, because of work, school, institutional, or childrearing responsibilities, it may be difficult to adjust sleep patterns. But there are many life adjustments that can usually be made in order to increase the likelihood of good sleep (for recommendations, see client information sheet 7.2, included at the end of this chapter and downloadable from www.newharbin-ger.com/42877).

Once again, the overall message is for you to counsel your clients not to take on complex, frustrating, important tasks, not to interact with difficult people, not to make important decisions, and not to engage in challenging social interactions when they are short on sleep. There are certainly some tasks that a client has to perform even when he or she is sleep-deprived, such as caring for an infant or a young child who is sick, or for a disabled parent who lives in the client's home. But it is probably unwise for a sleep-deprived client to ask for a raise or try to resolve a disagreement with a neighbor, spouse, or business partner.

Temperature

The relationship of temperature to anger and aggression is well established (for example, see Rotton & Cohn, 2000). Studies conducted in the fields of psychology, criminology, and political science have also established this relationship. Across the world, and over time, higher temperatures have been linked to anger and aggression. For example, Wei et al. (2017) found clear relationships between temperature and personality. People who lived in climates where the average temperature is about 72 degrees Fahrenheit scored higher on tests that measured agreeableness, emotional stability, extraversion, and openness to experience. These are positive characteristics that are helpful for people who are dealing with conflicts or who are feeling disrespected, rejected, or neglected. As environmental temperatures grew hotter, or cooler, the presence of these positive personality factors decreased.

Other studies have shown that anger and conflict rise as the temperature rises. You are more likely to honk at someone who cuts you off in traffic on a hot day than on a temperate day, and the number of crimes tends to go up in the hotter months of summer. The weather will certainly affect each client differently, and there will be wide variation in reactions to heat and cold. Nevertheless, the relationship holds true in many situations; as the temperature rises, so do anger and aggression. The relationship is curvilinear, however, rather than direct. Aggravated assaults increase in temperatures between 30 and 90 degrees Fahrenheit, but then they drop off as the heat rises even more. Apart from the general discomfort of heat, brain temperatures are also affected by ambient temperatures. Thus the phrase "He's an angry hothead" may be more meaningful than we thought.

We are not suggesting that heat is a primary cause of anger in your clients. Rather, as with the other variables discussed in this chapter, it may be wise for you to consider the environment in which your clients reside. For some clients who live in sweltering conditions in the summertime, an air conditioner may be of clear benefit in minimizing anger arousal. And at the institutional level, it would be wise to correct temperatures that are too high or too low. On a winter trip to Romania, for example, both of us toured a local prison and were impressed with what we saw. Much was being offered to the inmates—there was a gym as well as a library, classes were available, and a closed-circuit television studio broadcast programming to the various cell blocks. But temperatures in the facility varied widely. In the administrative offices there was plenty of heat, and working conditions and attitudes seemed good. The situation changed when we entered one of the inmate classrooms, which contained about ten prisoners who were learning basic mathematics skills. We asked the prisoners if they liked the class, and we inquired about what they were learning. Their response was immediate and perceptible annoyance, and they complained about how cold the classroom was. The cold temperature distracted them from learning, and their frustration was obvious.

Heating (and nutritious food, as noted earlier) can be costly to taxpayers at the institutional level, and these costs have to be reasonably balanced against money spent for personnel, supplies, and the equipment needed to keep institutions like prisons, hospitals, and schools secure. Nevertheless, whether we're dealing with a public facility or a private apartment or house, it is wise for us to at least consider the emotional and cognitive costs of underheating or overheating, both of which may contribute to anger and aggression.

Music

It has long been thought that music can influence attitudes, emotions, and behaviors, including those associated with anger and aggression. Support for this hypothesis was found in five experiments by C. A. Anderson, Carnagey, and Eubanks (2003), who showed that listening to songs with violent lyrics led to increases in hostility and aggressive thoughts. Fischer and Greitemeyer (2006) showed that male participants who listened to misogynistic songs (for example, "Superman," by Eminem) recalled more negative attributes of women, administered more hot chili sauce for women to eat, and reported more desire for vengeance against women. Similar effects were found for women who listened to songs with lyrics that expressed hatred toward men.

Brodsky, Olivieri, and Chekaluk (2018) examined the relationship of high-energy negative music to arousal and aggressive driving behavior. Using a driving simulator, they had fifty participants listen to music that had either hostile, aggressive lyrics or neutral lyrics, with both sets of lyrics sung by the same artists. The results showed that energetic music alone boosted excitement, led to decreased control of the automobile, increased deviations from the lane, and increased the tendency to stray onto the hard shoulder. Those participants who were exposed to high-energy hostile music with violent content demonstrated higher cruising speeds and spent more time exceeding speed limits.

There is also support for the positive effects of music. In four studies, Greitemeyer, Hollingdale, and Traut-Mattausch (2015) found that listening to music with "pro-equality" lyrics (such as "Respect," by Aretha Franklin) was associated both with positive attitudes and behavior toward women and with lower acceptance of interpersonal violence. Relaxing music, according to Bensimon, Einat, and Gilboa (2015), is thought to decrease the activity of the sympathetic nervous system and to dampen arousability of the central nervous system by synchronizing body rhythms with the rhythms of the musical selection. It seems likely, then, that the effects of powerful, extreme genres of music are different from those of soft, slow, romantic music.

Genres of high-intensity music that may influence anger include heavy metal, emotional hardcore, punk, and scream. This music is characterized by loud, powerful, chaotic, heavy sounds, and often by emotional vocals that contain themes of anxiety, anger, aggression, bitterness, depression, and loneliness. In contrast, it is possible that soft, slow music with romantic lyrics leads to relaxation and prosocial thoughts.

Our goal is not to disparage any form of high-intensity music. Rather, we are interested in whether soft, slow music might be of help in family, vocational, or institutional settings where there are many triggers for anger and aggression. A YouTube search on the phrase "relaxing music" returns many sites where clients can listen to calming, soft, meditation-oriented music. At https://www.youtube.com/watch?v=ss7EJ-PW2Uk, for example, clients can find a three-hour-long piece featuring soft piano and guitar; likewise, at https://www.youtube.com/watch?v=Cnfj6QCGLyA, they can find a three-hour piece for piano and flute that is exceptionally popular. These two pieces have each been accessed more than seventy-five million times. The fact that such sites in general are so exceptionally popular seems to indicate at least a belief that this kind of music can set the stage for relaxation. Music like this, played in the background of stressful, conflict-laden, aversive situations that are likely to elicit anger, may slow impulsive actions. Such situations include driving in heavy traffic, using machine tools with a disagreeable co-worker, or being in a state of physical pain.

As a practitioner, you might consider suggesting to clients in chaotic jobs and households, with high levels of anger and discord, that they have soft music playing in the background, at a low level. The financial cost would be minimal, and the downsides would be few to nonexistent. There are slow pieces with lyrics, of course, but it is probably best to use lyrics-free music so that conversations with family members and friends can continue.

If you are a practitioner in a jail or prison or at a school for disruptive adolescents or children, consider the use of relaxing music. Facilities like these are known for their high level of noise, and so slow, pleasant music may be of help. In support of this suggestion, Bensimon et al. (2015) completed a small study with forty-eight prisoners and found that self-reported anxiety and anger decreased in a group of participants who listened to relaxing music over a three-week period. In any case, given the low cost of this type of anger management strategy, there is little reason not to try it.

Lighting, Color, and Smell

Most of us prefer natural lighting from windows, or full-spectrum artificial lights. Full-spectrum lighting appears to help improve mood and increase motivation. These effects may then make clients more resilient in the face of disappointment, rejection, and other adversities. According to LeGates, Fernandez, and Hattar (2014), extreme light conditions, which may be experienced during shift-work schedules, during the short, light-deprived days of the winter months, or during transmeridian travel, can directly cause both cognitive deficits and mood alteration. Such negative effects of light, like the effects of sleep deficits, seem to be caused by upsets in normal circadian rhythm.

Colors also matter. That's why it's peculiar that many institutions have traditionally been painted gray or in drab colors associated with dirt, pollution, and malevolence. Except for very special colors or paint grades, costs do not vary by color. If you find yourself counseling clients who may be redecorating at home, or if you're making institutional decisions, it's a good idea to select colors for walls, doors, rugs, and furniture that are associated with calmness and happiness, such as purple, green, blue, and yellow. Red, in contrast, is generally associated with energy, passion, strength, danger, and hostility. Red can encourage alertness and action—it's often used for alarms and emergency buttons—but it may also lead to impulsive, nonthoughtful decisions. That is not the goal during an angry conflict.

Again, we recognize that this kind of discussion is unusual for psychologists. And yet empirical support for color effects was found in two experiments by Elliot and Aarts (2011). In the first one, children viewed and vocalized a number that was printed in red or gray, and then they were asked to pinch open a clasp. Results showed that participants who were exposed to the red number opened the clasp to a wider position, an action that required more effort and energy. This outcome reflected an initial effect of color exposure. In the second experiment, young adults who were exposed to black numbers on a red background squeezed with more force and at a faster rate than did those who were exposed to numbers on a blue or gray background. These findings confirmed the hypothesized effect between red and motor actions of strength and speed, and they highlighted the importance of attending to more than the aesthetic value of colors. The researchers concluded that red instills a feeling of threat, fear, and danger, which can affect muscular activity.

Most mental health practitioners view color therapy with skepticism and point out that the effects of color are often exaggerated. We agree. Certainly, there are gender variations as well as cultural and individual variations. For example, men seem to be less sensitive to color (although a woman in a red dress may stimulate male desire). And while red can be stimulating in Eastern cultures, it represents mourning in parts of Africa. In Europe, pink is the color of girls—except in Belgium, where it is associated with boys. Therefore, we urge caution in considering color effects across cultures.

We also want to say a word about smells. In the poll, mentioned earlier, that was conducted by the National Sleep Foundation (2013), more than 75 percent of respondents agreed with the statement "I feel more relaxed in my bed if my bedroom has a fresh, pleasant scent." More than 90 percent thought that the sleep environment affects the quality of sleep (and we have already shown that the sleep environment affects anger arousal). Lavender or jasmine was considered to be a good smell; smells considered bad were mold, body odor, and pet odor. Other factors thought to contribute to a relaxing bedroom environment were clean-smelling sheets, darkness, and a clean bedroom.

In a formal experiment, Mutic, Parma, Brünner, and Freiherr (2016) elicited chemosignals of aggression by having a set of participants engage in a boxing session and then collecting those participants' sweat and presenting it to new participants, for whom the smell of the collected sweat led to an anxiety response. This experiment indicated that angry adults may emit smells that lead others to feel anxious, which can be detrimental to relationships. Also, Croy, Olgun, and Joraschky (2011) found that most participants could name an olfactory elicitor of happiness and disgust, and about 50 percent could name an olfactory elicitor of anger (these included automobile exhaust, perfume, and cigarettes).

Takeaway Messages and Tools

Berkowitz and Harmon-Jones (2004), summing up what was known at the time, concluded that anger can be triggered by all kinds of uncomfortable conditions, including hot and cold temperatures, foul odors, pain, secondary smoke, social stress, noises, and so forth. In this chapter, we have briefly reviewed some effects of food, alcohol, sleep, temperature, music, lighting, colors, and smells. Some of these effects are likely to be subclinical. Nevertheless, taking these kinds of triggering background factors into account may be very useful in your work, at both the individual and the institutional level. The overall lesson here is that emotional behaviors related to these factors are worth considering. Hopefully, you will regard them as supplements to the other SMART strategies for change and acceptance that you will find in the chapters that follow.

We'll end this chapter by noting a study called the Blue Room Experiment (Nadkarni, Schnacker, Hasbach, Thys, & Crockett, 2017). Most readers of this book are probably seeking to help people manage anger that develops at home, in the workplace, in traffic, or with friends and family members in other situations. Many readers will have little familiarity with inmates of jails and prisons, and that's why we want to share this study with you—to reinforce the power of color, natural lighting, pleasant scenery, and calming music. As mentioned earlier, anger and aggression are frequent problems in jails and prisons; inmates often become agitated and threaten others, and about 25 percent of those incarcerated wind up being assaulted. In 2017, however, some inmates in solitary confinement at the Snake River Correctional Institution in Oregon were given an opportunity to watch nature videos that were projected on a wall for about one hour per day. These videos provided pleasant images and sounds for the inmates. The result? The inmates who had watched the videos ended up committing 26 percent fewer acts of violence. Impressive!

Although your angry clients may think all problems have to be faced head-on, it's sometimes a better approach to temporarily avoid and evade problems. In chapter 8, we'll consider when it is wise to address a problem directly and when it is wise to temporarily sidestep an issue.

CLIENT INFORMATION SHEET 7.1.
Are You Tired? Do You Have Sleep-Related Problems?

Are you tired? Do you experience slanger (sleep related anger)?
Here are the facts:

- Sleep is one of the most important considerations in maintaining good health.

- Among adults, 40 to 50 percent have trouble falling asleep, and 45 to 55 percent have trouble staying asleep.

- Adults require about eight hours of sleep per night but get only about six and one-half hours per night.

Some Outcomes of Poor Sleep

- General fatigue; feeling lousy

- Irritability, annoyance, anger, anxiety, rage

- Lack of tolerance for the actions of others

- Depression; mood disorders; general emotional dysfunction

- Impaired social interactions and moral judgments

- Difficulty remaining alert and being able to focus on tasks; memory loss

- Impaired thinking skills; confusion; impaired communication skills

- Impaired immune system; increased risk of infections and likelihood of catching a cold

- Increased risk of high blood pressure

- Increased risk for cardiovascular disease

- Increased hunger; increased risk of obesity and type 2 diabetes

- Increased risk of injury and death while driving

- Increased risk for colorectal cancer

- Increased substance use

Sleep deprivation is a one-way ticket to mental and emotional disturbance. Talk to your practitioner about your sleep concerns.

Howard Kassinove, PhD, and Raymond Chip Tafrate, PhD

CLIENT INFORMATION SHEET 7.2.
Recommendations to Improve Sleep

Eating and Drinking

- Don't eat a big meal right before bedtime, because it may prevent deep sleep. Consider making lunch the big meal of the day.

- Don't drink alcohol before bedtime. Alcohol makes most folks sleepy, but after a few hours it awakens you.

- Don't drink any liquids within three hours of going to sleep. Drinking anything before bedtime increases the need to urinate a few hours later.

- Be careful about consuming caffeine in any form when it is close to bedtime. Coffee, sodas, ice cream, energy water, and chocolate are some of the major offenders. Even decaffeinated coffee typically contains some caffeine. Be careful of pain relievers and cold medicines, too, because they often contain caffeine. Try noncaffeinated tea.

Lights and Noises

- Power down electronics. Cell phones, tablets, computers, TVs, and digital clocks near your bedside typically create a blue light that interferes with sleep. Turn them off, make them dim, or set them to "night shift" mode, if available, which produces a warmer light.

- Do you really need a bedside clock? Many people end up checking it repeatedly during the night because they worry about a business meeting or a school exam the next day. Have faith in the alarm by placing the clock out of sight—perhaps in the next room, under the bed, or in a drawer where you can hear the alarm but not see the display.

- Keep noise to a minimum. If there are distractions in your home, see if a white noise machine helps.

- No phone calls, text messages, and chats during your sleep hours.

Bedroom Hygiene

- If possible, go to sleep at roughly the same time every night, and wake up at roughly the same time every morning. This will help your brain and body get used to being on a healthy sleep-wake schedule.

- Your bed is for sleeping. Do not do work, watch TV, play games, or eat in bed.

- Keep your bed clean, and keep pets off of the bed. Mites, molds, dander, and other allergens can activate allergies, which will surely keep you up.

- Adjust your bedroom temperature. For most people, the best temperature range for sleeping is 68 to 72 degrees Fahrenheit.

Exercise and Pain

- Vigorous exercise is great—but not right before bedtime. It excites you, just when you want to be calm.

- Minor back pain may not wake you up, but it can disturb deeper sleep. Some people find that a pillow between their legs helps.

- Check pain medications with your physician.

Thoughts for Shift Workers

- Try not to work more than a single night shift in a row. You're more likely to recover if you can schedule days off in between shifts.

- When possible, avoid frequently rotating shifts. If that is impossible, it is typically easier to adjust to a schedule that rotates from a day shift to an evening shift to a night shift rather than from a night shift to an evening shift to a day shift.

- To promote alertness, keep your workplace brightly lit; it may be helpful to try a "bright light" box. Your body has an internal clock that tells you when to be awake and when to sleep, and it is controlled by light. Most of us wake up to light and go to sleep when it's dark. Light is associated with alertness.

- When you sleep during the day, use blackout blinds or heavy curtains to block sunlight. One of the strongest stimulators of your internal clock is sunlight, which goes right through your eyelids and stimulates you to stay awake.

Sleep deprivation is a one-way ticket to mental and emotional disturbance. Talk to your practitioner about your sleep concerns.

Howard Kassinove, PhD, and Raymond Chip Tafrate, PhD

CHAPTER 8

Sidestepping Provocations

Delay is the greatest remedy for anger.

—Seneca the Younger

As you probably know, in the world of anxiety treatment, avoidance is considered a poor strategy. Clients who are afraid of social situations, airplanes, physical sensations such as heart palpitations, dental offices, shopping malls, and so forth, typically avoid the things that trigger their anxiety symptoms. Therefore, practitioners routinely encourage clients to move *toward* those fear-inducing situations. The thinking behind the practice of facing fears is that anxiety causes avoidance behaviors. When the client avoids, it leads to a temporary reduction in the anxiety, and that reduction is in turn reinforcing. Thus the temporary anxiety reduction reinforces ongoing avoidance. This model evolved from the early days of strict animal behaviorism, and it has worked very well to produce highly effective clinical interventions that systematically expose individuals to their feared stimuli. There is good consensus that in the arena of anxiety, avoiding fearful situations does indeed make people worse.

The world of anger treatment is different. In many instances, there is little benefit to immediately facing a conflict or a problematic situation or person. Sometimes encouraging clients simply to avoid their anger triggers is the best medicine. And if they're already in a state of anger, then leaving the situation may be beneficial. If clients can avoid or escape and function for a while with less anger, they are often better able to generate solutions to their problems and implement those solutions at a later time. Facing anger-inducing problems before having the proper assertiveness or problem-solving skills, or without knowing how to control impulsive urges or think through situations in which dysfunctional anger appears, can lead to disaster.

Yet we also recognize that avoidance and escape are not permanent solutions to interpersonal conflicts and challenging life problems. Eventually it becomes important to talk to a husband suspected of having an affair, to a business partner who isn't carrying her workload, to a friend who gossips, or to a neighbor who has loud parties late into the night. Eventually it's important to talk to children about bad grades, inappropriate friends, sex, drugs, or morals. In these cases, the relationships with the other people are likely to continue for a long time. Therefore, an eventual resolution is important.

Avoidance and escape strategies do not develop or enhance the coping skills necessary to deal more effectively with unpleasant triggers. And, as in the case of anxiety problems, avoidance and escape reduce tension, and so they reinforce coping mechanisms that may easily become overused crutches in dealing with agitating people and situations. For some clients, avoidance and escape may already be overused in this way, and so it may seem strange to suggest that you entertain the options we're suggesting in this chapter. Nevertheless, these options are part of your SMART toolbox, since some clients believe that they must immediately face all of life's challenges, every time, and they never give themselves the opportunity to sit one out. This can lead to needless anger and aggression. Thoughtful avoidance and escape maneuvers may be especially critical in the beginning stages of intervention, with clients who are at risk of harming others, or with clients who are in jeopardy of suffering some type of loss (of a relationship or a job, for example) if they try to resolve problems impulsively and carelessly. Sometimes your immediate goal is simply to prevent further damage.

Which, When, and How

Determining the appropriateness of these strategies revolves around the key words "which," "when," and "how." With regard to "which," we ask you to consider whether *all* problems have to be addressed. Does your client really have to tell off a rude Uber or Lyft driver he'll never see again? Is it critical that your client confront and give negative feedback to a slow and unhelpful salesperson? Must your client give a piece of her mind to a person who jumps in front of her in line? Although everyone might experience some degree of annoyance in these situations, you'd be wise to talk with your clients about whether taking an impulsive, angry action will accomplish anything useful. Issues that have a likelihood of being resolved, and whose resolution might lead to better behavior in the future, may certainly warrant time and energy. For example, relationships with family members and close friends may justify corrective feedback and attempts to improve communication. But if your client will never see the person again, you may be better off encouraging your client to just let the situation go.

With regard to "when," the time to address a particular problem may not be at the moment when a client feels the angriest. Helping a client wait, or offering to schedule an earlier or extra session to consider a thoughtful response to a new problem, is likely to be more effective. Too many clients give in to the urge to act impulsively, and then they tell you about their problems after they've implemented a poor and ineffective solution—that is, a harmful one.

It's useful to stress to your clients that timing is important when they're dealing with difficult people and situations. Consider the outcomes of Matilda's angry action:

Matilda, a high school science teacher, was struggling with the disruptive behavior of one of her students. One afternoon, after this student made yet another disrespectful comment, Matilda became agitated and decided that she'd had enough. In front of the entire class, she impulsively launched into a loud, bitter scolding laced with profanity. One result was a formal reprimand from her principal. In addition, many parents and other students lost confidence in Matilda's ability to manage the classroom and communicate the science-based materials. It would have been much better if Matilda had not reacted in the moment and instead had confronted the disruptive student after she'd had a chance to cool off and consult with her principal and other teachers about ways in which this student might be handled.

"How" is related to "when." It's best to have clients delay reacting to unpleasant people and situations until they've mastered some of the skills we'll present in subsequent chapters. "How" requires knowing specific social problem-solving techniques. It consists of knowing how to best think about unpleasant people and situations in ways that are likely to lead to improvement. If it seems unlikely that a problem can be resolved, the best solution may be to know how to let it go. Often we want our clients to know how to relax. We want them to be able to use relaxation and mindfulness methods if they have to continue to experience annoying people like Aunt Mabel, who continues to nag your client about getting a better job, or situations like long checkout lines at the supermarket. And we want clients to know how to assertively let others know they are angry, in ways that will improve communication rather than increase arguments.

Being able to determine *which* people and situations are worth dealing with, *when* to approach them, and *how* to confront them is a useful skill to discuss with your clients. This is a practical first step in helping them skillfully sidestep unpleasant situations and navigate life's challenges.

The Practice of Avoidance

As you begin to understand the landscape of your clients' anger episodes, you will notice that some anger is likely to occur in response to known and predictable triggers. For example, clients may become angry when their children repeatedly resist doing their homework, play music very loudly, or keep their rooms messy, or when a spouse repeatedly asks the same accusatory questions, or when a co-worker asks again and again for help. If your clients can arrange to be absent from those situations, they will decrease their chance of becoming angry. The anger cycle will be delayed, and the problem can be dealt with at a later time.

Avoidance strategies do not produce long-lasting results. They may even make certain problems worse, if thoughtful avoidance isn't explained to others. For example, suppose that Jen has decided not to attend her niece's dance recital—Jen has had several conflicts with the mother of another child in her niece's dance class, and she knows that this woman will be at the recital. In this situation, it would be best if Jen told her sister why she isn't planning to attend. The larger point is that temporary avoidance can reduce the anger that develops in response to known and predictable anger triggers. Avoidance may give clients more time to develop better reactions and coping strategies.

If you are having difficulty accepting the benefit of temporary avoidance, you can think about this approach as being similar to what a doctor might recommend for a patient with an allergy. If the patient is allergic to cat dander but loves cats, for example, then the doctor may advise the patient to avoid this allergen as much as possible, starting with having no cats in the house. Then, during the period of total avoidance, desensitization injections can be started along with medications that provide long-term allergy relief. In the same way, anger avoidance is useful before other, longer-term anger management strategies have been learned.

You may be telling yourself that sometimes avoidance is impossible. We agree! And avoidance is certainly not a cure-all. Nevertheless, it can be useful because temporary avoidance gives clients time to rethink problems and, hopefully, handle them better. Some thoughtful avoidance on the part of your clients can go a long way toward preventing anger outbursts. Here are some possibilities for sidestepping problems and putting avoidance into action.

Planned Avoidance

Have your client identify a situation that consistently leads to anger, and ask him or her to decide to avoid it. For example, does the client become angry in crowded stores? While waiting for a long time at the doctor's office? When her young child spills food or leaves toys strewn around the house? When she has to travel on crowded roads or highways?

Sometimes clients can arrange their lives to avoid such hassles, but it just doesn't occur to them to do so. For example, your client can arrange to see her doctor during the first appointment of the day. If your client becomes angry upon seeing her child's toys scattered around the house when she returns from work, she can call her spouse who is already at home so there will be time to clean up before she arrives at home. And to avoid the potential anger trigger of rush hour, she can ask her employer to stagger her office hours, as many employers are now doing, or even allow her to work at home some of the time.

These examples may not apply to your particular clients, but almost everyone can occasionally avoid a dinner engagement where there's likely to be an angry blowup. And sometimes a client can avoid an argument simply by not asking a question that is likely to lead to a disagreement:

- To a teenage girl: "Why did you wear that outfit to the party last night?"

- To a business colleague: "I know you liked that salesperson who was caught stealing money. How come you didn't catch it sooner?"

- To another adult who openly identifies as a Republican or a Democrat: "Don't you think the Democrats [Republicans] are acting like morons?"

Consider the case of Allison:

Allison and her husband lived across the country from his parents. For the first few years of their marriage, they stayed for five or six days when they visited her husband's family.

A predictable pattern emerged. The first two days were usually enjoyable. By the third or fourth day, however, tension would start to build between Allison and her mother-in-law. The visits always ended on an unpleasant note.

After considering this pattern, Allison decided that it would be best if she and her husband limited their visits to three days. That way, she reasoned, their time with his parents would have a better chance of being enjoyable, and angry blowups would be less likely.

Avoidance by Delay

Since impulsive reactions can make difficult situations and problems worse, it's often valuable to coach a client to get in the habit of putting in a time delay before responding to annoying people or situations. For example, your client may be asked to do something that would require a large commitment of energy or time, such as serving on the board of a homeowners' association or driving a neighbor to a weekly doctor's appointment or watching a neighbor's dog while she goes on vacation. In these situations, the client can usually say, "Can I get back to you on that in a day or two?" This delay allows the client time to gain composure, consider more options, and develop a calmer and more reasonable response. University professors, high school teachers, and public speakers (such as press secretaries for politicians) regularly use delays to avoid friction with students and audience members. When a student voices a strong opinion about a topic that isn't relevant to the lesson, the professor might say, "Let me think about what you're saying. I'll get back to you next class." And when a reporter asks an uncomfortable question, the press secretary might say, "I'll check on that for you." This simple delay until the next day or the next press conference often defuses the situation.

Avoidance by Indirect Response

We're amazed at the number of people who think they have to respond to a difficult situation right in the moment. Often, with some thought, a more creative way to handle the problem can be found than might emerge during an immediate, face-to-face response. For example, one of us found when his children were growing up that it was often better for his wife to speak to them first if they had broken a rule; as the messenger, she was usually calmer and did a better job of dealing with the children in a constructive manner.

As another example, a client may be able to avoid direct contact with an angry employee or co-worker by responding with a thoughtful email, or with a memo or a letter, rather than dealing with the issue in person. This approach usually provides a helpful delay, allowing the client to express thoughts in a more reasonable manner. Avoidance is even possible when anger is triggered by a spouse or partner. After a breakfast confrontation, for instance, your client may be better able to express his or her ideas by sending a text from work than by continuing a conversation that isn't going anywhere.

Keep in mind, of course, that angry, impulsive emails and other types of social media communications can be destructive. Significant damage to careers and relationships via social media is becoming increasingly common. Therefore, we also recommend slowing down your clients' social media behavior, encouraging them to be less reactive, and teaching them to practice waiting until their anger has subsided before they send these types of communications. Personally, we routinely enlist the opinion of a trusted co-worker or friend before sending emails related to challenging and emotional issues.

The Practice of Escape

Some situations just can't be avoided. For example, your client may have to fire an underperforming employee, attend a distasteful family function, or appear at a stressful meeting. In these situations, if anger starts to increase, it's wise for your client to have legitimate options for leaving, interrupting the anger cycle, and, over time, developing better control.

Time-Outs

There are times when it's best to walk away from a disagreement. As anger gets worse, continued discussion may become unproductive and more damaging. Thus your angry client could take a break by telling a teenage child, "I'm upset now. I'd like us to talk about something else for a while [go out to eat, watch TV for an hour]. We can try to solve this problem later." Or in a heated conversation with a spouse or romantic partner, you might teach a client to say, "I don't like where this is headed right now. Why don't we each take the rest of the afternoon to think, and we can try to talk this out again later tonight." When the conflict is occurring on the telephone, it's even easier to say, "We probably shouldn't continue this right now. I'll call you back tonight."

We've found that, as a learning example, you can have clients practice using their internal experience of anger as the signal to remove themselves from a situation where anger is building. Then, as we've just described, they can practice calmly removing themselves from different types of conversations, or letting others know that a conversation can be continued at a later time. Of course, it's also important to follow up most of the time and attempt to actually resolve the problem. It usually takes some practice for clients to become aware of their internal experience of anger and stop an angry conversation, but this sequence often yields a feeling of success as well as better self-control.

Planned Escapes

It's difficult for a client to leave some situations when his presence is expected. But if he knows in advance that dealing with someone is likely to lead to anger, it makes sense for him to limit the time he spends with that person. Once the client becomes angry, he will tend to spend too much time and energy on unproductive, almost always unhelpful dialogue like this:

But you said…

No, I didn't.

Well, I heard that with my own ears.

What I *meant* was…

Well, you didn't *say* that.

Sometimes it's possible to schedule only a brief time for a problematic interaction. A client can say up front that she has time constraints. For example, at the very beginning of a difficult meeting or telephone conversation, the client might say, "I'm happy we can talk about this, but I want you to know that I only have half an hour before I need to meet with a customer." We're not suggesting that clients lie. Rather, we suggest that they organize their schedules in a way that builds planned time limits into potentially difficult interactions, as when a client schedules a challenging conversation to take place half an hour before an actual dental appointment or meeting with a customer.

Another possibility for a planned escape is to have a co-worker, friend, or family member help out. For example, your client's office assistant can be asked to interrupt a meeting after thirty minutes and to remind your client about the next appointment. In order to use this escape strategy, your client will have to anticipate situations in which anger may erupt and then have a plan in place to leave early.

The Practice of Distraction

Thinking over and over again about a problem tends to increase anger and doesn't usually produce good solutions. Therefore, there's a place for distraction. Of course, recommending that your clients put their heads in the sand for years will probably increase their anger because some problems do get worse with the passage of time. In the short term, however, this step can often be beneficial.

Distraction simply means absorption in a non-anger-related and preferably enjoyable activity. After an anger-filled workday, what this may mean for your client is going to a bowling alley, a baseball game, a movie, or dinner with a family member, or having a phone conversation with an old friend. During the distracting activity, it's important that the anger-related situation not be the sole focus of discussion. For example, a client who has had a conflict at work might say to her spouse, "I want to tell you about a problem I had with John today. As usual, he was rude to a customer and lost an order. I'll have to deal with him at some point. But I just wanted you to know about it, and I don't want to discuss it further. Instead, I was hoping we could go to that new movie. Is that okay with you?" Then, if anger-related thoughts intrude during the movie, the client may have to work at letting them pass and bringing her mental focus back to what's on the screen. The goal is to break the ruminative cycle connected to the event that led to the anger, and to place the focus on more positive thoughts and pleasurable activities. At the most basic level, we're suggesting that it's important for angry clients to take steps to create balance in their lives by engaging in enjoyable activities (see chapter 16 for more tips on living a happier life).

Takeaway Messages and Tools

Strategies for sidestepping problematic interactions involve knowing *which* ones actually have to be addressed as well as *when* and *how* to deal with them. By practicing temporary avoidance or escape in problematic situations, your clients can become more skillful at reducing their day-to-day anger experiences. (Client worksheet 8.1, included at the end of this chapter and downloadable from www.newharbinger.com/42877, is a practice exercise for sidestepping problems.)

The hope is that avoidance or escape will allow for the development of better solutions once anger has been naturally reduced. Eventually, however, many problems do have to be addressed. In chapter 9 we present a technique—social problem solving—to help clients see that they can, with some thoughtfulness, generate multiple solutions to problems and decide on actions that are likely to lead to success.

CLIENT WORKSHEET SHEET 8.1.
Temporarily Avoiding and Escaping from Anger Triggers

Part 1. Avoidance

Identify an ongoing problematic situation in which it *may* be beneficial to practice temporary avoidance.

_____

_____

_____

_____

Place a check mark in the box next to the type of avoidance you will use to cope with this situation.

☐   Planned avoidance

☐   Delay

☐   Indirect response

Part 2. Escape

Identify an ongoing problematic situation from which escape *may* represent a beneficial temporary strategy.

_____

_____

_____

_____

Place a check mark in the box next to the type of escape you will use to cope with this situation.

☐   Time-out

☐   Planned escape

☐   Distraction with an enjoyable activity

Howard Kassinove, PhD, and Raymond Chip Tafrate, PhD

CHAPTER 9

Social and Personal Problem Solving

If we fail to find a just and peaceful solution, history will judge us harshly.

—Lyndon Baines Johnson

Some people grow from interpersonal adversity and emerge stronger. Others do not. Those who lack growth are often stuck in their own anger. They ruminate, complain, and remain unhappy, which interferes with their ability to see a path forward. They react to daily struggles with a startling lack of awareness about the outcomes of their actions. It's as if they are stuck on an unfortunate autopilot setting that does not allow for the exploration of alternative actions that, if tried, might be helpful. They do not see that facing interpersonal problems provides opportunities to grow through the acquisition of new knowledge and skills. They seem oblivious to the fact that complaining without proposing a solution stifles growth and leads to nothing but more and continued interpersonal disharmony.

Learning how to react constructively in response to difficult people and situations requires a degree of personal awareness as well as the willingness to explore new approaches. It involves asking a key question: *Does what I'm doing work for me?* How your clients approach their problems is not a small matter—it sets the stage for their lives to improve, stay the same, or get worse.

Similarly, many people go through life with the unstated goal of trying to minimize their struggles and discomfort. Their energy is focused on moving the number of negative situations in life from many to none. They aspire to get to zero—a life with no problems or hassles. Of course, that's unrealistic because everyone's life is full of social difficulties and interpersonal challenges. Accepting this reality is a critical step in managing anger and having a more fulfilling life. We will say more about developing a flexible and realistic philosophy in chapter 10. Here, we focus on a strategy to help your clients build skills to productively face the inevitable challenges and problems that are part of living, as opposed to angrily demanding that such problems not exist.

The goal here is to teach your clients to calmly and objectively look at their problems, seek reasonable (but often not perfect) solutions, and gain wisdom through the process of being thoughtful and searching for options. It involves a focused and careful consideration of specific problematic situations and a search for realistic alternatives. This technique is practical and generally useful for social and interpersonal problems, such as those that commonly occur between dating or marital partners, business colleagues, neighbors, and friends. Situations that require the development of additional expertise (learning a foreign language to get a job as a translator, learning a new computer application, becoming a licensed electrician, and so forth) are best handled in other ways.

A social problem-solving intervention begins with the development of a positive, problem-solving orientation. This means fostering the view that challenges can be thought-provoking and interesting, and that only rarely are they insurmountable. It's important for clients to be optimistic and believe that they have the ability to work on a problem and find a solution. Therefore, your first goal is to move the client from ruminating and whining to the stage where possible solutions are generated. This can be as easy as telling your client, "Now that I understand what happened, I would like to work with you to generate some possible solutions." Alternatively, it may be difficult. Angry clients have the urge to react impulsively to aversive and unwanted triggers. They may be initially unwilling to consider potential alternatives to their usual autopilot reactions, and they often fail to think through the immediate and long-term outcomes of their actions. In these cases, the techniques presented in previous chapters to increase awareness and motivation will be helpful. (Also beneficial will be assertiveness training, developing an accepting philosophy, overcoming impulsive urges, and perspective taking, interventions that we will present in later chapters.) In many cases, however, clients will immediately respond very positively to the problem-solving approach alone, since it presents an optimistic and immediately useful strategy for resolving some of life's difficulties.

Five Steps of Social Problem Solving

The problem-solving model we recommend is adapted from the foundational work of D'Zurilla and Goldfried (1971) and from the later work of Chang, D'Zurilla, and Sanna (2004). Where your clients are concerned, there are two main goals of problem solving:

1. Helping them improve their decision-making skills

2. Helping them respond with better reactions to the inevitable hassles of life

As usual, we recommend that you pull back from giving advice and directly telling your clients what to do. Instead, listen carefully, and be patient, first as you help them through the initial phase, when they describe their problems in concrete terms, and then as they generate a menu of potential solutions, explore possible alternative behaviors, and make decisions about which option to implement. Each step of the problem-solving model is shown in figure 9.1.

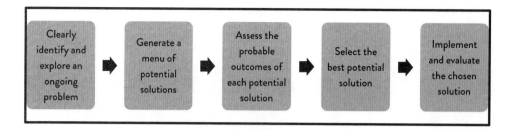

Figure 9.1. Steps of Social Problem Solving

Step 1. Clearly Identify and Explore an Ongoing Problem

The first step is to identify an ongoing interpersonal problem that is difficult or unpleasant. This problem will form the centerpiece of the session (or perhaps of a few sessions), and so it's important for you to be sure that you have an adequate understanding of the history of the problem, of the client's typical reactions, and of the effect that this problem is having on the client's life. If other, related problems are identified in the course of discussion, they can be worked on at a later time. It's quite important that you focus on only one problem at a time.

Describing the problem in concrete terms may not be so easy for your client. Some angry clients are not able to conceptualize their problems clearly, and so the amount of time required for this step will vary. The time needed for this step is often influenced by the complexity of the problem and by the verbal and conceptual abilities of the client as well as by the client's tendency to be repetitive when talking about the nasty behavior of the other person(s) involved. If a client spends excessive time blaming another person, listen attentively, and make statements like, "I hear how difficult this situation is for you. The problem-solving approach we are talking about may be very helpful, so let's keep going." The goal is to focus on the problem-solving steps and sidestep discussions of who is to blame, discussions that could go on for some time. To do this effectively and minimize global generalizations about how bad the situation or the other person is, you can use a *when…then* framework in your discussions. To see this framework in action, first consider the case of Janet:

> *Janet, forty-three years old, recently separated from her husband of nineteen years and is in the process of filing for a divorce. The couple has a fourteen-year-old son and two daughters, twelve and nine years old.*
>
> *After the separation, Janet's husband jumped quickly into a relationship with a younger woman who has two children and works as a fashion model. Janet is angered that he found somebody else so quickly. She is also threatened by the fact that the new woman seems to be in a glamorous profession. Janet feels abandoned and lonely and has been questioning her self-worth.*

To make matters worse, her husband is exposing the couple's three children to this new woman and her two children. According to Janet, their children seem confused and have said that they do not wish to spend time with their father, and especially with his "new family."

When Janet hears that her children have spent time with this other woman and her children, she becomes very angry and grows visibly upset in front of the kids, complaining directly to them that their father is a terrible person and has ruined her life. During these episodes, she also sends angry texts to her husband, suggesting that he is harming their children. She also threatens to confront the other woman and tell her in no uncertain terms to leave her children alone.

These angry reactions have developed into a pattern. Janet recognizes that the long-term outcomes of her behavior are bad for the children and for herself, and she has asked for guidance.

Now read the following dialogue, which demonstrates how to launch into a problem-solving discussion:

Practitioner: Janet, I like to think of problematic situations within a *when…then* framework. This helps me understand exactly what is going on. What I have been getting from you is that after the separation, your soon-to-be-ex-husband quickly found another woman who has two children. He has been taking your children over to her home and allowing them to get to know her and to play with her children. Your sense is that they are confused, and you react with anger. Do I have that right?

Janet: Yes, that's pretty much it.

Practitioner: Okay. I'd like you to think of a specific situation when that happened.

Janet: That's easy. It was just yesterday. They came home at 8 p.m., looking tired. It was a school night, and they still had homework to do. I was really pissed. I screamed at my husband when he dropped them off. I said, "What the hell is the matter with you? Don't you know the kids have school tomorrow, and they have homework to do? Are you *stupid?*"

Practitioner: Okay. Let's consider that to be the *when*. You screamed and questioned his intelligence. Now let's go to the *then*. What happened next?

Janet: Well, all hell broke loose. My girls began to cry and ran to their rooms. My son said, "Here come the bullcrap arguments again" and went next door to his friend's house. My husband called me immature for not being able to handle the situation. In the end, he left, and none of the kids did their homework, because they were so upset. It was midnight before any of them got to sleep.

Step 2. Generate a Menu of Potential Solutions

Once a problem is clearly identified and explored within in the *when...then* framework, a menu of potential solutions is collaboratively generated. This is a list of options, reactions, new behaviors, or available paths that may help resolve or reduce the problem and move the client forward. We use the word "menu" here to indicate that the generated solutions are not fully organized at first. Rather, the client will eventually choose one possible solution, just as we make a final dinner choice after looking at a restaurant menu. In the case of Janet, the question to ask is, "What could you do the next time your children come home late after spending time with their father's girlfriend and her children?" Then, after some discussion, some alternatives would be written down.

When you're working with your own clients, it's important to develop a range of potential solutions, guiding clients beyond their autopilot reactions and toward behaviors that they would not normally consider. Therefore, it's important not to stop at the first and most obvious solution.

As clients go through the process of generating potential solutions, they commonly come up with a few actions that are likely to be ineffective or to make their problems worse: "Call that bitch and tell her to stay away from my kids." But resist the temptation to spend time and energy criticizing potential solutions. Rather, continue gently nudging your client to come up with better possibilities, by asking, for example, "What else could you do?" Here, your goal is not to discuss the effectiveness of any particular alternative; it's simply to come up with a variety of alternative solutions. You can even suggest solutions that are silly and unlikely but still possible: "Here's a silly one—have some doughnuts ready to give your husband when he arrives, and ask the children to send his girlfriend and her kids your best wishes." The goal is to develop mental flexibility. With practice and repetition, the specific skill of *alternative-solution thinking* becomes easier. After the first time this strategy has been implemented, it becomes easier to use later with new problems.

Here are five of the solutions that Janet proposed:

1. Bad-mouth my husband to the kids after he leaves, and try to turn them against him.

2. Confront this bitch directly—drive to her house and warn her to stay away from my children.

3. In front of the kids, threaten my husband with loss of custody and more legal problems if he continues to expose our children to this woman.

4. Explain to my husband that the children say they're confused about being forced into seeing this woman at such an early point, and ask him for advice about what to say to them.

5. Tell the children that I love them, no matter what happens, and that it's okay if they like the other woman and want to have a relationship with her and her children—they get to decide what to do.

Step 3. Assess the Probable Outcomes of Each Potential Solution

In this step, the client is encouraged to thoughtfully consider what would be likely to happen, both in the short term and over the long term, if each potential solution were to be implemented, and if that course of action were to be pursued. *Short-term outcomes* are the immediate reactions that the client would probably get from others. *Long-term outcomes* are those that unfold over time.

The effects of long-term outcomes can last for hours, days, months, or even years. For example, angrily yelling at a child may cause the child to cease annoying behavior in the moment. Over the longer term, however, this action is likely to produce emotional distance in the parent-child relationship and provide a model of poor behavior for the child to follow. Similarly, physically shoving a colleague at work to teach him a lesson may feel good in the moment, but over the longer term it will surely create significant damage to the work relationship, diminish one's professional reputation in the office, and possibly lead to involvement with the criminal justice system. Therefore, it's usually a mistake to focus only on immediate outcomes.

Your job is to be curious about how the client views both the short- and the long-term consequences of each potential solution, and your client's perspective may initially be different from your own. It's okay to respectfully question or challenge a client's perspective if you believe it is too positive or negative regarding a potential outcome. The idea is to collaboratively agree on the most likely scenario for each path.

Once the likely outcomes have been discussed, write them down next to each alternative solution until each one has a corresponding short- and long-term outcome. Then review what has been discussed, to reinforce the idea that a whole range of alternative solutions can lead to different outcomes.

Client Worksheet 9.1, included at the end of this chapter and downloadable from www.newharbinger.com/42877, helps structure problem-solving discussions with your clients and follows the first three steps of the model we've been describing. Figure 9.2 shows Janet's completed worksheet, where she indicates what she might do when her children arrive home from a visit with their father and his new girlfriend.

Name _____

Date _____

A. Clearly Identify and Explore an Ongoing Problem

Use the *when...then* format. Include actions, thoughts, and words.

When...

My husband came home with the kids at 8 p.m. from his new girlfriend's house. The kids still had homework to do. I thought he was a jerk, screamed at him, and called him stupid.

Then...

All hell broke loose. The girls began to cry and ran to their room. My son ran to his friend's house, and my husband called me immature. We didn't get to bed until midnight, and the kids didn't do any of their homework.

B. Generate a Menu of Potential Solutions

In the space provided, describe at least five potential solutions to the problem you identified in part A.

1. Bad-mouth my husband to the kids after he leaves, and try to turn them against him.

2. Confront this bitch directly—drive to her house and warn her to stay away from my children.

3. In front of the kids, threaten my husband with loss of custody and more legal problems if he continues to expose our children to this woman.

4. Explain to my husband that the children say they're confused about being forced into seeing this woman at such an early point, and ask him for advice about what to say to them.

5. Tell the children that I love them, no matter what happens, and that it's okay if they like the other woman and want to have a relationship with her and her children—they get to decide what to do.

C. Assess the Probable Outcomes of Each Potential Solution

For each potential solution that you identified in part B, list the likely short-term outcomes and the likely long-term outcomes.

Potential Solution	Likely Short-Term Outcomes	Likely Long-Term Outcomes
1	Feels good because he gets what he deserves.	Creates more confusion for the children. He might fully withdraw from them, which would not be good for them, or me, in the long run.
2	Could escalate into a fight.	Creates a toxic relationship with this other woman, who may end up being in the picture for a long time.
3	He threatens to pull back from his financial support.	We get stuck in legal problems for years. All our money goes to attorneys' fees.
4	He doesn't seem to be open to my report about what the kids are saying and how they seem to be confused. He won't listen.	He may continue to blame me for poisoning the kids against him and his new relationship. Yet he may develop more of an understanding about how confused the kids are.
5	Puts the kids' well-being first. Won't make the problem worse. The focus will be on the kids' mental health, and they will be less conflicted. More inner peace for me.	During the next few years, the children will decide for themselves what type of relationship they want to have with their father.

Figure 9.2. Janet's Completed Social Problem-Solving Worksheet

Step 4. Select the Best Potential Solution

Once you and the client have agreed on the list of possible solutions and their potential outcomes, the next step is to choose the solution that is likely to bring about the best outcome. Again, resist the temptation to take the lead in selecting the solution. Instead, allow the client, after discussing the alternatives with you, to make an informed decision.

One way to start is to eliminate potential solutions that are likely to make the problem worse: "Which of these solutions will create more conflict for you and more turmoil for your children?" In the example of Janet, solutions 1, 2, and 3 would quickly be disregarded. As for Janet's other proposed solutions, more than one might produce a good outcome. Solutions 4 and 5 both have merit, but solution 5 seems more promising because it is likely to reduce conflict in the short run and be helpful to the well-being of the children over the longer term.

A consideration in selecting the most effective solution is to evaluate the client's ability to implement that solution; for example, there may be economic and situational factors that are out of the client's control, a potential solution may be contraindicated by the client's emotional state, or the client's resistance may be too high. It would make little sense to pick a solution that looks good on paper but has no chance of being properly executed because of the client's current level of skill or interest. In Janet's case, if she can't afford riding lessons for her children, it would not be helpful to suggest that she take the kids to a horse stable twice a week to keep them away from her soon-to-be-ex-husband and his girlfriend. In addition, Janet may not have the assertiveness skills even to talk with her husband in a productive manner (see chapters 14 and 15). And even though Janet has reached this point, she may still resist taking any kind of action. In that case, her practitioner might have to revert to motivational interviewing to help her move forward: "In what way might it be beneficial if you were to tell the children that they get to decide what to do?"

Keep in mind that even when a solution has been implemented with skill, there is no guarantee that the target of the client's anger will respond reasonably. One guiding principle is to agree on a solution that *seems practical*, given the situation, and to warn the client that although the proposed solution is likely to work, unexpected reactions from the other person may produce a roadblock to the desired outcome.

Step 5. Implement and Evaluate the Chosen Solution

Once a course of action has been agreed upon, the final step is to implement the chosen solution and evaluate it—that is, to have the client carry out the planned solution, observe what happens, and follow up in a subsequent session. Such follow-up leads to greater awareness and, hopefully, to better outcomes that are naturally reinforced, and that build a client's repertoire of effective behaviors for the future. Even if a solution turns out to produce a less than desirable outcome, it can still be a learning experience. In this situation, simply go back and start the process again, and search for another path forward.

Summary of the Five Steps of Social Problem Solving

We recommend that you go through client worksheet 9.1 with your client the first time it's used.

In step 1 (corresponding to part A of the worksheet), *clearly identify the problem*, and have the client provide a concise, concrete description of the situation. The discussion with your client can delve into the details and history of the problem, but it's best to present it succinctly on the worksheet—just capture the basics.

In step 2 (corresponding to part B of the worksheet), *identify potential solutions*, and discuss at least five alternatives with your client.

In step 3 (corresponding to part C of the worksheet), *list the corresponding short- and long-term outcomes*. Discuss in detail where each option is likely to lead, and put this basic information on the worksheet.

In step 4, work with your client to *choose the best solution*.

In step 5, have your client *implement and evaluate the chosen solution*. Troubleshoot any challenges that arise and, if necessary, coach the client on other skills that can make the implementation more successful. Follow up with a discussion of the outcomes, and of any adjustments that may be needed.

Takeaway Messages and Tools

Social problem solving is designed to help clients expand their skills for developing alternative solutions, thinking consequentially, and improving their decision making. We have found social problem solving to be among the most practical, helpful, and acceptable interventions for clients engaged in anger management. Implementing this simple and effective five-step model will help your clients face challenges and problems in a different way, with more effective behaviors and less anger. This approach also blends well with many of the interventions discussed in earlier chapters as well as with interventions to be discussed in the chapters to come. In chapter 10, we present ways to develop realistic (rather than exaggerated) thoughts about problems, a skill that can reduce anger-related reactivity and allow for continued generation of alternative solutions to problems.

CLIENT WORKSHEET 9.1. **Social Problem Solving**

Name _____

Date _____

A. Clearly Identify and Explore an Ongoing Problem

Use the *when...then* format. Include actions, thoughts, and words.

When...

_____

_____

_____

_____

_____

_____

_____

_____

_____

Then...

_____

_____

_____

_____

_____

_____

_____

_____

B. Generate a Menu of Potential Solutions

In the space provided, describe at least five potential solutions to the problem you identified in part A.

1. _____

_____

_____

2. _____

_____

_____

3. _____

_____

_____

4. _____

_____

_____

5. _____

_____

_____

6. _____

_____

_____

7. _____

_____

_____

8. _____

_____

_____

C. Assess the Probable Outcomes of Each Potential Solution

For each potential solution that you identified in part B, list the likely short-term outcomes and the likely long-term outcomes.

	Likely Short-Term Outcomes	Likely Long-Term Outcomes
1		
2		
3		
4		
5		
6		
7		
8		

Howard Kassinove, PhD, and Raymond Chip Tafrate, PhD

PART 5

Interventions to Change Thoughts: Accepting, Adapting, and Adjusting

CHAPTER 10

Promoting Realistic Thoughts and an Accepting Philosophy

A thought often makes us hotter than a fire.

—Henry Wadsworth Longfellow

Human beings are meaning-seeking creatures. We constantly perceive, evaluate, and try to make sense of our experiences. When angry clients show up in your office believing that their anger is automatically switched on by what they perceive as the negative and unwanted behavior of someone else, the reality is that they have more control over their anger than they realize. The way clients think about their interpersonal difficulties and life struggles has a powerful influence over their feelings and actions. Indeed, it is often clients' evaluative thoughts that are the real problem.

The good news is that, with your thoughtful guidance, clients can learn to think differently and reduce their anger. The not so good news is that, over time, and with years of repetition, clients' thinking patterns have become automatic and inflexible. And people in general take their own thoughts way too seriously; our thoughts often take on the aura of gospel truth, which further reinforces our cognitive rigidity. Thus it's common for angry clients to ooze with prickly confidence that they are interpreting events correctly and seeing the world accurately. Because their thinking has become an ingrained part of clients' inner worlds, it can be a challenging new experience for clients to pause and examine their thinking processes. Yet thought patterns can be changed. Therefore, one of the most common treatments for reducing anger is to help clients become more aware of the thoughts that typically occur to them during their anger episodes and then help clients work to change those thoughts.

In this chapter, we briefly review the leading cognitive behavioral therapy (CBT)–based intervention models that can be used to alter clients' thinking. We then describe three practical steps for restructuring the thoughts that lead to and maintain your clients' anger episodes. We also present a tool that clients can use to monitor their thinking as well as several strategies that clients can use to make rational, realistic thoughts more automatic in their day-to-day lives.

Cognitive Behavioral Therapy–Based Approaches to Addressing Clients' Thinking

There are three leading approaches to addressing the thinking that contributes to problematic anger reactions, and each approach is based on a particular type of CBT:

1. Acceptance and commitment therapy (ACT, discussed briefly in this chapter and at greater length in chapter 13)

2. Cognitive therapy

3. Rational-emotive behavior therapy (REBT)

Each of these approaches leads to a somewhat different intervention strategy, but there is a degree of conceptual overlap among them. In order to understand the subtle differences and similarities among these approaches, we'll consider the case of Yulia, then we'll briefly explain the unique features of each cognitive approach as it relates to her:

> Yulia, a thirty-two-year-old single mother of two daughters, twelve and ten, has sought treatment because her anger reactions, mostly elicited by her children, have been becoming increasingly severe. The children argue with each other when they are in the car with Yulia, and she struggles to drive safely while also bringing them under control. But the children's arguments typically continue even after Yulia has made repeated requests for them to cease their screaming and their verbal put-downs of each other. For Yulia, then, the most common trigger for anger is her children's yelling, screaming, and bickering during car rides.
>
> In this situation, Yulia has the following quick, automatic thoughts:
>
> - They must stop.
>
> - I can't stand this.
>
> In-depth discussion has helped Yulia reveal some other thoughts as well:
>
> - There is something wrong with my kids—they're always fighting.
>
> - If I can't get them to behave, it shows that I'm a bad, inadequate parent.
>
> On a scale of 0 (no anger) to 10 (extreme anger), the intensity of Yulia's anger in this situation often reaches 8 after just a few minutes, which means that Yulia becomes more than moderately angry. She notices muscle tension in her jaw and jitteriness in her body. She turns around and swears at her children, struggling not to smack them, too (she never has actually hit them while driving). The short-term outcome of her screaming and swearing at her children has been their litany of arguments about which of them is at fault. And as they blame each other, Yulia's

yelling and screaming escalate, producing even more noisy arguments from the children. As for the likely long-term outcome of these episodes, Yulia will probably find herself dreading the prospect of driving her children anywhere. In addition, she will probably feel disgusted with herself for not being able to hold it together. More conversation has made it clear that Yulia deeply desires to be a calm and more effective parent.

Acceptance and Commitment Therapy

In Yulia's case, the first approach to addressing her angry thoughts and feelings—ACT—would aim to teach her to become aware of her thoughts and feelings but not to act on or give in to them. Very often in daily life, all of us experience impulses, thoughts, and urges but do not follow through with verbal or motor behaviors; when we're on a diet, for example, we probably don't buy that great-smelling doughnut, and most of the time at work we don't express our disgust with long, boring, pointless meetings. Therefore, one option for clients is to distance themselves from their automatic angry thoughts and then deliberately pursue actions that are more consistent with their values and life priorities (these usually involve nonangry behaviors). The gist of this approach is to help the client become aware of internal processes but not focus too much on them; instead, the client learns to focus energy on those behavioral steps that will produce a valued outcome. As clients practice replacing their typical angry behaviors with behaviors that are likely to lead to better results, their internal symptoms of anger (that is, their angry thoughts, urges, and sensations) tend to diminish over time.

Because Yulia values being a calm, effective mother, one option for her is to work on not responding to her thoughts and sensations, and not yelling and screaming. If she is going to stop doing this, then a key question emerges: *What will she be doing instead?* She can start by identifying a behavioral path that is more in line with her value of being a calm, effective parent. In this scenario, for example, she can come up with a contingency system for dealing with the children during car rides, such as rewarding or praising them for making it to their destination without fighting, or calmly informing them that they are not allowed to use their cell phones for the rest of the day if an argument has broken out. To use this system, Yulia will need to accept a few basic facts:

- Her children will initially escalate their poor behavior when she enforces the new rules.

- Initially, she will continue to have the usual thoughts racing through her mind.

- Initially, she will still feel strong sensations in her body.

- She will still have the urge to yell and hit.

Nevertheless, regardless of these external and internal stimuli, Yulia will stay the course—that is, she will make a commitment to her behavioral plan and follow through with action. Over time, Yulia's anger will probably diminish, and the situation can be expected to improve.

Cognitive Therapy

The second approach, cognitive therapy, grows out of the work of Aaron Beck, a psychiatrist. It teaches clients the skills they need in order to assess the thoughts typically related to their anger triggers, and it helps them perceive situations more accurately and realistically. This approach can also involve identifying the basic assumptions (*I must not let others disrespect me*) and core beliefs (*Others can't be trusted*) that might predispose individuals to anger episodes.

As originally formulated by Beck (1967), cognitive therapy emphasizes common mistakes that people make in interpreting not only situations but also the actions and intentions of others. Such thinking errors, often associated with negative affect, take the form of distortions, exaggerations, negative assumptions, and misattributions. In this approach, the focus is on having clients become aware of their thoughts, weigh the evidence for and against the accuracy of their thoughts, and replace their distorted thinking with more realistic appraisals.

If this approach is used with Yulia, a place to start might be with her thinking that there's something wrong with her children because they argue. To examine the evidence for this thought, she will be asked to keep track of the number and severity of her children's arguments for a short time (maybe a week or so). Let's assume that her children bicker, on average, about ten times a day, and that their bickering consists mostly of negative comments and verbal arguing. There may also be occasional light pushing or shoving. Once this baseline information is established, Yulia will be asked to talk with several of her friends who have children around the same ages as her own kids, and to ask her friends about the frequency and intensity of the bickering in their households. Will Yulia's children be considered way out of the normal range in terms of this type of behavior? The answer is no. It may be that Yulia has distorted expectations of what normal behavior looks like for children in this age range. If so, she can replace her anger-prompting thought (*There is something wrong with my kids—they're always fighting*) with a new and more accurate counterthought: *Yes, they fight sometimes—it's annoying, but it's normal.*

Rational-Emotive Behavior Therapy

The third approach, REBT, was originally formulated by Albert Ellis, a psychologist. REBT places the focus on teaching clients to become less reactive to life's daily hassles and inconveniences by making a philosophical cognitive shift, moving away from a rigid, demanding life outlook and toward a more flexible, accepting view of the world. The approach developed by Ellis (1962, 1994) has become a popular intervention over the past fifty years and has been applied to a wide range of human problems, including anger (Ellis & Tafrate, 1997, 2016). Two main hallmarks distinguish REBT from cognitive therapy:

1. REBT focuses strongly on the thinking pattern of demandingness, which is reflected in a client's language by the use of phrases like "They must…" or "She should…" or "He has to…" Since these phrases suggest no alternative, the task is to shift the client toward a more flexible, preference-based mind-set: "I would prefer…" or "It would be nice if…" With this shift, the client can acknowledge the reality that things often do not unfold as desired, and that people (including children) do not always behave the way the client wants them to.

2. The emphasis in REBT is on the underlying logic of thoughts rather than on the objective evidence for their accuracy.

If this approach is used with Yulia, several of her thoughts will be directly questioned and discussed over the course of treatment (in REBT, this is called disputing):

•   Why must your children stop fighting in the car?

•   Most children argue and bicker—why can't yours?

•   Is there any evidence that you can't stand it, or are those just words that you say?

Through questioning and discussion, the goal will be to foster a more accepting and tolerant attitude toward the behavior (her children's arguing) that Yulia finds objectionable. Over time, her anger-prompting thoughts (*They must stop* and *I can't stand this*) will be replaced with less demanding counterthoughts: *It would be nice if they didn't argue in the car, but that doesn't seem likely at this stage of their lives. I can tolerate their bickering for short car rides. They will eventually outgrow this behavior.*

As for Yulia's thought that she's a bad parent, discussion would focus squarely on the logic of this thought. Does the fact that her children argue loudly during car rides make her a totally bad parent? The answer is no. Is children's arguing in the car the ultimate criterion of good or bad parenting? Again, the answer is no. Are there criteria besides children's behavior in the car that may be connected to good parenting? The answer this time is yes. And what if Yulia actually isn't such a good parent? As a single mom, maybe she's preoccupied with trying to support her household financially and has limited time and energy to devote to her children. Can children move forward with their lives even if they have parents who can't always put a lot of energy into parenting? Again, the answer is yes, assuming that serious forms of neglect and abuse are not present. In this scenario, Yulia's anger-prompting thought (*If I can't get them to behave, it shows that I'm a bad, inadequate parent*) will be replaced with a philosophically more logical and accepting counterthought: *In the big picture, the fact that my children argue has little to do with the kind of parent I am. Clearly, I'm not a perfect parent, but I do pretty well under difficult circumstances.*

Blending Approaches

You do not have to adhere to just one of the three intervention strategies just described. In actual practice, we tailor our approach to the client, to the context of the client's anger episodes, and to the content of the client's anger-prompting thoughts. Sometimes we embrace the philosophical approach of Ellis, and sometimes we favor the evidence-gathering techniques of Beck. There are also circumstances in which it's unproductive to tussle over the accuracy or logic of a client's thinking. In that situation, we shift gears to identify the client's underlying values, and we help the client discover more helpful behaviors. In other words, if one approach doesn't seem to be working, we switch to another—and that kind of flexibility is a major theme of the SMART program.

Steps for Cognitive Restructuring

The approaches of Ellis and Beck are designed to help the client reevaluate and change what he or she thinks, and so these approaches are often referred to as *cognitive restructuring interventions*. Both approaches incorporate the following basic steps:

1. Identify the typical thoughts that go through clients' minds when they are angry (anger-prompting thoughts).

2. Help the client replace anger-prompting thoughts with more accurate, flexible, reasonable thinking (rational, realistic counterthoughts).

3. Help the client practice new thinking in day-to-day life.

Identifying Anger-Prompting Thoughts

In chapters 3 and 4, we presented the Anger Episode Model and the Anger Episode Record. In those chapters, the client's thinking patterns were described as one critical element of his or her typical experiences during an anger episode. Before you move forward, you may want to quickly review those descriptions.

As a way of determining which thinking patterns are most relevant in a particular case, we recommend that you assess several anger episodes and pay close attention to part 2 ("Thoughts") of the Anger Episode Record. As you assist your clients in tracking their anger episodes, keep in mind that you are most interested in two kinds of thoughts:

1. Those that are *most immediately connected to* anger experiences during anger episodes

2. Those that *come up most often during* anger episodes

You may recall the six specific thought categories that the Anger Episode Record asks clients to consider (see client worksheet 4.1):

1. Awfulizing: *At the time, I thought this was one of the worst things that could be happening.*

2. Low frustration tolerance: *I thought I could not handle or deal with the situation.*

3. Demandingness: *I thought the other person(s) should have acted differently.*

4. Rating others: *I saw the other person(s) as* _____ .

5. Rating myself: *Deep down, I thought I was less important or worthwhile.*

6. Distortion or misinterpretation: *My thinking became distorted, and I didn't see things clearly.*

These six thinking patterns tend to be important because they are common and contribute to the development of anger; reducing their frequency and intensity helps people do better at managing their angry reactions. There are certainly many kinds of thoughts that can prompt anger episodes, and there may be times when it's appropriate to focus on a thinking pattern that is unrelated to these six, if that pattern (black-and-white thinking, for example, or blaming others) consistently prompts a client's anger.

Replacing Anger-Prompting Thoughts with More Accurate, Flexible, Reasonable Thinking

Formalizing new thinking to counter anger-prompting thoughts is a crucial step in cognitive restructuring. Each of the six anger-prompting thought patterns has a rational and realistic alternative that will help your clients think about difficult situations in a more flexible and moderate manner. The following sections present some general guidelines for coming up with more rational counterthoughts.

REPLACING AWFULIZING WITH MODERATE EVALUATIONS

If awfulizing, or making a mountain out of a molehill, is a common anger-prompting thought pattern for your client, then your goal will be to reinforce the client for labeling her negative anger triggers in a more moderate manner. The overwhelming majority of anger triggers are social in nature and are not life-threatening; therefore, the challenges that your client typically encounters in her day-to-day life are better described as being inconvenient, unfortunate, bad, or difficult. Most anger triggers, regardless of how negative they may seem in the moment, usually cause little more than loss of time, prestige, and/or money. The more moderate descriptions suggested in table 10.1 are not meant to minimize the reality of the struggles that your client may be facing. No one enjoys being rejected, disrespected, treated poorly, or losing money, a job, or social status, so it's important not to come across as minimizing your client's struggles. Rather, these moderate counterthoughts are simply offered as more realistic assessments.

Table 10.1. Cognitive Restructuring Examples for Awfulizing

Anger-Prompting Thought	Rational, Realistic Counterthought
It's awful that Debbie broke up with me.	Even though I hoped we would stay together, I recognize the breakup is realistically only unpleasant. While it may be temporarily bad, I am capable of moving on and meeting new people.
It's horrible that my children keep fighting with each other.	The constant bickering between the children is really unpleasant. Nothing more—just unpleasant.
It's terrible that I didn't get the job.	It's unfortunate that I was not selected. I'll keep looking. I know there will be other opportunities.

INCREASING FRUSTRATION TOLERANCE

If low frustration tolerance has emerged as a common pattern, your task is to shift your client away from telling himself that he cannot handle things and move him toward viewing his challenges and difficulties as manageable. It's okay for the client to say that he dislikes a situation, or that it's unpleasant, as long as he also recognizes that the situation is not overwhelming and can be handled. Your client will be better off learning to describe aversive triggers as difficult and frustrating than continuing to complain that he can't cope with his problems. Realistic counterthoughts (see table 10.2) bolster your client's faith in his ability to cope with adversity.

Table 10.2. Cognitive Restructuring Examples for Low Frustration Tolerance

Anger-Prompting Thought	Rational, Realistic Counterthought
I can't stand it when my partner criticizes me.	I'm capable of listening to my partner's complaints and perspectives. I may not like what I hear, but I can tolerate what is said.
I can't deal with this job anymore.	This job is unpleasant, and I am often frustrated. But I can certainly keep my cool while I look for another one.
I've had it with my ex!	I really don't like talking to my ex. That's why we're not together anymore. On the flip side, I certainly can manage communications that deal with stuff related to the children.

GIVING UP DEMANDS AND BECOMING MORE FLEXIBLE

Demandingness is one of the most common thinking patterns linked to a client's experiences during anger episodes. Restructuring this thinking pattern requires a change in perspective whereby the client is taught to replace, in his thinking and his speech, phrases like "They must…" or "She should…" or "He has to…" with language that emphasizes a less rigid stance. Here, the underlying philosophy is that it's okay for the client to *want* things to be different but less helpful for the client to *insist* that things be different. For example, it is perfectly acceptable for your client to want his boss to treat him with more respect, but behaving as if his boss *must* treat him with more respect is a different thing altogether. Table 10.3 presents some realistic counterthoughts to replace demanding thoughts.

Table 10.3. Cognitive Restructuring Examples for Demandingness

Anger-Prompting Thought	Rational, Realistic Counterthought
It's unfair! This shouldn't be happening.	It is definitely not fair. But, aside from wanting and expecting things to be fair, there is no reason why they must be so. Oh well—I can accept that things don't always go the way I want them to go.
Reginald has to start showing up on time for meetings.	It would be more professional if Reginald were on time. He's one of those people who is always ten minutes late. Eventually his chronic lateness will cause him problems.
My teacher should treat me with more respect.	It would be nice if she treated me with more respect. But she seems to have her own style of interacting with students. She's unlikely to change, so I'll just do my best while working with her.

REPLACING NEGATIVE LABELS WITH ACCEPTANCE

Making negative, sweeping, exaggerated judgments about others ("jerk," "dope," "ass," and so forth) is often automatic. If this pattern is connected to your client's anger, you can work toward helping the client replace such negative labels with more precise descriptions of other people's specific behavior. The underlying philosophy here is that it's okay for your client to view some kinds of behavior as negative but not to make totalizing, global judgments. Table 10.4 presents realistic alternatives to global ratings of others.

Table 10.4. Cognitive Restructuring Examples for Rating Others

Anger-Prompting Thought	Rational, Realistic Counterthought
My boss is a complete jerk.	My boss seems to be under a lot of stress, and he doesn't always talk to me the way I want. In the past he treated me well, but not now. His behavior is variable.
Jane is a selfish bitch.	Jane has some good qualities. However, one that I don't like is that sometimes she thinks only about herself.
All cops are assholes.	Some police officers are in the job for the wrong reasons. Others are well-meaning.

ACCEPTING PERSONAL FALLIBILITY

Some clients have the common pattern of labeling themselves harshly when they make mistakes, have setbacks, or act in a careless manner. (Recall Yulia, who labeled herself a bad parent when she became angry with her children for fighting in the car.) In some cases, your goal will be to help the client become more accepting of his or her fallibility and replace harsh self-labeling with self-descriptions that portray their behavior in a less extreme way. Several examples are presented in table 10.5.

Table 10.5. Cognitive Restructuring Examples for Self-Rating

Anger-Prompting Thought	Rational, Realistic Counterthought
I'm a horrible person for yelling at my elderly mother.	I made a mistake in how I treated my mother the other day. It was not nice to do that. I will apologize and do better in the future.
I can't believe I forgot the appointment. I'm such an idiot!	Lots of people forget appointments. I had a lot going on yesterday. I'll see if I can reschedule.
I texted something stupid to Tina. Now she won't talk to me. I can't believe I'm so dumb!	Dating can be difficult, and I will definitely make mistakes. I'll try to learn from them so I can have better connections with people in the future.

BEING MORE ACCURATE AND REALISTIC IN INTERPRETING THE NEGATIVE BEHAVIOR OF OTHERS

To change a pattern of distorted thoughts or misinterpretations on the part of a client, you can teach her to resist the urge to jump to conclusions about why others acted the way they did, and to consider alternative explanations—that is, to consider the facts and evidence related to the situation and then come up with an interpretation that seems more likely. In many problematic situations, the facts are not completely known, and so the client can be asked to suspend her judgment until more information becomes available. In restructuring this type of thinking, it can also be helpful to have your client consider the perspectives of the other people who are the targets of her anger. In most cases, the motive behind another person's unwanted behavior is that person's self-interest, not a malevolent intention (see table 10.6).

Table 10.6. Cognitive Restructuring Examples for Distortions and Misinterpretations

Anger-Prompting Thought	Rational, Realistic Counterthought
Leslie didn't respond to my text. She's blowing me off.	I don't know what's happening with Leslie. She might be busy with her children. I'll reach out again in a few days and see if she responds.
Jaden keeps interrupting me on purpose when I speak. He doesn't respect me.	I've noticed that Jaden is not a very good listener. He seems to interrupt people quite a bit.
Sharon got the promotion, not me. I'm sure it was based on politics.	I'm not sure why Sharon was chosen over me. I'll ask my supervisor to explain the reasoning behind the decision so I can be in a better position for the next opportunity.

Practicing New Thinking in Day-to-Day Life

Restructuring a client's thinking is definitely not a one-session endeavor. It will take time—sometimes a lot of time. And, unfortunately, it's usually not enough just to discuss changes in thinking, or just to talk about possible alternative appraisals of situations. Significant, lasting change in emotional and behavioral reactions—*real* change—requires practice and repetition of rational, realistic counterthoughts in order for clients to transfer new thinking to their day-to-day lives.

We often recommend working on one anger-prompting thought pattern at a time. After analyzing your client's Anger Episode Records, simply pick one of the six thought patterns presented in this chapter, choosing the one that seems to be most on target. Over the course of several meetings, a portion of each session can be devoted to reviewing homework related to that specific thinking pattern. Thus one option is to work on promoting one new rational, realistic thinking pattern until it becomes more automatic in response to real-life adversity, and then to address the next relevant pattern. Nevertheless, there may be situations in which it's appropriate to address multiple anger-prompting thought patterns at the same time. In any case, your job is to work on the anger-prompting thought pattern or patterns until rational, realistic counterthoughts become ingrained as automatic responses to adversity.

Client worksheet 10.1, included at the end of this chapter and downloadable from www.newharbinger.com/42877, is used to foster between-session practice and has been completed for the case of Yulia (see figure 10.1). To get started, in part 1, you, the practitioner, write the name of the anger-prompting thinking pattern that you want your client to monitor, or you write a brief description of a pattern that deviates from the list of six patterns presented earlier in this chapter but that nevertheless seems instrumental to your client's anger reactions. In Yulia's case, for example, the practitioner might write "Demandingness—others should act differently." It is usually best if you take the lead in identifying the thinking pattern of most concern, but it's equally important for the client to have not only some understanding of how the specific anger-prompting thought fits into the sequence of his or her anger reactions but also a conception of a more rational and realistic alternative. In Yulia's case, before she is asked to monitor her thinking pattern of demandingness, she and the practitioner might have a discussion of how this pattern emerges and intensifies her anger when her children bicker, and they could talk about potential alternative thoughts.

Parts 2 through 5 of the worksheet are completed by the client, who is asked to set aside a specific time at the end of each day to reflect on any events that may be applicable to the thinking pattern being monitored. Instruct the client to complete a copy of the worksheet for times when both the anger-prompting thought *and* the experience of anger occurred together in a real-life situation:

- In part 2, the client briefly describes the incident that instigated the thinking pattern. Phrases capturing the basics of the situation (who, what, where, and when) are fine.

- In part 3, the client describes, as accurately as possible, the specific self-talk that was related to the thinking pattern. This will usually take the form of a phrase or a sentence. (For example, Yulia might write: "My kids are ungrateful jerks—they should listen when I tell them to stop arguing.")

- In part 4, the client records the intensity of the experienced anger, using a scale of 0 (no anger) to 10 (extreme anger). The client also notes any action urge felt at the time and describes what he or she actually did. It's enough for the client to capture the basics of this information so that it can be discussed later. Keep in mind that the anger expressions reported on the worksheet may be self-defeating or destructive (the client acted on the anger-prompting thought), neutral (the client did not act on the anger-prompting thought), or positive (the client acted productively in spite of the anger-prompting thought and successfully countered it).

- In part 5, the client describes an alternative way of thinking that would lead to less anger in the situation.

Part 1. Thinking Pattern to Focus On (to be completed by the practitioner)

Demandingness—others should act differently

Part 2. Situation and Trigger

Briefly describe the situation in which the anger-prompting thought emerged. What happened? Where? Who was involved?

We were driving to the supermarket. The kids started to tease each other, and it got louder and louder. They kept at it even after I asked them to stop.

Part 3. Anger-Prompting Thought

Write a sentence or two that captures the anger-prompting thought as it was going through your mind in this situation.

My kids are ungrateful jerks. They should listen when I tell them to stop.

Part 4. Anger Rating, Action Urge, and Expressions

Describe how strong your anger was in this situation, along with any urges or impulses you felt, and describe how you expressed your anger.

At that moment, I felt strong anger. Maybe 8 on the 10-point scale. I wanted to stop the car and smack them both. Instead, I turned around and screamed even louder and said they were both immature jerks.

Part 5. Rational, Realistic Counterthought

Describe another way of thinking that could lead to less anger in this situation.

I could have recognized that their behavior was only unpleasant, and not what I wanted. I now see that I could have caused an accident if I had paid too much attention to them. Actually, some of their teasing was funny, as when my twelve-year-old called her sister a WOAT (worst of all time). I guess all kids, including my daughters, act like this. Now that I think about the incident, it was not a big deal. They will probably argue and tease each other many other times. I can just let it go and recognize that sometimes they will act in ways I like while at other times they will be silly with each other. I can learn to listen from afar and maybe even enjoy what they say to each other. I can tolerate not being in total control of their words.

Figure 10.1. Yulia's "Change Your Angry Thinking" Client Worksheet

Although the worksheet is designed to be completed by the client between sessions, we recommend that you use a real-life example to go through one or two worksheets the first time you assign it, to minimize any confusion regarding how the client is to complete it. Often it is helpful to have a "refresher" conversation about the worksheet after the client has completed one or two, to serve as a reminder of what is expected and why the assignment is important. Completion of the worksheet provides ongoing opportunities for clients to practice using rational and realistic alternatives to their anger-prompting thoughts.

Clients' motivation to complete a between-session assignment may vary according to the setting where you see them—a private practice, for example, or a clinic, school, hospital, or correctional center. We have been pleasantly surprised by how willing many clients are to complete the worksheet we've been describing. We suspect that they do so because the worksheet asks them about real-world situations, and because we present the worksheet in a way that is relatively straightforward and nonjudgmental.

Being realists, however, we know that there are inevitably times when clients fail to complete their homework. Often in this situation, practitioners simply reassign the homework for the following appointment and move on to something else to be covered in the current session. But we recommend that you avoid this option, since it can unintentionally reinforce the behavior of not following through on homework. In that situation, it is preferable to have the client complete the worksheet in the waiting room, or in front of you at the start of the next session. In cases of repeated noncompliance, an email reminder between sessions has been found to increase completion of homework assignments. For example, in a study by Lent (2017), participants were asked to report by text message that they had completed a daily homework assignment designed to help them practice a stress management exercise. In response, some of the participants received a congratulatory text from the clinician. Those participants who did receive the message of praise later demonstrated greater compliance with homework assignments than did participants who had not received the message of praise. For this reason, we believe that sending a reminder, and giving some type of immediate reinforcement for between-session practice, will be likely to increase clients' completion of the worksheet. This approach may seem rigid, but it emphasizes the importance we place on completing between-session assignments. It also provides potentially useful material for the next session and, hopefully, leads to greater diligence on the part of clients in future meetings.

Making Rational Counterthoughts More Automatic

For most angry clients, new ways of thinking and behaving will seem clunky and artificial at first. The trick is to get clients to try the new skills in real-life situations and then observe better outcomes and results (such as less conflict, closer relationships, and more inner peace). The hope is that, with enough trials, the new skills will become reinforced in the natural environment.

When it comes to helping clients take the skills they've discussed in treatment sessions and transfer those skills to the real world, a variety of cognitive behavioral techniques can be useful. In the sections that follow, we share three of our favorite tools for making new thinking patterns more automatic:

1. Coping statements

2. Role-playing with anger-prompting thoughts and rational counterthoughts

3. Rational role reversal

Coping Statements

Once rational counterthoughts have been discussed, specific coping statements can be created to help direct behavior in challenging situations. The underlying philosophy of this approach is that verbal self-instruction can interrupt dysfunctional thinking and behavior patterns and replace them with more adaptive responses. Such procedures have a long history in the anger treatment literature and grow out of the self-instructional training approach, pioneered by Meichenbaum and Cameron (1973) with schizophrenic patients and used later by Novaco (1975) with angry adults.

Coping statements are often written on index cards or entered into electronic notes applications on a cell phone or tablet. Over time, the client is asked to commit such statements to memory. An effective coping statement accomplishes two goals simultaneously:

1. It reinforces rational counterthoughts.

2. It guides improved behavior.

For example, Yulia's coping statements might include "I can tolerate my kids fighting in the car, and I do not have to lash out at them" and "My kids' arguing is normal, and they will eventually outgrow it. I don't have to confront them when they bicker." Over the course of several meetings, Yulia can be asked to rehearse her coping statements in session, write them down in a place where she can easily find them, and then commit them to memory so that she can quickly use them during car rides with her bickering children.

An advanced twist on this strategy is to use scenes involving anger imagery and verbal barbs (see chapter 13) as the context for in-session practice of coping statements. Exposure practice makes it more likely that the new skills will be transferred to real-life scenarios, and clients are always asked to apply the coping statements to their ongoing situations.

Given a specific anger-evoking situation, it may sometimes be quite easy to reinforce realistic coping in the natural environment:

Miguel, twenty-four years old, repeatedly became angry while driving. Even when traffic was light, he would flare up if someone ahead of him was driving at or below the speed limit. He would honk, yell, give the other driver the finger, experience muscle tension, and think about how to get even—by tailgating, or by speeding up and placing his car in front of the other vehicle and then slowing down. As an intervention, we had Miguel place a sign on his dashboard. It contained four sentences:

1. It's only unpleasant that I have to slow down for other drivers.

2. There is no reason why other drivers must do what I want.

3. No one appointed me police officer of the universe.

4. I can tolerate driving slowly.

After about two months, Miguel reported that he was much less angry while driving.

Role-Playing with Anger-Prompting Thoughts and Rational Counterthoughts

Another way to strengthen counterthoughts is to engage the client in a role-playing exercise in which rational and realistic thinking responses to anger-prompting thoughts can be practiced. We call this role-play the Two Voices Exercise. Initially it requires some time to explain to clients, but once they have gone through the exercise, they will need only a brief reminder about how it works.

The two competing voices are the anger-prompting thoughts and the rational, realistic counterthoughts. You, the practitioner, play the role of the anger-prompting thoughts or the angry voice, and you feed anger-prompting thoughts to the client; the client plays the role of the rational voice that attempts to come up with realistic counterresponses to the anger-prompting thoughts. Here is how it works:

1. Because you will be role-playing the anger-prompting thoughts, it is necessary for you to have an in-depth understanding of how the client thinks during a typical anger episode. Before starting the exercise, give yourself a few seconds to recall several examples of anger-prompting thoughts from your client's life.

2. Generate at least three examples that are at different levels of difficulty—easy, moderate, and hard—for the client to counter.

3. Begin with the easiest one by voicing a low-level anger-prompting thought and then asking the client to provide a rational counter to it.

4. If the client can successfully counter your anger-prompting thought with better thinking, offer congratulations, and determine whether you can move on to a more difficult example.

5. If the client is able to successfully counter your next example, repeat the process, and go for a third or even a fourth round, at increasing levels of difficulty.

6. If the client is unable to successfully counter your anger-prompting thought, avoid abruptly terminating the exercise. The goal is to have the client experience success and strengthen his or her rational thinking.

   • Give the client another chance to counter the anger-prompting thought.

   • If the client still struggles with a rational counterresponse, offer an example of one yourself.

   • Now voice a new anger-prompting thought, at a lower level of difficulty, so that the client can complete the exercise with an experience of success.

7. Close the exercise with a discussion of how the client can make the rational, realistic counterthoughts, or rational voice, stronger in his or her day-to-day life.

Let the client know that it's important to keep filling out copies of client worksheet 10.1, and tell the client that you will come back to this exercise in subsequent sessions.

Here is an example of how this exercise might be conducted with Yulia:

Practitioner: So, based on our discussions, it seems like there are these two voices in your head when your kids fight in the car. Let's be clear on what they sound like. First, at times when you get angry and yell at them, you have this tendency to think that your kids must stop fighting when you tell them to, and that you can't tolerate their behavior. Second, you also think that their fighting means there is something fundamentally wrong with them, and that because you can't get them to stop, you are a bad parent. At other times, when you are less angry, you tell yourself that you can tolerate their fighting in the car, and that you do not have to lash out at them. Also, when you are less angry, you say to yourself that they are normal and will outgrow this fighting behavior, and that it has nothing to do with being a bad parent. Does that capture it pretty well? Or would you describe it differently?

Yulia: No, that's good.

Practitioner: Okay. I'd like to try something with you. I'm going to ask you to be a bit of an actress for a few minutes. We're going to do a quick role-playing exercise. I'm going to play the angry voice and present some ideas that come from that voice. I want you to be the rational, less angry voice, and to counter what I say. So we're going to play these two voices. I'm going to

	be the angry voice, and I want you to be the rational voice and see if you can counter my thoughts, as we've been talking about.
Yulia:	So you're the bad voice and I'm the good voice?
Practitioner:	Right. Just give me a few seconds to think of what I'm going to say.... Okay. Ready? *Damn it! My kids shouldn't fight in the car.* Now you counter that angry voice.
Yulia:	*My kids are acting like kids. They're not going to just sit there quietly.*
Practitioner:	Good job! You countered that one nicely. Now I'm going to bump it up a notch. Ready? *I work hard all day. I can't handle their bickering.*
Yulia:	*I certainly can handle it and keep my cool for short car rides. That's what good moms do.*
Practitioner:	Very nice. How was that for you?
Yulia:	That was good. That was real.
Practitioner:	I'm going to bump it up another notch. Ready? *My kids don't listen to me. I'm not a good mother.*
Yulia:	*I try my best to be a good mother. I work all day and then spend my energy managing their activities. I do better than most women in my position.*
Practitioner:	Really good job being the rational, less angry voice! What do you think would be different about your interactions with your kids if you paid more attention to that voice? How can you strengthen that rational voice, moving forward?

Rational Role Reversal

In the Two Voices Exercise, as we've just seen, the client is presented with unhelpful, irrational thoughts and is asked to generate helpful counterthoughts. Rational role reversal (Kassinove & DiGiuseppe, 1975; Lipsky, Kassinove, & Miller, 1980), another classic technique that has worked very well for many years, also challenges clients to generate rational thinking reactions and verbalize better thinking patterns. Here, however, the practitioner unexpectedly presents an anger scenario, actual or not, in which the practitioner has experienced (or is assumed to have experienced) mild anger, and the practitioner then asks the client for help. Here is an example of how to use this technique (the client in the example has had some experience with cognitive interventions; clients at an earlier stage of intervention will need more support and guidance as well as simpler scenarios and praise for getting the exercise right):

Practitioner:	I'd like to try something that we haven't done before. I'm going to ask you to be my therapist and help me. Is that okay?
Johan:	Sure, I can give it a shot.
Practitioner:	Yesterday my phone went dead after it had been charging all night. When I saw that I had only 10 percent left at 10 a.m., I felt angry. Would you please help me?
Johan:	What were you saying to yourself when you saw that the charge was at 10 percent?
Practitioner:	Good. That's the way to begin. Well, I said, "That shouldn't happen! I paid a lot of money for this phone, and it should operate correctly!"
Johan:	What's the difference between telling yourself that the power drain shouldn't have happened and simply thinking that it was unexpected, and that unexpected things happen all the time, even to expensive items?
Practitioner:	Good! It's good to have me compare those two positions. To answer your question, if I simply accepted the reality that objects malfunction and break, even when they are expensive, I would probably feel less angry. I guess even super expensive cars break down now and then. That's just the reality of life. (*Practitioner models acceptance of reality.*)
Johan:	(*calling on his advanced skills*) So if you view it as inconvenient to have a phone with a bad battery, and if you see that you can tolerate the situation for a few days while the phone is being repaired, and that there is no reason why it *should not* have broken, you will probably feel better.
Practitioner:	Correct. I hear what you are saying. And thanks for bringing good thinking to my attention.

Takeaway Messages and Tools

Exaggerations and distortions are typically long held thinking patterns of angry clients. Therefor, it will take multiple sessions and techniques to create a cognitive shift. It requires time, effort and practice to develop more realistic perceptions, a less demanding philosophy, and a view of life's challenges as unpleasant but manageable. The interventions described in this chapter will help your clients develop a new perspective on their current everyday challenges and struggles.

But what about truly difficult situations from the past, or situations that for other reasons cannot be changed? A shift in perspective may be of value in those cases, too. We cover the very important topics of perspective taking and forgiveness in chapter 11.

CLIENT WORKSHEET 10.1. Change Your Angry Thinking

Part 1. Thinking Pattern to Focus On (*to be completed by the practitioner*)

_____

Part 2. Situation and Trigger

Briefly describe the situation in which the anger-prompting thought emerged. What happened? Where? Who was involved?

Part 3. Anger-Prompting Thought

Write a sentence or two that captures the anger-prompting thought as it was going through your mind in this situation.

Part 4. Anger Rating, Action Urge, and Expressions

Describe how strong your anger was in this situation, along with any urges or impulses you felt, and describe how you expressed your anger.

Part 5. Rational, Realistic Counterthought

Describe another way of thinking that could lead to less anger in this situation.

Howard Kassinove, PhD, and Raymond Chip Tafrate, PhD

Perspective Taking, Compassion, and Forgiveness as Antidotes to Anger and Resentment

As I walked out the door toward the gate that would lead to my freedom, I knew if I didn't leave my bitterness and hatred behind, I'd still be in prison.

—Nelson Mandela

As a consequence of his protests against the racially discriminatory policies of the South African government, Nelson Mandela was locked up for twenty-seven years in the highly restrictive Robben Island Prison. He was isolated from nonpolitical prisoners and was held in a small, damp concrete cell and was frequently harassed by the white wardens. Mandela was required to spend much of his time breaking rocks into gravel until he was reassigned to work in a lime quarry where the glare damaged his eyesight. He was also put in solitary confinement on several occasions for possessing smuggled newspaper clippings.

After his release, Mandela continued to work to eliminate discrimination, and in 1994 he was elected the first black president of South Africa. While in office, he focused on reconciliation between South Africa's racial groups. Finally, in 1996, twenty-four years after having been sent to Robben Island, Mandela presided over the creation of a new South African constitution that prohibited discrimination against minorities, including white South Africans. He worked with leaders of all races to promote peace and social justice until his death, in 2013.

Given his very long imprisonment, the years of forced labor, the damage to his eyesight, his solitary confinement, and his restricted access to information from the outside world, we might expect Mandela to have emerged a bitter, angry man set on revenge. Why didn't he? Was there something special about his personality that led him to move toward reconciliation rather than vengeance? Can people be taught to move forward as Mandela did? These are the issues we address in this chapter. And they are difficult issues.

The most common reactions to perceived unfairness are anger, bitterness, jealousy, rumination, and desire for revenge. These responses occur in reaction to transgressions or rule violations of all sorts, such as sexual infidelity, emotional infidelity, and deception by friends, family members, and business associates. They also occur in reaction to various kinds of rejections, misunderstandings, and neglect. Deception can take the form of outright lies, such as made-up information or information that is otherwise different from the truth ("No, I did not spend the rent money on drugs"). It can also consist of equivocations, such as indirect or ambiguous statements ("I can't really remember what I said") or concealments, as when important information is omitted: "I just went to put gas in the car and came right back" (with no mention about the quick stop for a beer). Deception can also include exaggerations of the truth ("The boss said I'm the best worker and am likely to get a big raise soon") or understatements that minimize the truth ("I wasn't fired—I was just told not to come in for a while until things get better"). These transgressions are perceived as unfair because they result from violations of formal or unspoken agreements to be open, honest, and trustworthy, especially with relatives, friends, and romantic partners.

Some of your clients, not unlike Nelson Mandela, will have experienced truly major suffering as a result of purposeful physical abuse, wrongful imprisonment, rape, a mugging, torture, and so forth. Survivors from war-torn nations marked by ethnic conflict certainly fit this profile. Sometimes the aggressive behavior against your client may have been intentional, as when a marital partner sought control through threats and actual physical violence. At other times, the offensive and hurtful behavior will not have been personally directed at your client, who may simply have been in the wrong place at the wrong time. This occurred in the 2004 case of a woman who suffered numerous broken bones, spent weeks in a medically induced coma, and required months of rehabilitation after a teenager dropped a twenty-pound frozen turkey from a freeway overpass and through her windshield (Vitello, 2005).

As a professional, you cannot restore years lost to wrongful imprisonment, nor can you make restitution for broken bones, stolen money, abuse, or violence. So how *can* you help your clients live better lives, whether they have been the victims of major or relatively minor offenses? To answer that question, you can look to religious and philosophical teachings for guidance, you can examine the natural reactions of victims, and you can consult the professional literature to see whether you can teach healing practices to those who have suffered. No matter where you search, however, the goal is for your clients to move forward and not live lives filled with anger, bitterness, hateful rumination, vengefulness, and psychological pain. In the end, the main goals of life are to be happy and to have a life worth living (see chapter 16). Anger, bitterness, and revenge are antithetical to those goals, whereas compassion and forgiveness will move your clients in the right direction. Mandela certainly knew that to nurture bitterness and hatred, and to live without forgiveness, would have been, for him, to remain in prison. Yet forgiveness may be an idea that your clients have never considered.

What Is Forgiveness?

Forgiveness is an intentional, voluntary process by which the victim of an offense undergoes a reduction in negative feelings and psychological suffering as well as a change in attitude toward the perpetrator of the offense. It's thought that at some point in the process of forgiveness, the victim decides to move forward, either with or without professional help or the help of family members, friends, or significant others. Moving forward means desiring to diminish the frequency, intensity, and duration of negative emotions and attitudes, such as anger, rage, and thoughts about revenge. This desire is often coupled with an increased desire to wish the offender well. That, for many people, is the shocking part of forgiveness—wishing the offender well. Yet it does occur. For example, the woman struck by the frozen turkey, although she did not absolve the offender of responsibility for his behavior, did ask the court to be lenient and spare him the twenty-five-year sentence recommended by the prosecutor (the offender served only six months, with five years on probation), and she asked the offender to do good works in the remainder of his life—she wished him well (Vitello, 2005).

To forgive, then, does not mean to absolve. It does not mean to condone, nor does it mean to fail to see that an action is wrong. It does not mean to excuse, to forget, or simply to eliminate conscious awareness of an offense, nor does it mean that the offender is granted a pardon, which in legal terms restores the offender's civil rights. It *does* mean holding the offender responsible for his or her actions, and it may or may not lead to reconciliation or to the restoration of a relationship with the offender. Reconciliation may be a desired goal, especially in cases of transgression within a family or between friends, but the offender may not be interested in meeting with the victim, may not be available because of long distance, may not apologize, or may have died. In the end, to grant forgiveness is a personal journey, whether the offense is minor or serious. And forgiveness does not occur quickly. Rather, it is a process that may take weeks, months, or years to complete.

Religious Teachings on Forgiveness

Religious doctrines and philosophies regarding human nature, offenses, victimization, and forgiveness have been around much longer than scientific and psychological approaches. It's wise for you to know a bit about those perspectives, and to have at least basic knowledge of religious teachings, since many clients are at least partially guided by such traditions. Indeed, if the offense that led to your client's anger was major in scope, as in cases of abuse or violent crimes, your angry client (the victim) may already have consulted a religious leader.

We do recognize that there is significant variability among and within religious traditions with respect to views and practices, and that no mental health practitioner can be an expert in all the variants of any religion. This is all the more true because there are thousands of religious traditions worldwide, and widespread immigration may lead you, as a practitioner, to work with persons of faiths that are both known and unknown to you. Therefore, gaining fundamental knowledge about religious traditions is worth your effort as you work with angry clients.

The world's six most popular religious traditions are Christianity, Islam, Hinduism, Buddhism, Sikhism, and Judaism. In the United States, approximately 74 percent of people identify with one of the various Christian traditions; 2 percent are Jewish, 1 percent are Muslim, and a significant number, about 18 percent, are not religiously affiliated at all. A survey of US adults by the Pew Research Center (2014) showed the importance of not making assumptions about clients; in that survey, 63 percent of respondents indicated their certainty that God exists, 9 percent did not believe in God at all, and others indicated varying degrees of certainty and uncertainty regarding God's existence. Women were more likely than men to describe themselves as believers, and belief in God tended to be inversely correlated with a respondent's higher educational achievement. Here are some other findings of importance to anger management:

- Respondents who expressed belief in God said that they were likely to look for guidance about right and wrong from religious teachings.

- Respondents who did not express belief in God were likely to seek guidance in philosophy, common sense, or science.

- With respect to moral questions of right and wrong where the entire sample of respondents was concerned, fewer than 40 percent of the believers from all religious traditions endorsed the notion of absolute standards of right and wrong, and more than 80 percent of the nonbelievers said that the question of right and wrong depends on the situation.

In some traditions, a switch in religious affiliation is not a major issue; in Islam, Mormonism, and orthodox sects of other faiths, however, the switch to a different faith may be considered blasphemous. For your client, then, a family member's switch to a different religion can be an anger trigger.

Because your clients probably come from different traditions, you are unlikely to have true expertise in each of their religions. We recommend that you tread lightly in this area. At the same time, whether you are personally guided mostly by scientific findings, seek guidance from a religious tradition different from your client's, or don't practice a religion at all, your gentle acceptance of your client's beliefs can do much to strengthen the therapeutic alliance.

Forgiveness in the Professional Literature

In the scripture and other writings of many religious traditions, passages can be found that seem unclear or even contradictory, and clients may come to you with different interpretations regarding how they should behave in specific situations. Sometimes you may find it helpful to consult with a minister, a priest, a rabbi, an imam, or another representative of your client's religion. But the bottom line is that even though religious traditions typically promote forgiveness, most do not prescribe *specific behavioral procedures* to help followers move in that direction. Rather, they rely on scriptural recommendations or commands to forgive. In most cases, then, you will have to turn to the professional literature to understand how to produce forgiveness and help clients move forward. In this section of the chapter, we offer examples of forgiveness for three different types of offenses—romantic betrayal, murder, and genocide. Later in the chapter, we present a six-step intervention that you can use to help clients move in the direction of reducing anger, bitterness, and the desire for revenge, thus freeing them to live constructive lives.

ROMANTIC BETRAYAL, EXAMPLE 1

Semi, a forty-four-year-old Buddhist, was born and raised in Vietnam. At the age of sixteen she moved to Chicago and later met her husband. They had two children.

They seemed to be happily married. Soon, however, Semi discovered that her husband was having affairs with her cousin and with many other women. Enraged, she had numerous arguments with her husband and finally divorced him.

Semi took the children and opened up her own successful business as a hair stylist. On the basis of her Buddhist and personal philosophy, she later decided to forgive both her husband and her cousin. She now talks to her former husband on the telephone, without agitation, when there are matters related to the children. She has decided to not tell the children about their father's affair in order to protect his relationship with them. Yes—she decided to protect him. She is also thankful for her relationship with her cousin, a connection that continues to be positive for Semi, since she believes that her cousin showed her a great deal about the faults of her former husband. Semi says that she forgave the two of them for herself, so that she could move forward in her life.

ROMANTIC BETRAYAL, EXAMPLE 2

John was seen in treatment after being rejected by his girlfriend, Sophie. The couple had been dating for a few years, and during that time John thought he and Sophie were firmly connected and in love.

At one point, Sophie decided to take a trip to Europe. She talked regularly with John by telephone and continued to profess her love, saying she could not wait to get back to him. But the night after she returned, she told John she had found another man in Europe, and she said their relationship was over.

John, stunned by this sudden turn of events, felt bitter and angry and wished bad things for Sophie. He wanted nothing to do with her, and he certainly did not want to talk with her. This situation lasted for months, until John embarked on a programmed path of forgiveness.

John was an atheist. Therefore, the gains he made were attributable to behavioral exercises and cognitive changes. Eventually we asked him to send Sophie a note, wishing her well. He agreed, but it took him seven months to do it. When he did, Sophie responded positively, and this exchange set the stage for forgiveness to occur.

John says he is now able to see Sophie in person and perhaps have coffee with her. He wishes her a good life. More important, he now experiences fewer negative thoughts about their past relationship.

MURDER, EXAMPLE 1

In 1992, Anthony's brother was murdered during a fight over drug-dealing turf. The suspect, Michael, was arrested, pleaded guilty, and was sentenced to twenty years in a state prison. He was released in 2013.

As would be expected, Anthony was initially filled with bitterness and rage toward his brother's killer. As time went on, however, Anthony began to go to church on a regular basis, read the Bible, and learn about forgiveness.

Still later, Anthony had occasion to visit the prison where Michael was confined. While he was there, he saw Michael and forgave him.

While still incarcerated, Michael eventually earned a master's degree, and Anthony went to the prison to see Michael graduate. He also spoke on Michael's behalf at his parole hearing. This may seem shocking to some readers, but Anthony and Michael are now friends (Dwyer, 2013). A short story about this case can be seen at http://religion.blogs.cnn.com/2013/04/13/from-anger-to-forgiveness-man -befriends-brothers-killer/.

MURDER, EXAMPLE 2

In 1987, Walt's twenty-four-year-old son was murdered by Mike, a chronic street criminal, violent drug addict, and drug dealer. Mike said, "I'm sorry" at his sentencing, and he received a plea deal leading to a five-year sentence.

Walt, a minister, was initially very distressed, but he eventually asked himself whether he was going to remain bitter and angry for the rest of his life, or whether there was a way to move forward. He decided that he would show God's love to Mike.

He began to write to his son's killer and eventually said, "I forgive you, Mike." He visited Mike in prison and thought that Mike had changed for the better. He said so to Mike's parole board, and Mike was released after thirty-five months.

Walt and Mike became friends. They now attend social events and baseball games together, and Walt even officiated at Mike's marriage. (See our video series Anger Management in Counseling and Psychotherapy at www.psychotherapy.net, where Raymond Chip Tafrate explores the entire forgiveness process in a full interview with Walt.)

GENOCIDE, EXAMPLE 1

The 1990s genocide in Rwanda led to the death of almost a million people, mostly Tutsis. In 1994, Iphigenia's husband, a Tutsi, and five of their children were murdered with machetes by Hutu extremists. One of the Hutu killers was Jean-Bosco, the husband of Ephiphania, and a neighbor of Iphigenia and her family. When the war was over, Jean-Bosco was sent to prison for seven years. Afterward, he was allowed to publicly confess, and he apologized to Iphigenia.

Although Iphigenia did not speak to Ephiphania or Jean-Bosco for four years, she believes that she was led to forgive them by her Christian faith as well as by the government-sponsored process whereby the murderers made public admissions of guilt and had the opportunity to apologize.

But there was another, overarching issue that led Iphigenia to forgive her family members' killers—the need for her to make money and survive. Iphigenia, Ephiphania, and Jean-Bosco now work together to make baskets, which are sold in the United States by Macy's. Their collaboration as partners and friends has fostered their continued reconciliation and keeps both families in close daily contact.

Iphigenia says, "The dead are dead, and they cannot come back again, so I have to get on with the others and forget what has happened." Reports about the families, including a video showing Iphigenia cooking and serving diner to Jean-Bosco, can be found at https://www.youtube.com/watch?v=q3revyWnbZM and http://www.cnn .com/2008/WORLD/africa/05/15/amanpour.rwanda.

GENOCIDE, EXAMPLE 2

The story of Eva Mozes Kor (Kor, 1995; Kor & Buccieri, 2009) presents an exceptionally powerful case of forgiveness. Kor, a Jewish woman, was born with a twin sister in Transylvania, Romania, in 1934. In 1944, the Nazis transported Eva and her family to the Auschwitz-Birkenau extermination camp.

Eva's parents and two older sisters were immediately exterminated, but she and her twin were held aside by the so-called Angel of Death—Josef Mengele, a Schutzstaffel (SS) physician—who was conducting a series of infamous medical experiments on more than a thousand sets of twins. In these experiments, Mengele's usual procedure was to inject one twin with poison, bacteria, or a virus and then watch to see how disease developed, and how long it took for death to occur. When that twin died, he would murder the other in order to determine, by comparison, the effects his injections had caused. Eva and Miriam were in Auschwitz for nine months, but they survived and were liberated in 1945, at the age of ten.

In 1950, Eva and her sister went to Israel, where Eva married an American tourist who was also a Holocaust survivor. Eva and her husband later moved to the United States. Both sisters continued to suffer the effects of Mengele's experiments. Eva developed tuberculosis and had miscarriages. Her sister had undeveloped kidneys and died of cancer in 1993.

Surely this is one case in which the expectation would be for Eva to live her life with ruminating bitterness and hatred. And yet, as a way of freeing herself from being a victim, she chose forgiveness and has made public declarations on many occasions about forgiving those who harmed her and her family.

For example, on the fiftieth anniversary of her liberation from Auschwitz, Eva returned to the site of the concentration camp with Hans Münch, a German physician who had worked there with Mengele, and she publicly declared her forgiveness. (Münch had been tried after the war but was found not guilty because he hadn't actually carried out Mengele's experiments.)

And some twenty years later, at the age of eighty-one, she went to Germany and testified at the trial of ninety-three-year-old Oskar Groening, the "Bookkeeper of Auschwitz." Groening was found guilty, but Eva did not want him to be sent to prison. Instead, she thanked him for accepting responsibility for what he had done, and she said that she thought it would be best if he spent the rest of his life making public statements and teaching others about the evils of Nazism. Groening was nevertheless sentenced to four years in prison.

There are Holocaust survivors who do not agree with Eva's position, but Eva continues to fully understand that forgiveness is for the forgiver, not for the offender. Her goal was to set herself free— to release herself from the past and move forward with her life.

Eva Kor's stance of forgiveness does not mean that she has forgotten what happened, or that she condones it. In fact, she has established a museum as a way of teaching about the Holocaust and has written books about her experience to educate others. Many videos about her story of forgiveness can be found on YouTube; see, for example, https://www.youtube.com/watch?v=xk1N7xAv9W8 and https://www.youtube.com/watch?v=wHZbiqMYb1M.

Outcomes Associated with Forgiveness

There is no doubt that forgiveness is difficult. Yet it is mentally and physically health-enhancing. It's associated with happiness, subjective well-being, resilience, and positive interpersonal outcomes.

Sometimes forgiveness occurs naturally. When it does, that's great. At other times, intervention by a practitioner is helpful. Several variables are predictive of forgiveness and may make the process shorter and easier to achieve:

- It's easier for clients to forgive when they are heavily invested in their relationships, as in a marriage or a business partnership.

- It's easier to forgive when restitution has been made, as when the offender has paid a fine.

- It's easier to forgive when the outcome of a transgression involves a new and positive experience, as when someone is wrongly fired and then finds a much better job.

- It's easier to forgive a trivial offense (such as lying about how much money was spent to purchase a piece of furniture) than a serious offense (such as emptying a joint savings account to pay off hidden gambling debts).

- Transgressions that are voluntarily revealed and admitted to are easier to forgive than those that are discovered by the injured party.

- It's easier to forgive an accidental transgression than one that was committed with malicious intent.

- It's easier to forgive an offense when the offender has offered an apology and seems sincerely remorseful.

- An increased capacity for forgiveness is associated with older age, emotional stability, the personality trait of agreeableness, and religious commitment.

Forgiveness is challenging, but we have used it successfully with difficult cases, when other interventions seemed doomed to fail. Despite the positive outcomes associated with forgiveness, however, it is often not even considered as an option for clients with long-term anger reactions, especially when there has been severe harm.

Steps Toward Forgiveness

A number of different models exist for producing forgiveness. The six steps we use to encourage and enhance forgiveness in those who suffer from long-standing anger and bitterness are similar to those found in the models of Enright and Fitzgibbons (2000) and Enright (2012). In this section of the chapter, we review those six steps:

1. Reviewing the event and uncovering anger

2. Developing the motivation to forgive

3. Defining forgiveness

4. Understanding what may have influenced the offender

5. Working toward empathy and compassion

6. Expanding and deepening forgiveness

In some ways, the goal here is to extend the natural outcome of moving forward that, with the passage of time, follows many types of transgression. Consider, for example, the case of a university student who finds that his romantic partner has transgressed, either sexually or emotionally; six months later, this student probably will have moved beyond his anger and his desire for revenge and will become involved in a new relationship. If a client has not moved forward in this way after a transgression, the practitioner can use strategies of forgiveness and perspective taking either to initiate the process of moving forward or to decrease the time required for it to occur.

Step 1. Reviewing the Event and Uncovering Anger

The first step involves the client's developing full awareness of exactly what happened. Since anger often leads to exaggerated and unclear statements, one goal is to determine whether the offense was objectively minor, moderate, or severe. Did a friend gossip behind the client's back? Did the client's partner engage in a sexual transgression? Did the client's family member die as a result of a needless medical procedure? The client is led to consider how the offense, transgression, or injustice has objectively affected his or her life. Because offenses are complex, you may also want to have discussions about how the event may be related to shame and guilt as well as to anger and revenge and to even larger philosophical issues regarding the nature of the world, justice, or God, if that is relevant to the particular client.

Step 2. Developing the Motivation to Forgive

For this step, the goal is to help the client realize that continued rumination about the specifics of the event, along with the associated inflammatory thoughts, will likely lead to ongoing anger, distress, and personal unhappiness. Your goal, while you continue to validate the client's objective report about what happened, is to lead the client to consider alternatives to harboring bitterness:

Lorraine is a thirty-seven-year-old woman whose husband had a short affair at work about six months ago, when Lorraine had the flu and was constantly tired. He calls it a two-night fling, and she calls it a major betrayal. Lorraine's husband apologized, but Lorraine is still angry. She and her husband were high school sweethearts, and they have three children in their teens. Given the couple's long history, Lorraine wants to stay with her husband. She says she still loves him, but she continues to feel angry and bitter, and she repeatedly brings up the affair up to him. As a result, they argue and give each other the silent treatment.

At this step of the process, Lorraine might be asked to consider the following questions for the purpose of increasing her motivation to change:

- *How much time and effort do you devote to recalling what happened? How does that help you?*

- *On a scale of 0 (bad) to 10 (wonderful), where do you see this event?*

- *How do your anger and your desire for revenge help your marriage?*

- *What might happen if you stopped ruminating about your husband's behavior?*

- *If you were to decide, here and now, to forgive your husband, how might that decision benefit you?*

- *If you were to decide, here and now, to forgive your husband, how might that decision affect your eating, your sleep, and your relationships with friends and with other family members?*

- *If you were to decide, here and now, to forgive your husband, how might that decision affect your children?*

- *What might happen if your thoughts about getting even were to disappear?*

Although a goal here is to help the client decide to forgive and commit herself to forgiving, a yellow flag of caution should be raised—the client may be able to read your intention and thus feel "forced" to forgive. She may also feel pressure from religious and cultural mandates to forgive the person who has wronged her. This is a problem because true forgiveness develops only when the client sees it as a personal choice that she deliberately makes. At this point, her commitment to forgiveness may be strong or weak, but the goal is for her to see forgiveness as her own decision to take the path of letting go.

Step 3. Defining Forgiveness

When forgiving is first brought up, it may come across as a shocking concept for your client. You may hear reactions like these:

- How can I forgive him?

- Would *you* forgive in my situation?

- You must be crazy to think I could forgive her for what she did!

- Never!

- Why should I let him off the hook?

Each of these reactions suggests that the client does not understand what forgiving means. The best way to help the client understand is to differentiate forgiving from similar concepts, such as accepting and condoning. This short dialogue with Lorraine demonstrates that type of conversation:

Lorraine: It sounds like you just want me to let my husband off the hook—to just forget about the affair.

Practitioner: Actually, I want you to remember what happened. As a situation that occurred twice, it was legitimately disruptive to your marriage. He violated your trust. But I'd like to help you think about it less often. And when you do think about it, I'd like to help you be less upset.

Lorraine: It sounds like you want me to just accept the affair.

Practitioner: For me, acceptance means a kind of indifference, and a lack of motivation to make changes. That's not what I mean. Forgiveness means not repeatedly dwelling on the negative aspects of his behavior, and it means asking how the event might even lead to some kind of unexpected improvement in your marriage. That might happen if both of you discussed your marital expectations—if you sort of put them on the table for discussion.

Lorraine: I still don't understand. It almost sounds like I am supposed to excuse his behavior and consider it OK. I don't think it was OK. Just because they worked late at the office together, and just because she came on to him, that doesn't make it right.

Practitioner: I agree. You legitimately expected that he would resist her approach. So the fact that she began the affair is not an excuse. It doesn't give him a pardon. Again, I just want you to be less angry and aroused when you think about what happened, and to move toward a resolution. And let me say a little more. I'm not suggesting that you be neutral about the whole thing. You have a legitimate position. And I am not asking you to somehow justify what he did. Certainly you could make excuses for him. For example, you said they had to work late, and they took a break for dinner with wine, and it was the wine that led him to act impulsively. But making excuses is not the goal, either. And I am not just telling you to calm down. What I *am* doing is asking you to figure out a way to hold on to your desire for a good marriage, to remember what happened, and to see it for what it was—a regrettable act of infidelity. Now, here is the key. I'd like to help you do all of this while not becoming too emotionally charged—while not being angry, and while not thinking about getting even.

Lorraine: Why not?

Practitioner: It seems that you want the marriage to continue. You seem to want to spend the rest of your life with him. And you want the best for your children. Also, consider all the time you spend thinking about his behavior and feeling angry. How does that help?

Lorraine: I know it doesn't help us.

At this point. the practitioner might return to the series of questions listed in step 2.

Practitioner: Let me ask you a question. Given what we have been talking about, would you be willing to make a direct decision, today, to forgive him? Not to forget, condone, accept, or approve of his behavior, but be able to think about it, and talk to him about it, without getting too emotionally charged?

As you will discover, steps 2 and 3 (and even step 4, which we're about to discuss) often operate in tandem for a particular client.

Step 4. Understanding What May Have Influenced the Offender

Most clients think that human beings almost always act volitionally. They attribute the behavior of an offender to conscious, thoughtful intent. Again, consider Lorraine. If she were asked why her husband had his brief affair, her most likely answer would be something like, "I was sick with the flu and was not interested in sex for about two weeks. He wanted satisfaction, so he decided to follow her to the motel. That was it. He did what he wanted to do." Clients often make similar attributions involving an offender's purposeful awareness when an offender abuses his partner, for example, or when an adolescent steals money from a parent. But are such attributions correct? Is conscious volition always the explanation for an offender's transgression?

Most of us strongly believe that we always act consciously and intentionally. We say, for example, "My car has been acting up—I think I'll look for a new one today" or "I'm going to get one of those muffins I see in that bakery." But neuroscientists, industrial psychologists, and practitioners know that this is not a completely accurate picture. Our reasons for looking for a new car today, for buying a particular car, or for entering a bakery and buying a muffin often do not reside solely in our conscious awareness. Thoughtful, conscious choice plays only a small part in our decisions and actions:

- Neuroscientists think that conscious volition explains only 5 percent of our decisions, and they attribute most of what we do to brain functions and biological urges.

- Behavioral psychologists, to explain current behavior, look for habits that have been reinforced.

- Industrial psychologists regard behavior as determined by desires that often are not conscious, such as the desire to remain young. Therefore, when a buyer leaves an automobile showroom with a red convertible instead of a gray van, it's because convertibles and the color red signify youth, attractiveness, and sexuality, whereas a gray van does not.

And what causes us to buy a certain breakfast cereal? We may enter a supermarket with a conscious decision to buy a particular brand of cereal, but industrial psychologists know that we will ultimately make our choice as a function of the size, shape, and color of the box, or because of the price, or because a popular athlete has endorsed the product as healthy, or even because of the cereal's location in the store. (We often find that this example works well in an introductory discussion with clients about how most behavior is determined by factors that are not conscious; most clients will agree that the cost, packaging, and even the location of an item in a supermarket enters into their decision making, if not consciously.)

In the case of Lorraine's husband, the biological drive for sexual satisfaction certainly would have contributed to his actions, as would the disinhibiting effects of the wine he had at dinner. Apart from simple, conscious volition, here are some possible explanations for his behavior:

- Brain functions

- Genetics

- Behavior encouraged by evolution

- Reinforced personal habits

- Behavior modeled by peers

- Pressure from social groups

- Cultural norms

- Being at the right place (his office) at the wrong time (when he was susceptible to being seduced by his female colleague)

- Socially reinforced thinking patterns ("I can get away with it—it's not really hurting anyone" or "It will just be a brief fling—casual fun, not a big deal")

And, again, his conscious volition would have played only a small part in his choice to have the affair. His behavior, like the behavior of most other people, was multiply determined, and its causes were mostly out of his conscious awareness.

In short, then, the goal at this step of the process is to help the client see the world from another perspective, starting with an understanding of the biological and environmental forces that may have influenced the transgressor or offender to act as he or she did. Again, however, this can be very difficult, since most clients do a lot of blaming, thus indicating that they think transgressors and offenders act with conscious, voluntary forethought and malicious intent.

Two ways to help the client in step 4 are to explain human drive states and to offer exercises in perspective taking. In the following dialogue, for example, the practitioner explains the difference between wants and needs:

Practitioner:	When a person like your husband has an affair, we say he is reacting to his drive. For us, that's a technical term.
Lorraine:	Yeah. I think he was somehow driven to do it.
Practitioner:	We break drives down into two categories—needs and wants. Needs are drives that must be fulfilled. It's like breathing or urinating. You can't just say, "I think I won't breathe today" or "I will wait until tomorrow to urinate." In contrast, wants are desires that can be postponed or ignored completely. You might want a new watch or a new sweater, but you can wait until next week or next month to get it. And sex is kind of in the middle between needs and wants. We will have to figure out how much of your husband's behavior was a response to a biological need like urinating, and how much was just something he wanted to do.
Lorraine:	I haven't thought about it that way before.
Practitioner:	Thinking about the difference between needs and wants, in percentages, how much of his behavior do you think was a need, and how much was a want?
Lorraine:	Maybe 20 percent was driven by a need.
Practitioner:	Okay. So he had some degree of choice for 80 percent of his behavior, and 20 percent of his behavior was beyond his control. Maybe you can be angry about the 80 percent but give him some forgiveness for the 20 percent. Would you be willing to think of the situation that way?
Lorraine:	That's certainly a different way of looking at what he did. I'll have to think about that a bit.

Here, the practitioner is just introducing the idea that some behavior is out of conscious control. And the client can always offer a retort to the idea that volitional control accounts for only a small portion of behavior. She might say, for example, "He could have waited to have sex with me" or "He could have satisfied himself"—and that's okay. At this point, the practitioner is just trying to introduce the fundamental idea that we don't have 100 percent conscious and voluntary control over our behavior.

Step 5. Working Toward Empathy and Compassion

In this step, the client is helped to understand the offender's life, with the goal of viewing the person differently, and with the practitioner's hope for a positive change in the client's affect. This reframing may involve seeing the offender from a new perspective—as a person who is a fallible human being and not motivated by evil intentions. As practitioners, we have found that a client usually begins to *think* differently about an offender before *feeling* more positively and letting go of anger and motivations for revenge.

Other goals will now include the client's working toward a degree of empathy and compassion for the offender. Of course, this shift to thinking and feeling differently cannot be forced on the client. It often takes time, and some clients who struggle to come to terms with severe offenses (abuse, assault, murder, and so forth) will only develop a lessening of bitterness and will never fully forgive. That is why it is so important for us to understand cases in which full forgiveness does develop, as it did for Eva Kor, the Holocaust survivor, and for Walt, whose son was murdered. Eventually such cases will lead us to better understand the forgiving process, and to develop more powerful techniques for helping clients.

STRUCTURED PERSPECTIVE TAKING

One technique that is useful at this point is structured perspective taking. Because clients understandably tell us about offenses from their own perspectives, it's from their perspectives that we first ask clients to tell us their stories. Clients are usually well practiced in doing so, and in most cases this will be easy for them. Consider the case of Francisco (we'll have more to say about him in chapter 15):

> *Francisco was a thirty-nine-year-old salesperson. His colleague, Merla, was taking sales leads off his desk.*
>
> *"She's such a bitch," Francisco said. "She knows she's hurting my chances of making a sale. What kind of person would do that? She's a real snake. She probably learned to do that from her family. They are probably all a bunch of untrustworthy losers. I'm done with her!"*
>
> *The practitioner gave Fernando this instruction: "I understand what happened and why you became angry. I'd like you to retell your story, but this time I'd like you to imagine that you are Merla. Tell me the story from her perspective—from her point of view, speaking as Merla. I know that you might not have all the facts, but do the best you can. And as you tell the story, I'd like you to make sure you answer four questions in your role as Merla. First, why might you, Merla, have taken Francisco's sales leads? Second, what might you have been thinking as you took his leads? Third, what factors in your life might have influenced you to take his leads? And, fourth, what were you feeling and thinking after you took his leads?"*
>
> *As co-workers, Francisco and Merla knew each other fairly well, and so even though Francisco was angry, he knew that Merla needed money because her car had*

broken down. Taking Merla's perspective, he said, "Francisco often comes in to work a little late. He has a lot of sales leads on his desk, and I could sure use some of them. He's a nice guy, but I need money to replace my old car. I'm going to take a few of his leads. I know that's not right, but I need the money more than he does. I'm feeling pretty bad about doing this. Maybe someday I'll be able to make it up to him. I'm very uncomfortable about this, but I have to do it."

The actual questions that you ask your client to consider will vary according to several factors, including the relationship between the offender and your client, the nature of the transgression, and so on. In any case, the questions themselves are intended to help the angry client understand some of the factors that led to the offensive behavior. It's also true that you may not quickly hear a retelling of the story that indicates your client's understanding of the offender's position. Nevertheless, we have found that our clients, with some creative prompting, begin to see other elements of their stories and start to broaden their views regarding why an offender acted the way he or she did. This is actually what Walt did, without professional help, as he began to forgive Mike, his son's murderer. Walt saw Mike's aggressive act not as something perpetrated by an evil man but as the outcome of a rough upbringing and the need for money to satisfy a drug habit. This change in perspective help set the stage for Walt to forgive Mike and become his friend.

Once a change in perspective has been achieved, the client is helped to respond to the question "What kind of person am I?" The client is asked to consider whether it is useful to be angry and bitter when the offense was not perpetrated on the basis of the offender's volitional, evil intent. The client considers—again, with your guidance—the value of letting go. In some cases, if the circumstances are appropriate, reconciliation may also be considered.

GIVING SOMETHING OF VALUE TO THE WRONGDOER

If the timing seems right, you can suggest that your client give a gift to the offender. This suggestion may constitute another moment of shock. Your goal here is to explain that your client, by continuing to harbor bitterness, is choosing to remain in the role of victim. In contrast, by giving a gift, your client can take control and move into the driver's seat. The client is also led to understand that a gift may be something very small, such as a statement made in your office to express the client's wish for the offender to move forward to a better life, or something larger and more tangible, such as a positive holiday card or email sent to the offender. The client's good wishes can be conveyed even if the offender has died. For example, we asked a fifty-six-year-old client how she might forgive her verbally abusive father, who had died three years earlier. Although she still harbored significant bitterness toward him, she agreed to write a letter of forgiveness and to place it at his gravesite. She then reported a significant reduction in her angry ruminations. The idea of giving a gift may be difficult for a client to understand. But forgiveness is not just a process that takes place in people's minds. It requires some type of *action*. When clients have taken this step, we've heard them say, "If I'm strong enough to give something to the person who harmed me, then I'm no longer a victim."

Step 6. Expanding and Deepening Forgiveness

In this step, with the practitioner's support or by themselves, clients find increased meaning in their suffering, reduce their negative affect even further, and, hopefully, discover renewed purpose in life. These changes occur through continued forgiveness work.

Many people who were victims of abuse and neglect have made public statements about their history in order to teach others or work to improve the lives of others and free themselves from continued victimhood:

- Eva Kor developed Children of Auschwitz Nazi Deadly Lab Experiments Survivors (CANDLES) and, as mentioned earlier, founded a Holocaust museum and educational center in addition to writing books and making films about her time as a prisoner of the Nazis, and she has regularly taken groups to Auschwitz to show them, in person, what life in a concentration camp was like.

- On the basis of his own experience in the Nazi death camps, Viktor Frankl, a psychiatrist, developed Logotherapy, a school of psychotherapy that emphasizes the importance of finding meaning in existence (Frankl, 1959).

- Primo Levi, a Jewish chemist and also an Auschwitz survivor, deepened his liberation from the past by writing such books as *The Periodic Table* (Levi, 1984), a collection of autobiographical stories covering everything from Levi's childhood to life in and after Auschwitz.

- In South Africa in the 1990s, a partial goal of the Truth and Reconciliation Commission (http://www.justice.gov.za/Trc) was the development of forgiveness so that the country could move beyond the atrocities of apartheid. Perpetrators who came before the commission and admitted their wrongdoing were granted amnesty from punishment.

- In 1967, as a navy pilot, John McCain was shot down over Hanoi, stabbed by his initial captors, and denied medical care for his wounds, which left him with lifelong disabilities. He then spent five and a half years in North Vietnamese prison camps, where he endured dysentery along with severe torture, routine beatings, and long-term solitary confinement. After North and South Vietnam were reconciled, McCain, who became a US senator, worked to restore diplomatic relations between the United States and Vietnam, and the two countries became allies. McCain publicly forgave his former captors and then made several trips to Vietnam (Danner, 2018).

Takeaway Messages and Tools

In this chapter, we have presented a six-step intervention model for helping angry clients forgive the offenses and transgressions of others. We all suffer from a variety of life events in which unfair, unexpected, and unwanted actions are taken against us. Although anger, bitterness, and the desire for revenge may result, the real goal in life is to move forward and be as happy as possible. Fortunately, there are many ways to move forward, including the interventions presented here. Many minor transgressions also resolve themselves with time, and even a relatively severe transgression, with significant anger and bitterness, may be resolved without professional assistance, although that resolution occurs over a longer time.

But, sadly, many angry clients hold on to their anger and their ruminations along with their desire to seek revenge. In these cases, specific forgiveness interventions can be considered, including those presented in this chapter, but clients may not have thought of this option, and they may bristle when forgiveness is first mentioned. One way to broach the subject is to provide them with client information sheet 11.1, included at the end of this chapter and downloadable from www.newharbinger.com/42877.

Anger, no matter what its objective trigger may be, is often associated with strong urges to act, usually against the source of the transgression. But such impulsive urges usually lead to nothing but more distress. Therefore, in chapter 12, we turn to an examination of urge reduction strategies.

CLIENT INFORMATION SHEET 11.1. Forgiveness as an Antidote to Anger, Bitterness, and the Desire for Revenge

Have you been lied to? Cheated on? Wrongly accused? Rejected? Abused?

After these kinds of transgressions, people often harbor anger and resentment for years. They believe that anger, bitterness, grudge holding, and a desire for revenge are appropriate reactions. They mentally review the situation that led to their anger, dwell on how wrong the other person was, and believe that the other person should somehow pay for the distress that was caused. The offended person sees no other option.

But this is not a healthy situation. Rather than enjoying the present, the offended person is living in the past and staying in the role of victim.

How long do you have to suffer with anger because of past negative events? To some extent, it's up to you. Of course, it would be unwise to just ignore the past injustices that led you to suffer. But current anger and bitterness are not useful. They lead to ruminative thoughts, bodily stress, sleep disturbances, heart problems, lack of trust, and other forms of life disruption.

Forgiveness education can be the first step in moving forward from the prison of the past. It involves the development of a clear and thoughtful differentiation between the healthy response of letting go and giving up the role of victim, on the one hand, and continuing, on the other hand, to believe that only persistent condemnation and retribution will make you feel better.

Forgiveness education gives you the power to control your own feelings, thoughts, and behavior. Forgiveness itself means living in the present, developing an understanding of what caused the other person to act offensively, and perhaps even understanding that this person was also a victim of life circumstances.

Forgiveness is a healing process that takes time. Ask your practitioner to help you understand why forgiveness is *not* the same as these actions and attitudes:

Accepting the offender's behavior

Excusing or condoning what the offender did

Just taking a neutral position regarding the offense that was committed

Forgetting about the offense

Justifying why the offender acted the way he or she did

Simply calming down or agreeing to a truce

Consider the words of Louise L. Hay, the late motivational author: "Forgiveness is for yourself because it frees you. It lets you out of that prison you put yourself in."

Discuss the benefits of forgiveness with your practitioner.

Howard Kassinove, PhD, and Raymond Chip Tafrate, PhD

PART 6

Interventions to Alter Internal Experiences and Urges

CHAPTER 12

Overcoming Impulsive Urges and Increasing Tolerance for Distress

Look before you leap.

—Traditional proverb

There are dangers in moving too fast, without thoughtfulness. Impulsiveness can have bad effects. Rash actions can lead to negative and unfortunate behavioral, cognitive, and emotional anger-oriented outcomes.

In this chapter, we again recognize the reality that life often consists of betrayals, disappointments, neglect, cheating, lying, and other forms of nastiness. In such situations, there is both cognitive and bodily arousal. Increases in heart rate, sweating, and hyperalertness may be attached to cognitions such as *I can't believe this is happening* or *I'm feeling really agitated* or *I'm not just going to take this*. Clients, recognizing their own bodily arousal and low-frustration-oriented thoughts, often show a hasty, immediate, impulsive urge to act. Indeed, angry clients often react on autopilot to negative situations. They behave speedily and nonthoughtfully, calling on previously reinforced provocative and vengeance-based responses. At the specific moment when they perceive an anger trigger, the urge to act kicks in. They don't even try for open-mindedness and don't slow down enough to think about the consequences of their anger-driven actions.

This commonly occurs in cases of intimate partner violence. For example, an angry, abusive woman (or man) may perceive the action of her (or his) partner as unwanted and intolerable. The partner may have interacted with a co-worker, verbally disagreed with the client about how to correct a misbehaving child, failed to make dinner, not kept the home organized, or refused a sexual approach. The client's negative response may be immediate and can include anything from a verbal put-down to a physical assault. The abuser acts impulsively, calling on a desire to be in control of the relationship as well as on the belief that the partner's disagreement or disobedience is intolerable. In fact, such individuals may see any perceived aversive behavior by others as unbearable.

This kind of reaction also occurs in cases of road rage. A client develops an instant sense of agitation if another driver follows too closely, drives too slowly, or cuts the client off. This reaction is thoughtlessly immediate and may include honking, glaring, forcing the other car off the road, or engaging in a physical altercation.

Several causes of these kinds of angry, explosive patterns have been hypothesized:

- Genetic and physiological factors, such as problems with the neurotransmitter serotonin

- Modeled behavior at home, such as past or current exposure to parents' or siblings' explosive anger

- Experiences of physical or emotional trauma during the formative years

Regardless of the exact etiology, an automated schema leading to anger arousal is generated; it is coupled with a lack of thoughtfulness, and there is an immediate urge to act.

When Clients Are Angry, Encourage Them to Slow Down

In this chapter, we are mostly talking about a time dimension in which reactions come about too quickly for thoughtful evaluation, with the result that anger and dysfunctional, quasi-automatic behavior emerges. The proverb "Look before you leap" is a way of saying that too little time between a perceived aversive stimulus and an angry reaction is often a recipe for disaster. We use the phrase "on autopilot" to suggest that anger and aggressive reactions to perceived aversive stimuli often occur without forethought and are typically based on a client's learning history. Such impulsive actions may occur in conjunction with a number of behaviors, situations, characteristics, sensations, and tendencies:

- Alcohol intake or drug use

- Fatigue

- Stress

- A feeling of being overwhelmed by life's hassles

- Sleep deprivation

- Hunger

- Aggressive music

- Emotional and behavioral problems like post-traumatic stress disorder or generalized anxiety disorder

- A sensation-seeking personality

- Suicidal behavior

- Characteristics of antisocial or borderline personality disorder

- An overall tendency toward impulsiveness (in shopping, for example, or in gambling or sex)

Impulsivity certainly has some positive aspects, of course. For example, the gut impulse to duck and raise your hands when an object is hurled at you may very well save your life. You may also know that when you're taking a difficult multiple-choice test, the first answer that comes to mind is often the correct one; in that situation, making a snap decision is typically better than pondering the answer, since you may not be able to finish the test in time unless you make some snap decisions. Top professional athletes also make snap decisions on the field. But the impulsive decisions of good test-takers and top athletes are essentially nonconscious, learned reactions that have developed over years, whereas the snap decisions of abusers and road ragers pay off, if they do, only in the short run. Spouses, children, and work colleagues may comply with an impulsive, screaming partner, parent, or boss, but relationships are damaged in the long run. With proper interventions, however, many maladaptive, impulsive reactions can be modified or completely unlearned.

Why do people respond to urges so quickly, impulsively, quasi-instinctively, and without forethought? One reason is that the human brain evolved in such a way that we tend to take the quickest and most efficient route to a decision, since there is sometimes little opportunity to consider the available choices in conflict situations. The brain slows down when we stop to consider too much information about the consequences of our actions, and so in conflict situations we use rules of thumb (heuristics) to negotiate the social environment. Simplicity, according to Gigerenzer and Gaissmaier (2011), is an evolutionary adaptation to uncertainty. If short-term accuracy is the goal, then automated impulsivity is better than thoughtful reflection in some situations. Gladwell (2005) has referred to intuitive acting as "thinking without thinking," and he notes that this process can be both helpful and unhelpful because it narrows the range of the variables to be considered in making a decision.

One heuristic is called the *recognition* rule of thumb. Here is a situation in which it would be unhelpful. Imagine that you are a contestant on a game show where you can earn a million dollars by answering eight out of ten questions correctly, and that there is a time limit for you to respond after the host says, "For each pair of cities, identify which one has more inhabitants." The choices are as follows:

- Pune or Rome

- Shenzhen or Mexico City

- New York City or Kinshasa

- Rio de Janeiro or Harbin

- Guangzhou or Paris

- Athens or Surat

- El Paso or New Orleans

- Austin or Boston

- Taos or Henderson

- Newark or Bakersfield

Many people who live in the Western hemisphere pick Rome, Mexico City, New York City, Rio de Janeiro, Paris, Athens, New Orleans, Boston, Taos, and Newark, since these are the more recognizable choices. Yet the correct answers are Pune, Shenzhen, Kinshasa, Harbin, Guangzhou, Surat, El Paso, Austin, Henderson, and Bakersfield. The recognition rule of thumb would serve you poorly in this situation.

In other situations, heuristics are helpful. Less is often more, and simple rules of thumb such as "Never hit your child" or "Minimize conflicts at work" or "On an academic test, go with the first answer that comes to mind, and leave it alone" can often guide behavior in positive ways. Clients who need to manage their anger often need to relearn rule-of-thumb reactions to provocative and challenging life situations.

But it's also crucial for clients to learn to go beyond rules of thumb, since doing so will help them make slower, more thoughtful choices about their behavior. Slowing their reactions also helps clients actually experience their angry feelings and avoid moving straight toward an outward, antagonistic verbal response or physical aggression. According to Gardner and Moore (2014, 37), "The problem is not actually the experience of anger, even if that anger is incredibly intense. Rather, the real concern is the maladaptive need to inhibit the experience of anger, and/or maladaptive efforts to avoid/escape from the experience of anger." In other words, they believe that it is better to help clients *experience* their anger, accept it, and behave in more adaptive ways than to directly help clients *reduce* their anger. We agree that what can be problematic is a client's lack of tolerance for the experience of feeling angry, followed by the client's rapid and dysfunctional expression of anger; that is, we think the problem is emotion dysregulation. But whereas Gardner and Moore focus on building awareness and acceptance of anger, we focus on directly minimizing angry reactions to aversive situations. In the end, though, there is overlap between our approaches; helping clients slow down and get off autopilot will go a long way toward helping them improve their lives.

Urge-driven impulsive reactions become dysfunctional when we disregard rational consideration of the shorter- and longer-term consequences of our behavior. The truth is that we don't spend most of our lives taking multiple-choice tests or competing on game shows; in most interpersonal situations, we really do have time to be thoughtful, and life will be better if we wait. When spur-of-the-moment reactions lead to harmful personal, family, or vocational problems, intervention is called for to slow reactions down.

Adolescents and Brain Biology

As we saw in chapter 1, the prefrontal cortex is associated with executive functioning, such as predicting the risks and rewards of our actions. Our prefrontal cortex reaches full development when we reach the age of about twenty-five. As a result, those brain structures (such as the amygdala) that account for impulsive, emotional reactions can operate relatively unchecked until the prefrontal cortex is ready to do its job. Therefore, the types of impulsive, reckless decisions that come from brain immaturity are more likely to be seen in adolescents and younger adults; recall Shakespeare's *Romeo and Juliet*, with its story of an impulsive teenager who heedlessly kills his paramour's cousin and goes on to kill himself, even though his death could have been averted if he had simply waited long enough to acquire a true picture of his situation. Unfortunately, our angry and aggressive young clients may be the impulsive Romeos of the mental health landscape. All of this suggests that behavioral interventions for anger management may work better as clients get older. This is well known among mental health practitioners, who often comment that adolescents are more challenging to work with than adults. And yet there are marked individual differences related to urges and impulsivity in clients, and some younger clients may profit more from intervention than some clients who are older. This means that you will have to use your personal judgment about which anger management interventions are best suited to a particular client.

In any case, here is the basic lesson to be taught to clients: learning to go slow, and even to occasionally be nonresponsive, can take you a long way toward emotional happiness. As noted by Yutang (cited in Agel & Glanze, 1987, 162, 10), "Besides the noble art of getting things done, there is the noble art of leaving things undone," since "the wisdom of life consists in the elimination of non-essentials."

Interventions for Slowing Down Angry Reactions

As a first step, it will be useful to put the label "impulsive" on the table. Some angry clients do see themselves as reacting too quickly by flying off the handle, and they readily admit to being hotheads. But others tend to minimize or justify such reactions. Therefore, a first step for them is to recognize their impulsive behavior.

A second step is to assist clients in identifying the most common stimuli or triggers that are likely to lead to impulsive anger on their part (refer to figure 3.1). The Anger Episode Record may be helpful in logging the people, places, and situations that evoke a client's impulsive anger.

A third step is to discuss the bodily or personal vulnerabilities that increase the probability of impulsive anger (see "Pre-Anger Lifestyle Issues" in chapter 3). These may include fatigue, hunger, job hassles, sleep deprivation, or just a feeling of being unappreciated. A meal or a nap may be a quick fix for some kinds of situational anger.

A fourth step is to have a client review the shorter- and longer-term consequences of his or her impulsive reactions. Some short-term consequences, such as others' compliance with a client's demands, reinforce the client's angry behavior. In cases where a client's anger reactions produce compliance from others ("My employees seem to work harder when I come down on them"), it's useful to focus on the longer-term effects that the client's anger is having on his or her relationships.

But none of these four steps is a true fix for impulsive anger. Instead, interventions that slow reactions down, and that can be practiced in imagination and in vivo, are most likely to yield beneficial results. We suggest that you consider two possible interventions that can be geared to slowing anger reactions down: *mindfulness meditation* and *progressive muscle relaxation*.

Mindfulness Meditation

In recent years, the proponents of various popular forms of meditation have made claims that their approaches can increase happiness while reducing anxiety, chronic pain, depression, stress, disordered eating, borderline personality symptoms, gambling, medical problems like asthma and arthritis, and so forth. Kabat-Zinn (1994) has described one such approach—mindfulness meditation, often simply called *mindfulness*—as a process of purposefully and nonjudgmentally paying attention to the present moment. This kind of meditation may consist of a mental scan of one's body, a sitting meditation, yoga, or a walking meditation. Other writers, such as Goyal et al. (2014), have not found convincing evidence for the clinical effectiveness of mindfulness. In addition, Wampold, Mondin, Moody, Stich, and Hyun-nie (1997) have noted that many nonspecific factors in this approach, including the practitioner's enthusiasm and expectations of success, may account for its outcomes. As a result, there have been calls for research using active control conditions to better answer the question of mindfulness's efficacy.

We do not want to get into the question of whether mindfulness works. There are too many complexities in that question. Besides, procedures in the mindfulness genre were never meant to solve health-related problems. Practitioners of mindfulness understand that pain is a natural consequence of illness and aging, and they make no claims to directly reduce pain; rather, they believe that mindfulness can reduce the needless *suffering* that often accompanies pain. Therefore, they use acceptance and related procedures to help people work on reducing their excessive focus on pain. Readers who are interested in an in-depth presentation of the issues surrounding mindfulness are referred to the October 2015 issue of *American Psychologist*.

Our goal here is to present mindfulness as an outgrowth of other philosophies and procedures, and to note that one of its central features is the purposeful bringing of attention, focus, and appreciation to the present moment, without evaluation. This feature tends to slow angry clients' reactions down, since clients are not engaged in such future-oriented thoughts as *I wonder if he will ever become more caring* or *I can see bad things happening to us* or *This is going to land us in court.* Nor do clients focus on past-oriented thoughts like *This has been going on for too long—I should have recognized the problem long ago* or *Anger is part of my upbringing—it's how we deal with conflict in my family.* In contrast to future- and past-oriented ruminations, a mindful perspective entails living in the current moment and appreciating what is happening now, even if things were bad in the past. The goal is not to learn to eradicate such thoughts; instead, the goal is to make rational decisions and respond to those thoughts with different behavior. There is, of course, much that is positive about recalling the past and imagining the future, but clients of all sorts do this far too often and thereby miss opportunities to live in the present.

Mindfulness as a psychotherapeutic intervention emerged in part from the 1950s-era study and popularity of Zen Buddhism, or simply Zen, as it was often called. Zen, considered an antiauthoritarian philosophy and practice, focused on experiencing the world as it "really is." Zen purported to be a way of gaining access to the "true" world and moving beyond a dichotomous conception of right and wrong. Older readers will recall that the 1950s were a time when citizens were expected to conform to family- and gender-role norms, to go to work and produce, and to keep the gross national product rising through consumption and the constant purchasing of new products. In a sense, the 1950s were a time of "shoulds." This rigidity led to the existential problems and spiritual concerns that were said, in the following decade, to be addressed by Zen. Psychotherapists of the 1960s questioned the medical model of mental health, wherein anxiety, depression, and other problems were considered illnesses to be cured. Zen practitioners replaced that model with one that focused on the emptiness of living in a society where happiness was supposed to come from conformity to rigidly prescribed roles and from the acquisition of tangible goods. Indeed, a phrase of the era, distasteful to many of the younger generation, was "He who has the most toys at the end, wins." It represented a Western way of thinking and was antithetical to Eastern traditions that focused on values rather than on consumption. The psychoanalyst Karen Horney, among others, thought Zen was a good model for the kind of nonjudgmental listening that was central to psychoanalytic practice.

The 1960s also saw the popularization of LSD, a hallucinogenic and reputedly mind-expanding drug originally synthesized in the late 1930s at the Sandoz Laboratories in Switzerland. This was also the era of transcendental meditation (TM) and the so-called relaxation response, conceived as antithetical to the fight-or-flight response. TM, promoted as a quick, easy form of meditation, challenged the notion that reaching a mindful state had to take a long time. As in Zen, the goal in TM was to produce a person who was more peaceful, creative, and intelligent, and who did not respond impulsively to the adversities of life.

Scientists eventually began to look for objective, measurable changes that could be attributed to TM practice. Some studies associated TM with changes in resting heart rate, oxygen consumption, and electroencephalogram patterns. These findings suggested that TM could lead to something like a new state of consciousness, but they had little effect on mental health practice until Herbert Benson, a cardiology professor at Harvard University, began to investigate the hypothesis that TM could lead to a voluntary reduction in blood pressure, to the relaxation response, and perhaps to a reduction in heart disease. Regarding the relaxation response, Benson claimed that it could be induced through the simple chanting of any word that was used as a mantra, and that this response could be produced without recourse to any kind of religious or spiritual tradition or explanation. In this way, the practice of mindfulness began to be separated from the Eastern religions. A person did not have to become a Buddhist, wear special robes, or give up worldly possessions in order to profit from the practice of mindfulness.

In 1979, Jon Kabat-Zinn set up a self-care training program at the University of Massachusetts Medical Center to help patients suffering from chronic pain. He named his program Mindfulness-Based Stress Reduction (MBSR), and he worked to distance it from Buddhist and so-called New Age or mystical philosophies. It was important for him to do this, since he hoped to establish mindfulness practices in a medical facility. MBSR was a blend of different philosophies and traditions. As noted earlier, it is based on the idea that excessive suffering is associated with physical illness, and that this suffering is caused by unwise affective and attitudinal components that are brought to the illness. Mindfulness practitioners believe that if these components can be recognized and accepted, then the medical condition, even though it will still exist, will be less associated with anxiety, anger, depression, guilt, self-criticism, and catastrophizing.

Mindfulness, then, is basically a state of active, open attention to the present moment, with little dwelling on the past or the future. When clients learn to be mindful, they simply observe their present thoughts and feelings from a distance. It's as if they were in a helicopter looking down on themselves. Their thoughts and feelings are not judged to be good or bad. Rather, clients are awakened to the current moment, which they are taught to radically accept. At its root, mindfulness practice teaches clients to experience things as they are, unbound by judgments, opinions, or the desire to change things to better suit expectations.

Many people's meditation practice is informed by the Buddhist idea that one cause of suffering is attachment to objects, ideas, and emotions like anger. Attachments are colored by judgments, opinions, and the desire to change the external world. Desire itself, or an attachment to desire, is cited as another cause of suffering. Not accepting things as they are, and insisting that things be different, can be a cause of significant emotional distress. This outlook is similar to the ideas underlying the common practice of cognitive behavioral therapists who try to reduce the "shoulds" that reflect a client's insistence on making his or her world different from what it actually is.

Many of these ideas are unfamiliar to and thus difficult for people living in Western societies. We certainly are not trying to convert the readers of this book to Eastern philosophies or religions, and we hope that you will not try to convert your clients. Rather, we simply want to help you embrace a fundamental idea that we think is helpful in efforts to teach clients to slow down and look before they leap into anger and aggression. It is useful to live in the moment without judgment, appreciate the current moment, and decrease attachment to ideal images or demands for perfection. The actions and attitudes likely to increase anger and distress are living in the past or the future; evaluating and judging friends, family members, and others; and being attached to the idea that you are right and they are wrong. When a client learns and practices mindfulness, her mindfulness practice counteracts her autopilot responses to unwanted situations; thus, mindfulness is likely to enrich her life and decrease her tendency to become angry. But, as we've just implied, mindfulness does require learning and practice. This means that reading a book is not enough. Mindfulness, just like any other new behavior, is something that clients have to understand before they can practice it—by themselves, with others, or with you. Here, repetition and reinforcement are key. A good way to begin is to have clients watch some videos, which can then be discussed in session. You may be working with clients of different backgrounds, ages, and levels of intellectual and linguistic sophistication, and so you would be wise to match your recommendations to your clients' characteristics. Here are a few videos that we recommend:

- *The Healing Power of Mindfulness* (2011). This two-hour lecture presented at Dartmouth University by Jon Kabat-Zinn, founder of the Mindfulness-Based Stress Reduction program at the University of Massachusetts, is useful for clients who want to learn about the elements of a mindfulness experience (https://www .youtube.com/watch?v=_If4a-gHg_I).

- *Meditation for Working with Difficulties* (2014). This is a seven-minute video by Diana Winston, director of mindfulness education at the UCLA Mindful Awareness Research Center (https://www.youtube.com/watch?v=XInJoYvy_ew).

- *9 Attitudes* (2015). In this twenty-six-minute video, Jon Kabat-Zinn talks about the nine central attitudes of mindfulness that can be used in daily life (https:// www.youtube.com/watch?v=2n7FOBFMvXg).

- *Why Mindfulness Is a Superpower* (2015). This is a three-minute animated explanation of mindfulness, using driving anger as an example (https://www.youtube .com/watch?v=w6TO2g5hnT4).

- *Mindfulness for Beginners* (2017). This three-hour-plus video presents an opportunity to learn about and practice mindfulness with Jon Kabat-Zinn (https:// www.youtube.com/watch?v=FgweXc5G2xc).

Progressive Muscle Relaxation

Progressive muscle relaxation (PMR) has been around for a long time. PMR is used for learning to monitor and control the state of muscular tension in the body. It was developed in the late 1920s by an American physician, Edmund Jacobson, and was originally a long and laborious procedure. Over the years, Jacobson's cumbersome version of PMR was reduced to a procedure that can be completed in about twenty minutes and is often used for anxiety management. Since part of anxiety is tense muscles, PMR is useful for anxious clients. In this instance, anxiety stimuli are paired with a state of relaxation, with the goal of reducing reactivity to the feared stimuli. It works very well, and the same model can be applied to anger. Anger-evoking stimuli (such as mental images of friends talking negatively about a client, or the client being insulted or ignored) can be paired with a state of muscle relaxation in order to reduce immediate and excessive reactivity to the anger-evoking trigger.

But PMR involves a few caveats. The Internet is full of sites purporting to show how to do PMR, but they typically do not discuss PMR's limitations. For example, a site may sell PMR recordings for children, but it is unlikely that these recordings will have the same effect on children that we see in adults. With an adult, as the PMR procedure goes along, you will often see spontaneous sighs and other signs of relaxation. Some adult clients even fall asleep during PMR. Also, human beings vary quite a bit in their capacity to respond to PMR training, and they may or may not accept or want to practice it. Therefore, PMR may not work as well with obsessive and compulsive adults, with people who are highly suspicious, with people who suffer from major mental illness, and so forth. For the majority of adult clients, however, PMR is very effective and acceptable.

For angry clients, we usually pair relaxation with visual imagery. The goal is to have clients imagine one or more of their anger triggers while in a relaxed state. We also suggest to clients that, as they practice PMR, they not react to their anger triggers as they normally would. Rather, clients are asked to take a moment to imagine their anger triggers and to recognize that these triggers are tolerable and do not have to be responded to. They are asked to live with their anger-inducing images for a moment and to experience them without flying off the handle. This is the part of PMR that involves distress tolerance. Clients are then asked to imagine engaging in more effective behavior, such as assertively asking for clarification about an unwanted event or just allowing a slow driver to continue being slow for a while.

There are three general steps for PMR as used in the office with an angry client:

1. The client gets as naturally comfortable as possible.

2. The client engages in the tension-relaxation contrasts that are central to PMR.

3. The client imagines having more distress tolerance and more acceptance of an unwanted event.

We begin by setting an expectation for change:

Practitioner: Today we are going to do progressive muscle relaxation, or PMR. The goal is to help you quickly learn to recognize and distinguish how it feels to have tense muscles, which are often part of anger, and how it feels to be in a state of complete muscular relaxation. PMR is quite easy to learn, and it's very effective. With practice, you will be able to bring about physical relaxation at the first signs of the muscle tension that accompanies your anger. This will also increase your overall feelings of calmness.

The client is then asked to relax as much as possible in his or her chair:

Practitioner: Let's begin by having you loosen any tight clothing [*tie, belt, top button of a shirt, and so forth*]. You can take off your glasses and set them on the table. If you want to, you can take off your shoes, too, and just settle comfortably into your chair. Now find a nice resting place for your hands. It would be best if you also closed your eyes, so you can focus all your attention on your muscles.

The main part of the PMR procedure, then, is to repeatedly do a series of tension-and-relaxation contrasts, and to give the expectation that relaxation is a voluntary action that can be called on at times when anger may emerge. Although the various muscle groups can be addressed in any order, we usually go from the arms and legs to the stomach and chest and then to the facial area. Clients often like to hear instructions in the voice of their practitioner, and so practitioner script 12.1, included at the end of this chapter and downloadable from www.newharbinger.com/42877, may be useful if you record it for your clients so that they can practice between sessions. Remember, PMR takes time, and multiple practice sessions will provide the greatest payoff for clients.

Some of your clients may have medical problems that prevent them from tensing some of their muscle groups, and it's wise to ask about that before beginning, so that your instructions can be modified and your client will not experience pain or other harm in a particular area. Remember to periodically intersperse messages to breathe deeply and slowly, since this enhances the process. As mentioned earlier, PMR proper usually requires about twenty minutes, and we hope you can learn the basic procedure by visiting www.newharbinger.com/42877. We also offer a visual demonstration of PMR, and of how we incorporate imagery into the procedure, in our video series *Anger Management in Counseling and Psychotherapy* at www.psychotherapy.net.

Although practitioners often have preferences and beliefs regarding which techniques are best, we hope that you will see the significant overlap between relaxation and mindfulness. In our opinion, the more you read about and review audio and video presentations about mindfulness and PMR, the more overlap you will see. In both procedures, the goal is to live in and experience the present moment. Both involve repeated, guided practice so that clients can learn to reach the desired relaxed state on their own. Meditators are asked to simply accept the present moment without judgment, whereas those engaging in PMR are told to focus on the difference between tense and relaxed muscles. In both procedures, clients are discouraged from dwelling on the past, fantasizing about the future, and engaging in evaluative thoughts. In both procedures, clients are actively practicing distress tolerance. They learn key skills for becoming nonreactive. Once the nonreactive state has been learned, it can be purposefully paired with relevant anger triggers. Through repeated practice, diminished reactivity to perceived aversive stimuli is ultimately transferred to the real world.

In one empirically supported intervention in which PMR was used with angry clients, Deffenbacher and McKay (2000) paired images of client-relevant aversive stimuli with relaxation in order to slow down impulsive actions. In some ways, this direct pairing is easy to do with PMR, but we recommend that imaginal exposure be introduced under your guidance. See practitioner script 12.2, where an imaginal scene of relaxation is paired with a typical trigger for road rage.

Progressive muscle relaxation has been part of our general toolbox for many years. In its application to angry clients, it has much to offer by way of helping slow down the process of reacting to aversive stimuli. Once the process is slowed, clients can develop new and more effective ways of reacting.

Takeaway Messages and Tools

The techniques presented in this chapter—mindfulness meditation and progressive muscle relaxation—are used to slow the action down and help your clients become more present in the moment so that they will not suffer serious losses by acting too quickly. In chapter 13, we present additional strategies to assist your clients in tolerating negative words and thoughts so that they can further reduce their impulsive urges to react.

PRACTITIONER SCRIPT 12.1. Instructions for Progressive Muscle Relaxation

You can use these instructions to make a personalized relaxation recording for your clients. Do not go too quickly through the following procedure. After each section, allow the time indicated in italics within the square brackets.

We recommend that you instruct your client to play the recording in a comfortable, quiet place away from your office, taking plenty of time and without worrying that the phone will ring or that another distraction will occur. The client can listen to the recording while sitting in a comfortable chair or while lying on a bed, a couch, or the floor. The client will also find it useful to remove his or her glasses, loosen his tie, open the top button of his or her shirt, and loosen any other tight clothing.

[START *recording here.*]

Close your eyes, sit quietly for a few seconds, and focus on smooth breathing.

[*Pause ten seconds.*]

Notice that you are in control. You can regulate yourself to breathe slowly, smoothly, and deeply.

[*Pause five seconds.*]

Good. You are doing very well.

[*Pause three seconds.*]

Now make fists with both of your hands, and feel the tension building in your lower arms, hands, and fingers. Focus on that tension, and silently describe the uncomfortable pulling sensations to yourself. That's what happens when you are angry. Okay, hold the tension.

[*Pause three to five seconds.*]

Now release the tension, and let your hands and arms relax. Focus on the warm, heavy, relaxed feelings in your hands, and notice the contrast with the tension. Just focus for a while on your relaxed hands, and continue to breathe slowly, smoothly, and deeply.

[*Pause three to five seconds.*]

Now bend your arms, and press both of your elbows firmly into your sides. While pressing your elbows inward, also flex your arm muscles. Notice the tension building up throughout your arms, shoulders, and back. Hold that tension.

[*Pause three to five seconds.*]

Okay. Now release your arms, and let them fall heavily to your sides. Focus on the heavy, warm, relaxed feelings in your arms, and continue to breathe slowly, smoothly, and deeply.

[*Pause three to five seconds.*]

Moving to your lower legs, flex your feet by trying to point your toes toward your nose. Notice the tension spreading through your feet, ankles, and calves. Hold the tension.

[*Pause three to five seconds.*]

Okay. Now release the tension in your lower legs, and focus on your sense of comfort as your lower legs become more relaxed. Continue to breathe slowly, smoothly, and deeply.

[*Pause five to ten seconds.*]

You are doing very well.

[*Pause three to five seconds.*]

Now build tension in your upper legs by pressing both your knees together and lifting your legs off your bed or chair. Focus on the tension in your thighs and the pulling sensations in your hips. Describe those uncomfortable feelings to yourself.

[*Pause three to five seconds.*]

Now release the tension, and let your legs fall slowly and heavily onto the bed or chair. Focus on letting go of all the tension in your legs, arms, and shoulders. Just let go. Breathe slowly, smoothly, and deeply.

[*Pause three to five seconds.*]

Now pull your stomach in toward your spine. Notice the tension in your stomach.

[*Pause three to five seconds.*]

Now voluntarily let your stomach relax. Breathe slowly, smoothly, and deeply, and focus on the relaxation you can produce in your stomach, in your legs, and in your arms and shoulders.

[*Pause three to five seconds.*]

Now take in a very deep breath, and hold it.

[*Pause ten to fifteen seconds, until some discomfort is likely.*]

Notice the tension in your expanded chest. Now slowly let the air out, and feel the tension gradually disappear. Notice that you can voluntarily relax your body, and you can breathe slowly, rhythmically, and deeply. And with each breath that you take, you can allow yourself to relax even more. Focus on relaxing and just letting go of all of your tension.

[*Pause five to ten seconds.*]

Now imagine that your shoulders are on strings and are being pulled up toward your ears. Feel the tension building in your shoulders, your upper back, and neck. Hold that tension.

[*Pause three to five seconds.*]

Okay. Now just let the tension go. Allow your shoulders to droop down. Let them droop down as far as they can go. Notice the difference between the feelings of tension and relaxation.

[*Pause three to five seconds.*]

Pull your chin down, and try to touch your chest with it. Notice the pulling and tension in the back of your neck.

[*Pause three to five seconds.*]

Now relax. Let go of the tension in your neck. Focus on letting your neck muscles relax. Let your arms and legs relax. Breathe slowly, rhythmically, and deeply.

[*Pause three to five seconds.*]

Now clench your teeth, and focus on the tension in your jaw. Feel the tight pulling sensation.

[*Pause three to five seconds.*]

Okay. Release. Allow your mouth to drop open, and relax all of the muscles around your face and jaw.

[*Pause three to five seconds.*]

Very good.

[*Pause three to five seconds.*]

Build up the tension in your forehead by forcing yourself to frown. Try to pull your eyebrows toward each other. Focus on the tension in your forehead.

[*Pause three to five seconds.*]

Now release. Smooth out all of the wrinkles, and let your forehead relax.

[*Pause three to five seconds.*]

At this point, allow your whole body to feel relaxed and heavy. Breathe deeply and rhythmically, and voluntarily relax your arms, legs, stomach, shoulder, and facial muscles. You are in control. Every time you breathe out, silently say the word "relax" to yourself, and imagine that you are breathing out all of the tension in your body. Breathe in and out deeply five times, say the word "relax" to yourself, and voluntarily let all of the tension disappear. Just let go and relax. I am going to stop talking for a while and allow you to enjoy the pleasant relaxed feeling you can let yourself have.

[*STOP recording here.*]

Howard Kassinove, PhD, and Raymond Chip Tafrate, PhD

PRACTITIONER SCRIPT 12.2. **Sample Imagery Scene**

Okay, now that you are relaxed, let's imagine you're driving on a two-lane highway where the speed limit is sixty miles per hour. Suddenly you come up to two cars in front of you that are both driving about forty miles per hour. They take up both lanes, and it is impossible to get beyond them.

At that moment you start to think, *Damn it! I'm in a rush*, and you notice your body start to get tense. You take a deep, calming breath in through your nose and let it out through your mouth, and you start to relax. Look at that car in front of you. Notice how slowly it is going. You also notice the color of the car and the sound of its engine. Surprisingly, you take another deep breath, and you say to yourself, *How interesting, I can tolerate not driving any faster right now. Although I usually get upset, I don't have to.* Then you take another deep, calming breath. All the tension seems to be draining out of your body.

You start to play with your jaw, raising and lowering your head until it takes no muscle tension to keep your jaw closed. The slow car is still in front of you, but you do not seem to be getting angry. This is a new experience for you. You find all the tension in your body floating away.

As you take another deep breath, the car finally pulls over to the other lane, and you can pass. You congratulate yourself on how well you did. Also, you realize that when bad things happen on the road, you can take calming breaths and relax and not become angry.

Now I'd like you to slowly open your eyes and return to this room.

Howard Kassinove, PhD, and Raymond Chip Tafrate, PhD

CHAPTER 13

Tolerating Negative Words and Thoughts: Barb Exposure

It is the mark of an educated mind to be able to entertain a thought without accepting it.

—Aristotle

Wouldn't it be great if harsh words would somehow just roll off our backs, like water off the backs of ducks? Instead, most of us respond to words as if they were fused with reality. And we respond to them immediately, without much thought. On the positive side, it's common to hear a parent say to a child, "You're the best." In response, the child may feel good and experience a rise in self-image. Or, in a serious dating relationship, a partner may say, "You're the greatest on the planet." Again, that may lead to good feelings. Of course, objectively, it's just an opinion. The partner is not really the greatest, since many other great people exist in the world.

There is an interesting puzzle here for us to consider. If your client were to hear "You are applesauce" from an acquaintance, it's likely there would be only confusion, and there would be no thought that the recipient had turned into that delightful mush that smells of apples. Certainly there would be no anger or rage. But if the same client were to hear from the acquaintance "You are a jerk," then all kinds of reactions might occur, ranging from internal seething to verbal lashing out at the person. Why does this happen? In this chapter, we present our ideas about this issue and suggest some possible interventions. We also focus on helpful tools to use when negative verbalizations, which are the most common triggers for most people, lead to anger and discord. As always, our goal is to provide you with usable SMART change strategies.

When we are faced with insults, or with statements that are otherwise demeaning, our responses almost always seem *reflexive*. Here's an example of a typical interaction:

Aspasia: You're an idiot.

Ben: *(in quick response)* Drop dead. You're an ass!

This kind of interaction happens so fast that it's easy to think of it as an automatic reflex. But it is not. A reflex is an involuntary, almost instantaneous, biologically based reaction to a stimulus. The term "reflex" usually refers to a motor reaction, as in the pupillary light reflex, when pupil size shrinks in response to light, or the knee jerk (patellar) reflex, which occurs when a physician hits your tendon just below the knee, or the sucking reflex, which occurs when anything touches the roof of an infant's mouth, or the corneal reflex of blinking both eyes when the cornea of either eye is touched. In reflexes, no learning is involved. Reflexes just occur naturally and are products of our evolutionary history. As biological responses, they work to our benefit.

But at some point in our evolutionary history, we developed the capacity for language. We began to associate objects with sounds. This led to huge advantages for our species, since we could now say, "Tomorrow I plan to eat a steak and a baked potato," and others knew what we were talking about. No one then or now thought or thinks that eating a steak and a baked potato turns us into a steak or a potato. We know (or at least we have an implicit cognitive theory about) what happens when we eat: food is taken in, it gets digested, and it provides nutrients and energy for us. Yet when someone calls us an idiot, all hell breaks loose. That's because we are now talking about a different set of learned cognitive appraisals and habits in response to sounds.

In the end, words are just sounds. It's our conditioning and the meanings we attach to these sounds that give us great joy ("You are brilliant, marvelous, and attractive") as well as significant psychological pain ("You are so stupid that I can't stand to be around you"). In view of this analysis, it would be best for treatment to focus both on changing an angry client's learned automatic reaction patterns and his or her deeper philosophies regarding how to deal with verbal negativity. Consider the case of Luther:

Luther, eighteen years old, had grown up in a struggling family. In many ways, he was trying to make a good life for himself. After having bounced around and attended different schools at various locations, he now lived with his grandmother and his twelve-year-old sister. When we saw him in our clinic, he was working in a fast-food restaurant and trying to earn his high school general-equivalency diploma.

Luther had a small group of friends in the neighborhood who often teased him. Specifically, they called him a pussy and a retard, since he admitted to having great difficulty with arithmetic, and he spoke very slowly. (He had spent years in a rural southern town where the speaking pace was much slower than that in his current urban environment.) On more than one occasion he had gotten into fistfights with other boys when he was called these names.

Two elements are significant here. First, Luther had learned to be immediately reactive to such provocations. Over time, and with repetition, he began to react impulsively and without forethought. And, second, he appeared to have developed something close to a cognitive philosophy regarding how to react to a perceived provocation. He told us, "You can't just take disrespect! You have to stand up for yourself and hit back." Unfortunately, Luther's conditioned reactions and implicit strategy had not worked well for him. He had wound up on probation and was sent to us for treatment.

The Barb Technique: Tolerating Negative Statements from Others

What might happen if we repeatedly exposed clients to some of the nasty verbalizations that they experience in their daily lives but also had them practice different reactions to these verbalizations? We tested that question by bringing into our university clinic forty-five men from the community between the ages of twenty and fifty-six (Tafrate & Kassinove, 1998). About half were married; the rest were single, divorced, separated, or cohabitating. They were mostly white, worked full time, and had a few years of college to their credit. They all admitted to having had personal problems with anger, and they had all scored higher than the 75th percentile on the Trait Anger Scale (Spielberger, 1999). About 66 percent had engaged in at least one act of physical aggression during the previous year, and 13 percent had been arrested. They had suffered significant relationship and family problems as a function of their anger. In sum, we were working with a difficult group of men who were suffering significant consequences of their dysfunctional anger. We divided the men into three groups and then conducted a twelve-week intervention. During the treatment sessions, the men were exposed to negative verbalizations (barbs) and were taught to respond in one of three ways:

1. Men in the first group listened to the barbs and responded with one of four rational statements about themselves (for example, "I can stand hearing this stuff, and I don't have to respond with anger").

2. Men in the second group responded with one of four irrational statements about themselves (for example, "I can't stand hearing this stuff").

3. Men in the third group responded with one of four irrelevant statements (for example, "When in doubt about who will win, be neutral").

The barbs were generic, nasty, and normatively expected to elicit anger. Interspersed with the barbs were a few positive and neutral verbalizations. All the verbalizations were delivered in a moderately forceful manner. Thirty verbalizations were delivered in each session; five of them were positive (for example, "I admire your decision to work on your anger"), five were neutral (for example, "I think the clothes you are wearing are appropriate"), and twenty were aversive. The aversive barbs encompassed five areas:

1. Physical appearance: "You look unkempt and sloppy, like you don't care about yourself."

2. Intelligence: "Your low intelligence seems obvious to everyone who meets you."

3. Personality: "I'm sure you don't have any friends, since you are so dammed irritating."

4. Athletic ability: "You just look like such a fucking wimp."

5. Achievement: "You know, you're really a loser."

Over the course of the twelve sessions, each man heard almost five hundred aversive statements. In keeping with a learning-theory model in which fading was an important variable, the men were permitted to read and recite their responses from notecards during the first four sessions; they recited their responses from memory during the next four sessions, and they said their statements silently to themselves during the final four sessions. The results were as follows:

1. Men in all three groups showed improvement, an indication that it had been useful for them to repeatedly hear and respond to verbal barbs in our supportive environment.

2. By comparison with the other two groups, the men who had responded with rational statements about themselves reported less outward expression of anger after the twelve treatment sessions, an indication that this type of exposure intervention was a promising approach.

3. There were no indications that this type of intervention had impaired the therapeutic alliance, which, as we have indicated, is central to SMART treatment. All the men completed a therapeutic-alliance scale, and no differences were found among the groups. In addition, their scores were in the range that indicated an effective working alliance.

These results were supported by subsequent studies that used very similar procedures (see McDermott, 1998; Terracciano, 2000).

The technique of using verbal barbs, then, can be very effective. Obviously, however, it is not suitable in every case, and it is best applied by practitioners who are comfortable using a learning-theory approach to intervention. The delivery of barbs can also be preceded by training in progressive muscle relaxation or other calming techniques, which may make the procedure more acceptable to clients and practitioners alike. It's good to remember that barbs can be either generic or taken directly from the client's life. Because the verbal barbs used in this technique are the kinds of statements that clients are likely to hear in real life, it can be of great benefit to work directly with clients on developing such statements during sessions. In many cases, for example, you will notice that a tit-for-tat communication style is common:

Jack: You're stupid.

Fran: No, *you're* stupid.

Chad: You're a nasty, lying bitch!

Lola: I hope you rot in hell!

When that response strategy is replaced with a variety of alternative reactions, as in the work we reported earlier (Tafrate & Kassinove, 1998), more productive reactions can be developed:

Jack:	You're really stupid.
Fran:	*(without sarcasm)* Thanks for sharing your opinion.
Jack:	You're really stupid.
Fran:	*(without sarcasm)* I can only say that you are wonderful, and I admire your talents.
Jack:	You're really stupid.
Fran:	Love is a many-splendored thing.
Jack:	You're really stupid.
Fran:	Sometimes I know a lot. But there are some things I know nothing about. Please help me understand what you are talking about.

We understand that this technique may seem odd or unusual to some readers. Yet it's useful to recall that reinforcing interchanges are shapers of behavior as well as of anger reactions. Surprising though this idea may be, the back-and-forth banter of angry clients is often reinforcing, at least in the short term, for both parties because of issues related to compliance with the behavior of others and to the self-righteousness that accompanies angry responding.

The idea that words are just words, and that being called stupid is like being called applesauce, does take some getting used to. Words have no real meanings aside from whatever meanings are imposed by the listener. The goal in this technique is for your clients to distance themselves from the conditioned meanings of words and to generate new, more useful responses (and sometimes silly responses). If this technique is carried out well, it can lead to laughter rather than anger. Sometimes these types of more positive reactions occur naturally. For example, in a training group we run for therapists, we spend some of our time learning about our trainees' lives, and then (with their permission) we deliberately say nasty things about them. The goal is to build up trainees' resilience in the face of such statements. One year we had a trainee who just kept saying "Thank you" to our negative statements. It turned out that he had been doing this for years, as a naturally developed response to criticism; we found it so disarming that we were unable to keep up our teasing.

And what about Luther?

As our sessions with Luther continued, we discovered that the word he found most disrespectful was "pussy," and so we called in Mike, one of our graduate trainees.

First we explained to Luther what we were going to do, and we got his permission—although he couldn't believe we were really going to do it.

We began by calling Mike a pussy. Then we increased the volume and added to the barb: "You know, Mike, you are a real pussy" and "You're more of a pussy than anyone I have ever met!" We did that a few times, waiting a few seconds between barbs, and then it was Luther's turn to barb Mike by repeatedly calling him a pussy.

Luther was incredulous. He said to Mike, "How can you take that?"

Mike said, "It's easy. These are only words, and remember—sticks and stones can break our bones, but words can never hurt us, unless we let them."

We then asked Luther if he would accept some barbs from us. He agreed, and off we went. Luther began to see that words did not cause him to react with anger, and that he had response options when people called him unpleasant names.

Acceptance and Commitment Therapy: Tolerating Negative Internal Stimuli

Proponents of acceptance and commitment therapy (ACT), such as Eifert, McKay, Forsyth, and Hayes (2006), believe that cognitive fusion is a major problem for clients of all sorts, and that ACT is a useful intervention for anger. In cognitive fusion, it's hypothesized, we get bullied by our thoughts because we attend to their contents rather than just experiencing them. Then, as though our internal thoughts were somehow objectively real, we often make bad decisions about friends, lovers, employers, neighbors, and others. This is in contrast to making decisions and taking action on the basis of what is really going on in the external world. When our thoughts are fused with us, we are susceptible to the illusion that our thoughts are absolute truths. This phenomenon becomes easier to understand when we consider the opposite process, *defusion* (or *deliteralization*). In defusion, clients can be taught that thoughts like *John thinks I'm a lying bitch* or *My friend Julio doesn't respect me* may or may not reflect reality. Thoughts are not actually threatening to your client; they are not something concrete outside the client in the physical world. Clients can allow their thoughts to come and go, without acting on them.

In the ACT framework, then, *acceptance* is the choice to adopt an open, curious, receptive attitude toward thoughts, emotional arousal, urges, and memories, even when they are unpleasant. The opposite process is trying to evade or eliminate internal experiences like anger in what is called *experiential avoidance*. Avoidance of negative internal stimuli may take lots of time and energy, and it leads to not interacting with family members, friends, and others in order to keep angry arousal out of the picture as much as possible. It can lead to loss of assertiveness in interactions and to the inability to generate solutions to problems, out of fear that acknowledgment and acceptance of anger will erupt into poor behavior or aggression. In the ACT model, you teach your clients to stop turning abstractions (that is, their thoughts) into concrete entities; in other words, you help them reduce their tendency to *reify* thoughts, images, emotions, and memories. Clients learn that thinking and experiencing are ongoing processes, not realities, and that thoughts can just be allowed to come and go, without a struggle and without efforts to change them. In ACT, some importance is placed on the process of unhooking the relationships among thoughts, feelings, and behaviors, an outcome achieved through the use of procedures like engaging in mindfulness exercises, learning to be present, and examining metaphors (some of these techniques were described in chapter 12).

Cognitive defusion and acceptance are two processes that you can help clients develop as they move toward the more general, overarching goal of *psychological flexibility*, meaning the ability to shift perspectives, adapt to the ever-changing demands of life's situations, and balance competing stressors. The flexible client has the skills to face challenging private experiences in an open, aware, focused, values-oriented manner. Again, this concept may be better understood in contrast to its opposite, *psychological inflexibility*, meaning rigidity that is inconsistent with a client's values, goals, and committed actions and that is due to excessive influence of the client's private experiences on his or her patterns of behavior. The basic concept here is that it's best for clients to develop skills for moving toward the things they value most. For an angry client, psychological flexibility would mean the ability to use the right resources, at the right time, in order to create the kind of life the client wants to live.

Aside from defusion and acceptance, other processes are important in the quest for psychological flexibility. For example, *awareness of personal values* is important. Clients are asked to examine four questions as they go through life:

1. What do I value?

2. What forces are pulling or pushing me away from moving toward what I value?

3. What action can I take now to move myself closer to what I value?

4. How do I continue in the future to move toward what I value?

The client is helped to discover what will be most important over his or her life span, and to explore his or her desired life directions. What is it that gives meaning to the client's life? Is it his or her career? Family? Living an eco-friendly life? Something else? Or, to ask a more provocative question, what might the client like others to read in his or her obituary?

It's also important to help clients increase their *presence in the moment* and to accept stressful thoughts and emotions through nonjudgmental contact with events. They are taught to use language as a tool for simply noting and describing events rather than judging or predicting them. Your goal, then, is to teach clients to just notice, accept, and embrace their private events, especially those that have been unwanted.

In addition, clients are also taught to develop an *observing self*. They are to become aware of an unchanging sense of self, a self-image that does not vary in response to momentary events. Clients are taught to view their identity as separate from the content of their experiences. And, again, they are helped to experience the here and now with openness, interest, and receptiveness rather than living in the past ("Last week at the party he insulted me, and I will never forgive him") or the future ("I bet there will be lots of arguing at dinner later tonight").

Committed action is another key. A core learning for angry clients is to accept what is out of their personal control and commit themselves to actions that will improve and enrich their lives. As in other forms of intervention, an aim of ACT is to maximize the human potential for a rich, full, meaningful life. As a final goal, therefore, you can teach clients to set psychological destinations that correspond to their values, and to carry them out.

In learning to be present with what life brings and to move toward valued life directions, clients learn not to overreact to unpleasant thoughts and feelings and not to avoid situations in which such thoughts and feelings appear. They are taught instead to choose behavior that is consistent with their life priorities. In sum, at the core of this approach is the idea that psychological suffering, including anger, is caused by clients' avoidance of difficult internal experiences and by clients' failure to take reasonable steps to move toward their most fundamental desires. They learn to accept their reactions, be present, and take action to move toward what they see as most important in their lives. To help clients develop psychological flexibility, mindfulness and acceptance processes (such as defusion and contact with the present moment) are integrated into treatment, as are commitment and the behavioral change processes of identifying core values and taking committed action.

Translating values into action has long been a goal of many therapies, including cognitive behavioral therapies (CBT), although that goal has not always been stated directly. At the same time, translating values into action does not come easy. In keeping with that idea, we offer four practical steps that you can implement in your anger interventions, as reflected through a practitioner's dialogues with William, a forty-eight-year-old married lawyer who had frequent angry flare-ups with his business partner of seven years.

Step 1. Help Your Client Choose a Life Domain That Is a High Priority for Change

Practitioner: William, you've been telling me about some of the pros and cons of your marriage, your business relationship with Kentaro, and your concerns about getting older. I'd like you to pick one area that we can focus on. Which one of these are you most concerned about?

William: There's so much going on in my life with the kids, my marriage, my concerns about my health, and my business. But if I had to pick one, it would be my relationship with Kentaro, my business partner.

Practitioner:	What's the issue here?
William:	We just do things differently. He's from an Asian background. He likes to work independently and does not express his feelings or communicate about work issues. When he won't talk to me, I become angry and just seethe inside. I can see that some of his cases are not going well. On others, he does a great job. But a few of his clients have actually left him, giving our firm a bad name.

Step 2. Help Your Client Choose Values Worth Pursuing

Practitioner:	Okay. I hear your concerns and understand that you sometimes react to Kentaro with anger. What is it that you desire? What do you value?
William:	I value openness and collaboration. For me, a partnership means talking, a lot, about what's going on. It means talking about successes and being open when things go off the rails with our cases.

Step 3. Help Your Client Develop Values-Guided Goals

Practitioner:	In this specific situation, what have you done so far?
William:	Not much. I just stew a lot. I tried a few times to tell Kentaro what he was doing wrong, but he didn't listen. He just got even more quiet for the next few days.
Practitioner:	That sounds frustrating.
William:	Yeah.
Practitioner:	What would be an acceptable goal at this point?
William:	He's a good, well-trained lawyer. I want to continue to work with him. But I also want to stop being so angry.

Step 4. Help Your Client Take Action

Practitioner:	It seems like there would be two parts to this goal. First, you want to talk to Kentaro to see if communication can be improved, and you don't want to act in a way that shuts him down more. Second, you want to be more accepting of his personal style, which is different from yours, and you want to be less angry about this fact.

William: That's exactly correct.

Practitioner: Maybe when you told him what he was doing wrong, there could have been a better way to do it. If you would like to, we can work on some assertiveness skills. They would help you learn how to express yourself while respecting Kentaro's right to be himself.

William: I'll try anything.

Practitioner: You can begin by doing some reading, as a foundation for what we will practice here in the office. There's a book I recommend called *Your Perfect Right*, by two psychologists—I'll write the title down for you. (*Practitioner recommends Alberti and Emmons, 1970, 2008, 2017.*)

William: Okay. I'll look for it tonight.

Practitioner: Since you value a more open relationship with Kentaro, we can try out some different ways of seeing whether communication can be improved.

William: That sounds good.

Practitioner: In the meantime, that leaves the acceptance part—accepting that your thoughts are just thoughts, which may or may not reflect reality. After all, you have been working together for seven years, and you said he does a great job on most cases.

William: That's true. But sometimes I let my thoughts get away from me. I let them upset me.

Practitioner: Let's continue with an exercise to show you where you are with regard to your thoughts. (*Practitioner continues to work on unhooking William's thoughts from his anger reactions, reinforcing William's behaviors in a valued direction, and using metaphors as appropriate.*)

A Note on Tolerating Negativity

An initial goal of all counseling and psychotherapy programs is to identify what can be changed, what cannot be changed, and when the client should seek change instead of working toward acceptance. For many problems of life, short-term tolerance and acceptance play an important role. Some unwanted or unpleasant issues (such as a physical handicap, very short stature, or a historical event like a previous divorce or a physical trauma) are best *fully* accepted or accepted for a period of time with an expectation of eventual change (as when a teenager suffers from acne). Other unwanted or unpleasant issues (such as an unreliable automobile or an unfulfilling, conflict-laden job) are best dealt with in the present.

METAPHORS

Practitioners often use metaphors, in the form of stories or illustrations, to help clients develop alternative ways of looking at the types of personal problems that may lead to angry arousal. You probably use a number of metaphors to reflect on your own life. In fact, all cultures and religions use stories, analogies, and parables to improve understanding of the world, and to make rules of behavior more memorable so they can provide guidance while encouraging understanding and change. When you use a metaphor, your goal is to help the client see things in a different light. A metaphor can help the client shift perspectives and make better, more objective life decisions. Metaphors are more effective with larger issues (such as an overall relationship) than with single interactions (such as a specific anger-provoking event). When they work, metaphors can bring on an "aha" moment for your client. A metaphor may even evoke laughter and positive emotion when a client grasps it, since many metaphors are playful. It may be that metaphors are helpful because they rely both on visualization and on words. Consider these two metaphors, which are commonly used by ACT practitioners (for a full description of these and other metaphors, see Hayes, Strosahl, & Wilson, 1999, and Stoddard & Afari, 2014):

1. Passengers on your bus: As if you were driving a bus, you can stay behind the wheel, at the front of this large vehicle, while the passengers (your thoughts) are being critical, abusive, intrusive, and distracting or shouting out nonsense. You can allow the passengers to continue shouting while you keep your attention focused on the road ahead and go on driving toward your personal goal. An effective bus driver understands that such thoughts are nothing more than background noise; an incompetent bus driver can't tolerate such thoughts without acting on them and is likely to stop the bus or drive it into a ditch. You don't have to react to your thoughts (Hayes, Strosahl, & Wilson, 1999, 157–158).

2. The mountain: You can think of yourself as being like a mountain—observing your thoughts, feelings, and sensations while also keeping an inner stillness and a stable sense of self. Whatever the weather, rain or snow, and whatever is happening on the surface, such as a rockslide, the mountain stands firm, strong, grounded, and permanent.

Readers may have some concerns about the concept of having a client tolerate external negative stimuli (such as verbal barbs) or internal negative stimuli (such as unpleasant thoughts). When you're engaging in the interventions described in this chapter, you would be wise not to insist that your client accept every external situation, or stay stuck in an unsatisfying relationship or career, or remain passive in the face of verbal or physical harm or abuse. Indeed, where such situations are concerned, we have already presented active change strategies in chapters 8 and 9. Our position, simply put, is that once a client has developed less reactivity to challenging situations, the client will be in a better position to transcend such problems, make thoughtful decisions, and have greater control over his or her own actions. The ultimate goal is for the client to develop a more satisfying life.

Deciding Between Acceptance Interventions and Change Interventions

ACT is sometimes described as a third-wave cognitive behavioral therapy intervention. A key feature of ACT and similar approaches is that they are more aligned with the so-called Eastern philosophical perspectives of acceptance and mindfulness.

In contrast, first-wave CBT consisted of techniques based on the works of Ivan Pavlov, John B. Watson, Clark L. Hull, Joseph Wolpe, Hans Eysenck, and B. F. Skinner. They focused on behavior-change methods as produced by learning theory–oriented procedures, including progressive muscle relaxation, systematic desensitization, operant conditioning, exposure (barbing), and extinction techniques. These remain popular and effective treatments, used today for anger management, and we integrate them into our SMART intervention program.

In the 1950s and 1960s, second-wave social-cognitive procedures were developed by Albert Bandura, Aaron Beck, Albert Ellis, Julian Rotter, and others. They showed that thoughts, cognitions, and interpersonal schemas, which had been avoided by Skinner and his first-wave colleagues, contribute both to behavior change and to acceptance. The second-wave interventions also remain very useful in the treatment of anger, and we have already discussed them as part of our SMART program. Eventually, everything merged into what is generically called *cognitive behavioral therapy*, which is an umbrella term for a wide variety of interventions. We hope that you, as a SMART anger manager, will be open to using any reasonably validated procedure that seems to be a good fit for your individual client. As always, the key to deciding between an acceptance-based intervention and a change-based intervention is to utilize relevant assessment information and exercise your professional judgment about which approach fits best for the client you are working with, in the context of his or her anger episodes.

Takeaway Messages and Tools

An important goal in SMART anger management is to help clients become less reactive both to the negative external stimuli and to the negative internal stimuli that typically trigger their anger reactions. If your clients are high-functioning, literate, well educated, and bright, then acceptance-based procedures (that is, procedures for helping them tolerate internal stimuli) may work well for them. These clients may immediately understand the metaphors that you present, and they may change rapidly by means of the insights your metaphors provide. These clients can understand, for example, that stopping a thought that has nasty content may be impossible, like trying to hold a beach ball under the water—it just keeps popping up. They may also understand that they can allow the ball to float around them, just letting it be while they swim or engage in other activities.

In contrast, if your clients have relatively poor language skills, are comparatively less well educated, and have difficulty with abstractions, then they may be much better served by more direct behavioral methods that can help them tolerate or be less reactive to external stimuli. Once impulsive urges have been brought a bit under control, and clients are better able to tolerate negative words and thoughts, other interventions to address social and interpersonal problems can be introduced. We deal with those interventions in chapters 14, 15, and 16.

PART 7

Interventions to Alter Anger Expression

CHAPTER 14

Social and Interpersonal Skills

The basis of social skill is the ability to relate to the situation of the "other."

—Neil Fligstein

We begin this section of the book, and this chapter, with a focus on the basic interpersonal skills that are often not addressed in treatment programs. If your clients come across as angry, aggressive, dismissive, or uninterested during social interactions, then they have little chance of resolving their conflicts with others. Yet this is exactly how angry clients do come across. They then feel hurt and disrespected, believe that their ideas and opinions are being ignored or disregarded, and, as a result, act in an antagonistic or threatening manner. These attitudes are shown not only in their words but also in their body language. In many cases, you will have to spend some time working to help a client develop a presentation style that is more open and inviting. In chapter 15, we will focus on how words can increase or decrease anger during an interpersonal interaction. In this chapter, our focus is on body language.

If you're like most other practitioners, your focus is on words as the primary medium of communication. We have been brought up to believe that good interventions are based on shaping thoughts and words so as to improve relationships. Yet many scholars believe that words account only for only about 7 percent of what occurs in communication. The rest is accounted for by vocal features, such as intonation, pauses, pitch, and volume (about 38 percent), and body language (about 55 percent). These figures are based on older publications (see, for example, Mehrabian, 1970) that stressed attitudes toward a speaker. Later scholars have disagreed with these figures, suggesting that, in many situations, words account for more than 7 percent of communication. We will not resolve that issue in this book. Instead, we'll simply point out that clients are usually unaware that their bodies and the vocal features of the messages they deliver are critical parts of the communication process. This may be particularly true in the case of anger; for example, Elgin (1993) states that more than 90 percent of the communication of emotions occurs nonverbally. To best resolve interpersonal anger and negotiate beneficial outcomes, it's important that your clients learn how to talk to others with whom they are angry and learn to adjust their body language and verbalization features so that their messages can be received as nonthreatening. In university training programs, this kind of work is usually left to drama departments and schools of communication. But if a client is perceived to be angry and about to pounce, then anger reduction, conflict resolution, and improved relationships are unlikely. Therefore, we recommend that you pay close attention to the physical actions and vocal tones of your clients.

Often you will need to have an initial discussion with a client about his or her goals with respect to a conflict. As usual, this discussion is best conducted within the framework of motivational interviewing. The first step is to increase the client's awareness and foster motivation to change those elements of his or her communication style that are ineffective and likely to increase conflict. Here are some issues to consider:

- Does your client tend to approach disagreements with a desire to forcefully convince the others involved that he is right?

- Does your client try to find common ground with others in order to solve problems?

- Does your client have a dictatorial style or a curious problem-solving orientation?

- Is your client more likely to try to control the situation or to work collaboratively?

- Is your client trying to be the boss, or does she make a real attempt to include others in the decision-making process?

A positive outcome will be impeded by any part of the communication process that suggests strong anger, the possibility of aggression, or unwillingness to listen. If your client's words are asking for conflict resolution but her body language is suggesting a different goal, then the recipients of her message will sense the discrepancy and probably become defensive.

Body Language: Kinesics, Proxemics, and Haptics

Body language consists of *kinesics, proxemics,* and *haptics.* The term "kinesics" refers to the way in which body movements and gestures act as elements of communication. The term "proxemics" refers to the amount of space people want between themselves and others. The term "haptics" refers to elements of touch. Factors related to each of these dimensions may signal anger and bring up anger in others or, alternatively, they may signal attention, warmth, and caring. You can help your clients practice and increase their effectiveness with skills related to each of these three dimensions.

Kinesics

Here, we'll consider four elements related specifically to kinesics:

1. Eye contact

2. Facial expressions

3. Gestures

4. Posture

EYE CONTACT

Regarding eye contact, the goal for your client is to show attention to and interest in the perspective of the other person, without generating discomfort. Therefore, you'll want to help your client come across as inviting rather than domineering. In general, although cultural differences will come into play, too much eye contact can be experienced as domineering, threatening, and even insulting. This means that after five or six seconds, it's important that your client look away for a bit. Also, teaching your client to shift his or her gaze between the two eyes and the mouth of the other person is a good plan for helping your client show interest in that person.

In contrast, too little eye contact can be experienced as impolite and may suggest lack of interest and inattentiveness. If your client is talking to a small group (perhaps two or three colleagues from work), it will also be important for him or her not to focus on one person for too long, since that leads the others to feel left out and increases their sense of being ignored. Of course, suggest that your client not look at his or her cell phone after breaking eye contact. Common though this behavior is today, it's still a sure sign of disrespect.

FACIAL EXPRESSIONS

Facial expressions are very important. The muscles of the face can communicate interest or indifference, happiness or anger, fear or aggression. A disapproving frown, pursed lips, eyebrows pulled toward each other, a smirk, and similar expressions will impede communication. Figure 14.1 depicts six expressive facial patterns. As noted in chapter 1, we agree with Salter (1949) that there is much to be gained by practicing facial talk with clients. It's likely that they have never experienced it before.

Figure 14.1. Facial Expression of Emotions

Key: (top row, left to right) angry, surprised, neutral;
(bottom row, left to right) sad, angry, happy.

Adapted by the authors from Anggi Sukardi's depiction of Steven Gerrard, an English association football player; see https://commons.wikimedia.org/wiki/File:Steven-Gerrard-profile.jpg.

For a visual presentation of the relationship between facial muscles and feelings, we recommend that you watch season, 1, episode 7 of the YouTube series *Mind Field.* In that episode, participants are first asked to hold a piece of wood (similar to a tongue depressor or a pencil) either between their teeth, thus causing the sides of their lips to extend as in a smile, or between their lips with their teeth shut, as in frowning. The participants, while continuing to hold the wood in their mouths, are then asked to imagine engaging in an objectively pleasant task (such as playing with puppies and taking a picture with them) or an objectively unpleasant task (such as touching and looking through poop for hard protein deposits). Finally, they are asked to rate the pleasantness or unpleasantness of their assigned imaginal tasks. Participants who have been induced to simulate a smile find it more pleasant to imagine playing with puppies, and less unpleasant to imagine looking through poop; likewise, participants who have been induced to simulate a frown find it less pleasant to imagine playing with puppies, and more unpleasant to imagine looking through poop.

Zilioli et al. (2015) found that anger is shown by the facial width-to-height ratio. Sell, Cosmides, and Tooby (2014) showed that movements of seven facial muscle groups—which produce a lowered brow, raised cheekbones, thinned and pushed-out lips, a raised mouth, a flared nose, and a chin pushed out and up—led to faces being judged as angrier;

as a corollary, observers assumed that the person was physically stronger. From the perspective of animal evolution, the purpose of anger is to make one appear stronger so as to potentially scare off competitors and gain more in a conflict. That was fine when the stakes included the preservation of food sources, the safety of offspring, and protection from attacks during mating. Today, however, with the stakes in a conflict less likely to involve physical harm and survival, and more likely to be social in nature (as during a marital or family conflict or a business negotiation), coming across as more powerful is likely to push others away and lead to increased animosity rather than conflict resolution. Therefore, helping your client develop a less angry face can be a very useful basic intervention.

GESTURES

A shrug of the shoulders, especially combined with a smirk, typically indicates an "I don't know" attitude and does not suggest agreement with the other party. Keeping one's hands in one's pockets, or on one's hips, may suggest lack of openness to discussion and negotiation. A closed attitude can also be indicated by pointing at others or showing a clenched fist. Stroking one's chin may indicate positive thoughtfulness, whereas placing one's chin in one's hand may indicate boredom. What about the thumbs-up sign? Doesn't it usually indicate something positive? And nodding may indicate that an agreement or a compromise has been reached. In general, it's good to teach an angry client to keep her hands and arms in her lap, or at her sides, while listening to feedback from others. Your client's crossed arms may indicate that she feels annoyed or angry. Hand movements are usually okay for accenting a few points, but constant movement of the hands is distracting and may come across as domineering. Tapping the fingers can indicate annoyance, whereas waving the fingers may be seen as condescending or demeaning.

When it comes to gestures, culture matters. In the United States, closing your eyes while someone is talking suggests lack of interest or boredom; for the Japanese, in contrast, closing the eyes suggests concentration on what the other person is saying. Also in the United States, the thumbs-up sign clearly indicates approval, whereas in Russia, Israel, Greece, Iran, and West Africa, it may (or may not) be interpreted as meaning "Up yours," and in some Arab countries it may be threatening and can mean "Just wait— you'll see." There are wide within-country differences in the use and understanding of these and other gestures, and so caution is warranted. When you're working with a client whose cultural background is different from your own, be sure to ask whether particular gestures are appropriate.

POSTURE

A client's standing or sitting posture may give information about his or her attitudes and feelings. It may be good to ask your client to lean forward a bit when receiving feedback from others, to suggest that he is open and listening. Leaning back and away may suggest unwillingness to discuss a problem in a collaborative manner.

Proxemics and Haptics

With respect to distances between people, space is traditionally broken up into *public, social, personal*, and *intimate* dimensions (see figure 14.2). In North America, well-attended formal events like lectures and concerts are held in public space, which involves twelve or more feet of interpersonal distance. Obviously, no matter how enjoyable a lecture or a concert may be, audience members have little real connection with the speaker or performers.

When people are standing or sitting four to twelve feet from each other, they are in social space—a small gathering like a cocktail party or a picnic. Most conversation in social space is casual and is not perceived as threatening. Highly personal information is not likely to be revealed or discussed in social space.

In personal space, people stand or sit eighteen inches to four feet from each other. Personal space is reserved for interactions among family members and good friends, as in a private conversation with a sibling about sensitive issues. When personal space is invaded by a stranger, or by someone with whom there is a history of conflict or discord, there is an increase in arousal and perceived threat. As an exception, however, we'll note that this is also the space in which we shake hands with someone.

In intimate space, people stand or sit no farther than eighteen inches apart. Usually we reserve this intimate space for romantic partners and very close friends, and we feel quite threatened when this space is invaded by those we do not consider close to us. Intimate space is for whispering, sensual touching, hugging, and kissing, but it's also the space that is acceptable between parents and young children, as when parents wash the faces of their children or read to them in bed.

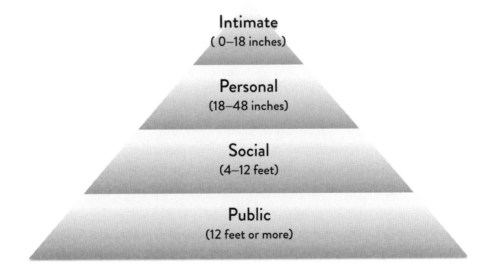

Intimate
(0–18 inches)

Personal
(18–48 inches)

Social
(4–12 feet)

Public
(12 feet or more)

Figure 14.2. Social Distance Norms

Moving too close to others is distracting, inhibits attentive verbal interactions, and can cause alarm, agitation, annoyance, and anger. Violations of space can occur for many reasons, including a desire to be domineering as well as lack of knowledge about the norms of interpersonal space. Recently at an outdoor social gathering, one of us was approached by a woman who could best be considered an acquaintance. She got very close—about twelve inches away—and she talked in a loud voice while touching incessantly. Although her behavior did not come across as angry, it did increase vigilance, and internal alarm bells were going off. What was going on? It was a challenge to focus on the content of her words, since her spatial invasiveness was distracting and was bringing up too many possibilities. Soon, however, it became clear that she'd simply had too much to drink. On another occasion, one of us experienced repeated space violations during interactions with a colleague who regularly moved to an uncomfortable distance of only twelve to twenty-four inches away during conversations. After a while, however, it became clear that he was legally blind, and it became more relaxing to talk with him.

The lesson is clear—it is important for clients to know and attend to conventions regarding interpersonal space and relationships with others. And yet the issue of proxemics is rarely discussed outside academic environments. In addition, it's helpful for a client to know and understand *general* norms, but norms also vary in terms of the individual client, the nature of the client's relationship with a *specific* person, and the client's (or the other person's) culture. In North America, for example, we might engage in friendly physical contact like hugging when we greet someone, or touching another person's arm while we're talking. But Japanese people consider this behavior an invasion of personal space; indeed, we worked with a Japanese colleague for more than twenty years and felt quite emotionally close to her, but whenever we moved to hug her, she turned her head away. An invasion of personal space, actual or perceived, may seem like a threat and can lead to mild discomfort and awkwardness in some situations; in others, it can quickly fuel anger reactions and lead to a physical altercation.

In our travels around the world, we have become very much aware of the tacit rules regarding interpersonal space. In Russia, for example, we've noticed that people in line at a grocery store or a bank get very close, almost touching us; it's distracting, feels like a threat, and has led us to check our wallets and wish for greater interpersonal distance. And men in India often hold hands and stand quite close together, but no romantic or sexual interest is implied. There are times when North Americans do accept invasions of personal space without much sense of alarm, as in a crowded elevator or in the coach section of a plane, but even in these instances people are more easily irritated, and flare-ups of anger are more common.

Takeaway Messages and Tools

If your clients want to communicate effectively, diminish threats, and resolve conflicts, then it makes sense for them to understand how they can (and cannot) use their bodies to say what they mean. Body language and verbalizations come in clusters of signals, as Gestalts. Recognizing a cluster of kinesics, proxemics, and haptics in a relationship offers a more reliable way of understanding than do efforts to interpret any individual element of body language.

In the end it will be up to you, in your office, to help your clients practice dealing with contrived and real conflicts, and to teach your clients to use their bodies in an open and inviting manner. You can do this by using the method of contrasts. Begin by presenting a conflict scenario to your client. Perhaps you can take the role of someone who is asking for an unreasonable favor, or the role of a spouse or other family member who has treated your client disrespectfully. Ask your client to talk to you about the problem as you play the role of the person who was disrespectful. First have the client adopt an angry behavioral stance, and then have the client adopt a friendly, openhearted stance that indicates a desire to resolve the problem. Repeat the exercise a few times, over a few sessions, and give plenty of verbal reinforcement for open and inviting behaviors.

The body language–related issues that you can highlight as you practice with your clients can include interpersonal distance, eye contact, facial expressions, gestures, touch, posture, and stance. Verbal elements of communication, such as pauses, pitch, and tone, can also be rehearsed. Clients can develop the behavioral skills of seeming accepting and cooperative (rather than threatening, angry, and uncooperative) in every type of interpersonal communication. An understanding of the rules of kinesics, proxemics, and haptics is the basis of these skills. In chapter 15, we tackle the second part of this process by presenting the rules of helpful and effective verbal communication.

Assertiveness Training: Awareness, Actions, and Words

Most people do not listen with the intent to understand; they listen with the intent to reply.

—Stephen R. Covey

For many clients, perhaps most, anger follows interpersonal conflict. Employees become angry when they are required to do something they perceived as unreasonable, such as working extra hours without pay. Adolescents feel angry when their parents or teachers require them to do schoolwork at a time when they want to do something else, such as playing a video game. Parents sometimes lose it when their children act in ways considered inappropriate, as when they repeatedly use profanity. Clients involved with the criminal justice system are often annoyed when the demands of a new job conflict with the requirement to report in person to the probation office. And of course spouses become angry with each other for so many reasons that we cannot begin to list them all. Reacting with anger rarely produces anything helpful, however, and so clients can often benefit from learning not only anger expression but also conflict-resolution skills.

Each type of conflict is unique and has its own potential resolution pattern. But before a client can resolve any conflict, two elements usually have to be present:

1. The client's awareness of his or her personal emotional reaction to the problem

2. Full, proper, and appropriate communication between the client and the other party or parties involved in the conflict

These two elements constitute the assertiveness skills we describe in this chapter.

At the same time, we do recognize that some conflicts may not be resolvable, and that clients may also benefit from skills that can help them accept some of the negative aspects of life. In earlier chapters, we discussed ways to think about ongoing struggles. Here, we take an optimistic outlook. If clients know what they are feeling and know how to present their concerns reasonably, then they stand a good chance of resolving many of their problems, with minimal anger.

The word "assertiveness" is often misunderstood. Many people think it means letting others know that they are not pushovers, that they can't be taken advantage of, or that others will be in for a real argument or a physical fight if they mess with them. If clients want to be assertive, they may think this means that they must be loud and defensive, and that they must advocate strongly for their positions and *win*, no matter what. Clients may also confuse being assertive with discrediting their adversaries. To provide some clarity about the concept of assertiveness, we'll place its development in its historical context.

A Brief History of Assertiveness

There hasn't always been as much emphasis as there is today in the United States on the individual person, or on the free and appropriate experience and expression of emotions. Before the 1960s, for example, women were assumed to want the life of a homemaker, and girls—future homemakers—were expected to be sweet and innocent, and to exercise sexual restraint in addition to tact, diplomacy, good manners, self-denial, and modesty. As for men, it was considered acceptable for them to be tough and aggressive in the business world and in sports, to get ahead by stepping on and over others, and not to have much awareness of or ability to express their inner feelings. These expectations and prescriptions were seen as the way to personal happiness, although they did squelch the aspirations of the individual, not to mention those of minority groups.

Things started changing in the 1960s, partly as an effect of the civil rights movement of the mid-1950s and the larger social changes it had begun to bring about. Humanistic psychology developed, too, and with it came an interest in the conscious motivations of individuals. The human potential movement was growing. People everywhere, at all levels and in all sectors of society, wanted self-improvement. They wanted to realize their potential and live at full capacity, without being held back by society's conventional expectations and prejudices.

In the 1970s, as psychologists began paying more attention to assertiveness as a means of achieving and protecting individual rights, books and articles on the topic began to appear. Alberti and Emmons (1970, 2008, 2017) created the first program of assertiveness training intended for the activation of human potential. They believed that all people have equal rights, regardless of social status, and they argued that in families and friendships, as in community relationships, it is wrong to put oneself above others; all people, they believed, have the right to be masters of their own lives, to act according to their personal desires, interests, and beliefs, and to freely express their views and feelings. During the same period, Jakubowski and Lange (1978) even published a list of basic rights that they saw as pertaining to all people, irrespective of gender, race, religious affiliation, or social class (see figure 15.1).

1. The right to act in a manner that promotes our dignity and self-respect, as long as we do not violate the rights of others.

2. The right to be treated with respect, not only by family members and friends but also by all the people with whom we interact.

3. The right to say no and refuse requests without feeling guilty.

4. The right to experience and express feelings, both negative and positive.

5. The right to take time to calm down and think about goals and actions.

6. The right to be adaptable, flexible, and change our mind, given that we are all subject to the receipt of new information, and given the belief that it is a responsible action to consider evolving information.

7. The right to ask for whatever we want, without embarrassment.

8. The right to do less than what we could do, not to escape responsibility but to spread efforts among the many life tasks required of everyone.

9. The right to ask for information, without being demeaned or disrespected, given the complexity of the world and our inability to be knowledgeable in all spheres of life.

10. The right to make mistakes, and not be discouraged by them, since all human beings are mistake-making creatures and mistakes can lead to knowledge and improvement.

11. The right to feel good about ourselves, as a basic human right and not as a sign of selfishness.

Figure 15.1. Jakubowski and Lange's List of Basic Rights

*Adapted from P. Jakubowski and A. Lange, The Assertive Option
(Champaign, IL: Research Press, 1978), p. 80.*

By the 1990s, assertiveness training had come to be seen as a solid means of achieving and/or strengthening the human potential of all individuals. It had also moved firmly into the arena of psychotherapy, with behavior therapists now incorporating assertiveness training into their theory-based learning packages.

Nevertheless, many individuals today remain unable to deal constructively with interpersonal conflicts and disappointments, in part because they have learned in various ways to be unassertive, as we've noted in earlier chapters. And yet, just as people learn to be unassertive, they can also be taught to become assertive. This is why assertiveness training continues to be an important intervention in in SMART anger management and in cognitive behavioral therapy as a whole.

Six Steps for Fostering Assertive Skills in Your Clients

For us, assertiveness involves the direct, honest, appropriate expression of feelings, especially annoyance and anger. The goal is to try to reduce conflict and work with others to find mutually acceptable solutions to problems. Notice that we said "try." We believe that assertive communication provides the best chance of working things out, but it isn't a guarantee. It is just one tool in the SMART package.

Step 1. Raising the Client's Awareness of Personal Anger Reactions

Recall the case of Francisco (chapter 11), who discovered that Merla, his friend and colleague at a home-improvement sales company, was stealing leads from his desk whenever he got to work a few minutes late. Merla did this even though their boss was scrupulous about giving both her and Francisco the same number of leads every morning, since every lead was potentially worth a bonus of $250. What might have been the best way for Francisco to handle this situation?

It would have been important for Francisco first to look into himself and gauge his internal reaction. Assuming that he was experiencing some degree of negative arousal, Francisco might have needed some help to become fully and appropriately aware of his feelings.

Some clients deny their anger because they do not want to upset the applecart of relationships, or perhaps they fear losing control of their words or actions if they try to express their angry feelings. In Francisco's position, they might say, "It's no big deal, and so it's better to let it go—I don't want to upset the boss" or "She deserves a break, since her car broke down and she has extra expenses" or "I just refuse to believe she would do something like that." Avoidance of the anger experience would not be good for Francisco or for his relationships with others. This kind of reaction usually means a client does not have the skills of *emotional intelligence*, a term coined by Salovey and Mayer (1990) that refers to the recognition of one's own and others' personal feelings and to the skills needed to manage feelings in relationships. People strong in emotional intelligence are self-aware, engage in self-evaluation, and are self-confident. When people are responding in an emotionally intelligent manner, they can classify their feelings by category (anger versus anxiety versus shame) and intensity (mildly annoyed versus angry versus truly furious). They are aware of their body language, can regulate the tone of their verbalizations, and use humor to communicate that the other person is not an enemy. They also have conflict-resolution skills, a positive problem-solving orientation (see chapter 9), and the ability to negotiate beneficial outcomes.

The goal for Francisco would have been to become, with the practitioner's help, fully aware of his reactions, to express them constructively, and to maintain and even improve his relationship with Merla. The practitioner might simply have asked, "When you discovered that Merla was taking your leads, how angry did you feel on a scale of 1 to 10, where 1 is almost no anger and 10 is the most anger you have ever experienced?"

During this type of discussion, we recommend that you start your questioning with a "When..." clause. Consider these examples involving other situations:

- When you discovered that your son lied to you about his test grade, how did you feel?

- When your husband called you distant, how did you feel?

- When your boss said that you did not have the skill to be a supervisor, how did you feel?

- When you were accused of being a thief, how did you feel?

The situations to which these statements refer would normatively lead to some degree of anger. If your client minimizes or denies his anger, you can use a few strategies to build awareness. You might, for example, use the 1-to-10 scaling technique just described, and if your client rates his anger as 3, you might say, "I wonder why you didn't say 1 or 2." That might lead the client to describe the reasons why he was angry and might therefore create more awareness. Alternatively, you could use an imaginal exercise. You can say, "Imagine that..." and insert an example that is somewhat relevant to the client's life. Here are a few "Imagine that..." ideas concerning family relationships:

- ...your adolescent tells his friends that you are an uncaring parent.

- ...your wife tells a friend that you have become lazy and boring.

- ...your husband tells his friends that you are lousy in bed.

- ...your cousins gossip about your lack of intelligence, and they laugh at you behind your back.

Since such statements would normatively lead to some degree of negative arousal, you would ask your client to rate the arousal. Focus on muscle tension, heart rate, thoughts, and fantasies of revenge. In cases where a client says, "It wouldn't bother me at all," you can ask, "Did the imagery cause happiness or joy or exhilaration?" Clients almost always say no to this suggestion, and this may help put them in touch with their anger.

Sometimes imaginal exercises don't work. Therefore, another technique—to be used carefully—is to ask the client if it would be okay for you to practice delivering insults to him in the therapy office (or in a therapy group). This can lead to real awareness of emotional arousal, and it works even though clients know it's a simulation. Begin by saying, "You know, I enjoy working with you, and I think quite highly of you. But today, with your permission, I would like to lie about my thoughts and insult you, so we can practice something new. Would that be okay?" After you get permission, stand behind the client and deliver one of the following verbal prods, speaking as if you mean what you are saying (deliver these prods slowly, and at a medium level of loudness):

- Sometimes I think about your lack of basic intelligence. You just don't seem to be very smart.

- Sometimes you just don't get what I am saying. It's like your brain doesn't work well.

- Your face often seems unattractive and distorted to me.

- I've noticed a smell coming from you, like you don't brush your teeth.

- I can understand why you have social problems. I don't like you much, either.

Even though you will have begun the exercise by telling the client that you are going to lie, you will usually notice head movements, a scrunching of the face, tensing of the shoulders, and minor overall body movements. That's an opportunity to teach the client about emotional reactivity, and to build awareness by asking the client what it felt like for him to hear the insults. It's a difficult exercise, not to be used except by skilled practitioners and in select cases in which there is a good working relationship, but it can provide a very powerful learning experience and can put the client more in touch with his angry feelings.

Step 2. Raising the Client's Awareness of Body Language

In this step, your goal is to use all the material presented in chapter 14, both to introduce the client to the importance of body language in interpersonal interactions and to teach him how to modify his use of facial expressions, space, and touch so that he is perceived as welcoming.

Step 3. Providing Assertiveness Education

In this step, your goal is to teach the client what it means to be assertive, and to distinguish assertiveness both from unassertiveness and from aggressiveness. For example, a dialogue with Denis, twenty-four years old, might go something like this:

Practitioner: You've told me that you often have difficulty expressing anger, and that you sometimes explode at your girlfriend. Today I'd like to begin the process of teaching you how to assertively express those kinds of feelings. Would that be okay?

Denis: Sure.

Practitioner: First it would be good if we could agree on what it means to be assertive when you interact with her. Assertiveness means direct, honest, appropriate expression of your feelings. So the goal is for you to communicate your anger directly to her rather than complaining to your friends about her. It also means being honest—that is, expressing the feeling without minimizing it, and also without exaggerating it. Finally, it means expressing it appropriately. You've told me that sometimes you yell, wave your hands, point at her, and threaten to leave her. What's the usual outcome of that?

Denis: First she yells back. Then she cries and tells me our problems are all my fault. Then she locks herself in the bedroom. It ends with both of us feeling lousy. I love her and want to have a life with her. I know that there will always be conflicts in relationships. I don't know what to do.

Practitioner: Seems like you're concerned about the arguments and want things to go better. And you are correct. Life is filled with differences with those we like and love. Sometimes romantic partners don't appreciate what we do, or they don't understand us. You said your girlfriend accused you of neglecting her when you went out with some friends from work. She called you uncaring and selfish. Those are strong words, and that's what led to your anger, right?

Denis: Yeah, that's right. My friends and I decided to go out at the last minute. That's my right. I deserve some freedom, too.

Practitioner: Okay, thanks for sharing. In these kinds of situations, you can be unassertive, aggressive, or assertive. Being unassertive means giving up your personal desires. You come home and say, "I was totally wrong. There must be something wrong with me. I will never do anything like that again. I was a real jerk." Unfortunately, that would not be the truth, and you would be wrongly putting yourself down and suppressing your anger. In contrast, if you acted aggressively, you might say, "You are such a bitch! I work hard to make money for us, and all you ever do is attack me. You are the unappreciative one, not me. You better learn to control yourself, if you know what's good for you." In this case, you are strongly reacting at the expense of your partner, whom you love. Her response is likely to be fear, hurt, and a desire to get some distance from you. Finally, there is the assertive response. It would go something like this: "Since we have a little time now, I'd like to talk to you. When you yelled at me and called me uncaring and selfish, I felt angry. I am still feeling a bit of that. But I love you and care about your feelings and reactions. Sometimes I just want some time with friends from work. I'm sorry that I didn't call you. I hope we can work this out. Let's talk more about how we can be respectful of each other." In this case, you would have expressed your feelings and desires and even apologized, without putting your partner down. How does all this sound?

Denis: It sounds fine. As long as I can express myself, I think I can do it. I don't want to be put down, and I'd like some personal space. At the same time, I am in love with her and looking toward a long-term future. That last one, the assertive one, sounds good.

Step 4. Identifying the Client's Rights and the Rights of Others

In this step, your goal is to teach the client that he has rights, and so do others. The goal is for both sides to feel respected and understood. You typically do this by having your client repeat, or reflect back, what the other person is saying:

Practitioner: You have repeatedly told me about your love for your partner and how much this relationship means to you. Yet you want your rights to be respected. You want to be able to go out with friends occasionally and not feel trapped in the relationship. What do you think your partner wants?

Denis: Probably the same thing. We both want to be respected, and we both want some freedom. Also, we both probably want to be treated well and not be yelled at.

Practitioner: So the goal is for you to identify your rights and the rights of your partner. You both have desires, goals, and wishes about the relationship. You might say something like this: "I understand that you were disappointed and even a bit concerned when I didn't come home at the usual time. I just want to be able to be free once in a while. I understand that you might want the same thing. Maybe the best way to do that is to be sure to inform each other in advance when that's likely to happen. We can work on a plan to accomplish that." How does that sound?

Step 5. Reducing the Client's Cognitive and Affective Blocks

The next step is to explore any obstacles that may prevent the development of assertive responding:

Denis: What you have been talking about seems great. But I have a concern. I think I am supposed to be supportive, no matter what. I guess that's the way I was brought up. My dad was a very supportive man, and I want to be the same way.

Practitioner: Sounds good. Being a supportive partner is important. Life is tough, and we all want support during tough times. But being supportive doesn't mean giving up all your desires related to friends, hobbies, or work. You're entitled to get what you desire also. The goal here is to work collaboratively with others so that you are cooperative and supportive, but without giving up your own desires. Good relationships involve compromises.

Denis: Okay. I get it. But I am also afraid. What if I act in too much of a self-centered way?

Practitioner: You may. This relationship is a journey. Listen to your partner's viewpoint, consult others, use me as a sounding board. In the end, you will figure out what's best for you. You can have self-interest without being totally self-centered. You can devote some time and energy to your own interests *and* devote some time and energy to the interests of your partner. It would not be right to totally sacrifice what you desire. Does that make sense?

Denis: Yes. The idea is that we both get what we want, probably at different times, by working out a plan and being honest with each other.

Step 6. Helping the Client Practice Assertive Behaviors

This is the active learning phase. The goal is to make assertive responding the automatic default reaction in your client. You accomplish this goal by developing relevant interpersonal problematic scenarios to be used in session and coupled with lots of practice. Behavioral rehearsal and modeling are the two most important techniques you can use. This means using role-playing exercises (to rehearse assertive responses) and role reversals (where you play the role of the client, to demonstrate assertive reactions). Although your clients will naturally want to talk about real issues in their lives, it's important to also use contrived scenarios in developing assertiveness skills. Here are some situations you might consider using for practice in the office:

- Refusing an invitation to join a group when the person who invited you has political or religious views that are very different from yours and tries to convince you of his position

- Refusing repeated requests for a favor

- Replying to a put-down

- Responding to an employer who says you are not working hard enough

- Responding when you learn that your friends have not included you in an outing

- Talking to a teacher who accuses you of plagiarism

- Dealing with a friend who is always late and keeps you waiting

- Sending food back in a restaurant even though the server says it was cooked perfectly

- Telling a co-worker that he has body odor

- Informing a lover that there are better ways to satisfy you sexually

- Telling a coach it's unfair that you are not in the starting lineup

It is also useful to have clients write out assertive, verbally aggressive, and passive responses, so as to highlight the contrasts, in addition to having clients verbally practice such responses with you. If the client fills out a worksheet in the waiting area, just before seeing you, he can think through his answers while not in your presence (see client worksheet 15.1, included at the end of this chapter and downloadable from www.newharbin ger.com/42877).

Assertiveness training can be conducted with individual clients, or it can be conducted in groups. One advantage of the group method is that it allows for feedback from people other than the practitioner. Here are some additional exercises that work well in groups:

- Introduce yourself by highlighting your best attributes (this exercise builds self-confidence)

- Introduce yourself by highlighting your negative attributes (this exercise reduces shame and increases self-acceptance)

- Give compliments to others (this exercise reduces self-involvement)

- Give negative feedback to a number of other group members (this exercise reduces anxiety)

- Ask for and accept positive feedback from others (this exercise builds self-confidence)

- Ask for and accept negative feedback from others (this exercise builds openness to experience)

- Make boring small talk, such as about your favorite supermarket, your favorite kind of light bulb, or your favorite kind of picture frame (this exercise gives opportunities to be emotionally honest because you can teach clients to say, "I am feeling uninvolved in this conversation," and clients then have to figure out what to do)

- Change the subject in a small-group conversation (this exercise gives an opportunity to express emotional discomfort and desires)

- Disagree when others in the group talk about childless marriages, extramarital affairs, LGBT issues, and the accomplishments of the current president of the United States (this exercise provides opportunities to disagree while learning to respect the opinions of others)

Takeaway Messages and Tools

In this chapter, we've stressed the importance of emotional awareness and verbal assertiveness training as a means of reducing anger to improve communication. Anger-related feelings that result from interpersonal disagreements, rejection, unfair treatment, and the like can be reduced by building awareness of personal anger reactions, identifying personal rights as well as the rights of others, and practicing assertive behaviors.

At the same time, even if it is done perfectly, assertiveness training will not always work. That is just the nature of human interaction. For that reason, the SMART program also encourages the use of techniques for simply accepting the reality that not every situation or relationship can be fixed or improved. The hope is that, by thoughtfully selecting relevant acceptance procedures as well as relevant change procedures, you will be able to help your clients reduce their angry reactivity to aversive situations.

One of our core convictions is that clients have the right to be emotionally expressive, and to share positive as well as negative feelings with others, in the quest for reduced anger and improved interpersonal relationships. Yet helping clients learn to be assertive is only one aspect of helping them live in a fulfilling way. Another aspect, which we tackle in the chapter 16, is nurturing happiness.

CLIENT WORKSHEET 15.1.
Practicing Assertive Responding

Assertiveness involves the direct, honest, appropriate expression of feelings and desires. Assertive responding to others often helps you achieve your goals. In contrast, verbally aversive or aggressive responding represents a forceful attempt to get your own way, no matter what, at the expense of others. In the long run, angry and verbally aggressive responding leads to poor relationships with others.

The situations described here have the potential for conflict with others. Consider each one. Then, in the space provided, write an angry/aggressive response, a passive/unassertive response, and an assertive response.

1. You've made it clear to your partner that you are tired after a long workweek, and that you do not want to plan more than one social activity per weekend, but when you arrive home on Friday evening your partner says, "Please get ready quickly. We are going to our neighbors' house for dinner, and then out to a movie. Tomorrow my parents are coming over to go shopping with us, and on Sunday I invited the neighbors to watch football with us all afternoon. It will be fun!" You say...

    Your angry/aggressive response: _____

    _____

    _____

    Your passive/unassertive response: _____

    _____

    _____

    Your assertive response: _____

    _____

    _____

2. For the past hour, you've been preparing an important report for work. It's only halfway done, and it requires concentration on your part. All of a sudden your teenage son and his friend start playing YouTube videos and begin to

laugh loudly. You ask them to keep it down, but after a minute or so the laughter begins again. You can't concentrate, and so you go into the TV room and say...

Your angry/aggressive response: _____

_____

_____

Your passive/unassertive response: _____

_____

_____

Your assertive response: _____

_____

_____

3. You live in a condominium community that has strict rules about pets. You have two small dogs, and you walk them twice a day. Yesterday you got a warning letter indicating that you will be fined $500 because the dogs make too much noise, and because poop was found on a community path near your unit. There are other, much bigger dogs in the community, and they seem to bark all the time. Right after opening the letter, you run into one of your condominium board members, who says, "I hope our letter shows you that we're serious about the rules for pets." You say...

Your angry/aggressive response: _____

_____

_____

Your passive/unassertive response: _____

_____

_____

Your assertive response: _____

_____

_____

PART 8

Going Beyond Anger Management and Putting It All Together

CHAPTER 16

Happiness

In order to be happy oneself, it is necessary to make at least one other person happy.
—Theodor Reik

The topic of happiness is both important and complex and is almost always missing from books about anger management. Reducing anger doesn't guarantee happier living. But anger reduction does set the stage for increased happiness. The task of cultivating happiness, and going beyond anger management, is addressed in this chapter.

What Is Happiness?

What is this thing called happiness that we want for our clients and ourselves? Certainly it's more than just a positive mood. It's not simply the momentary state of good feeling that comes from eating a good steak, reading an exciting novel, or having an orgasm. It's more than bouncing from one joyous moment to another and then looking for the next exciting life event. The happiness we seek for ourselves and our clients is something larger.

Happy people consider themselves to be living good, meaningful, satisfying lives. They experience many positive and uplifting emotions but also some annoying, sad, and concerning moments. That's normal in anyone's existence, including the lives of happy people. So if happiness is not just a matter of accumulating more and more distinct happy moments, then much of happiness must be based on our subjective judgments regarding our overall positive well-being. It's the totality of our judgments that counts. Our sense of happiness reflects an evaluation of the self that leads us to the conclusion that we are content with a life that we see as good, meaningful, and worthwhile.

Our conclusion that we are happy (or not) is based in part on a genetic propensity to see the proverbial glass as half empty or half full. According to Lyubomirsky (2008, 2013), genetics (that is, tendencies determined by the chromosomal material passed down to us by our parents) accounts for about 50 percent of our happiness; 10 percent is determined by our life circumstances (where we live, whether we're good-looking, whether we've found the "right" partner, and whether we have enough money, a university degree, a nice home, a fancy car, a good job, a healthy baby, and so forth); and 40 percent is a function of our state of mind and our intentional activities (that is, how we choose to think and act).

Religious and Philosophical Perspectives on Happiness

Prescriptions for happiness have come from religious teachings and schools of philosophy and, more recently, from schools of psychotherapy and academic psychology. Within each of these perspectives the aim is to influence the portion of our happiness that we can control by modifying how we think and behave. Since correlational data suggest a somewhat positive relationship between religiously committed adults and life satisfaction, we'll begin by looking at several religious perspectives on happiness.

In Buddhism and other Eastern religions, it is thought that, in order to achieve happiness and Nirvana (everlasting peace), one must overcome cravings for worldly objects, become less attached to them, and follow the Noble Eightfold Path:

1. Right understanding (seeing the world as it really is, rather than how one wants it to be, and recognizing that personal actions have consequences)

2. Right intent (developing loving-kindness, compassion, and non–illwill toward others)

3. Right speech (awareness of the effects of idle gossip, combined with not lying, not being rude, and not using language that comes from anger)

4. Right conduct (being ethical, with no thievery, injuring, killing, sexual misconduct, or use of drugs or intoxicants)

5. Right livelihood (respecting life by possessing and eating only what is needed to sustain existence, and avoiding activities that might involve weapons, slavery, or alcohol)

6. Right effort (cultivating an enthusiastic but fair and balanced life that minimizes unwholesome actions, just as good music is produced when the strings of a musical instrument are plucked neither too lightly nor too intensely)

7. Right mindfulness (being undistracted from, clearly aware of, and focused on the present moment)

8. Right *samadhi* (practicing meditation to concentrate and unify the mind)

This path is considered to comprise a moral code like others, such as the Ten Commandments. In the Eastern religions, however, the code is associated with much less of a sense of authoritarianism.

Within the Judeo-Christian perspective, the Ten Commandments represent divine rules that one should live by:

1. Have no other God but me.

2. Do not worship idols, only God.

3. Be respectful, and do not misuse God's name.

4. Keep the day of the Sabbath without work.

5. Respect parents.

6. Do not hurt others.

7. Be faithful in marriage.

8. Do not steal.

9. Do not lie.

10. Do not be envious of what others have.

In Catholicism, it is accepted that the faculties of reason and cognition can improve happiness as a function of love of God, love of one's neighbor, and love of Christ. This happiness is considered transitory, however, because true and perfect happiness and complete well-being can be expected only in the next life.

In Judaism, happiness is considered a commandment, or a *mitzvah*, since happiness allows one to be more capable of serving God, which in itself is expected to produce happiness. Jews recognize that it's easier to fulfill the requirements of daily life if emotional distress (such as anger) is not present. Judaism promotes marriage, the rituals of bar (and bat) mitzvah, and the happiness of dancing (*tzahala*) and being together (*chedva*). To be happy during Jewish holidays is considered a special commandment.

Some of these age-old religious teachings correspond to contemporary scientific principles. In fact, many religious leaders believe that some of the ideas about happiness developed by modern-day positive psychologists have already been promoted for thousands of years within religious traditions. We agree. Nevertheless, a downside for mental health practitioners to consider is that even though religions typically offer prescriptions for happiness in life, they do not provide specific mechanisms for achieving happiness, other than prayer and attendance at services. In addition, religions are based on concepts about gods and spirituality that may be rejected by clients who choose no religion, or who practice outside traditional religious frameworks.

As mentioned earlier, correlational data suggest that religious people may have a bit of an advantage when it comes to happiness. But correlation, of course, does not imply causation, and we have little understanding of whether religious thinking causes happiness, whether happy people seek out religion, or whether other variables account for the relationship between religious practice and happiness. For example, if happiness is reflected in the absence of stress and negative emotionality, then it may be that prayer is helpful in reducing stress and negative emotions. For Buddhists, prayer is a meditative experience. For Jews, prayer (known as *davening*) involves repeating verses and making repetitive body movements. For Catholics, prayer may mean reciting the Rosary. For Protestants, it's the centering prayer. The repetition of words and bodily movements not only may reduce tension but also may contribute to happiness. This suggests that the observed positive relationship between religion and happiness may be due to a third variable—the repetitious and rhythmical nature of many religious sounds and behaviors, rather than religious belief itself.

Psychotherapeutic and Psychological Perspectives on Happiness

Aside from religious models of happiness, scientific and practice-oriented scholars have also had much to say about happiness. In this section, we cover two psychological perspectives.

Rational-Emotive Behavior Therapy

Albert Ellis, the founder of rational-emotive behavior therapy (REBT), promoted the philosophical principles of *ethical humanism* in his approach to human suffering and happiness. As a perspective, ethical humanism emphasizes the *agency* of human beings (that is, our capacity to behave intentionally as we seek our goals) as well as the idea that we can use thoughtful reasoning to explain and modify our actions. From this perspective, our judgments and actions are at least partially self-determined, and this is why ethical humanists and rational-emotive behavior therapists believe that we can thoughtfully bring about change in our lives and thus reduce unhappiness and promote more joy. (Methods derived from the REBT approach to reducing anger and unhappiness were reviewed in chapter 10.) The REBT perspective suggests that it is our responsibility to lead ethical lives, not only for personal fulfillment but also for the greater good of humanity. For ethical humanists, the ultimate questions have to do with how we can create meaningfulness in life and discover the best ways to treat each other. Ethical humanism promotes insight-based belief, actions that bring out the best in ourselves and others, and respect for human worth as evidenced by treating others with fairness and kindness. It also focuses on ethical behaving as evidenced by acting with love, justice, honesty, and forgiveness, and it aims to cultivate spiritualism through the experienced interdependence of humanity, nature, and positive values.

The ethical humanistic perspective contrasts with other deterministic views, such as those associated with psychodynamic theory and methodological or pure behaviorism, wherein our thoughts, feelings, and behaviors are considered outcomes of such biological and social forces as genetics and the pressures of the environment. The ethical humanistic perspective also contrasts with some religious views, since it shuns the influences of supernatural forces. REBT gives cognitive power to freethinking clients, who are seen as having the personal capacity to forge both their own dissatisfaction and their own happiness. From this perspective, there are two main life goals: *survival* and *enjoyment*.

Ellis thought that REBT practitioners would be wise to promote happiness by taking this ethical, humanistic, rational, scientific stance toward the resolution of human problems. In addition, given the focus of REBT on free will and choice, Ellis promoted the importance of long-range goals, as opposed to short-term hedonism. He believed that humans are happiest when we have personal life goals and work to achieve them. This belief is consonant with the conclusions of modern-day academic psychologists who study happiness.

Ellis notably recognized that we live in a social world, and that there are many forces influencing us to act in multiple ways. Therefore, in REBT, clients are taught to put themselves and their desires first and to allow the desires of others to come second. This perspective is sometimes viewed as selfishness. But that is not what Ellis intended. He thought the goals of others are important in clients' lives, and we agree. There are clearly times when attending to the discomfort of an infant child, an ailing parent, or a job-related problem is more important than going to the theater, taking a weeklong vacation, or taking care of one's own body by exercising. But in the longer run, survival and enjoyment occur as a result of eating right, sleeping right, exercising, having occupational goals, and attending to personal desires. It's the conscious, *agentic* balance of these activities that makes for long-term happiness, according to rational-emotive thinking. Self-interest, we note, is different from selfishness; the word "selfishness" suggests lack of interest in or concern for the satisfaction and survival of others, whereas the term "self-interest" suggests often putting oneself first while remaining aware of others' life situations and sometimes putting others first.

In many ways, the rational-emotive approach to enhancing happiness is consonant with the larger perspective of humanistic psychology. This approach emphasizes a drive toward self-awareness, self-actualization, mindfulness, and creativity along with the parallel goal of changing less fulfilling patterns to patterns that are more satisfying. As a practitioner, you will probably have many unhappy clients who are living their lives for others. Clients in this situation are being dishonest with themselves and spending significant time trying to please others, thus minimizing their moments of happiness. Consider the case of Frank:

> For many years, Frank, now in his early forties, had been keeping his homosexual desires and activities a secret. He harbored great fear of how his family members and friends might react if they knew about his true desires. He secretly had anonymous sex with other men, each time feeling guilty. Then a strange thing happened—he fell in love with a woman, and they became engaged to be married.

In couples therapy, we encouraged Frank to be honest with his fiancée and begin living a genuine, authentic life. He was asked to take charge of his life and become fully aware of his goals. Finally, after ten individual sessions, and with careful guidance, we asked Frank to bring his fiancée into the sessions and take the risk of telling her about his desire to have sex with men.

We certainly recognize that every case is different, and that practitioners need to exercise careful judgment in their efforts to help clients make decisions like the one we asked Frank to make. Fortunately, a stance of honest authenticity worked out very well for Frank. He told his fiancée that he wanted to occasionally see other men even after they were married. He focused on his deep love for his partner and indicated that his having sex with men had nothing to do with affection. She accepted this, acknowledging that her love for Frank was very strong. She also thought that being married to a man who had occasional flings would be less problematic than being married to one who would spend significant time and money to attend sporting events, gamble, drink, or acquire fancy cars.

When we followed up with Frank five years later, we found that he was still happily married. More important, he was living his life as he wanted to live it, rather than living only by how society pressured him to live.

There are many other examples of why it's better to live life openly and honestly, and we often advocate for clients to live authentic and self-interested lives rather than automatically doing what others want. Being a good mother, for example, does not have to mean giving up friendships and personal goals to make sure a child has "every opportunity" in life. It may be better for a parent who is allergic to cats and dogs to deny a child a pet, even if the child is too young to understand the medical implications of the decision. And if finances are difficult, it may be best not to spend large amounts of money on ice skating or skiing lessons if it means the parent is required to take on a second or third job to afford them.

Time and attention may also be an issue in some families. Many medical and shift workers go to sleep quite early because their day begins before dawn. When their children want to engage with them late in the evening or go to a late movie, it may be necessary to forcefully tell them no. If happiness, successful functioning, and safety the next day are the goals, then paying attention to self-interest and adequate rest becomes paramount. It's important for you as a practitioner to help clients balance their personal life goals with those of others. Total self-denial rarely leads to happiness.

In the REBT approach, which is based on Stoic philosophy, clients are taught to reduce their demands regarding how they and others should act and how the world should be. Once they have managed to do this, they often experience a reduction in their inappropriate negative affect, including a reduction in their anger experiences and anger expressions and in their desire for revenge. But these changes alone will not make your clients happy. That's why it's important for you to help your clients develop personal goals, work to achieve them, place themselves first (much but not all of the time), and adopt a long-range perspective.

Positive Psychology

In recent years, as part of the positive psychology movement, a science of happiness has developed within academic psychology. Using both correlational and experimental studies, researchers have examined the thinking patterns and behaviors of happy people, with the aim of developing intervention strategies to increase happiness. Seligman (2011) and others at the University of Pennsylvania's Positive Psychology Center have noted that full happiness is not simply the result of momentary pleasures; using the acronym PERMA, Seligman has suggested that happiness is the result of five variables that can be cultivated to promote happiness and well-being:

1. Positive emotions: This variable is associated with the pleasure, joy, or exhilaration that comes from doing things that are fun. This might include playing in a basketball game, connecting with nature on a long walk, or pursuing intellectual stimulation and creative activities.

2. Engagement and absorption: This component is found in the common experiences of being profoundly involved in reading a novel or a biography, solving a jigsaw puzzle, playing a video game, skiing down a challenging trail, or learning to play a piece of music.

3. Relationships that are authentic: This variable is linked to close, meaningful, intimate bonds with others that center on openness and trust, and which may be a source of joy.

4. Meaningful existence: This element has to do with loving and being loved, giving to others through involvement in a charity or a social movement, setting and meeting professional goals, and having a higher purpose or meaning in life than the simple acquisition of money and material goods. For the two of us, it has been meaningful and life-enhancing to learn and give lectures about anger, develop programs for reducing anger, train practitioners, and help clients.

5. Achievements and accomplishments: This variable is often involved in setting and meeting relatively small, short-term goals, such as painting a room, repairing a broken door, or completing the day's assignments at work or at school. To be happy, it's important to believe that you can meet goals and then look back over your life and see what you have actually accomplished.

In the end, it will be wise for you to look beyond the momentary discomforts of your clients if helping them to be happy is the goal. Reducing what is negative (anger, anxiety, sadness) will not in itself guarantee a happy and flourishing life. Helping your clients cultivate the PERMA values to enhance well-being is what will be called for.

Recommendations

With so many issues to consider, what advice do we have for you in your work with angry clients?

- Remember that you will have limited time with most of the people you work with. Unless you have the luxury of a very long treatment trajectory, your primary goal will be to use the SMART toolbox to reduce anger and just touch on the development of happiness.

- Many people will not see happiness development as part of the therapeutic enterprise. Even bringing the topic up may lead to discord regarding the goals of treatment.

- There is also the question of payment for happiness-based interventions and services. Many individuals, institutions, and insurance companies will not want to pay for such services. Mental health inpatient facilities, community mental health centers, and our jails and prisons are filled with people in distress, and working on happiness enhancement may not be seen as a practical endeavor. Our recommendation, therefore, is to tread carefully in this area. At the same time, we believe that happiness development is important, and so we think that in most situations you can at least raise the subject and review what we've said about the habits of happy people. The following sections highlight what's most important.

Developing and Nurturing Close Relationships

Think about times you've been alone, with friends, and with family members. It turns out that happiness is most associated with times when we're with friends and family members. If you think back on the periods in your own life when you were most happy, those times probably involved other people. Certainly there are variations across individuals and time. There are times when all of us want some peace and quiet and some alone time. Some people like going shopping alone, or taking solitary walks, or spending hours quietly reading by themselves. That's fine. And some people can be quite happy when they're alone, although those folks are more the exception. But for most of us, most of the time, being with friends and family members increases happiness.

Yet it's not so simple, and just being with others is not the full answer. Your clients may protest that they have a large group of friends, or that they often see their family members but find themselves continually angry and unhappy. This suggests another issue: *ask clients what they talk about when they're with friends and family.* We have been at many dinners where the topic of conversation was the latest TV program, the latest music star, sports, politics, or the most dreaded topic of all—the weather. Sometimes, if you are an avid music or sports fan, such conversations are interesting, but after a short time they're mostly not. It's generally less satisfying when group conversation is reduced to the lowest common denominator of what people will find least offensive. Happiness comes from talking about highly personal and meaningful issues, disclosing feelings, and being willing to listen carefully to the problems of others (as well as having people in our lives who listen carefully to us). These are issues worth exploring with your clients. Not everything has to be revealed to everyone. But you can guide your clients, in a systematic and progressive way, to become more open and genuine with their partners and friends.

Giving to Others and Engaging in Acts of Kindness

Angry clients are usually quite self-involved. They're not just self-interested; they too often place themselves first and do not consider the perspectives of others at all. But happiness does not come from always focusing on the self. People who genuinely care for others are much happier.

Have conversations with your clients to determine whether they are helping others in any meaningful way. Perhaps there are opportunities to volunteer, or to be giving on a day-to-day basis, that can be encouraged. This is easier in some environments than in others. For anger management practitioners who work in independent practices, there may be boundless opportunities for you to help clients identify ways they can reach out and help others. Yet even in a restrictive environment like a prison, there may be opportunities for your clients to help others learn to read, help others make art, or be helpful to aging inmates. Also, some jobs (such as teaching and mentoring) naturally provide opportunities to help people, whereas others (such as being a day trader) generally do not.

Many clients, immersed in their anger and the pursuit of vengeance, have never thought about kindness. Therefore, we recommend that you suggest the idea of engaging in acts of kindness and then incorporate that idea into treatment. The goal is not for your clients to be kind simply in order to get something back. Rather, the goal is for your clients to engage in *random* acts of kindness. Talk with clients about paying a bridge toll for the next driver, or paying for someone else's coffee and muffin, or covering someone else's bus fare. And don't forget the classic example of helping an elderly person cross the street. Most angry individuals have never considered performing random acts of kindness, but it's an activity that can greatly enhance happiness.

Exercising and Moving

That old adage about a sound body and a sound mind is still as useful as ever. Regular exercise is associated with mental well-being, although mental health practitioners often overlook this fact. Physical exercise helps distract from negative thoughts. It's difficult to focus for any sustained amount of time on problems at work or on family problems while counting laps in a pool or trying to improve your running stride. Exercise also stimulates the release of the brain chemicals called *endorphins*, which are known to produce good feelings. In addition, many physical activities involve a goal to be attained and can lead to a sense of satisfaction. And even though some kinds of exercise are solitary, many kinds of exercise are social; for example, weight lifters use spotters, cyclists often go on group rides, and sometimes people go on group walks. The goal here is to recommend and encourage about thirty minutes a day of moderately intense physical activity for your clients. Some folks ride a bicycle to work, and there are even rare reports of canoeing to work. Even parking a car farther from work or taking a few flights of stairs may be helpful. Although each case will be different, regular exercise will be a real contributor to happiness.

Going with the Flow

The term "flow" (Csikszentmihalyi, 1975, 1990; Nakamura & Csikszentmihalyi, 2014) refers to the state of happiness that comes from being totally immersed in an activity or completely involved in trying to reach a goal. The goal itself may be connected to leisure, professional, or occupational activities, but it has to be realistic and voluntary; happiness will not come from being forced to do homework, play the tuba, or become a grand chess master. Consider how much time some children spend perfecting their performance on a skateboard or a bicycle; their parents may wish their kids did more schoolwork, but no one can deny the long-term happiness these children feel when they're absorbed in their self-motivated activities.

Flow has eight characteristics:

1. Focused concentration on the present moment

2. Balance between challenge and skills

3. Merging of action and awareness

4. Loss of reflective self-consciousness

5. Clarity of goals

6. Distortion of the experience of time

7. A sense of personal control (agency) over the situation or activity

8. Experience of the activity as effortless and intrinsically rewarding

We recommend talking with clients about their larger life goals, and about the activities they are passionately interested in. Given the many pressures of daily life, it's all too easy to lose sight of the development of flow. Whenever it's realistic and possible, encourage your clients to go with the flow.

Cultivating Spirituality

The term "spirituality" can have different meanings for different clients. For many, it will refer to a specific religious persuasion. These clients may note that religious writings generally promote prosocial thinking and activities. And who can disagree with certain recommendations from Buddhism's Noble Eightfold Path, or with many of the Ten Commandments? At the same time, many wars have been fought and many atrocities have been committed in the name of religions, and some religious organizations promote intolerance of what they regard as deviant lifestyles. Therefore, it's useful to remember that spirituality does not have to entail faith in a supernatural power or adherence to the rules of a specific organized religion. It can mean something as simple as placing one's focus on the agentic ability to live a better life. Humanism, as discussed earlier, fits this tradition. According to the American Humanist Association (https://americanhuman ist.org/what-is-humanism/definition-of-humanism), humanism is "a progressive philosophy of life that, without theism or other supernatural beliefs, affirms our ability and responsibility to lead ethical lives of personal fulfillment that aspire to the greater good." Humanists believe that this is the only life of which we have certain knowledge, that we owe it to ourselves and others to make it the best life possible, and that when people are free to think for themselves, using reason and knowledge as their tools, they are best able to solve this world's problems.

But this is another area where we suggest that you tread lightly. Care has to be taken not to suggest that spiritual or religious involvement is a must for happiness, although it may be useful for some people. Clients can choose whether to get involved in organized religious activities. They can choose whether to believe in a supernatural power. They can choose a formal religion, a less formal religion, or no religion at all.

For angry clients, this is a place where your motivational interviewing skills can be integrated into discussions. If you decide to approach spirituality, and if your client is repeatedly angry with a partner, child, or colleague, you can use the following questions to launch into a discussion about your client's spiritual beliefs:

- Tell me about what kind of wisdom your religious or spiritual beliefs might offer for handling this type of life challenge.

- In what ways would your spiritual beliefs help you live with more peace and less anger?

- Given that you are angry at your friend, how does your belief system help you get over the transgression?

- I understand that what happened seems very bad. Which part of your spiritual system aids you in reducing your anger and moving forward with your life?

As always in the SMART program, it's up to you to decide whether you even want to mention spirituality. Many times, and in many environments, it's a topic better left untouched, since it can easily throw treatment off track and weaken the therapeutic alliance. But clients often bring it up, and that's why we mention it here.

Incorporating Strengths into Daily Activities

Most angry clients are so involved in the anger that surrounds their day-to-day lives that they rarely consider their own character strengths. These are the globally defined virtues that they demonstrate in different situations, and in unique ways. Here are some of the strengths that your clients may possess:

compassion	trust	humility
respect	flexibility	empathy
honesty	kindness	gratitude
patience	tolerance	commitment
optimism	fairness	adaptability
gratitude	generosity	cooperation
forgiveness	restraint	integrity
consideration	loyalty	assertiveness

One of the better ways to boost long-term happiness is to help clients recognize their positive attributes instead of just focusing on their weaknesses. It's also helpful to have clients pursue activities that capitalize on their strengths and abilities.

The first step is to identify strengths. This can be done in a verbal dialogue: "I know that we spend lots of time talking about your anger and life difficulties, but I'd also like to know a bit about your character strengths and personality assets. What would you say are the five best parts of your personality?" A review of these positive attributes, along with a discussion of where and when they have appeared, can contribute to a sense of positive self-regard. The upside of such a dialogue is that it's quick and easy and allows for immediate discussion during a session. The downside is the lack of reliability that comes from self-judgments.

A better way to help clients understand their character assets is to have them complete a survey that contains multiple questions about each asset. One such survey can be found at http://www.viacharacter.org. Of the twenty-four character virtues measured by this survey, one of us scored highest on the following assets:

- Love (valuing close relations with others; sharing and caring)

- Gratitude (being aware of and thankful for the good things that happen)

- Love of learning (mastering new skills, topics, and bodies of knowledge; tendency to add systematically to what one knows)

- Appreciation of beauty and excellence (noticing and appreciating beauty, excellence, and skilled performance in such areas as nature, art, mathematics and science)

- Honesty (being genuine and sincere, without pretense; taking responsibility for feelings and actions)

The other scored highest on these assets:

- Creativity (thinking of novel and productive ways to conceptualize and do things, including but not limited to artistic achievement)

- Perseverance (maintaining a course of action in spite of obstacles)

- Curiosity (taking an interest in ongoing experience; exploring and discovering)

- Social intelligence (being aware of the motives and feelings of others and oneself)

- Hope (expecting the best in the future, and working to achieve it)

Both of us were pleased with our results. Of course, we recognize that a survey like this one assesses only character strengths, not flaws—which we certainly have. We also know that our strengths may manifest in only some situations. Yet we find ourselves most happy when we're engaged in activities that naturally correspond with our strengths. Surveys like this one set the stage for clients to become aware of their own positive attributes and to make better use of their strengths in their day-to-day lives.

Takeaway Messages and Tools

In the end, the most significant issue for practitioners is to figure out how to use the SMART intervention toolbox to encourage good thinking and behaving in clients. Most of your focus will surely be on the reduction of anger, yet your attention to issues related to happiness, as presented in this chapter, may well support your clients not just in reducing their anger but also in living their lives with greater meaning and fulfillment.

SMART anger management is based on a high-quality relationship with engaged clients who are aware, involved, and motivated. Anger reduction combined with happiness enhancement will lead to the overarching goal of the treatment process—to help the client live a better life. In chapter 17, we show you how to put all of what we have presented into a plan of action.

Applying the SMART Model to a Sample Case

Not everything that is faced can be changed. But nothing can be changed until it is faced.

—James Baldwin

In some ways, this book ends where it began. As noted in the introduction, ours is not a session-by-session, cookie-cutter approach to treatment. Rather, as a SMART anger manager, you will be innovative in developing a unique treatment plan for each client. In this, the final chapter, we use the case of Justin to walk you through our decision-making process, and we provide general guidelines for you to consider as you make your own selections from the menu of interventions. Because good treatment is as much an art as a science, and because you have not seen Justin in real life, you may fully agree, partially agree, or completely disagree with our decisions in his case. But we hope that as you review this chapter, you will gain a better understanding of how to integrate the various tools that are part of the SMART anger program.

Selection Menu Guidelines

You are now familiar with the foundational elements of high-quality anger treatment. This section offers a few additional tips for selecting interventions.

Include an Intervention for Each Element of the Anger Episode Model

To provide a complete and well-rounded treatment program, select interventions that cut across the various elements of treatment. Be sure to include at least one intervention that enhances awareness, engagement, and motivation; one that aims to alter anger triggers; one that can enhance acceptance, and that introduces techniques for restructuring the cognitions that are typically present in anger episodes; one that aims to reduce and minimize internal anger experiences and urges; and one that utilizes some strategy to alter the expression of anger. The relative emphasis (number of interventions) on each of the elements will depend on the level of the client's skills (or deficits) and on the context of the specific case.

Tailor Preparation Time to the Level of the Client's Intrinsic Motivation

The reality of working with angry adults and adolescents is that great variability exists regarding their degree of insight and motivation. We suggest that you resist the temptation to paint all angry clients with a broad, pessimistic brush. You will find that successful engagement is often a matter of how these individuals are initially approached. Clients who arrive ready to work on their anger can move more quickly to action-oriented interventions. As a rule, the more the person's presence in treatment has been coerced, the more time we spend on preparation activities. Also remember that angry clients are often less avoidant than are anxious individuals, and they have more energy than do clients who are depressed. Therefore, once angry clients decide to reduce their anger-related reactions, they are often willing to jump right into learning and practicing new skills in their day-to-day lives. In general, it's best to make the transition to active behavior-change interventions after a degree of motivation and commitment to improving anger reactions has been developed.

Recognize the Anger Episode as the Unit of Analysis for Guiding Treatment

As we've said throughout this book, we have found it more useful to focus on specific episodes of anger than to have philosophical or fuzzy discussions about the underlying factors that may have led to a client's anger. Analysis of the anger episode forms the groundwork for building awareness, for developing a shared understanding with the client of how anger is experienced and expressed in real-life interactions, and for establishing treatment targets and goals. The greater the number of specific episodes that you and the client review, with in-session practice aimed at developing better reactions in the future, the more likely it is that the client will show improvement in the face of actual challenges.

Be Thoughtfully Cautious with Exposure and Assertiveness Interventions

In treatment studies with angry participants, and in clinical practice with angry clients, we have not encountered difficulties in the use of exposure procedures. Nevertheless, we recognize that you may work with violent offenders, individuals with traumatic brain injuries, schizophrenic-spectrum clients, and others who carry more risk. We believe that exposure procedures are a valuable component of effective anger treatment, but these procedures have not been widely described in the treatment literature. Therefore, before you implement an exposure exercise, make sure that the client has developed a commitment to reducing his or her anger, that the client has achieved a therapeutic alliance with you, and that the client understands the rationale for using exposure exercises. Of course, it's also wise to consider comorbidity issues that may impede the client's self-control. During an exposure session, check in frequently with the client about his or her ability to maintain control, and respect any objections the client may voice (again, we have not heard any).

Regarding assertiveness, there are times when teaching an angry client to express himself more assertively can make a bad situation worse by further disrupting a relationship, increasing a conflict with a supervisor, triggering a negative reaction from the police or a probation officer, and so forth. Also consider that a client's attempts to be assertive may be unsuccessful if his anger has escalated beyond a certain level. Angry thoughts and sensations will overpower new skills and propel poor behavior. Therefore, sometimes it's helpful for clients to reduce their reactivity to their triggers through exposure practice before they're taught assertiveness skills and asked to try transferring those skills to real-life situations. In addition, good judgment may be required with respect to the question of which situations call for assertiveness. It's not crucial that all unpleasant behavior be confronted, that all disagreements be discussed, and that all problems be resolved. Your thoughtful input, and your wisdom, regarding which situations call for an assertive response, and which ones can be let go, will often be very helpful to your clients.

Tailor Cognitive Interventions to the Characteristics of the Client

When you select a specific cognitive intervention, consider the thinking styles that emerge during anger episodes, and take note of the client's abstract reasoning abilities. You will find anger episode analysis helpful in identifying cognitive targets. For example, an adult who approaches situations with a negative bias toward others' intentions and behavior will probably benefit from learning to examine the evidence and consider alternative explanations for others' behavior. Clients whose outlook is demanding may benefit from a rational-emotive behavior therapy approach. Forgiveness might be considered for clients with longer-term anger reactions related to themes of past mistreatment.

Don't Try to Change Everything at Once

Thoughtfully prioritize the life areas (work, school, family, parenting, romantic relationships, friendships, and so forth) to be addressed with respect to improved anger management. In some cases, it may be best to initially address the life area that is creating the most turmoil. In other cases, the life area most likely to produce the quickest success might be prioritized as the initial focus so as to increase the client's confidence in the treatment process. Remember that collaboratively established treatment goals will hold the greatest value for clients and boost the likelihood of their active participation. Once improvement has been made in a specific life area, skills like relaxation, problem solving, assertiveness, and forgiveness can be applied to other areas of the client's life.

Be Selective: More May Not Be Better

There is no reason to believe that all the interventions we have described must be applied to each case. In the treatment outcome literature, complex multicomponent interventions often achieve treatment effects similar to those of single-modality treatments (DiGiuseppe & Tafrate, 2003), and so there is little support for the idea that the addition of numerous interventions (the "kitchen sink" approach) will result in increased overall effectiveness. When the two of us observe others conducting anger treatment interventions, we are often dismayed to see practitioners skimming along, in surface fashion, from one intervention to another: "Today we are doing cognitive restructuring, so pull out your thinking worksheet. Next session we will cover assertiveness." Such an approach is likely to have minimal effects in the long run because not enough time is devoted to practice, repetition, and real-world application of new skills. Therefore, resist the temptation to cover all the interventions. Rather, thoughtful selection of interventions, with sufficient time to practice and review progress, will be optimal for most clients. Another benefit of the SMART approach, however, is that if a specific intervention does not seem to be working, you can reasonably select a different option from the same treatment phase.

The Case of Justin

Justin, a current client, is forty-seven years old and has been a high school history teacher at the same school for the past twenty years. He says that the early years of his career were enjoyable—he liked the students and got pleasure from teaching his classes.

Unfortunately, however, over the past decade Justin has developed a reputation in his school district for being volatile, insensitive to students, and oppositional toward colleagues and the administration. He now describes his students as disrespectful, their parents as enablers of poor behavior, and the school administrators as out to get him. As an example, he cites the fact that each summer when class schedules are sent out, a few parents advocate for their children to be moved from his class to a different history teacher's class. Justin dismisses these parents' complaints as evidence that they are meddling too much in their children's lives, and he says the administration is afraid to stand up to what he describes as these entitled parents.

Justin has been passed over for leadership positions in the history department at his school, and he has been gently asked not to participate in any of the school clubs or extracurricular history-related events. Recently there have also been changes in the school district, with a new superintendent and a new administration. The new administrators are taking a more direct and adversarial stance toward Justin. They have created a new system of teacher evaluation, which involves classroom observations and feedback, and they are encouraging more detailed documentation of complaints. Justin's angry reactions toward the students in his classroom have been noted, and his behavior has been identified as in need of change if Justin is to continue teaching in the district. This is the immediate reason why Justin has sought treatment.

As for Justin's family life, he is divorced, with a sixteen-year-old son, a fourteen-year-old son, and a thirteen-year-old daughter. He reports a reasonably good relationship with his sons and occasional problems connecting with his daughter. Justin describes a contentious relationship with his ex-wife. Although things have settled down since the divorce, he complains that paying child support is contributing to his financial stress. Apparently his ex-wife is dating someone who is well off financially, but she is choosing not to remarry because she wants Justin to continue the payments until their youngest child reaches the age of eighteen. Justin describes the legal system as unfairly tilted toward women.

Justin occasionally takes on carpentry jobs, such as bathroom remodeling after school hours, to bring in extra income. He says that his dating life is hampered by financial and time constraints. His most successful relationship since the divorce lasted only a few weeks. He says that most of the women he has dated were unstable and difficult, and that these relationships typically ended after a verbal argument about money, politics, or parenting issues.

Justin also acknowledges that he drinks daily to relax. His drinking has fluctuated over the years, but he is beginning to see his alcohol use as a problem.

Setting the Stage for Treatment: Engagement and Enhancing Awareness and Motivation

It was important in the initial sessions to spend more time listening than conducting assessments or trying to teach new skills. Since Justin was coerced into treatment by his employer and sees the school administration as out to get him, we pulled back from an active-directive stance in the first few sessions and focused instead on meeting Justin where he was, gaining his trust, and developing a relationship with him. An additional objective in the early sessions was to explore and reinforce, through open questions and reflective statements, Justin's own arguments in favor of anger reduction. Since his initial motivation to change his anger reactions was low, we did three things:

1. Spent significant time in the preparation phase of treatment

2. Included heavy use of motivational interviewing

3. Incorporated awareness building into assessment

Before making the transition into active change interventions, we guided Justin toward the development of his own rationale for pursuing anger reduction. Even though Justin might have been thinking *I have to come to treatment or lose my job*, we wanted him to come to another realization as well: *There are some changes I would like to make anyway that will help me be more effective and happier in life.*

THE INITIAL APPROACH

Practitioner: (*opening statement*) Hi, Justin. I'm Dr. Kassinove. It's a pleasure to meet you. As you know, I'm a psychologist, and I work to help people develop skills to improve their lives. These skills often involve different ways of solving problems and reacting better to life's challenges. I know there have been some recent difficulties at work that have brought you here. I'd like to hear your perspective on those problems and also find out what is most urgent for you right now so I might be able to be helpful. Tell me, what's been happening?

Justin: I've been a high school teacher for almost twenty years. It's a good job, but the environment has really changed. The students have become more disrespectful, the parents all think their kids are special butterflies, and the administration's top priority is to be liked by the parents. I guess I'm not good at playing politics. So that gets me in trouble sometimes with the parents and the principal.

Practitioner: (*reflection to elicit more information*) So you're thinking it's not the same job as when you started.

Justin: Yeah. I don't enjoy going to work anymore. I end up clashing with students for using their cell phones in class and talking to each other. The kids complain, and the first reaction of the principal is to take their side.

Practitioner: (*reflection to elicit more information*) Sounds like the joy of the job has faded, and you don't feel much support from your administration.

Justin: It's worse than that. They're out to get me. It's already been decided they want me gone. Honestly, they sent me here because they are hoping you will tell them that I shouldn't be a teacher anymore.

Practitioner: (*reflection to grasp the client's perspective and reduce defensiveness*) Sounds like this has gotten serious. Also, you think coming here is not about trying to help you in any way. It's about providing some type of reason to get you fired.

Justin: Yeah.

Practitioner: *(providing information to reinforce confidentiality; instilling hope; reinforcing client's freedom of choice)* Thanks for being honest with me. Actually, I'm hoping our sessions together might be helpful to you. I'd like you to know that what we talk about stays between you and me. I don't share any information unless I have your permission to do so. The only exception is if you tell me you might physically harm yourself or someone else. Also, I want to mention that I have helped other people better manage work problems such as the one you described. Finally, since it's your life, you get to make the decision whether you want to try to improve things at work or not. I'm not sure if that's something you want to do.

Justin: I guess I need to think about it.

Practitioner: *(open question to steer the conversation toward specific anger episodes and elicit more information)* Okay, but for now, tell me more about the problems that happen with students in class—what kinds of things are happening?

The engagement skills demonstrated in the preceding dialogue are presented in more detail in chapter 2. In this case, on the basis of Justin's observed level of comfort and willingness to talk, we maintained a client-centered and exploratory stance for the first two to three sessions and then made the transition to assessment activities.

ASSESSMENT: ADMINISTERING STANDARDIZED TESTS AND PROVIDING FEEDBACK

As part of the standard intake process, Justin was given an intake interview and one of the specialty anger instruments described in chapter 4. The advantage of standardized testing was that we were able to quickly learn how Justin's scores on important anger dimensions compared to those of other men his age. Justin's highest scores on the Anger Disorders Scale (DiGiuseppe & Tafrate, 2004) were on the following subscales:

- Verbal expression: 91st percentile

- Suspiciousness: 90th percentile

- Coercion: 87th percentile

This suggested that Justin engages in a range of negative verbal behaviors (insults, sarcasm, threats) when angry, believes that other people harbor hostile intentions toward him, and uses his anger to control others in relationships.

We provided Justin with feedback on his scores in order to set the stage for exploring the impact of these anger patterns on different areas of his life—that is, work as well as family and romantic relationships. (As discussed in chapter 5, when feedback is provided, anger dimensions are always described in easy-to-understand language.) We presented one score at a time, and we discussed Justin's scores in terms of percentiles, since that is an approach that most clients easily understand (keep in mind that your goal is not to convince the client to *accept* the feedback but rather to *consider* the information; you also want to reinforce and evoke change talk as the discussion unfolds):

Practitioner: Justin, would it be okay if we took a few minutes to talk about the results of the test you took during our last meeting?

Justin: Yeah.

Practitioner: First let's talk about a scale called "Verbal Expression," which measures the level at which you express your anger toward others. You know— things like shouting, arguing, and making sarcastic comments. Based on your responses, this score was high. You scored at the 91st percentile. This means that you express anger at a level higher than that of 91 percent of other men your age. What do you think about that?

Strategic open questions can be used to further explore the anger dimension being discussed, and to evoke change talk:

- How has being so verbally expressive with your anger influenced your life?

- Give me some examples of how your anger reactions have affected your career.

- How have these anger reactions affected your romantic relationships?

ASSESSMENT: ANGER EPISODES AND ENHANCING AWARENESS OF ANGER PATTERNS

Using the Anger Episode Model, we examined specific components and consequences of Justin's individual episodes of anger. This was done in the spirit of exploration, with no evaluative judgments about whether Justin had an anger "problem." For most clients like Justin, anger does not emerge automatically. It follows a predictable pattern. Breaking anger experiences into components makes the task of altering those experiences less daunting and can be a good place to start in terms of collaboratively identifying treatment targets, such as exaggerated thinking and/or verbal behaviors like yelling and arguing.

We placed emphasis on the "Outcomes" part of the Anger Episode Model. As always during such discussions, speech that favored better anger control (change talk) was reinforced. The goal was to increase Justin's awareness of the costs associated with his anger reactions and to further develop and strengthen his own arguments for better managing his anger in the future.

Figure 17.1 shows one of Justin's completed Anger Episode Records. When we reviewed about seven of Justin's specific anger episodes across several early sessions, a few important patterns were revealed:

Fill out one record for each episode of anger. Provide information in each of the six parts.

Part 1. Trigger

Place a check mark in the box next to the word(s) indicating the area of your life in which your anger was triggered.

- ☑ Work
- ☐ School
- ☐ Family
- ☐ Parenting
- ☐ Romantic relationship
- ☐ Friendship
- ☐ Other: _____

In one simple sentence, report the event that led to your anger. (Example: "My son forgot again to clean his room.")

Emily was using her cell phone during class.

Part 2. Thoughts

Place a check mark in the box next to every statement that applies to this anger episode.

- ☐ *Awfulizing:* At the time, I thought this was one of the worst things that could be happening.
- ☑ *Low frustration tolerance:* I thought I could not handle or deal with the situation.
- ☑ *Demandingness:* I thought the other person(s) should have acted differently.
- ☐ *Rating others:* I saw the other person(s) as _____.
- ☐ *Rating myself:* Deep down, I thought I was less important or worthwhile.
- ☐ *Distortion or misinterpretation:* My thinking became distorted, and I didn't see things clearly.

Part 3. Experience

Place a check mark in the box next to the number that corresponds to the intensity and degree of your anger, and to how you felt in this situation.

Intensity of Your Anger	Extent of Your Anger	How You Felt
☐ 1	Almost no anger	Calm, indifferent
☐ 2	Slight anger	Jarred, moved, stirred, ruffled, challenged
☐ 3	Mild anger	Annoyed, bothered, irritated, perturbed, flustered, uneasy, provoked, impelled, cranky, crotchety, distressed, disturbed
☐ 4		
☐ 5	Moderate anger	Mad, agitated, pissed off, irked, aggravated, fired up, riled up, all worked up, peeved, indignant
☐ 6		
☑ 7	Strong anger	Irate, inflamed, exasperated, fuming, burned up, incensed, infuriated, enraged, hysterical
☐ 8		
☐ 9	Extreme anger	Frenzied, vicious, unhinged, up in arms, rabid, crazed, maniacal, wild, violent, demented
☐ 10		

Now complete the following sentence: *At the time of this specific event, I felt...*

very angry, and disrespected

How long did your anger last? Place a check mark in the box next to the word indicating the duration of your anger.

☑ Minutes   ☐ Days

☐ Hours   ☐ Ongoing

What physical sensations did you notice? Place a check mark in the box next to the word(s) describing your physical sensations.

☑ Fluttering/upset stomach   ☐ Sweating

☑ Indigestion   ☐ Warmth/flushing

☐ Rapid heart rate   ☐ Nausea

☐ Dizziness   ☐ Rapid breathing

☐ Fuzziness/feelings of unreality   ☐ Headache

☐ Muscle tension   ☐ Tingling

☐ Fatigue   ☐ Trembling

☐ Other: _____

Part 4. Action Urge

Place a check mark in the box next to the word or phrase corresponding to your action urge in this situation. Then, on the line that follows that word or phrase, briefly describe the impulse that arose for you. (Examples: "I just wanted to get in his face" or "I couldn't wait to get away from her.")

☑ Confront: *Wanted to get in her face and scream at her.*

☐ Withdraw: _____

☐ Resolve problem: _____

☐ Other: _____

Part 5. Anger Expression

Place a check mark in the box next to every behavior you engaged in during this anger episode.

☐ No expression (kept things in, boiled inside, held grudges and didn't tell anyone)

☐ Indirect expression (secretly did something to harm the other person, spread rumors, ignored what the other person wanted)

☐ Outward verbal expression (yelled, screamed, argued, threatened; made sarcastic, nasty, or abusive remarks)

☑ Outward expression against an object (broke, threw, slammed, or destroyed an object)

☐ Outward expression against a person (fought, hit, kicked, or shoved someone)

☑ Outward expression through bodily gestures (rolled eyes, crossed arms, glared, frowned, gave a stern look)

☐ Avoidance (escaped or walked away from the situation; distracted myself by reading, watching TV, listening to music)

☐ Substance use (drank alcohol; took medications; used other drugs, such as marijuana or cocaine)

☐ Attempt at resolution (compromised, discussed, or came to some agreement with the other person)

☐ Other: _____

Part 6. Outcomes

What was a *positive short-term* outcome of this anger episode?

When I slammed my hand on her desk, she stopped using her phone for the rest of the class period.

What was a *positive long-term* outcome of this anger episode?

Nothing positive in the long run.

What was a *negative short-term* outcome of this anger episode?

The other students in the class looked uncomfortable.

What was a *negative long-term* outcome of this anger episode?

Students think I'm a hothead.

Some students told their parents—the principal talked to me about the incident the next day.

Figure 17.1. Justin's Completed Anger Episode Record

- The largest number of Justin's anger episodes occurred with students; the second largest number of his anger episodes followed his interactions with his ex-wife.

- *Demandingness* and *low frustration tolerance* were the most common thinking patterns that Justin reported.

- Justin's anger episodes were usually of moderate intensity (ranging from 5 to 7 on a 10-point scale).

- Gastrointestinal and stomach sensations were common for Justin when he was angry.

- Justin had the urge to confront when he was angry.

- Verbal behaviors, bodily gestures, and hitting objects (such as his desk) were common for Justin.

- Positive outcomes of Justin's anger episodes were that students stopped their bad behavior after he confronted them, and that he felt justified expressing himself.

- Negative outcomes included increased conflict, damage to relationships, and loss of respect from colleagues at work.

In cases like Justin's, we consider the phase of preparation and engagement to be critical. Without sufficient motivation and a good therapeutic alliance, change-oriented interventions are unlikely to succeed.

Case Conceptualization and Development of a Treatment Plan

Synthesizing relevant information to create a tailored treatment plan is called *case conceptualization* or *case formulation*. As discussed throughout this book, the SMART menu of active change interventions is based on the general principles of traditional behavioral therapy as well as on the general principles of cognitive behavioral therapy. Therefore, we focus on modifying previously reinforced maladaptive behaviors and on changing thoughts that are problematic. The goal of this two-pronged approach is to reduce both the internal experience and the external expression of anger and to produce a more generalized pattern of reduced reactivity to existing anger triggers.

Given the context of Justin's referral to treatment, our initial interview with him, analysis of his anger episodes, the specialized anger testing that we administered, and information that we gathered during the initial sessions, we recommended the following general treatment plan for Justin:

- We identified the *work area* of Justin's life as the top treatment priority, starting with his classroom interactions with students and moving on to his exchanges with administrators and colleagues. We identified Justin's *interactions with his ex-wife and with potential romantic partners* as the second area of focus, to be addressed once progress had been made in the work area of Justin's life. We also recommended that Justin's *substance use* be further assessed and monitored as a potential additional focus of treatment.

- We identified Justin's *negative verbalizations* and his *use of anger expressions to coerce others* as key behaviors to be targeted for change. We saw the goal as reducing such behaviors and replacing them with more effective alternatives.

- We identified Justin's *negative bias in interpreting the intentions and actions of others* and his *demandingness* as the focal points for cognitive restructuring. Specific cognitive skills to be enhanced were *generation of alternative explanations for the actions of others* (perspective taking) and *development of a more flexible life philosophy*.

- We identified *improvement in Justin's lifestyle patterns* (especially regarding sleep and nutrition) and an *increase in his overall happiness* as the final treatment component. We saw that Justin would also have to address some larger questions, including what he wanted his future to look like in terms of work, his connection with his children, and his romantic relationships.

In the remainder of this chapter, we discuss specific interventions with Justin that corresponded to this treatment plan.

Altering Negative and Coercive Verbal Behaviors

As a starting point, we wanted to learn more details about the verbal arguments Justin was having with students in his classes and about the context surrounding his automatic, nonthoughtful, impulsive reactions. We began with the mindfulness procedures described in chapter 12 and asked Justin to become, in the classroom, an observer of his own anger. We wanted him to simply observe his thoughts, feelings, and actions in the present moment, from a distance.

MINDFULNESS

Practitioner: Justin, you have done a great job of tracking your anger episodes over the last few sessions. This week I want to have you try something a little different. I'd like you to focus on exactly what happens in the classroom and then become an observer of your own anger—kind of like you are standing outside yourself, watching the action. Don't try to change anything yet. Just see if you can describe what is happening to yourself as it unfolds.

Justin: You mean sort of like the anger records?

Practitioner: Yes, but with a more in-the-moment focus. With the anger records, you completed them at the end of the day, after you'd had an anger experience. You were looking back in time. Now I'm asking you to describe your anger, to yourself, as it's happening.

Justin: Like talking to myself as I'm feeling it?

Practitioner: Yes, exactly. So if I were you, it might sound like this in my head: *Oh, here comes Emily,* and I'm already thinking, *She's going to be a disrespectful brat again today and be on her phone.* I find myself focused on what she is doing and looking for signs that she is texting. There goes my mind again—I'm thinking, *She is so disrespectful—her parents haven't taught her how to behave in the real world.* I notice the knot in my stomach. Now she's looking down at her lap as I'm teaching. My mind quickly goes to *I know she is looking at her phone—I need to shut this down before it gets worse.* I find myself glaring at her as I feel my anger build. I'm resisting the urge to yell at her in front of the class, and I'm thinking, *Don't cause another scene.* She ignores me and keeps looking at her lap and smiles while typing something. My stomach gets tight. I think, *I must make her stop.* Like in a dream, I walk over and slam my hand on her desk to get her attention and make her stop. She looks up and stops. I quickly glance around the room and notice that the other students seem uncomfortable. I go back to teaching.

Justin: It's like telling a story. I think I can do that.

Practitioner: Try it. After you have fully observed your anger, find a place by yourself, and record the story with as much detail as you can, using the voice memo app on your phone. We will review the recording the next time you come in.

As a follow-up step, one that was more challenging, we asked Justin to become aware of his angry thoughts and feelings but not act on or give in to them. In this approach, Justin attempted to deliberately disengage from his automatic angry behavior and to step back from verbally or physically confronting his students in the classroom, even though he had angry thoughts and sensations. The emphasis then moved to replacing Justin's typical angry behaviors with behaviors likely to produce better outcomes.

PROBLEM SOLVING: DEVELOPING BETTER CLASSROOM MANAGEMENT SKILLS

In SMART anger management, the goal of problem solving is to find better solutions to ongoing life problems. To review, the problem-solving model described in chapter 9 comprises five steps:

1.   Clearly identify and explore an ongoing problem.

2.   Generate a menu of potential solutions.

3.   Assess the probable outcomes of each potential solution.

4.   Select the best potential solution.

5.   Implement and evaluate the chosen solution.

Like many other clients, Justin gets caught up in his anger and behaves impulsively and carelessly, and this behavior does not bring about the long-term outcomes he desires. The greatest classroom challenge for Justin seems to be students' cell phone use (see figure 17.2, which shows Justin's completed worksheet for social problem solving; refer to client worksheet 9.1, a blank copy of which is downloadable from www.newharbinger .com/42877). During our discussion, Justin identified several solutions that, when combined, formed the foundation for a workable classroom policy regarding mobile devices. Justin quickly eliminated the potential solution of assigning a detention, because that was likely to lead to more conflict and complaints. To put the new policy into practice, Justin decided that at the beginning of each class he would ask students to place their phones where they could not see them (such as in a backpack). Then, as the second part of the policy, he would offer the students a four-minute cell phone break during class time, when they could quickly check their texts, emails, and social media accounts. If students used their cell phones outside the breaks, he would gently remind the entire class of the policy by saying, in a calm voice, "I just want to remind everyone of the class rules, so please put your phones away. I will let you know when it is time for our cell phone break." If a student persisted, Justin would not confront the student but instead would remind him or her specifically of the policy by saying, again in a calm voice, "Emily, if you don't abide by the class rules, I will send you to the assistant principal's office." Discussion with Justin revealed several advantages to this approach:

- Justin would have his own reasonable policy to guide his expectations and behaviors regarding students' use of mobile devices.

- Instead of confronting students, Justin could fall back on stating the policy.

- He would be able to take himself out of the disciplinarian role.

- He would be able to take the negative focus off himself and place it on students' problematic behavior.

- Offering a cell phone break during class would help Justin be viewed as more accommodating, current, and cool in the students' eyes.

Name _____

Date _____

A. Clearly Identify and Explore an Ongoing Problem

Use the *when...then* format. Include actions, thoughts, and words.

When...

students use their cell phones in class while I'm teaching

Then...

I scold them, glare at them, or sometimes slam my hand on their desks. I think the students need to stop. My reaction makes things worse.

B. Generate a Menu of Potential Solutions

In the space provided, describe at least five potential solutions to the problem you identified in part A.

1. Ask students to put phones out of sight

2. Give the class a brief cell phone break

3. Give them a detention

4. State cell phone policy briefly at the start of class; repeat

5. Refer problem students to assistant principal

C. Assess the Probable Outcomes of Each Potential Solution

For each potential solution that you identified in part B, list the likely short-term outcomes and the likely long-term outcomes.

	Likely Short-Term Outcomes	Likely Long-Term Outcomes
1.	They won't be tempted	Less conflict
2.	Less need to check phones	Students will see me positively
3.	Conflict; students are unhappy	Parents complain
4.	Most students will comply	Less conflict
5.	I'm no longer the enforcer	It's not my problem; focus on teaching

Figure 17.2. Justin's Problem-Solving Worksheet

PRACTICING NEW SKILLS AND REDUCING REACTIVITY THROUGH IMAGINAL AND VERBAL BARB EXPOSURE

Exposure-based methods attempt to address the underlying conditioning and automatic nature of some anger reactions. In a conditioning model of treatment, the goal is to associate anger triggers with new, competing responses, such as relaxation, statements of cognitive coping, verbal assertiveness, and calm. New responses require repeated rehearsal of anger triggers, of course. Apart from producing both habituation to anger triggers and extinction of dysfunctional responses, the goal of systematic exposure is to create opportunities for the new responses to be practiced and reinforced, first in treatment sessions and ultimately in daily interactions.

In Justin's case, the emphasis is on more effective classroom management skills. Over the course of several sessions, we implemented an imaginal exposure intervention like the one described in chapter 12. The first step was to collaborate with Justin on creating an anger imagery scene related to students' cell phone use in the classroom, a scene that included details regarding a disrespectful student. Justin's recorded story of his anger was a good starting point for the development of his scene (see "Mindfulness," earlier in this chapter). We then asked Justin to review his scene each evening, to experience its imagery, and to imagine himself telling his students, without anger, about the new policy on cell phone use in the classroom.

As a follow-up, we developed a graded series of barbs (see chapter 13), which consisted of imagined statements from students:

- I don't have to listen to you. I can look at my phone whenever I want.

- I can listen to you teach and look at my phone at the same time. It's called multitasking. Haven't you heard of it?

- Cell phones are a part of life. You're just old and out of touch.

Justin was asked to stay calm and relaxed, to take a deep breath as the first barb was delivered in session, and to practice responding by repeating the classroom policy in a calm voice and, as necessary, saying that he was going to send a student to the assistant principal's office. The initial barb was repeated at increasing levels of intensity. Once the first barb no longer produced angry arousal, Justin worked on the second barb. (As always in this type of approach, additional barbs can be created, if necessary, from details related to a client's real-world anger situation.) We expect that Justin, through repeated practice both with his imaginal scene and with the in-session verbal barbs, will become less reactive to students' cell phone use and perceived disrespect and will be prepared to respond more effectively.

Restructuring Angry Thinking

With respect to interventions that involved accepting, adapting, and adjusting, we stayed focused on Justin's anger reactions in the classroom. Following a brief psychoeducational component, we moved our emphasis to replacing Justin's anger-prompting thoughts with more flexible, reasonable, and accurate thinking, and to having Justin practice new thinking in the classroom.

PSYCHOEDUCATION

Since students' cell phone use in the classroom emerged as an important anger trigger for Justin, we decided that a short psychoeducational component would set the stage for altering his cognitive reactions. Justin was asked to do some Internet research on students' use of smartphones so as to better understand how today's students differ from students of his own generation and from the students he taught at the beginning of his career. Justin discovered the following facts (see M. Anderson & Jiang, 2018; Lenhart, 2010, 2015; Pew Research Center & University of Michigan, 2010):

- Smartphone ownership has become a nearly ubiquitous element of teen life.

- 95 percent of teens now report they have a smartphone or access to one.

- 45 percent of teens say they are online on a near-constant basis.

- Another 44 percent say they go online several times a day, meaning roughly 90 percent of teens go online multiple times per day.

- Girls typically send and receive more than twice as many messages per day as do boys.

- 84 percent of teens sleep with their phones.

- 65 percent of cell-phone-owning teens at schools that completely ban phones still bring their phones to school every day.

- 58 percent of cell-phone-owning teens at schools that ban phones have still sent a text message during class.

- 43 percent of all teens who take their phones to school say they text in class at least once a day.

- Adults differ from teens—teens send and receive, on average, five times more texts per day than do adult texters.

PERSPECTIVE TAKING: UNDERSTANDING THE INTENTIONS AND ACTIONS OF OTHERS

Like many clients, Justin has difficulty seeing things from others' perspectives when he's angry. Because perspective taking can aid in the development of empathy, foster a more realistic view of others' intentions, and enhance overall anger reduction (see chapter 11), we asked Justin to explain his students' cell phone use from their perspective:

Practitioner:	Based on our discussions, during the times when you get angry and confront students about their cell phone use, you have this tendency to think that they are being disrespectful to you and you must make them stop. Does that sound about right?
Justin:	Yeah, that's it exactly.
Practitioner:	I'd like to try something with you. Can you take the students' perspective for a minute? See if you can view the situation from their point of view. For example, what is Emily thinking right before she looks at her cell phone in class?
Justin:	She's probably not thinking anything. She just reaches for her phone when she gets bored.
Practitioner:	Right. So she might be thinking, *Let me just check and see what is going on with my friends.* For her, and students from her generation, it's normal and automatic.
Justin:	I think so.
Practitioner:	So she doesn't look at her cell phone with the intention of being disrespectful to you. In fact, she is not thinking about you at all.
Justin:	That's probably right.
Practitioner:	When students look at their cell phones in class, what can you say to yourself that would be more accurate about what's happening? What could you say that would make it less personal?
Justin:	I could say that this is what these students do automatically. It's how they go through their lives.
Practitioner:	That's very good. So what does it mean about you?
Justin:	It means nothing about me. It's just the way it is now.

Practitioner: Seems like you've got it. Do you think you could say that to yourself the next time the issue comes up in class?

Justin: Yes.

Practitioner: Let's practice a bit. Let me hear you repeat it out loud.

In subsequent sessions, we used the Two Voices Exercise (see chapter 10) to provide Justin with practice opportunities to counter his own anger-prompting thoughts. We played the angry thinking voice (*She is being disrespectful—I must make her stop*), and Justin practiced countering that thought with more realistic and rational alternatives based on our discussion about perspective taking (*Cell phone use is automatic for this group—she doesn't mean any disrespect, and it has nothing to do with me*). Alternatively, we could have used the technique of rational role reversal (see chapter 10), pretending to be a classroom teacher and asking Justin to help us.

For many clients, the ability to see things from the other person's perspective can be developed as a skill that becomes easier with practice. A higher level of this intervention involves fostering compassion. At a very basic level, all people, from their own perspectives, are trying to be happy and avoid suffering. This means that even when people do things that are perceived as inconsiderate, unfair, or harmful, they are often doing those things to avoid pain and enhance their own happiness (Kolts & Chodron, 2013). Learning to see things from another's point of view is often an antidote to anger.

DEVELOPING A MORE FLEXIBLE PHILOSOPHY

The aim of rational-emotive behavior therapy (REBT; see chapter 10) is to teach clients to think realistically about negative situations and view them as what they are— unpleasant, problematic inconveniences. Most anger triggers, regardless of how negative they may seem in the moment, are not life-threatening and usually cause little more than loss of time, prestige, or money. This was certainly the case with the students who were using their cell phones in Justin's classroom.

We used the "Change Your Angry Thinking" worksheet (refer to client worksheet 10.1, a blank copy of which is downloadable from www.newharbinger.com/42877) and had Justin track and monitor the thinking pattern of demandingness as it occurred during his teaching (see figure 17.3). After a discussion of how this thinking pattern prompts and intensifies his anger, we entered it at the top of the worksheet: "Demandingness: Students must not use their cell phones in class." Justin completed the remainder of the worksheet on his own for times when he caught himself having that specific thought in class. Completing the worksheet in this way provided an ongoing opportunity for Justin to practice a more rational alternative to his demand that students behave the way he thinks they must.

Part 1. Thinking Pattern to Focus On (to be completed by the practitioner)

Demandingness: Students must not use their cell phones in class

---

Part 2. Situation and Trigger

Briefly describe the situation in which the anger-prompting thought emerged. What happened? Where? Who was involved?

Doug was looking at his phone on his lap. He acted like I wouldn't notice.

Part 3. Anger-Prompting Thought

Write a sentence or two that captures the anger-prompting thought as it was going through your mind in this situation.

He knows the classroom policy. He shouldn't be on his phone. I must get him to stop.

Part 4. Anger Rating, Action Urge, and Expressions

Describe how strong your anger was in this situation, along with any urges or impulses you felt, and describe how you expressed your anger.

My anger was like a 7. I wanted to go up to him and confront him. I kept my cool and repeated the policy to the class and reminded everyone of the break. He stopped.

Part 5. Rational Counterthought

Describe another way of thinking that could lead to less anger in this situation.

Students are going to use their phones even though I'm trying to create a classroom that limits distractions. All teachers have this challenge. It is only unpleasant and temporarily distracting. No point in getting upset and angry about it.

Figure 17.3. Justin's Completed "Change Your Angry Thinking" Worksheet

Consolidating Gains and Going Beyond Traditional Anger Management

Over the full course of Justin's treatment, we shifted the focus to his other anger triggers, such as his interactions with school administrators and his dealings with his ex-wife. Making the transition to those areas went smoothly, as we expected, because

Justin had been socialized into the treatment model, and so it was possible for us to apply many of the strategies he was already familiar with to help him improve his reactions to school administrators and his ex-wife. (Other SMART menu options could also have been selected as good fits with these new anger triggers; for example, forgiveness might have been a helpful intervention for reducing Justin's longer-term anger at his ex-wife.)

We used several additional SMART interventions—which are not usually considered in other anger management programs, and which go beyond conventional anger treatment—to help Justin make improvements regarding lifestyle issues, to appraise his risk for relapse, and to foster his overall happiness.

REDUCING IRRITABILITY: IMPROVED SLEEP AND NUTRITION

Justin is more vulnerable to reacting with anger when he stays up late and has not eaten a morning meal. Therefore, as we became more familiar with Justin's life, we addressed several lifestyle issues and worked to help him cultivate better habits, such as sleeping and eating well.

EXPECTING AND PREVENTING OCCASIONAL RELAPSES

Even in the most successful cases, we like to set realistic expectations regarding improvement. Steady and consistent progress is not the norm, and lapses into old angry behavior are common when difficult and unexpected challenges emerge. We adopt a relapse-prevention orientation and encourage our clients not to lose confidence when a negative anger episode occurs, but instead to look for overall patterns of improvement (such as a decline in the frequency and intensity of anger episodes and their associated behaviors). It's important to encourage clients to notice small steps toward progress as they work to improve their anger reactions.

We also ask clients to contemplate where and when high-risk anger situations are most likely to occur, and to develop plans (such as avoidance strategies) for dealing with them. In Justin's case, we told him that ups and downs are to be expected, that meaningful improvement is judged over the long run, and that overreacting to a specific lapse can undermine longer-term progress. As Justin's treatment is winding down, we are going through a process of helping him identify future high-risk triggers and develop a plan for dealing with each one.

ENHANCING OVERALL HAPPINESS

Another way we have assisted Justin in maintaining his treatment gains is by helping him create more joy and balance in his life so that struggles and disappointments will become less bothersome. We have asked Justin to pursue activities that increase his happiness, such as developing and nurturing close relationships, devoting some time to physical exercise, and cultivating a more giving stance toward others.

WORKING TOWARD TERMINATION

The length of treatment for any client will depend on the client's reactions and on how much progress the client makes outside of sessions (as well as on practical considerations regarding factors like the client's finances, the nature of the treatment program, the treatment setting, and insurance constraints). Termination of treatment begins with increased time between sessions. Depending on the client, bimonthly sessions are often a good starting point. The frequency of sessions can then be further reduced, until they take place once a month or on a quarterly "booster" basis. At the same time, clients are always informed that they have the option of once again increasing the frequency of their treatment sessions if new and unexpected aversive events appear, or if old patterns reemerge.

Final Thoughts

We want to thank you for spending time with this book, and we wish you much success as a SMART anger manager. We leave you with a quote from Deffenbacher (2011, 220), our colleague and friend from Colorado State University, who has conducted more anger treatment outcome studies than any other researcher in the world; his advice captures much of what we have attempted to describe in this book:

> Be gently tenacious. It often takes many repetitions to make new cognitive and behavioral strategies second nature. Perhaps like a puppy pulling on a cloth toy, practitioners should be ready to sink their teeth into the fabric of the client's life, warmly and playfully hang on, growl occasionally, and repeat as necessary.

References

Agel, J., & Glanze, W. D. (1987). *Pearls of wisdom: A harvest of quotations from all ages.* New York, NY: William Morrow.

Alberti, R., & Emmons, M. (1970). *Your perfect right.* San Luis Obispo, CA: Impact.

Alberti, R., & Emmons, M. (2008). *Your perfect right* (2nd ed.). Atascadero, CA: Impact.

Alberti, R., & Emmons, M. (2017). *Your perfect right: Assertiveness and equality in your life and relationships* (3rd ed.). Oakland, CA: New Harbinger.

Allen, R. (2015, July 10). Cancer doctor sentenced to 45 years for "horrific" fraud. *Detroit Free Press.*

Anderson, C. A., Carnagey, N. L., & Eubanks, J. (2003). Exposure to violent media: The effects of songs with violent lyrics on aggressive thoughts and feelings. *Journal of Personality and Social Psychology, 84*(5), 960–971.

Anderson, M., & Jiang, J. (2018, May 31). Teens, social media & technology 2018. Pew Research Center. Retrieved from https://www.pewinternet.org/2018/05/31/teens-social-media-technology-2018/.

Averill, J. R. (1983). Studies on anger and aggression: Implications for theories of emotion. *American Psychologist, 38*(11), 1145–1160.

Ax, A. F. (1953). The physiological differentiation between fear and anger in humans. *Psychosomatic Medicine, 15,* 433–442.

Barrett, E. L., Mills, K. L., & Teesson, M. (2013). Mental health correlates of anger in the general population: Findings from the 2007 National Survey of Mental Health and Wellbeing. *Australian and New Zealand Journal of Psychiatry, 47*(5), 470–476.

Beck, A. T. (1967). *Depression: Causes and treatment.* Philadelphia, PA: University of Pennsylvania Press.

Bensimon, M., Einat, T., & Gilboa, A. (2015). The impact of relaxing music on prisoners' levels of anxiety and anger. *International Journal of Offender Therapy and Comparative Criminology, 59*(4), 406–423.

Berkowitz, L. (1993). *Aggression: Its causes, consequences, and control.* Philadelphia, PA: Temple University Press.

Berkowitz, L., & Harmon-Jones, E. (2004). Toward an understanding of the determinants of anger. *Emotion, 4*(2), 107–130.

Bitsas, C. (2004). Food for thought: The role of nutrients in reducing aggression, violence, and criminal behavior. *Corrections Today, 66,* 110–115.

Bordin, E. (1979). The generalizability of the psychoanalytic concept of the working alliance. *Psychotherapy: Theory, Research and Practice, 16,* 252–260.

Boudreaux, D. J., Dahlen, E. R., Madson, M. B., & Bullock-Yowell, E. (2014). Attitudes toward anger management scale: Development and initial validation. *Measurement and Evaluation in Counseling and Development, 47*(1), 14–26.

Brodsky, W., Olivieri, D., & Chekaluk, E. (2018). Music genre–induced driver aggression: A case of media delinquency and risk-promoting popular culture. *Music & Science.* doi: 10.1177/2059204317743118

Brondolo, E., DiGiuseppe, R., & Tafrate, R. C. (1997). Exposure-based treatment for anger problems: Focus on the feeling. *Cognitive and Behavioral Practice, 4,* 75–98.

Buckley, T., Hoo, S. Y. S., Fethney, J., Shaw, E., Hanson, P. S., & Tofler, G. H. (2015). Triggering of acute coronary occlusion by episodes of anger. *European Heart Journal: Acute Cardiovascular Care, 4*(6), 493–498.

Burns, J. W., Gerhart, J. I., Bruehl, S., Peterson, K. M., Smith, D. A., Porter, L. S.,… Keefe, F. J. (2015). Anger arousal and behavioral anger regulation in everyday life among patients with chronic low back pain: Relationships to patient pain and function. *Health Psychology: Official Journal of the Division of Health Psychology, American Psychological Association, 34*(5), 547–555.

Bushman, B. J. (2002). Does venting anger feed or extinguish the flame? Catharsis, rumination, distraction, anger and aggressive responding. *Personality and Social Psychology Bulletin, 28*(6), 724–731. doi:10.1177/0146167202289002

Bushman, B. J., DeWall, C. N., Pond, R. S., & Hanus, M. D. (2014). Low glucose relates to greater aggression in married couples. *Proceedings of the National Academy of Sciences of the United States of America, 111*(17), 6254–6257.

Butcher, J. N., Graham, J. R., Yossef, Y. S., Tellegen, A., & Kraemmer, B. (2009). *Minnesota multiphasic personality inventory-2.* San Antonio, TX: Pearson Assessments.

Carver, C. S., & Johnson, S. L. (2018). Impulsive reactivity to emotion and vulnerability to psychopathology. *American Psychologist, 73*(9), 1067–1078.

Cattell, H. E. P., & Mead, A. D. (2008). The Sixteen Personality Factor Questionnaire (16PF). In G. J. Boyle, G. Matthews, & D. H. Saklofske (Eds.), *The Sage handbook of personality theory and assessment: Vol. 2. Personality measurement and testing.* Los Angeles, CA: Sage.

Chang, E. C., D'Zurilla, T. J., & Sanna, L. J. (2004). *Social problem solving: Theory, research, and training.* Washington, DC: American Psychological Association.

Cohen, S., Janicki-Deverts, D., Turner, R. B., & Doyle, W. J. (2015). Does hugging provide stress-buffering social support? A study of susceptibility to upper respiratory infection and illness. *Psychological Science, 26*(2), 135–174.

Croy, I., Olgun, S., & Joraschky, P. (2011). Basic emotions elicited by odors and pictures. *Emotion, 11*(6), 1331–1335.

Csikszentmihalyi, M. (1975). *Beyond boredom and anxiety.* San Francisco, CA: Jossey-Bass.

Csikszentmihalyi, M. (1990). Flow: The psychology of optimal experience. *Journal of Leisure Research, 24*(1), 93–94.

Danner, C. (2018, August 25). Senator John McCain dead at 81. *New York.* Retrieved from http://nymag.com/intelligencer/2018/08/senator-john-mccain-dead-at-81.html.

Darch, K., Ellett, L., & Fox, S. (2015). Anger and paranoia in mentally disordered offenders. *Journal of Nervous and Mental Disease, 203*(11), 878–882.

Darwin, C. R. (1872). *The expression of the emotions in man and animals.* London: John Murray.

Deffenbacher, J. L. (2011). Cognitive-behavioral conceptualization and treatment of anger. *Cognitive and Behavioral Practice, 18*(2), 212–221.

Deffenbacher, J. L., & McKay, M. (2000). *Overcoming situational and general anger: A protocol for the treatment of anger based on relaxation, cognitive restructuring, and coping skills training.* Oakland, CA: New Harbinger.

Deffenbacher, J. L., Oetting, E. E., & Lynch, R. S. (1994). Development of a driving anger scale. *OPsychological Reports, 74*(1), 83–91.

Derogatis, L. (1994). *Symptom checklist-90, revised.* San Antonio, TX: Pearson Clinical Psychology.

DeWall, C. N., Deckman, T., Gailliot, M. T., & Bushman, B. J. (2011). Sweetened blood cools hot tempers: Physiological self-control and aggression. *Aggressive Behavior, 37*(1), 73–80)

DiGiuseppe, R., & Tafrate, R. C. (2003). Anger treatment for adults: A meta-analytic view. *Clinical Psychology: Science and Practice, 10*(1), 70–74.

DiGiuseppe, R., & Tafrate, R. C. (2004). *Anger disorders scale.* North Tonawanda, NY: Multi-Health Systems.

DiGiuseppe, R., & Tafrate, R. C. (2007). *Understanding anger disorders.* New York, NY: Oxford University Press.

DiGiuseppe, R., & Tafrate, R. C. (2011). *Anger regulation and expression scale (ARES) for youth.* North Tonawanda, NY: Multi-Health Systems.

Distel, M. A., Roeling, M. P., Tielbeek, J. J., van Toor, D., Derom, C. A., Trull, T. J., & Boomsma, D. I. (2012). The covariation of trait anger and borderline personality: A bivariate twin-siblings study. *Journal of Abnormal Psychology, 121*(2), 458–466.

Dwyer, J. (2013, April 11). Two lives linked by murder, coincidence and reconciliation. *New York Times.*

D'Zurilla, T. J., & Goldfried, M. R. (1971). Problem solving and behavior modification. *Journal of Abnormal Psychology, 78*(1), 107–126.

Eifert, G., McKay, M., Forsyth, J. P., & Hayes, S. C. (2006). *ACT on life, not on anger: The new acceptance and commitment therapy guide to problem anger.* Oakland, CA: New Harbinger.

Ekman, P. (1984). Expression and the nature of emotion. In K. Scherer & P. Ekman (Eds.), *Approaches to emotion.* Hillsdale, NJ: Erlbaum.

Elgin, S. H. (1993). *Men, women, and the gentle art of verbal self-defense.* New York, NY: Wiley.

Elliot, A. J., & Aarts, H. (2011). Perception of the color red enhances the force and velocity of motor output. *Emotion, 11*(2), 445–449.

Ellis, A. (1962). *Reason and emotion in psychotherapy.* New York, NY: Stuart.

Ellis, A. (1994). *Reason and emotion in psychotherapy* (rev. ed.). Secaucus, NJ: Carol Publishing Group.

Ellis, A., & Tafrate, R. C. (1997). *How to control your anger before it controls you.* Secaucus, NJ: Carol Publishing Group.

Ellis, A., & Tafrate, R. C. (2016). *How to control your anger before it controls you* (2nd ed.). New York, NY: Citadel.

Enright, R. D. (2012). *The forgiving life.* Washington, DC: APA Books.

Enright, R. D., & Fitzgibbons, R. P. (2000). *Helping clients forgive: An empirical guide for resolving anger and restoring hope.* Washington, DC: APA Books.

Fernandez, E., Arevalo, I., Vargas, R., & Torralba, A. (2014). Norms for five parameters of anger: How do incarcerated adults differ from the community? *International Journal of Forensic Mental Health, 13*(1), 18–24.

Fernandez, E., Kiageri, V., Guharajan, D., & Day, A. (2017). Anger parameters in parolees undergoing psychoeducation. *Criminal Behavior and Mental Health, 28,* 174–186.

Fernandez, E., & Wasan, A. (2010). The anger of pain sufferers: Attributions to agents and appraisals of wrongdoing. In M. Potegal, G. Stemmler, & C. Spielberger (Eds.), *The international handbook of anger: Constituent and concomitant biological, psychological, and social processes.* New York, NY: Springer-Verlag.

Finkel, E. J. (2014). The I³ Model: Metatheory, theory, and evidence. In J. M. Olson & M. P. Zanna (Eds.), *Advances in experimental social psychology*. San Diego, CA: Academic Press.

Finkel E. J., & Eckhardt, C. I. (2013). Intimate partner violence. In J. A. Simpson & L. Campbell (Eds.), *The Oxford handbook of close relationships*. New York, NY: Oxford University Press.

Fischer, P., & Greitemeyer, T. (2006). Music and aggression: The impact of sexual-aggressive song lyrics on aggression-related thoughts, emotions, and behavior toward the same and the opposite sex. *Personality & Social Psychology Bulletin, 32*(9), 1165–1176.

Frankl, V. (1959). *Man's search for meaning*. Boston, MA: Beacon Press.

Gardner, F., & Moore, Z. (2014). *Contextual anger regulation therapy: A mindfulness- and acceptance-based approach*. New York, NY: Routledge.

Gesch, B. (2013). Adolescence: Does good nutrition = good behaviour? *Nutrition and Health, 22*(1), 55–65.

Gigerenzer, G., & Gaissmaier, W. (2011). Heuristic decision making. *Annual Review of Psychology, 62*(1), 451–482.

Gladwell, M. (2005). *Blink: The power of thinking without thinking*. Boston, MA: Little, Brown.

Glynn, L. H., & Moyers, T. B. (2010). Chasing change talk: The clinician's role in evoking client language about change. *Journal of Substance Abuse Treatment, 39*(1), 65–70.

Gonzalez, O. I., Novaco, R. W., Reger, M. A., & Gahm, G. A. (2016). Anger intensification with combat-related PTSD and depression comorbidity. *Psychological Trauma: Theory, Research, Practice and Policy, 8*(1), 9–16.

Goyal, M., Singh, S., Sibinga, E. M. S., Gould, N. F., Rowland-Seymour, A., Sharma, R.,… Haythornthwaite, J. A. (2014). Meditation programs for psychological stress and well-being: A systematic review and meta-analysis. *JAMA Internal Medicine, 174*(3), 357–368.

Greenbaum, Z. (2018). A greater role in nutritional health. *Monitor on Psychology, 49*, 54.

Greitemeyer, T., Hollingdale, J., & Traut-Mattausch, E. (2015). Changing the track in music and misogyny: Listening to music with pro-equality lyrics improves attitudes and behavior toward women. *Psychology of Popular Media Culture, 4*(1), 56–67.

Grodnitzky, G. R., & Tafrate, R. C. (2000). Imaginal exposure for anger reduction in adult outpatients: A pilot study. *Journal of Behavior Therapy and Experimental Psychiatry, 31*, 259–279.

Hayes, S. C., Strosahl, K. D., & Wilson, K. G. (1999). *Acceptance and commitment therapy: An experiential approach to behavior change*. New York, NY: Guilford Press.

Heather, N., Rollnick, S., & Bell, A. (1993). Predictive validity of the Readiness to Change questionnaire. *Addiction, 88*(12), 1667–1677.

Hemenover, S. H., & Zhang, S. (2004). Anger, personality and optimistic stress appraisals. *Cognition & Emotion, 18*(3), 363–382.

Honyashiki, M., Furukawa, T. A., Noma, H., Tanaka, S., Chen, P., Ichikawa, K.,… Caldwell, D. M. (2014). Specificity of CBT for depression: A contribution from multiple treatments meta-analyses. *Cognitive Therapy and Research, 38,* 249–260. doi:10.1007 /s10608-014-9599-7

Ireland, J. L., & Culpin, V. (2006). The relationship between sleeping problems and aggression, anger, and impulsivity in a population of juvenile and young offenders. *Journal of Adolescent Health: Official Publication of the Society for Adolescent Medicine, 38*(6), 649–655.

Irving, L. M., Snyder, C. R., Cheavens, J., Gravel, L., Hanke, J., Hilberg, P., & Nelson, N. (2004). The relationships between hope and outcomes at the pretreatment, beginning, and later phases of psychotherapy. *Journal of Psychotherapy Integration, 14*(4), 419–443.

Izard, C. E. (1977). *Human emotions.* New York, NY: Plenum Press.

Jakubowski, P., & Lange, A. (1978). *The assertive option.* Champaign, IL: Research Press.

Johnsen, T. J., & Friborg, O. (2015). The effect of cognitive behavioral therapy as an anti-depressive treatment is falling: A meta-analysis. *Psychological Bulletin, 141*(4), 747–768.

Kabat-Zinn, J. (1994). *Mindfulness meditation for everyday life.* Loughton, England: Piatkus.

Kassinove, H. (Ed.). (1995). *Anger disorders: Definition, diagnosis, and treatment.* Philadelphia, PA: Taylor & Francis.

Kassinove, H., & DiGiuseppe, R. (1975). Rational role reversal. *Rational Living, 10,* 44–45.

Kassinove, H., & Sukhodolsky, D. G. (1995). Anger disorders: Basic science and practice issues. In H. Kassinove (Ed.), *Anger Disorders: Assessment, Diagnosis, and Treatment.* Philadelphia, PA: Taylor & Francis.

Kassinove, H., Sukhodolsky, D. G., Tsytsarev, S. V., & Solovyova, S. (1997). Self-reported anger episodes in Russia and America. *Journal of Social Behavior & Personality, 12*(2), 301–324.

Kassinove, H., & Tafrate, R. C. (2002). *Anger management: The complete treatment guidebook for practitioners.* Atascadero, CA: Impact.

Kassinove, H., & Tafrate, R. C. (2006). Anger-related disorders: Basic issues, models, and diagnostic considerations. In E. L. Feindler (Ed.), *Anger-related disorders: A practitioner's guide to comparative treatments.* New York, NY: Springer.

Kassinove, H., & Tafrate, R. C. (2009). Anger. In D. McKay, J. Abramowitz, & S. Taylor (Eds.), *Cognitive behavior therapy for refractory cases: Turning failure into success.* Washington, DC: APA Books.

Kassinove, H., & Tafrate, R. C. (2010). Anger: Successful and non-successful treatment. In D. McKay, J. Abramowitz, & S. Taylor (Eds.), *The expanded scope of cognitive behavior therapy: Lessons learned from refractory cases.* Washington, DC: APA Press.

Kassinove, H., & Tafrate, R. C. (2014). *Anger management in counseling and psychotherapy.* DVD. Available from www.psychotherapy.net.

Kennedy, H. G. (1992). Anger and irritability. *British Journal of Psychiatry, 161*(2), 145–153.

Kichuk, S. A., Lebowitz, M. S., & Adams, T. G. (2015). Can biomedical models of psychopathology interfere with cognitive-behavioral treatment processes? *Behavior Therapist, 38*(7), 181–186.

Kolts, R., & Chodron, T. (2013). *Living with an open heart: How to cultivate compassion in everyday life.* London, England: Constable & Robinson.

Kor, E. M. (1995). *Echoes from Auschwitz: Dr. Mengele's twins.* Terre Haute, IN: CANDLES.

Kor, E. M., & Buccieri, L. R. (2009). *Surviving the angel of death: The story of a Mengele twin in Auschwitz.* Terre Haute, IN: Tanglewood.

Kowalski, R. M. (Ed.). (2001). *Behaving badly: Aversive behaviors in interpersonal relationships.* Washington, DC: American Psychological Association.

Krizan, Z., & Herlache, A. D. (2016). Sleep disruption and aggression: Implications for violence and its prevention. *Psychology of Violence, 6*(4), 542–552.

Krizan, Z., & Hisler, G. (2018). Sleepy anger: Restricted sleep amplifies angry feelings. *Journal of Experimental Psychology.* doi:10.1037/xge0000522

Lee, A. H., & DiGiuseppe, R. (2018). Anger and aggression treatments: A review of meta-analyses. *Current Opinion in Psychology, 19,* 65–74.

LeGates, T., Fernandez, D., & Hattar, S. (2014). Light as a central modulator of circadian rhythms, sleep and affect. *Nature Reviews Neuroscience, 15*(7), 443–454. doi:10.1038/nrn3743

Lenhart, A. (2010, September 2). Cell phones and American adults. Pew Research Center. Retrieved from https://www.pewinternet.org/2010/09/02/cell-phones-and-american-adults.

Lenhart, A. (2015, April 9). Teens, social media & technology overview 2015. Pew Research Center. Retrieved from https://www.pewinternet.org/2015/04/09/teens-social-media-technology-2015.

Lent, M. A. (2017). *Effects of text message reporting and reinforcement on mental health homework compliance* (Unpublished doctoral dissertation, Hofstra University).

Lerner, J. S., Gonzalez, R. M., & Small, D. A. (2003). Effects of fear and anger on perceived risks of terrorism: A national field experiment. *Psychological Science, 14,* 144–150. doi:10.1111/1467-9280.01433

Levi, P. (1984). *The periodic table.* New York, NY: Schocken Books.

Lipsky, M. J., Kassinove, H., & Miller, N. J. (1980). Effects of rational-emotive therapy, rational role reversal, and rational-emotive imagery on the emotional adjustment of community mental health center patients. *Journal of Consulting and Clinical Psychology,* 48(3), 366–374.

Litvak, P. M., Lerner, J. J., Tiedens, L. Z., & Shonk, K. (2010). Fuel in the fire: How anger impacts judgment and decision making. In M. Potegal, G. Stemmler, & C. Spielberger (Eds.), *The international handbook of anger: Constituent and concomitant biological, psychological, and social processes.* New York, NY: Springer-Verlag.

Lohr, J. M., Olatunji, B. O., Baumeister, R. F., & Bushman, B. J. (2007). The psychology of anger venting and empirically supported alternatives that do no harm. *Scientific Review of Mental Health Practice: Objective Investigations of Controversial and Unorthodox Claims in Clinical Psychology, Psychiatry, and Social Work,* 5(1), 53–64.

Lyubomirsky, S. (2008). *The how of happiness: A scientific approach to getting the life you want.* New York, NY: Penguin.

Lyubomirsky, S. (2013). *The myths of happiness: What should make you happy, but doesn't, what shouldn't make you happy, but does.* New York, NY: Penguin.

McDermott, S. (1998). *Effects of rational, typical, and irrelevant self-statements with barb exposure on anger in adult men* (Unpublished doctoral dissertation, Hofstra University).

McIntyre, K. M., Mogle, J. A., Scodes, J. M., Pavlicova, M., Shapiro, P. A., Gorenstein, E. E.,...Sloan, R. P. (2018). Anger-reduction treatment reduces negative affect reactivity to daily stressors. *Journal of Consulting and Clinical Psychology.* Advance online publication. doi:10.1037/ccp0000359

McLaughlin, K. A., Green, J. G., Hwang, I., Sampson, M. A., Zaslavsky, A. M., & Kessler, R. C. (2012). Intermittent explosive disorder in the National Comorbidity Survey Replication Adolescent Supplement. *Archives of General Psychiatry* 69(11), 1131–1139. doi:10.1001/archgenpsychiatry.2012.592

Mehrabian, A. (1970). *Tactics of social influence.* Englewood Cliffs, NJ: Prentice Hall.

Meichenbaum, D., & Cameron, R. (1973). Training schizophrenics to talk to themselves: A means of developing attentional controls. *Behavior Therapy, 4*(4), 515–534.

Miller, W. R., & Rollnick, S. (2013). *Motivational interviewing: Helping people change* (3rd ed.). New York, NY: Guilford Press.

Millon, T., Grossman, S., & Millon, C. (2015). *Millon Clinical Multiaxial Inventory (MCMI-III).* San Antonio, TX: Pearson Clinical Psychology.

Mills, J. F., Loza, W., & Kroner, D. G. (2003). Predictive validity despite social desirability: Evidence for the robustness of self-report among offenders. *Criminal Behaviour and Mental Health, 13*(2), 140–150.

Mitchell, D., Tafrate, R. C., Hogan, T., & Olver, M. E. (2013). An exploration of the association between criminal thinking and community program attrition. *Journal of Criminal Justice, 41*(2), 81–89.

Mostofsky, E., Penner, E. A., & Mittleman, M. A. (2014). Outbursts of anger as a trigger of acute cardiovascular events: A systematic review and meta-analysis. *European Heart Journal, 35*(21), 1404–1410.

Moyers, T. B., Martin, T., Houck, J. M., Christopher, P. J., & Tonigan, J. S. (2009). From in-session behaviors to drinking outcomes: A causal chain for motivational interviewing. *Journal of Consulting and Clinical Psychology, 77*(6), 1113–1124.

Moyers, T. B., & Miller, W. R. (2013). Is low therapist empathy toxic? *Psychology of Addictive Behaviors, 27*(3), 878–884. doi:10.1037/a0030274

Muran, J. C., & Barber, J. P. (Eds.). (2010). *The therapeutic alliance: An evidence-based guide to practice.* New York, NY: Guilford Press.

Mutic, S., Parma, V., Brünner, Y. F., & Freiherr, J. (2016). You smell dangerous: Communicating fight responses through human chemosignals of aggression. *Chemical Senses, 41*(1), 35–43.

Nadkarni, N., Schnacker, L., Hasbach, P., Thys, T., & Crockett, E. (2017, January–February). From orange to blue: How nature imagery affects inmates in the blue room. *Corrections Today*, 36–40.

Nakamura, J., & Csikszentmihalyi, M. (2014). The concept of flow. In C. R. Snyder & S. J. Lopez (Eds.), *Handbook of positive psychology.* New York, NY: Oxford University Press.

National Sleep Foundation. (2013). 2013 International bedroom poll: Summary of findings. Arlington, VA: Author.

Novaco, R. W. (1975). *Anger control: The development and evaluation of an experimental treatment.* Oxford, England: Lexington.

Novaco, R. W. (2003). *The Novaco anger scale and provocation inventory (NAS-PI).* Los Angeles, CA: Western Psychological Services.

Novaco, R. W., & Taylor, J. L. (2015). Reduction of assaultive behavior following anger treatment of forensic hospital patients with intellectual disabilities. *Behaviour Research and Therapy, 65*, 52–59.

Okuda, M., Picazo, J., Olfson, M., Hasin, D. S., Liu, S. M., Bernardi, S., & Blanco, C. (2015). Prevalence and correlates of anger in the community: Results from a national survey. *CNS Spectrums, 20*(2), 130–139.

Olatunji, B. O., & Lohr, J. M. (2004). Nonspecific factors and the efficacy of psychosocial treatments for anger. *Scientific Review of Mental Health Practice: Objective Investigations of Controversial and Unorthodox Claims in Clinical Psychology, Psychiatry, and Social Work, 3*(2), 3–18.

Paulhus, D. L. (1998). *Paulhus deception scales (PDS): The balanced inventory of desirable responding-7 user's manual.* North Tonawanda, NY: Multi-Health Systems.

Peterson, C., Seligman, M. E. P., Yurko, K. H., Martin, L. R., & Friedman, H. S. (1998). Catastrophizing and untimely death. *Psychological Science, 9*(2), 127–130.

Pew Research Center. (2014). Belief in God. Washington, DC: Author. Retrieved May 20, 2019, from https://www.pewforum.org/religious-landscape-study/belief-in-god.

Pew Research Center & University of Michigan. (2010, April 10). Teens and mobile phones. Washington, DC: Pew Research Center. Retrieved from https://www.pewinternet.org /2010/04/20/teens-and-mobile-phones-3.

Potegal, M., & Novaco, R. W. (2010). A brief history of anger. In M. Potegal, G. Stemmler, & C. Spielberger (Eds.), *The international handbook of anger: Constituent and concomitant biological, psychological, and social processes.* New York, NY: Springer-Verlag.

Potegal, M., Stemmler, G., & Spielberger, C. D. (Eds.). (2010). *The international handbook of anger: Constituent and concomitant biological, psychological, and social processes.* New York, NY: Springer-Verlag.

Ramsbotham, L. D., & Gesch, B. (2009). Crime and nourishment. *Prison Service Journal, 182*, 3–9.

Richardson, C., & Halliwell, E. (2008). *Boiling point: Anger and what we can do about it.* London, England: Mental Health Foundation.

Rosenberg, E. L., Ekman, P., Jiang, W., Babyak, M., Coleman, R. E., Hanson, M.,… Blumenthal, J. A. (2001). Linkages between facial expressions of anger and transient myocardial ischemia in men with coronary artery disease. *Emotion, 1*(2), 107–115. doi:10.1037/1528-3542.1.2.107

Rosengren, D. B. (2018). *Building motivational interviewing skills: A practitioner workbook* (2nd ed.). New York, NY: Guilford Press.

Rotton, J., & Cohn, E. G. (2000). Violence is a curvilinear function of temperature in Dallas: A replication. *Journal of Personality and Social Psychology, 78*(6), 1074–1081.

Saini, M. (2009). A meta-analysis of psychological treatment of anger: Developing guidelines for evidence-based practice. *Journal of the American Academy of Psychiatry and the Law, 37*(4), 438–441.

Salovey, P., & Mayer, J. D. (1990). Emotional intelligence. *Imagination, Cognition, and Personality, 9*(3), 185–211.

Salter, A. (1949). *Conditioned reflex therapy.* New York, NY: Creative Age Press.

Sawada, T., Konomi, A., & Yokoi, K. (2014). Iron deficiency without anemia is associated with anger and fatigue in young Japanese women. *Biological Trace Element Research, 159*(1–3), 22–31.

Schachter, J. (1957). Pain, fear, and anger in hypertensives and normotensives: A psycho-physiological study. *Psychosomatic Medicine, 19,* 17–29. doi:10.1097/00006842-195701000-00003

Scherer, K. R., & Wallbott, H. G. (1994). Evidence for universality and cultural variation of differential emotion response patterning. *Journal of Personality and Social Psychology, 66*(2), 310–328.

Schiller, J. S., Lucas, J. W., Ward, B. W., & Peregoy, J. A. (2012). *Summary health statistics for U.S. adults: National health interview survey, 2010.* Hyattsville, MD: US Department of Health and Human Services, Centers for Disease Control and Prevention.

Schoenthaler, S. J. (1983). The Northern California diet-behavior program: An empirical examination of 3,000 incarcerated juveniles in Stanislaus County Juvenile Hall. *International Journal of Biosocial Research, 5*(2), 99–106.

Seligman, M. E. P. (2011). *Flourish: A visionary new understanding of happiness and well-being.* New York, NY: Free Press.

Sell, A., Cosmides, L., & Tooby, J. (2014). The human anger face evolved to enhance cues of strength. *Evolution and Human Behavior, 35*(5), 425–429.

Sheehan, D. V. (2015). *The mini-international neuropsychiatric interview for DSM 5 (M.I.N.I.).* St. Petersberg, FL: University of South Florida.

Skinner, B. F. (1974). *About behaviorism.* Oxford, England: Knopf.

Spielberger, C. D. (1999). *Professional manual for the State-Trait Anger Expression Inventory-2 (STAXI-2).* Odessa, FL: Psychological Assessment Resources.

Stemmler, G. (2004). Physiological processes during emotion. In P. Philippot & R. S. Feldman (Eds.), *The regulation of emotion.* Mahwah, NJ: Erlbaum.

Stoddard, J. A., & Afari, N. (2014). *The big book of ACT metaphors.* Oakland, CA: New Harbinger.

Sukhodolsky, D. G., Golub, A., & Cromwell, E. N. (2001). Development and validation of the Anger Rumination Scale. *Personality and Individual Differences, 31*(5), 689–700.

Sullman, M. J. M. (2006) Anger amongst New Zealand drivers. *Transportation Research Part F: Traffic Psychology and Behaviour, 9*(3) 173–184.

Sullman, M. J. M., Stephens, A. N., & Yong, M. (2015). Anger, aggression and road rage behaviour in Malaysian drivers. *Transportation Research, Part F: Traffic Psychology and Behaviour, 29,* 70–82.

Swanson, J. W., Sampson, N. A., Petukhova, M. V., Zaslavsky, A. M., Appelbaum, P. S., Swartz, M. S., & Kessler, R. C. (2015). Guns, impulsive angry behavior, and mental disorders: Results from the National Comorbidity Survey Replication (NCS-R). *Behavioral Sciences & the Law.* doi:10.1002/bsl.2172

Tafrate, R. C., & Kassinove, H. (1998). Anger control in men: Barb exposure with rational, irrational, and irrelevant self-statements. *Journal of Cognitive Psychotherapy, 12*(3), 187–211.

Tafrate, R. C., & Kassinove, H. (2003). Angry patients: Strategies for beginning treatment. In R. Leahy (Ed.), *Overcoming roadblocks in cognitive-behavioral therapy.* New York, NY: Guilford Press.

Tafrate, R. C., & Kassinove, H. (2006). Anger management for adults: A menu-driven cognitive-behavioral approach to the treatment of anger disorders. In E. L. Feindler (Ed.), *Anger-related disorders: A practitioner's guide to comparative treatments.* New York, NY: Springer.

Tafrate, R. C., & Kassinove, H. (2009). *Anger management for everyone: Seven proven ways to control anger and live a happier life.* Oakland, CA: New Harbinger.

Tafrate, R. C., & Kassinove, H. (2019). *Anger management for everyone: Ten proven strategies to help you control anger and live a happier life* (2nd ed.). Oakland, CA: Impact.

Tafrate, R. C., Kassinove, H., & Dundin, L. (2002). Anger episodes in high- and low-trait-anger community adults. *Journal of Clinical Psychology, 58*(12), 1573–1590.

Tafrate, R. C., Mitchell, D., & Simourd, D. J. (2018). *CBT with justice-involved clients: Interventions for antisocial and self-destructive behaviors.* New York: Guilford Press.

Taylor, J. L., & Novaco, R. W. (2005). *Anger treatment for people with developmental disabilities: A theory, evidence, and manual-based approach.* London, England: Wiley.

Terracciano, S. (2000). *Effects of barb exposure and rational statement rehearsal on anger and articulated thoughts in angry married men: Extinction or cognitive restructuring?* (Unpublished doctoral dissertation, Hofstra University).

Truijens, F., Zühlke-van Hulzen, L., & Vanheule, S. (2019). To manualize, or not to manualize: Is that still the question? A systematic review of empirical evidence for manual superiority in psychological treatment. *Journal of Clinical Psychology, 75*(3), 323–327.

Van Kleef, G. A., De Dreu, C. K. W., & Manstead, A. S. R. (2004). The interpersonal effects of anger and happiness in negotiations. *Journal of Personality and Social Psychology, 86*(1), 57–76.

Vitello, P. (2005, October 17). L.I. teenager is sentenced to six months in turkey case. *New York Times.*

Walitzer, K. S., Deffenbacher, J. L., & Shyhalla, K. (2015). Alcohol-adapted anger management treatment: A randomized controlled trial of an innovative therapy for alcohol dependence. *Journal of Substance Abuse Treatment, 59,* 83–93.

Wampold, B. E., Mondin, G. W., Moody, M., Stich, F., & Hyun-nie, A. (1997). A meta-analysis of outcome studies comparing bona fide psychotherapies: Empiricially, "all must have prizes." *Psychological Bulletin, 122*(3), 203–215.

Wei, W., Lu, J. G., Galinsky, A. D., Wu, H., Gosling, S. D., Rentfrow, P. J.,…Wang, L. (2017). Regional ambient temperature is associated with human personality. *Nature Human Behaviour,* 1, 890–895.

Weiner, M. D., Pentz, M. A., Turner, G. E., & Dwyer, J. H. (2001). From early to late adolescence: Alcohol use and anger relationships. *Journal of Adolescent Health: Official Publication of the Society for Adolescent Medicine, 28*(6), 450–457.

Williams, J. E., Paton, C. C., Siegler, I. C., Eigenbrodt, M. L., Nieto, F. J., & Tyroler, H. A. (2000). Anger proneness predicts coronary heart disease risk. *Circulation 101*(17), 2034–2039.

Williamson, P., Day, A., Howells, K., Bubner, S., & Jauncey, S. (2003). Assessing offender readiness to change problems with anger. *Psychology, Crime & Law, 9*(4), 295–307.

Wranik, T., & Scherer, K. R. (2010). Why do I get angry? A componential appraisal approach. In M. Potegal, G. Stemmler, & C. Spielberger (Eds.), *The international handbook of anger: Constituent and concomitant biological, psychological, and social processes.* New York, NY: Springer-Verlag.

Zilioli, S., Sell, A. N., Stirrat, M., Jagore, J., Vickerman, W., & Watson, N. V. (2015). Face of a fighter: Bizygomatic width as a cue of formidability. *Aggressive Behavior, 41*(4), 322–330.

Howard Kassinove, PhD, ABPP, is a board-certified clinical psychologist, former chairperson of the psychology department at Hofstra University, and past director of their PhD program in clinical and school psychology. Kassinove is a fellow of the American Psychological Association, the American Psychological Society, the Albert Ellis Institute, and the Behavior Therapy and Research Society. Editor of *Anger Disorders*, he has published more than sixty papers, and has lectured widely in the United States, Europe, and Asia.

Raymond Chip Tafrate, PhD, is a clinical psychologist, and professor in the criminology and criminal justice department at Central Connecticut State University. He is a fellow and supervisor at the Albert Ellis Institute in New York City, NY; and a member of the Motivational Interviewing Network of Trainers. He frequently consults with criminal justice agencies and programs regarding difficult-to-change problems such as anger dysregulation and criminal behavior. He has coauthored numerous books, and has presented his research throughout North America, Europe, Asia, and Australia. He is coauthor, with Howard Kassinove, of the popular self-help classic, *Anger Management for Everyone*.

Index

MORE BOOKS *from*
NEW HARBINGER PUBLICATIONS

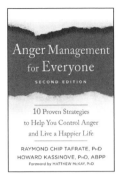

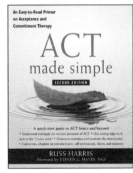